ary
wars
2
—Love & War—

STORY & ART BY Kiiro Yumi   ORIGINAL CONCEPT BY Hiro Arikawa

Library Wars
Love & War

Contents

The Library Freedom Act

Libraries have the freedom to acquire their collections.

Libraries have the freedom to circulate
materials in their collections.

Libraries guarantee the privacy of their patrons.

Libraries oppose any type of censorship.

When libraries are imperiled,
librarians will join together
to secure their freedom.

library wars

Love & War

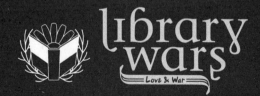

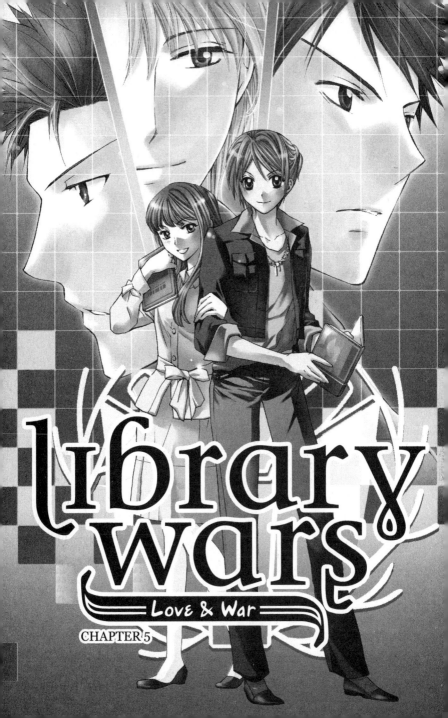

library wars

Love & War

CHAPTER 5

Library Wars LOVE & WAR 2

time

is

It

to

begin!

Hope you enjoy the story!

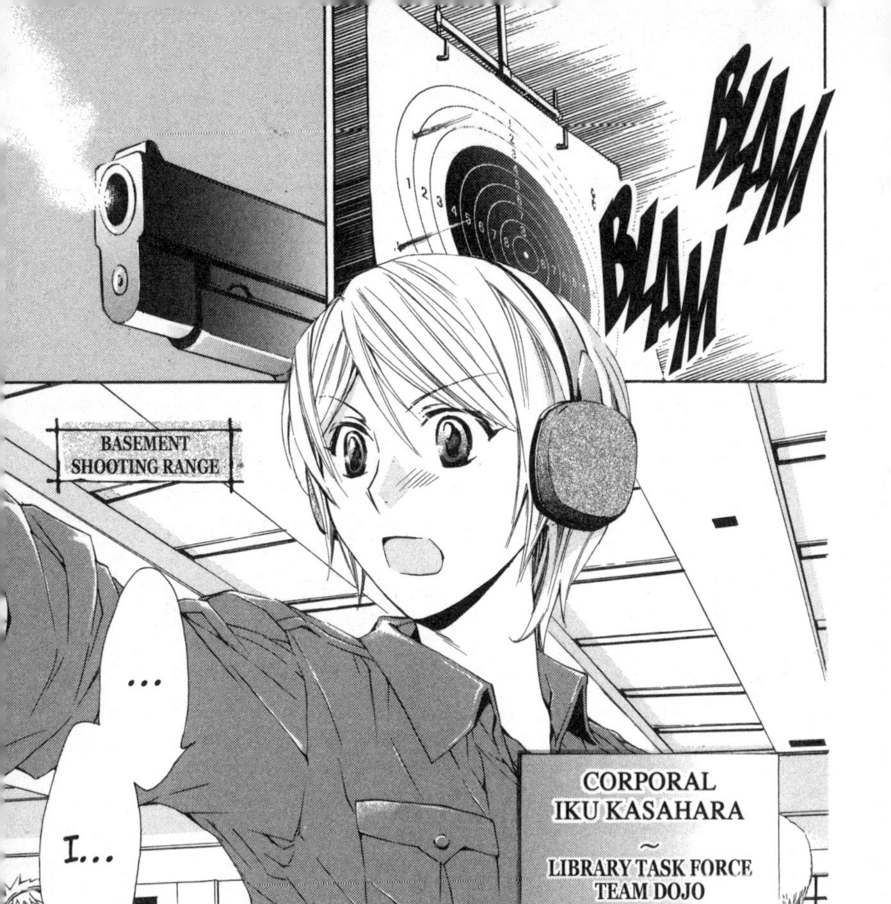
BLAM BLAM
BASEMENT SHOOTING RANGE
CORPORAL IKU KASAHARA ~ LIBRARY TASK FORCE TEAM DOJO
... I...

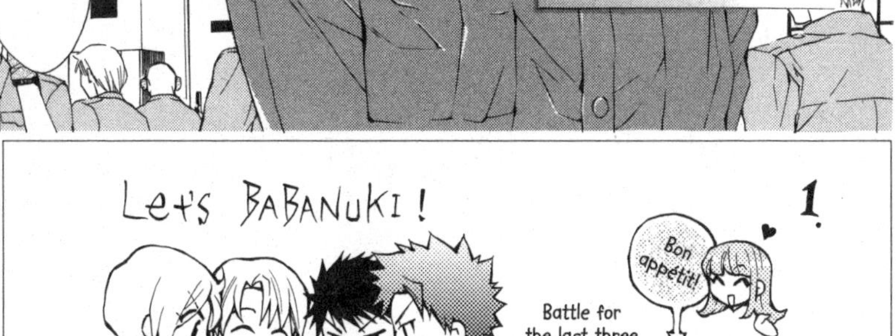
Let's BABANUKI!
1
Bon appétit!
Battle for the last three steamed buns!

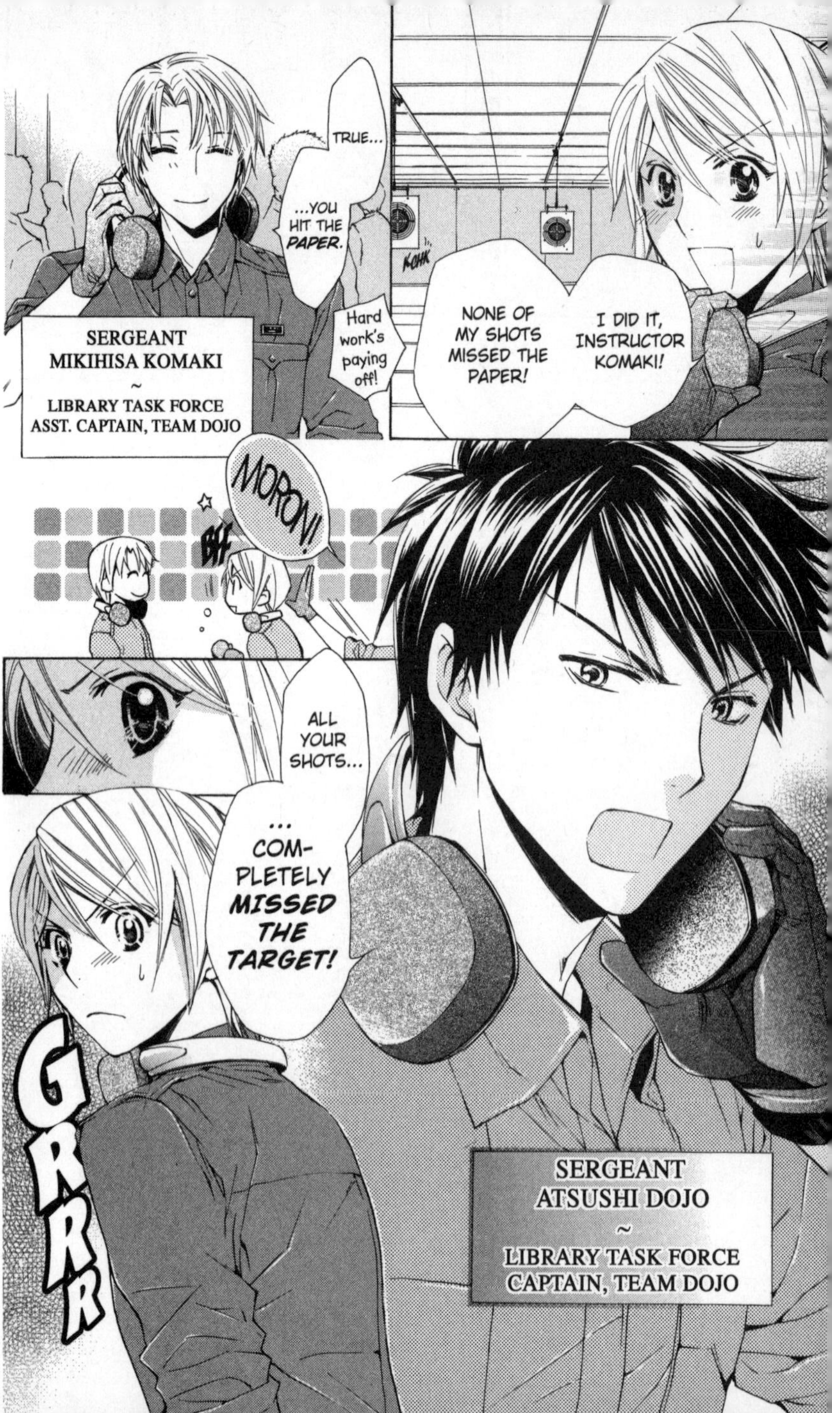
I DID IT, INSTRUCTOR KOMAKI!
NONE OF MY SHOTS MISSED THE PAPER!
K-CHK
TRUE...
...YOU HIT THE PAPER.
Hard work's paying off!
SERGEANT MIKIHISA KOMAKI ~ LIBRARY TASK FORCE ASST. CAPTAIN, TEAM DOJO
MORON!
BH
ALL YOUR SHOTS...
...COMPLETELY MISSED THE TARGET!
SERGEANT ATSUSHI DOJO ~ LIBRARY TASK FORCE CAPTAIN, TEAM DOJO
GRRR

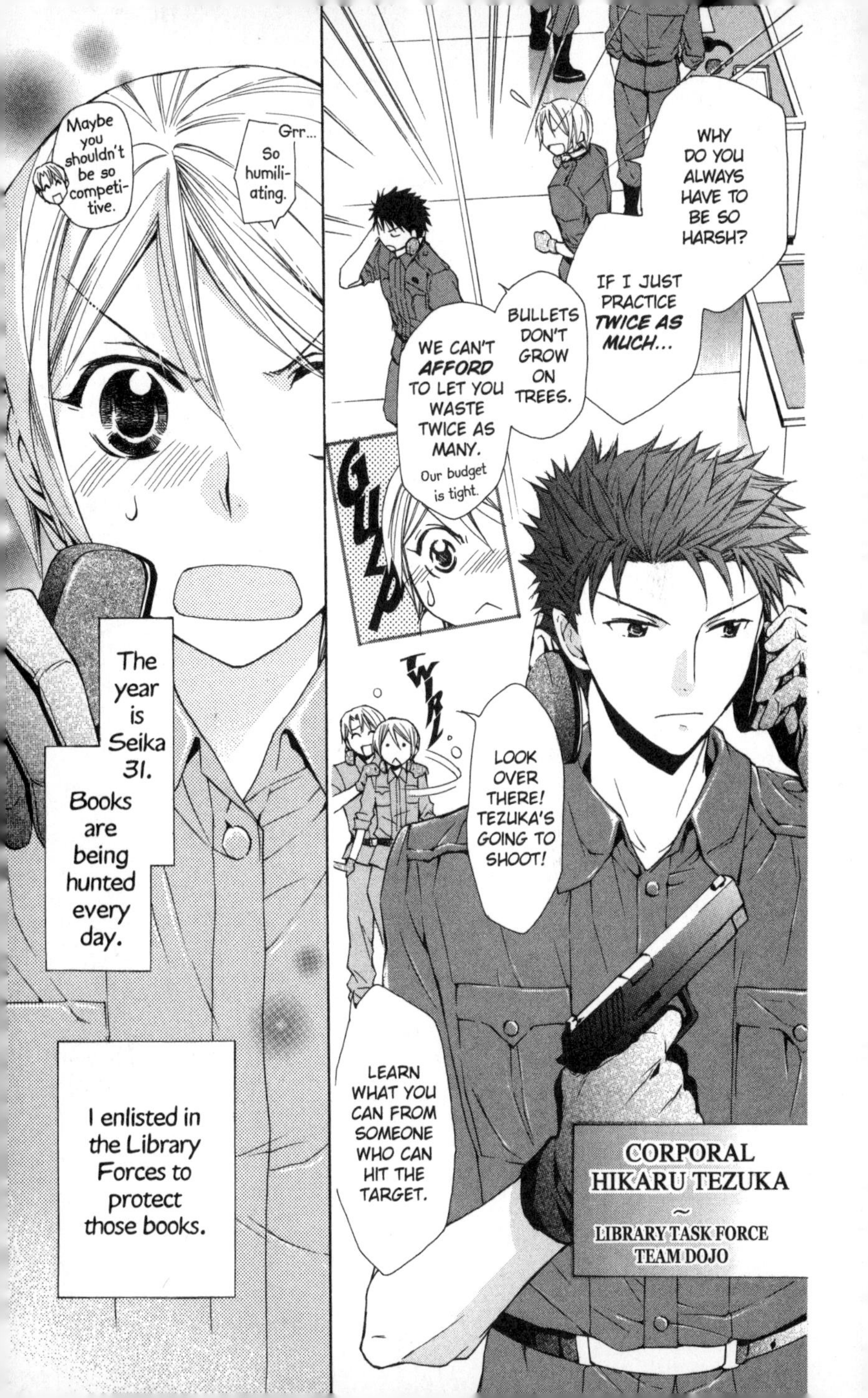
WHY DO YOU ALWAYS HAVE TO BE SO HARSH?
IF I JUST PRACTICE *TWICE AS MUCH*...
BULLETS DON'T GROW ON TREES.
WE CAN'T *AFFORD* TO LET YOU WASTE TWICE AS MANY.
Our budget is tight.
GULP
TWIRL
LOOK OVER THERE! TEZUKA'S GOING TO SHOOT!
LEARN WHAT YOU CAN FROM SOMEONE WHO CAN HIT THE TARGET.
CORPORAL HIKARU TEZUKA ~ LIBRARY TASK FORCE TEAM DOJO
Grr... So humiliating.
Maybe you shouldn't be so competitive.
The year is Seika 31. Books are being hunted every day.
I enlisted in the Library Forces to protect those books.

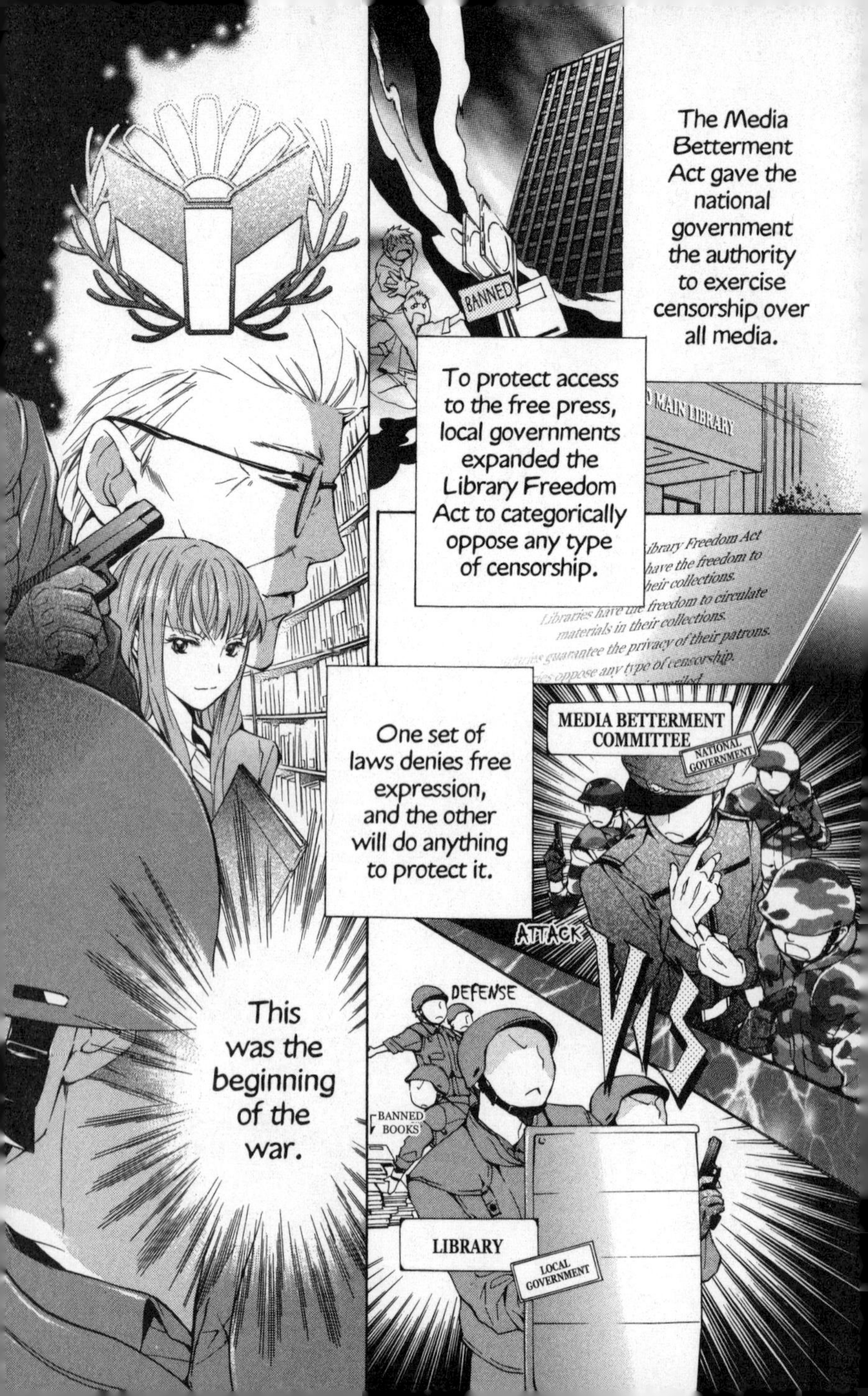
The Media Betterment Act gave the national government the authority to exercise censorship over all media.
BANNED
MAIN LIBRARY
To protect access to the free press, local governments expanded the Library Freedom Act to categorically oppose any type of censorship.
ibrary Freedom Act
have the freedom to
heir collections.
Libraries have the freedom to circulate
materials in their collections.
guarantee the privacy of their patrons.
oppose any type of censorship.
One set of laws denies free expression, and the other will do anything to protect it.
MEDIA BETTERMENT COMMITTEE
NATIONAL GOVERNMENT
ATTACK
VS
DEFENSE
BANNED BOOKS
LIBRARY
LOCAL GOVERNMENT
This was the beginning of the war.

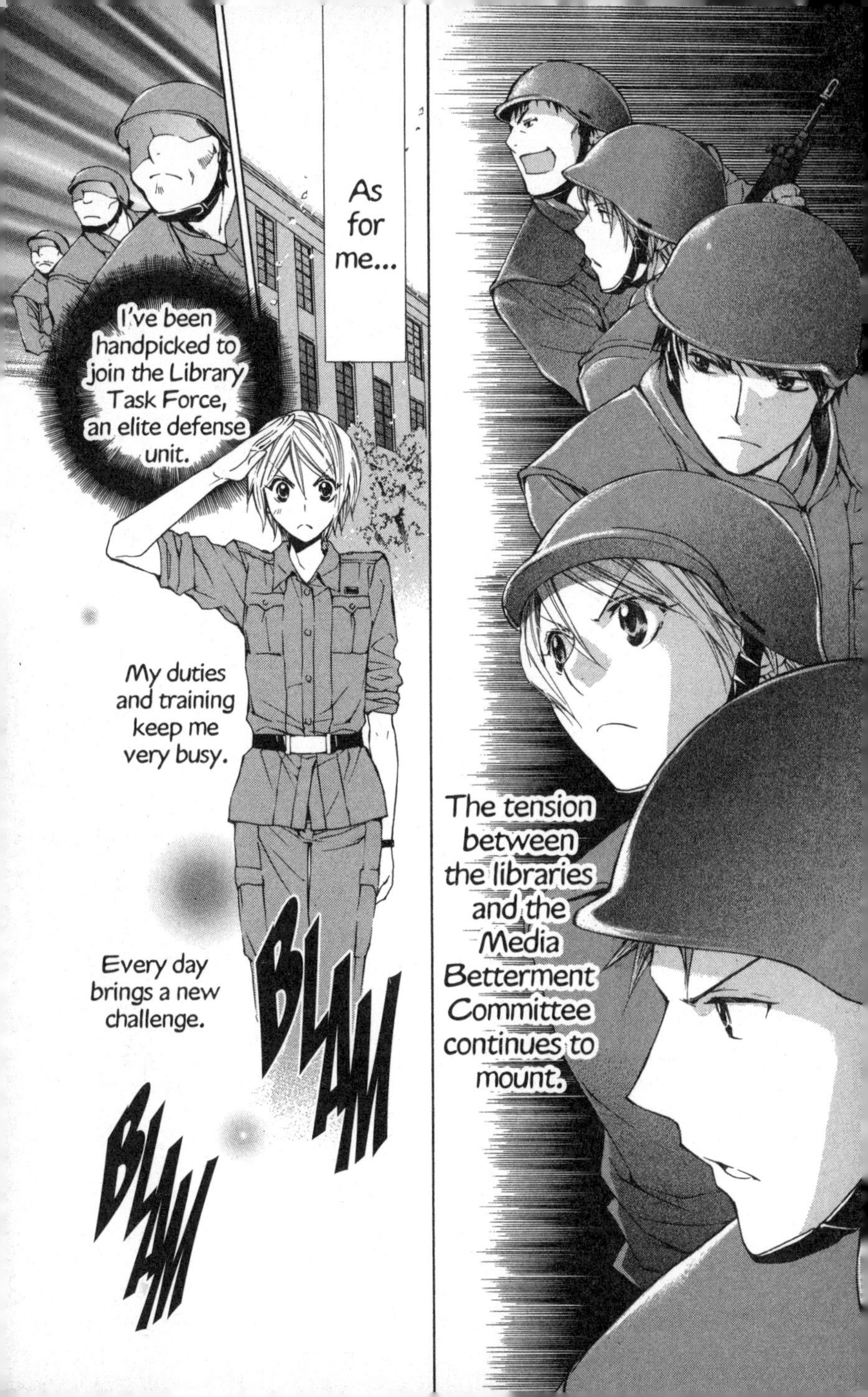
The tension between the libraries and the Media Betterment Committee continues to mount.
As for me...
I've been handpicked to join the Library Task Force, an elite defense unit.
My duties and training keep me very busy.
BLAM
Every day brings a new challenge.
BLAM

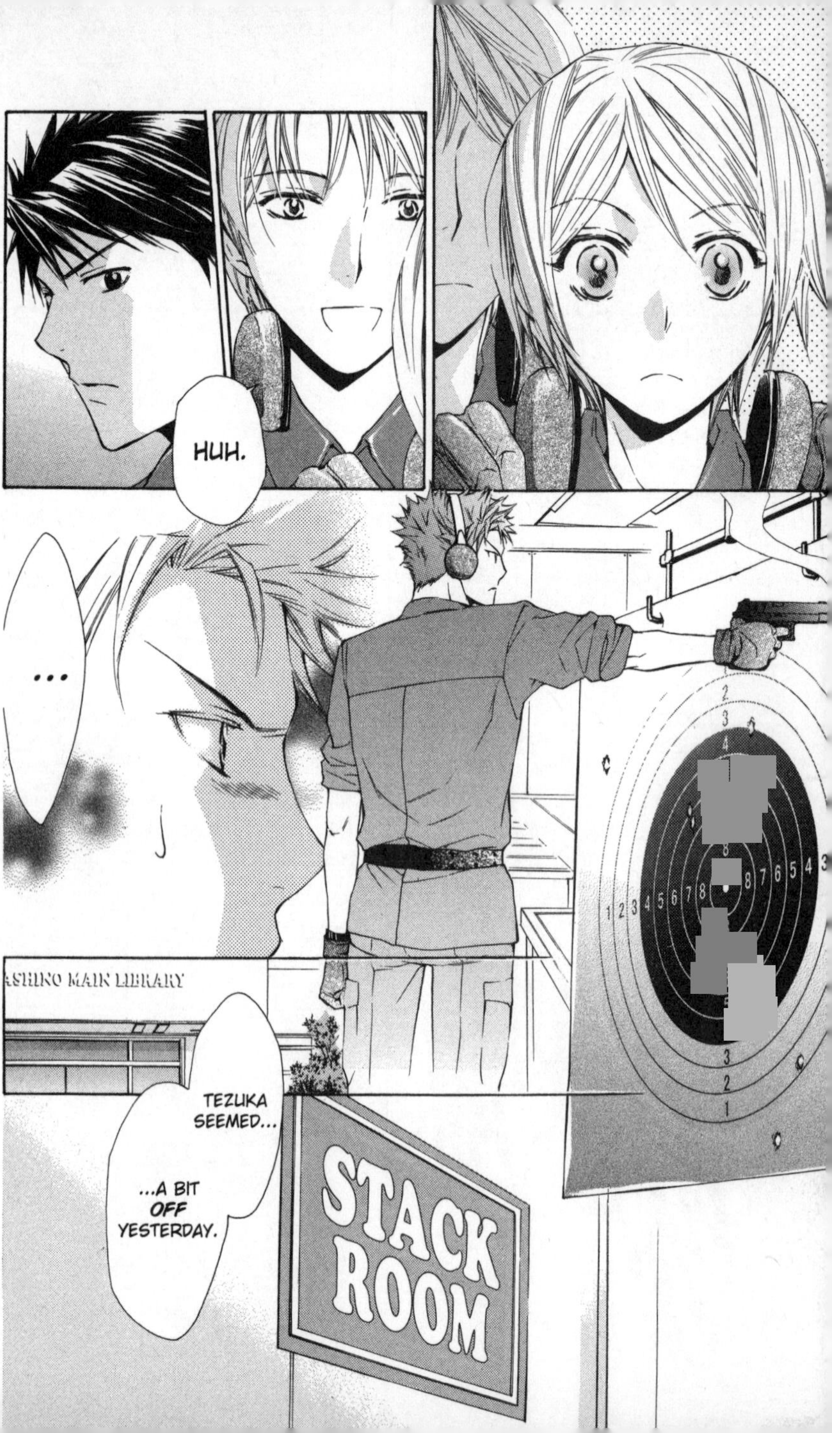
HUH.
...
ASHINO MAIN LIBRARY
TEZUKA SEEMED...
...A BIT OFF YESTERDAY.
STACK ROOM

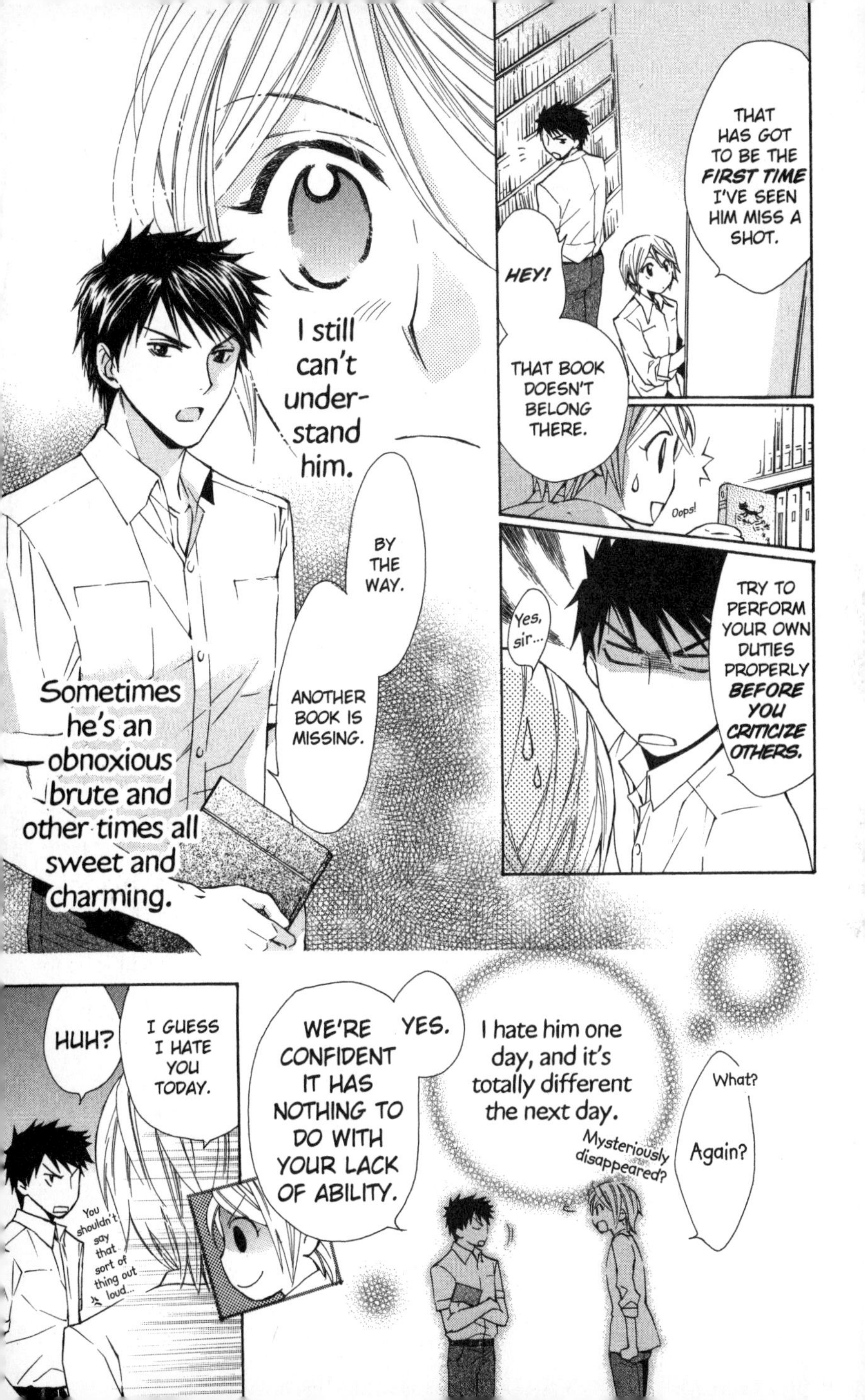
THAT HAS GOT TO BE THE **FIRST TIME** I'VE SEEN HIM MISS A SHOT.
HEY!
THAT BOOK DOESN'T BELONG THERE.
Oops!
TRY TO PERFORM YOUR OWN DUTIES PROPERLY **BEFORE YOU CRITICIZE OTHERS.**
Yes, sir...
I still can't under-stand him.
BY THE WAY.
ANOTHER BOOK IS MISSING.
Sometimes he's an obnoxious brute and other times all sweet and charming.
I hate him one day, and it's totally different the next day.
What?
Again?
Mysteriously disappeared?
YES.
WE'RE CONFIDENT IT HAS NOTHING TO DO WITH YOUR LACK OF ABILITY.
I GUESS I HATE YOU TODAY.
HUH?
You shouldn't say that sort of thing out loud...

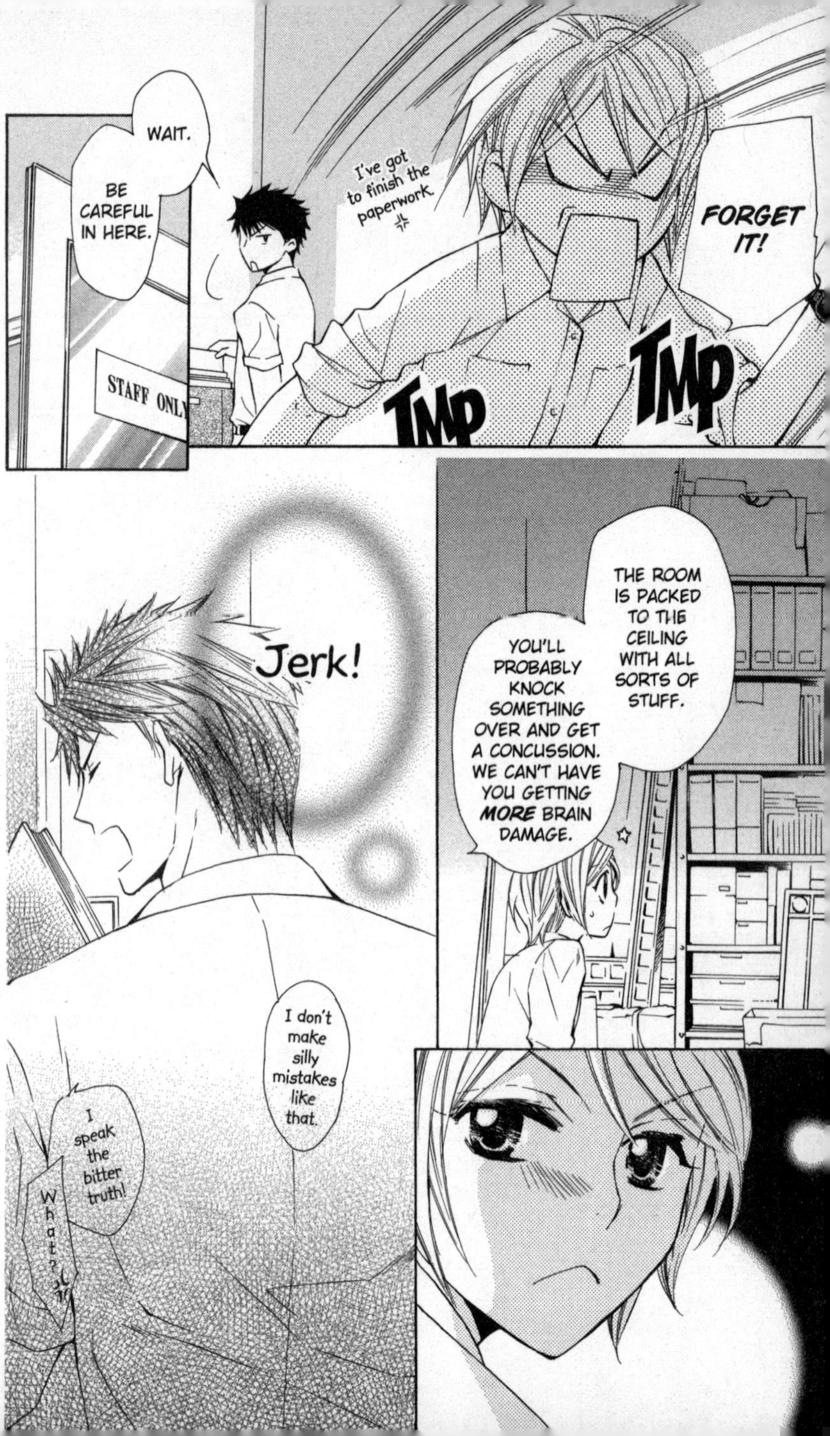
FORGET IT!
TMP
TMP
I've got to finish the paperwork.
WAIT.
BE CAREFUL IN HERE.
STAFF ONLY
THE ROOM IS PACKED TO THE CEILING WITH ALL SORTS OF STUFF.
YOU'LL PROBABLY KNOCK SOMETHING OVER AND GET A CONCUSSION. WE CAN'T HAVE YOU GETTING *MORE* BRAIN DAMAGE.
Jerk!
I don't make silly mistakes like that.
I speak the bitter truth!
What?!

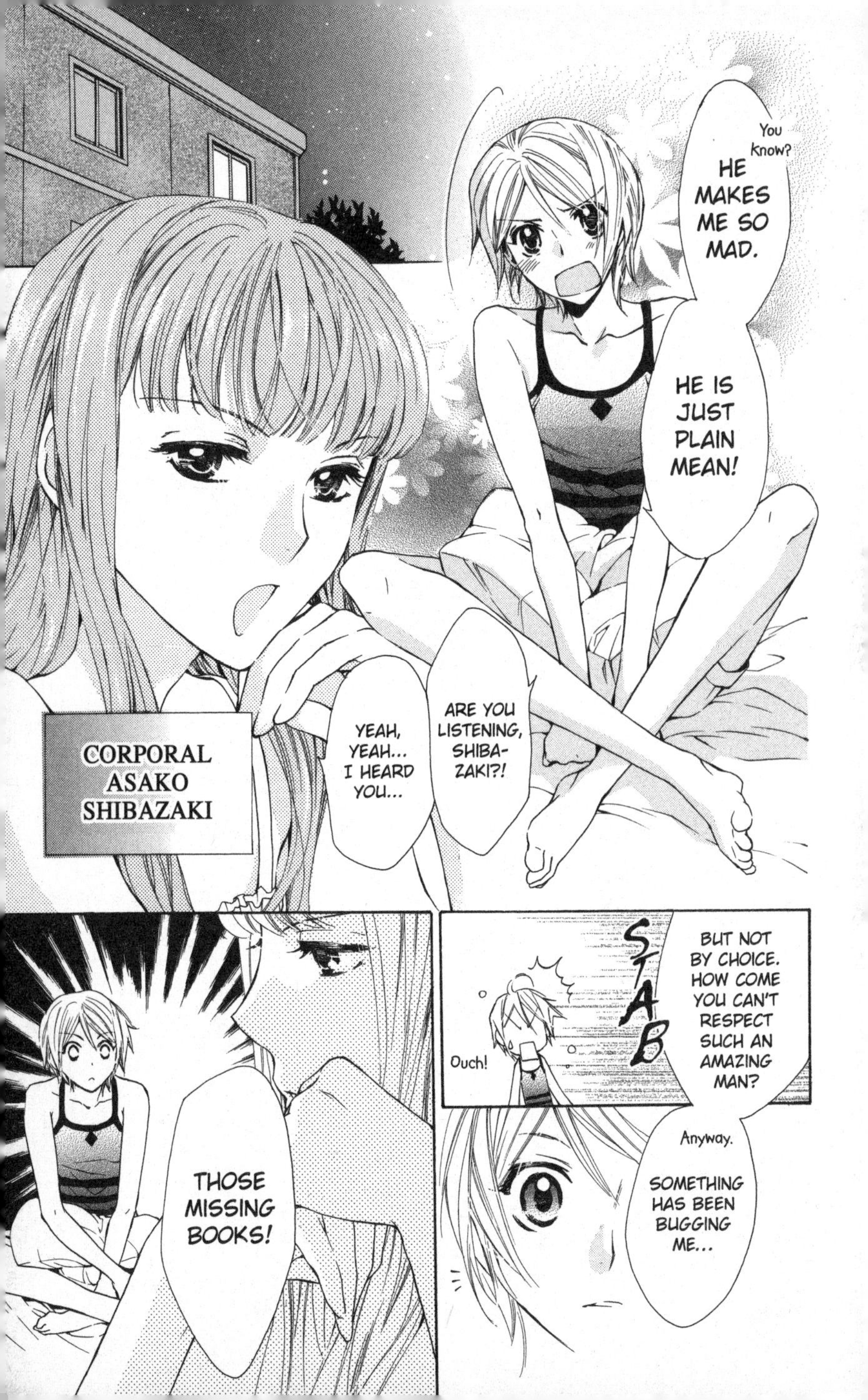
You know?
HE MAKES ME SO MAD.
HE IS JUST PLAIN MEAN!
ARE YOU LISTENING, SHIBAZAKI?!
YEAH, YEAH... I HEARD YOU...
CORPORAL ASAKO SHIBAZAKI
BUT NOT BY CHOICE. HOW COME YOU CAN'T RESPECT SUCH AN AMAZING MAN?
STAB
Ouch!
Anyway.
SOMETHING HAS BEEN BUGGING ME...
THOSE MISSING BOOKS!

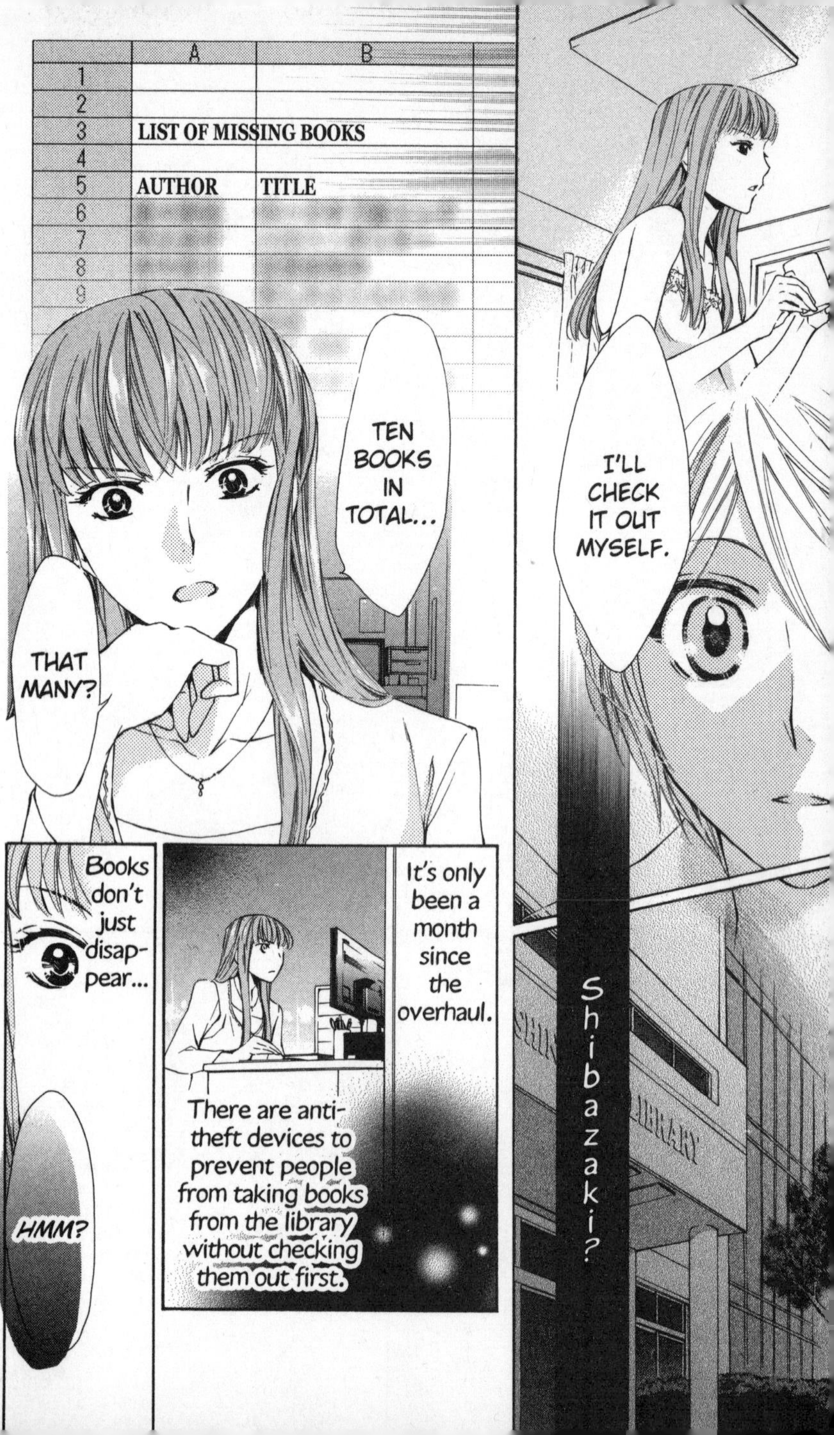
I'LL CHECK IT OUT MYSELF.
Shibazaki?
A
B
1
2
3 LIST OF MISSING BOOKS
4
5 AUTHOR TITLE
6
7
8
9
TEN BOOKS IN TOTAL...
THAT MANY?
It's only been a month since the overhaul.
There are anti-theft devices to prevent people from taking books from the library without checking them out first.
Books don't just disappear...
HMM?

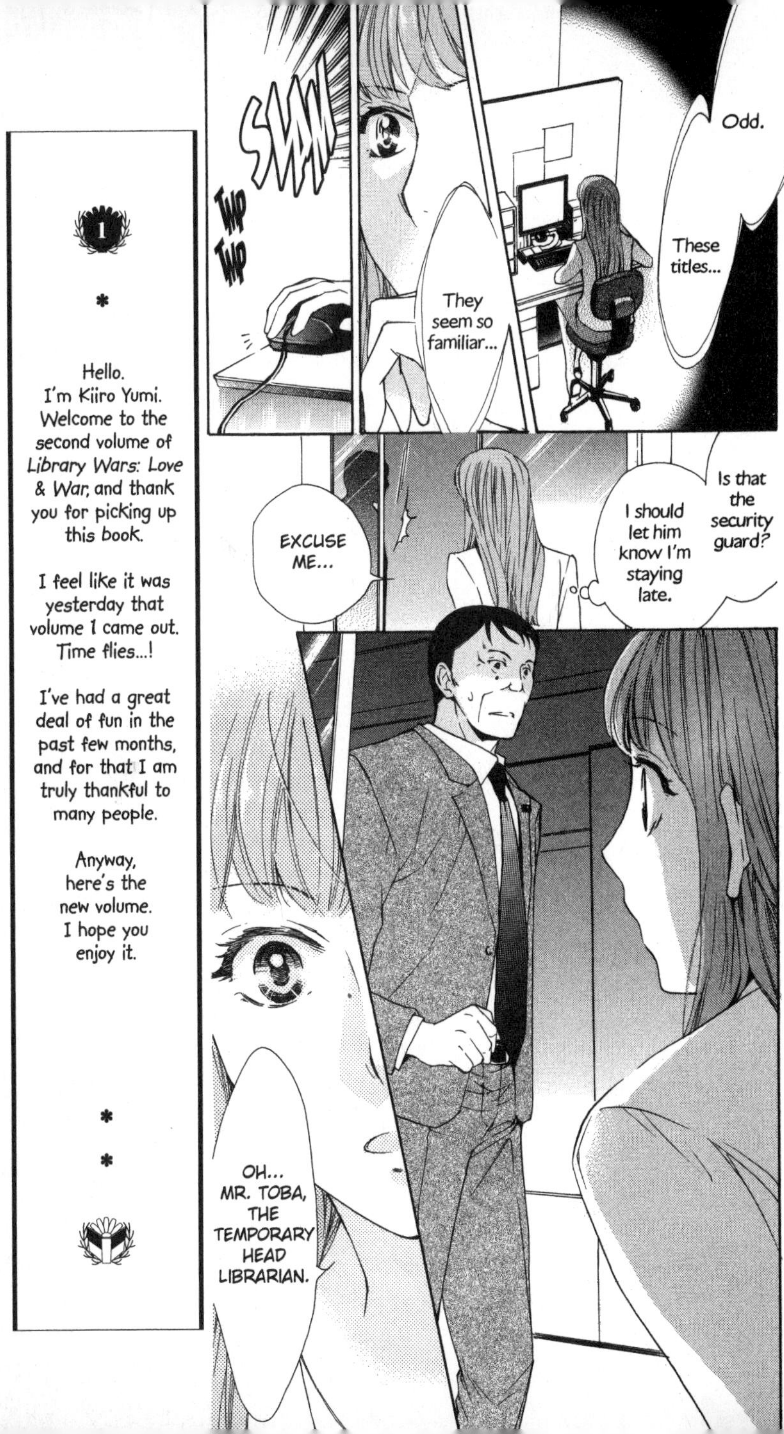
Odd.
These titles...
They seem so familiar...
SLAM
TMP TMP
Is that the security guard?
I should let him know I'm staying late.
EXCUSE ME...
OH... MR. TOBA, THE TEMPORARY HEAD LIBRARIAN.

1

*

Hello.
I'm Kiiro Yumi.
Welcome to the second volume of *Library Wars: Love & War*, and thank you for picking up this book.

I feel like it was yesterday that volume 1 came out. Time flies...!

I've had a great deal of fun in the past few months, and for that I am truly thankful to many people.

Anyway, here's the new volume. I hope you enjoy it.

*

*

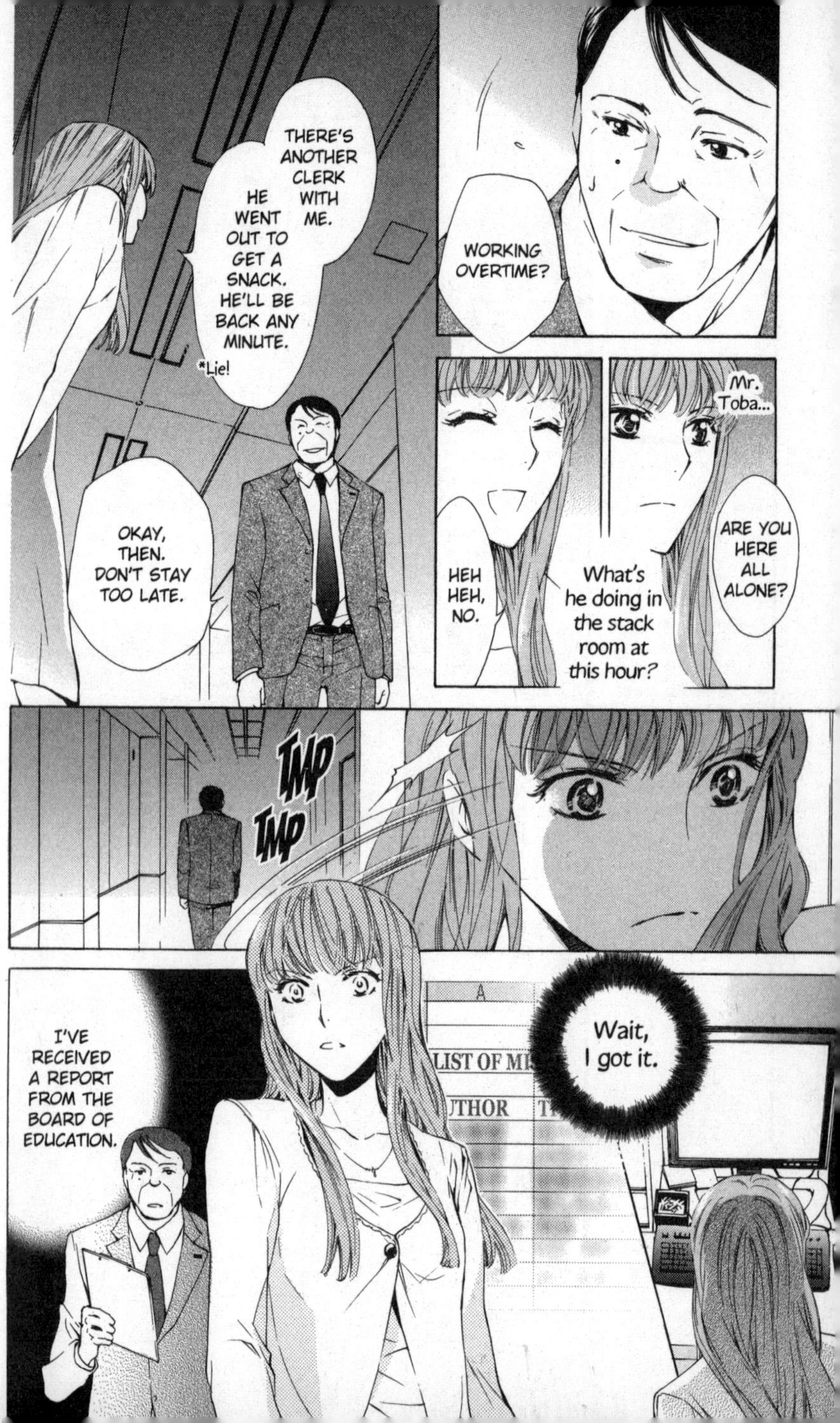
WORKING OVERTIME?
Mr. Toba...
ARE YOU HERE ALL ALONE?
HEH HEH, NO.
What's he doing in the stack room at this hour?
THERE'S ANOTHER CLERK WITH ME.
HE WENT OUT TO GET A SNACK. HE'LL BE BACK ANY MINUTE.
*Lie!
OKAY, THEN. DON'T STAY TOO LATE.
TMP
TMP
Wait, I got it.
I'VE RECEIVED A REPORT FROM THE BOARD OF EDUCATION.

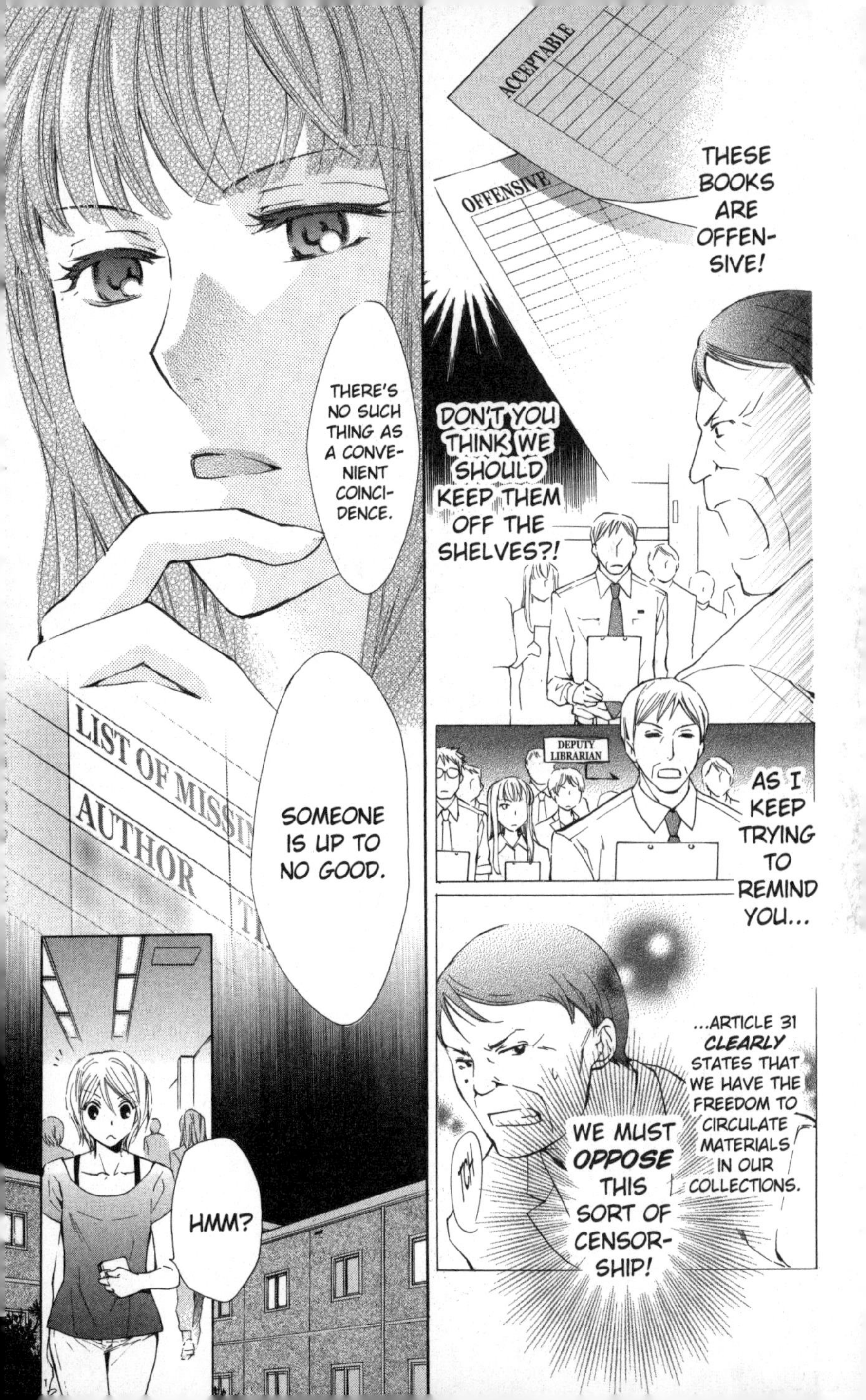
ACCEPTABLE
OFFENSIVE
THESE BOOKS ARE OFFEN-SIVE!
DON'T YOU THINK WE SHOULD KEEP THEM OFF THE SHELVES?!
DEPUTY LIBRARIAN
AS I KEEP TRYING TO REMIND YOU...
...ARTICLE 31 CLEARLY STATES THAT WE HAVE THE FREEDOM TO CIRCULATE MATERIALS IN OUR COLLECTIONS.
WE MUST OPPOSE THIS SORT OF CENSOR-SHIP!
TCH
THERE'S NO SUCH THING AS A CONVE-NIENT COINCI-DENCE.
LIST OF MISSI
AUTHOR
SOMEONE IS UP TO NO GOOD.
HMM?

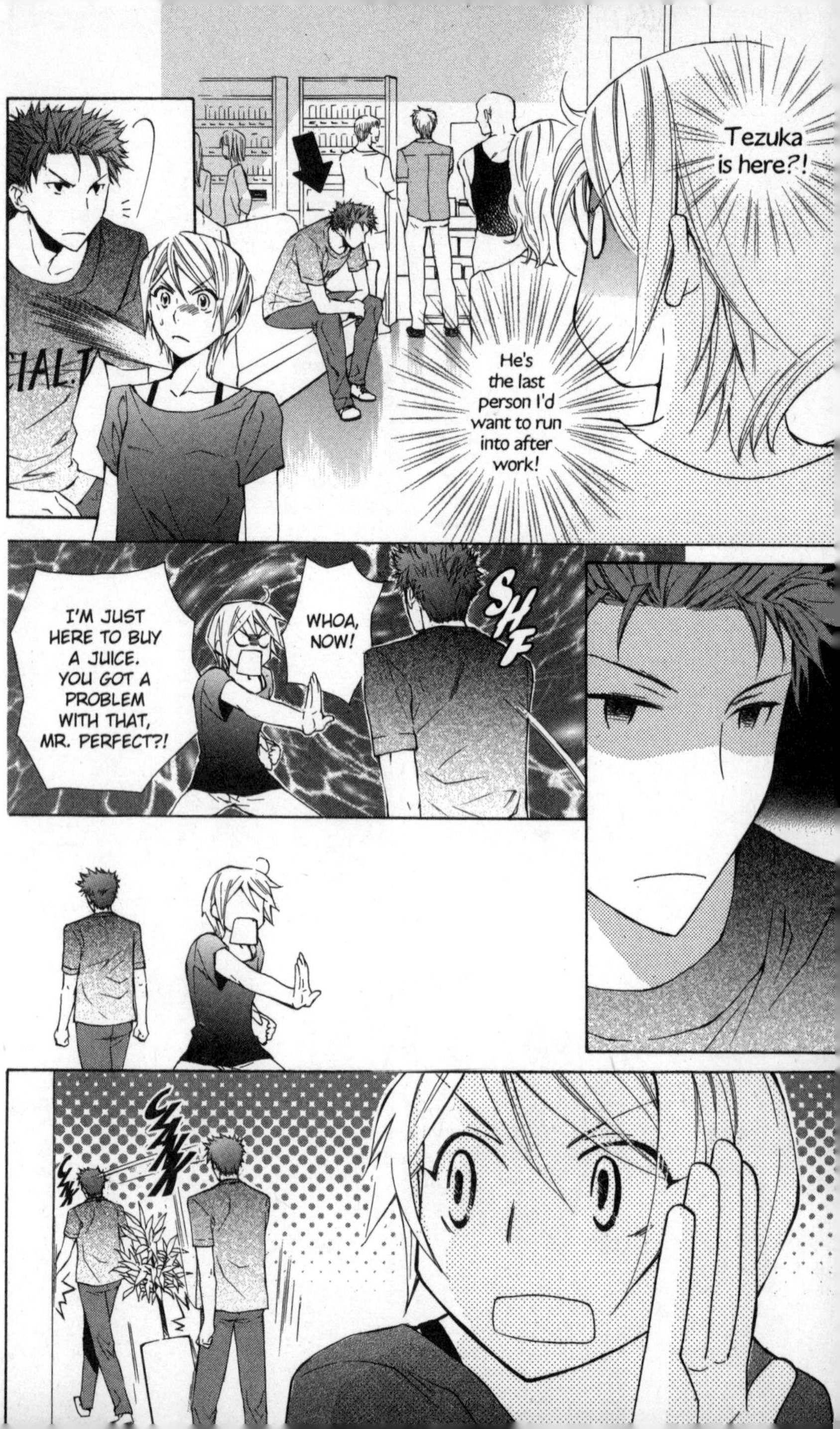
Tezuka is here?!
He's the last person I'd want to run into after work!
SHF
WHOA, NOW!
I'M JUST HERE TO BUY A JUICE. YOU GOT A PROBLEM WITH THAT, MR. PERFECT?!

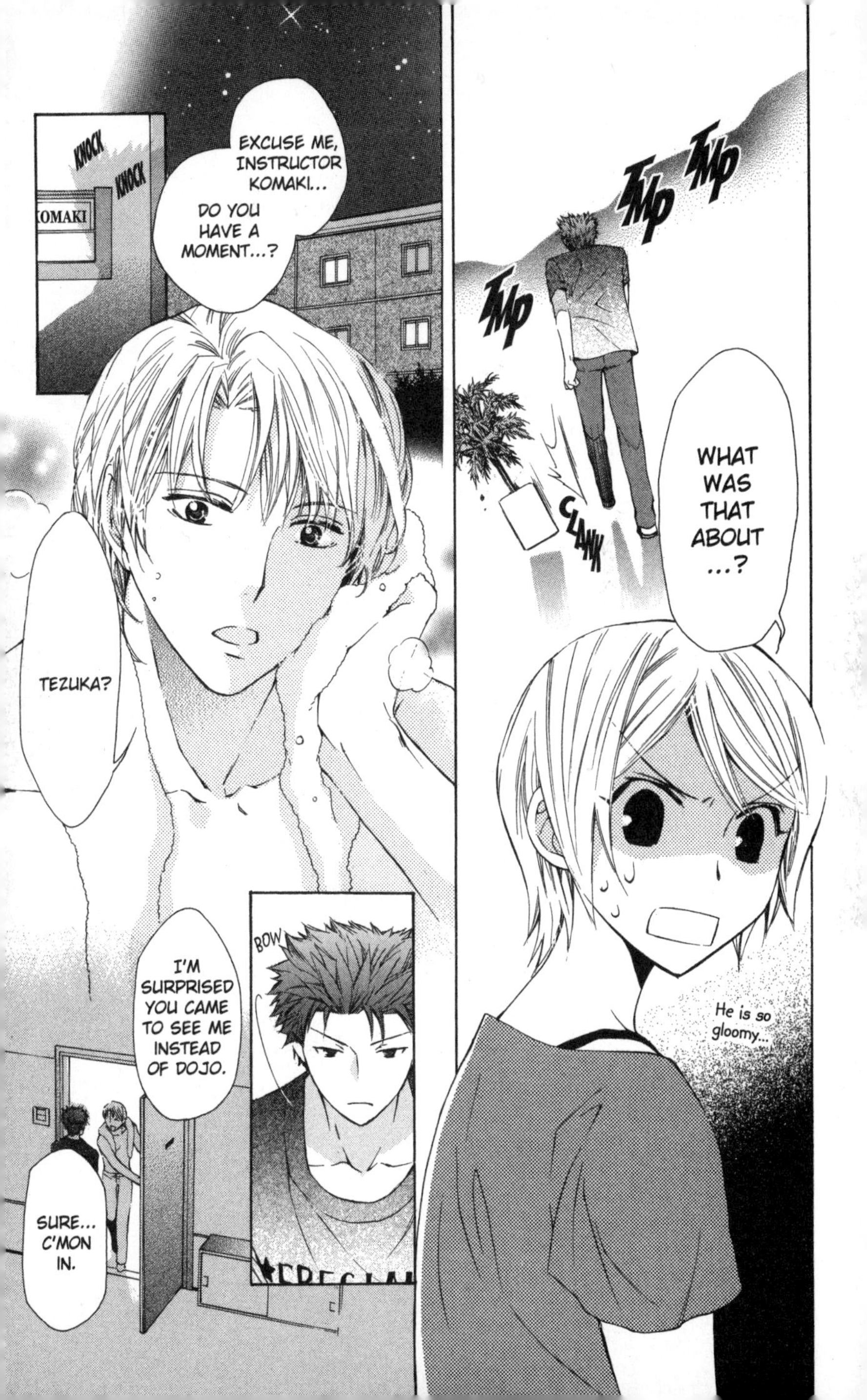
TMP
TMP
TMP
CLANK
WHAT WAS THAT ABOUT ...?
He is so gloomy...
KNOCK
KNOCK
KOMAKI
EXCUSE ME, INSTRUCTOR KOMAKI...
DO YOU HAVE A MOMENT...?
TEZUKA?
BOW
I'M SURPRISED YOU CAME TO SEE ME INSTEAD OF DOJO.
SURE... C'MON IN.

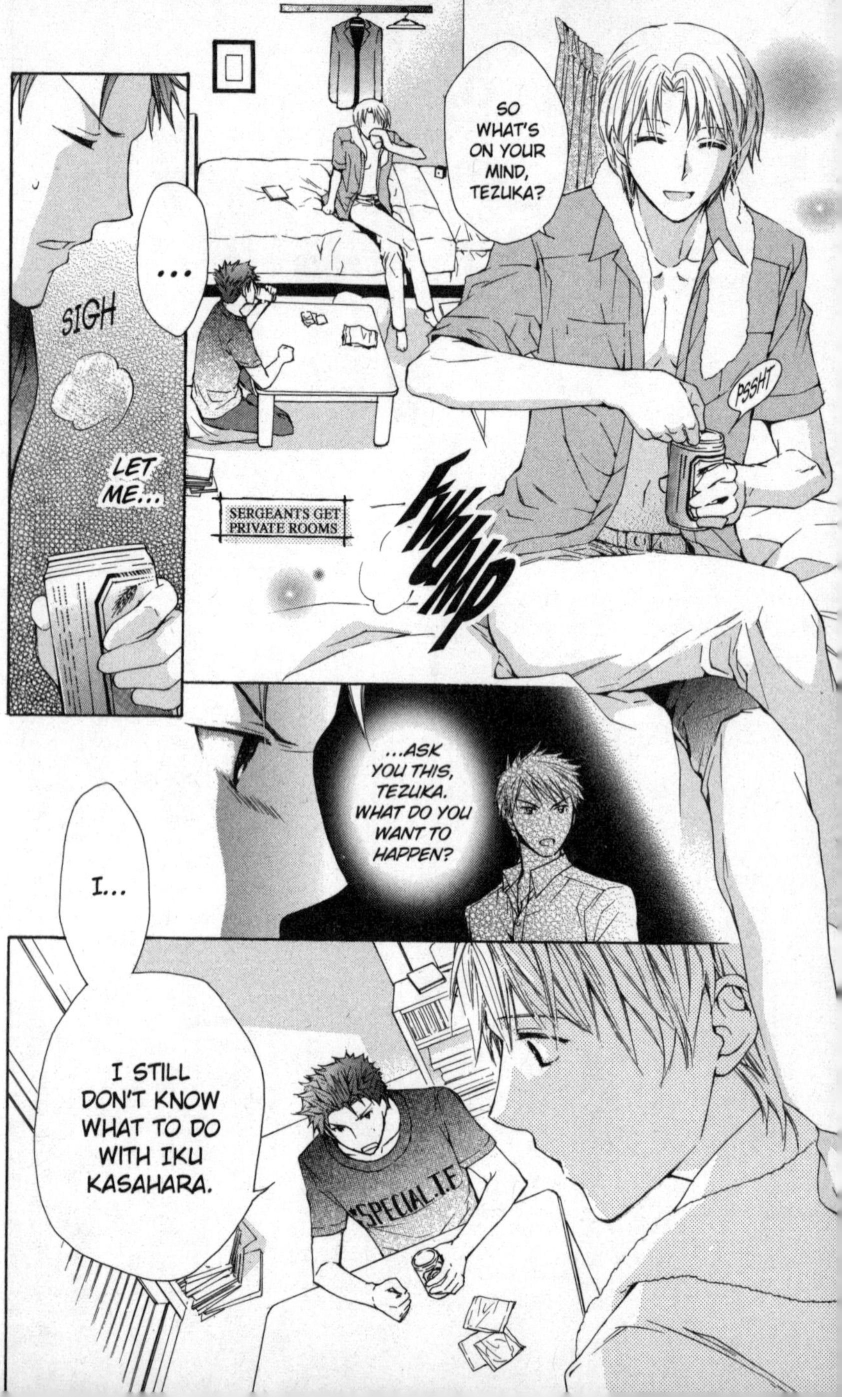
SO WHAT'S ON YOUR MIND, TEZUKA?
PSSHT
SERGEANTS GET PRIVATE ROOMS
KWUMP
...
SIGH
LET ME...
...ASK YOU THIS, TEZUKA. WHAT DO YOU WANT TO HAPPEN?
I...
I STILL DON'T KNOW WHAT TO DO WITH IKU KASAHARA.
SPECIAL T.F

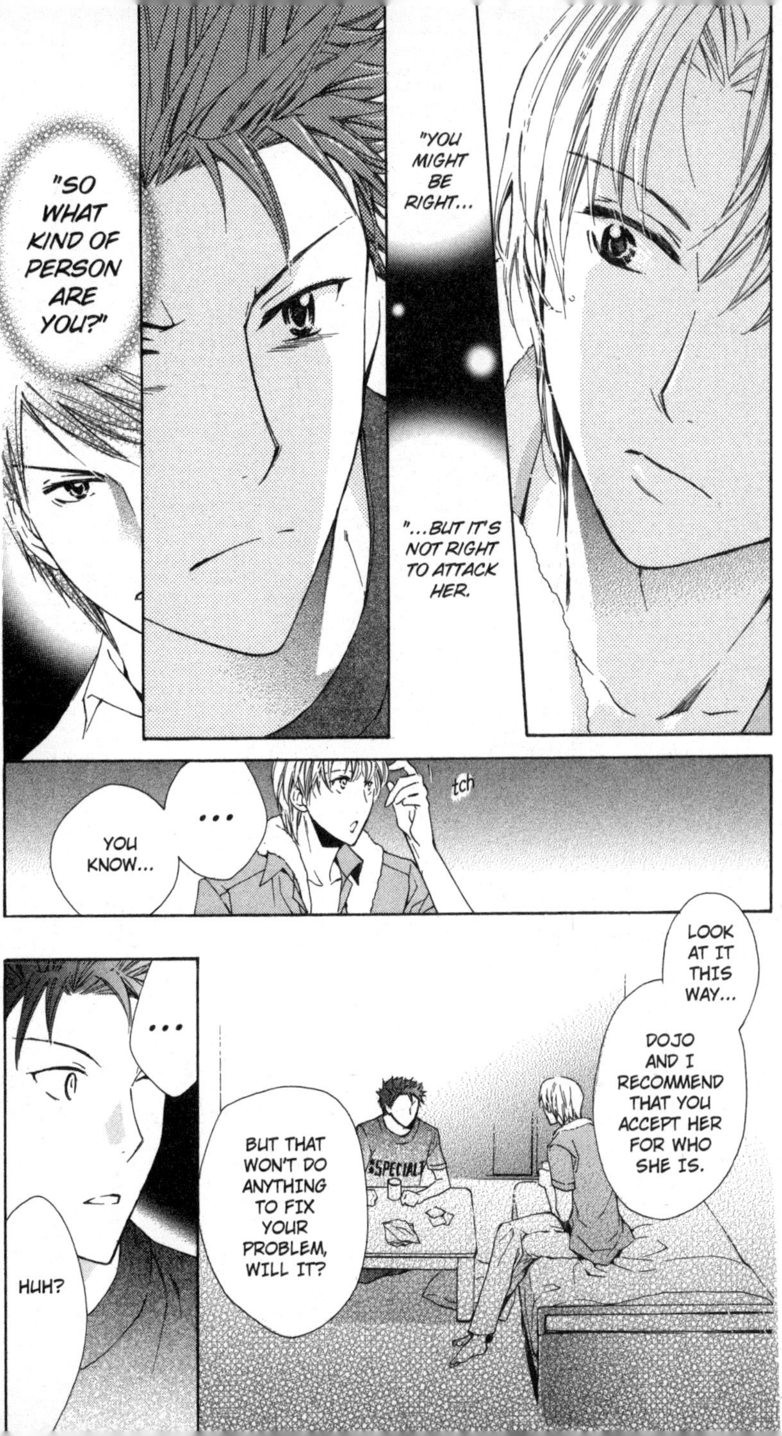
"YOU MIGHT BE RIGHT...
"...BUT IT'S NOT RIGHT TO ATTACK HER.
"SO WHAT KIND OF PERSON ARE YOU?"
tch
...
YOU KNOW...
LOOK AT IT THIS WAY...
DOJO AND I RECOMMEND THAT YOU ACCEPT HER FOR WHO SHE IS.
BUT THAT WON'T DO ANYTHING TO FIX YOUR PROBLEM, WILL IT?
...
HUH?

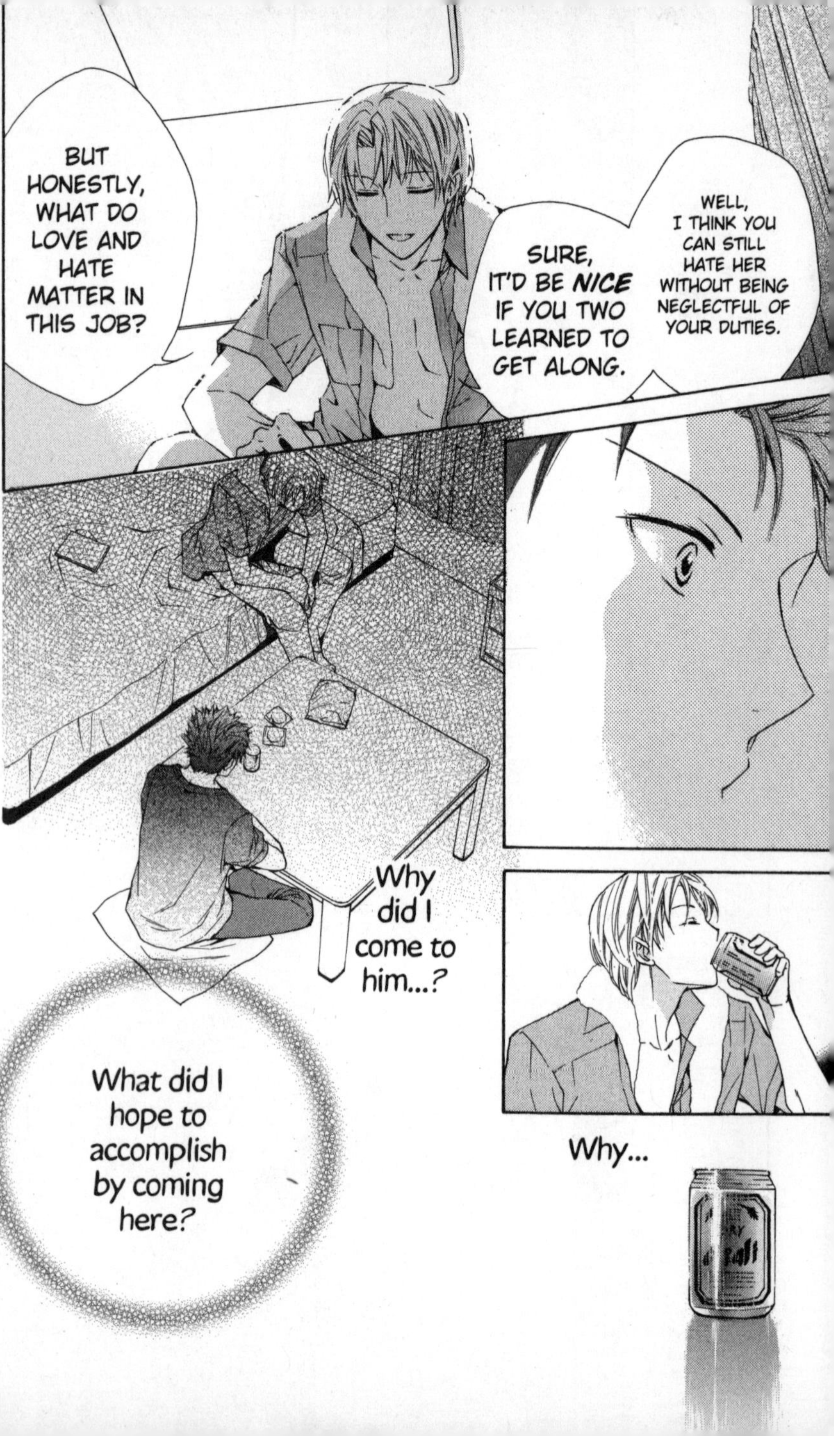
WELL, I THINK YOU CAN STILL HATE HER WITHOUT BEING NEGLECTFUL OF YOUR DUTIES.
SURE, IT'D BE **NICE** IF YOU TWO LEARNED TO GET ALONG.
BUT HONESTLY, WHAT DO LOVE AND HATE MATTER IN THIS JOB?
Why did I come to him...?
Why...
What did I hope to accomplish by coming here?

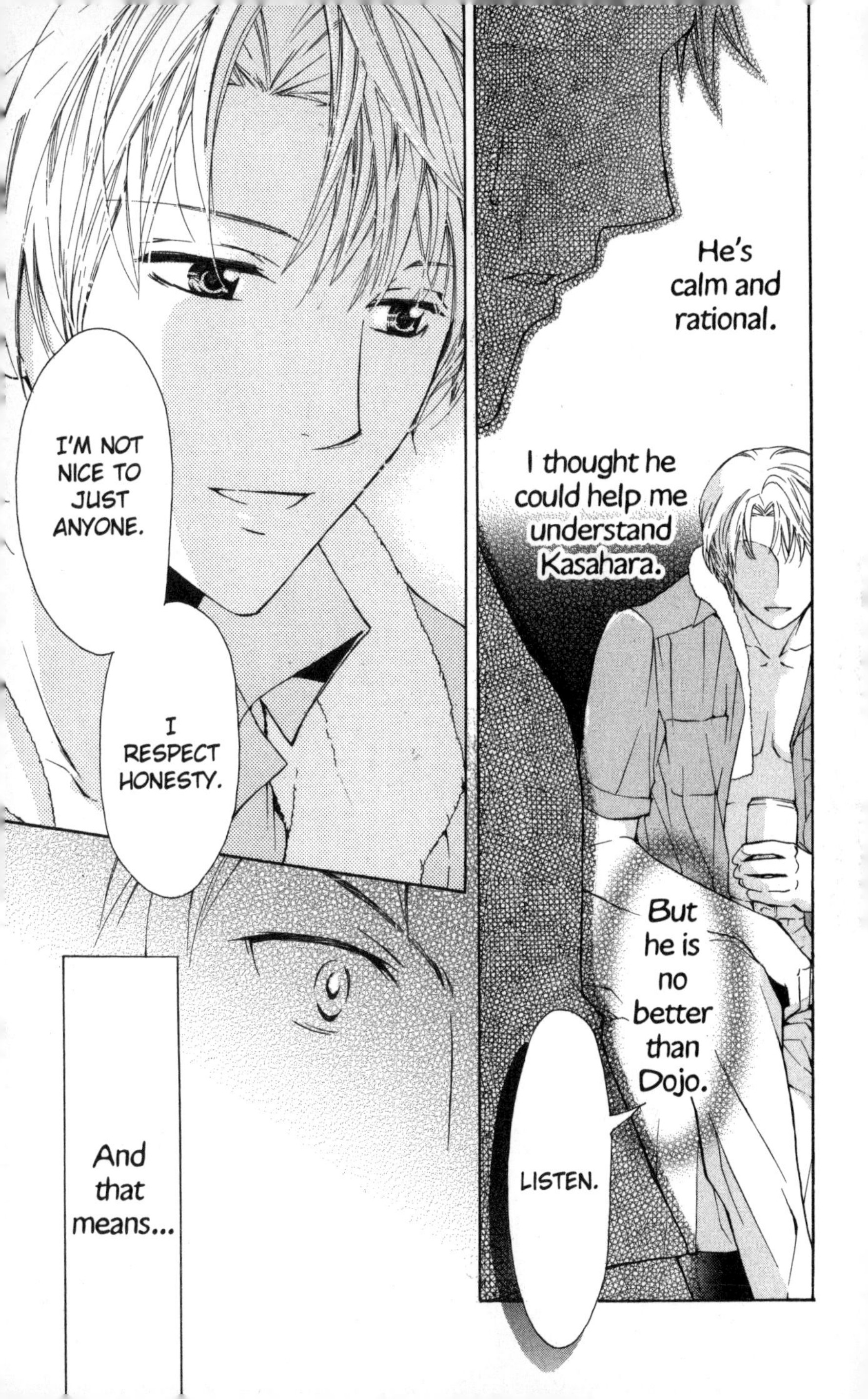
He's calm and rational.
I thought he could help me understand Kasahara.
But he is no better than Dojo.
LISTEN.
I'M NOT NICE TO JUST ANYONE.
I RESPECT HONESTY.
And that means...

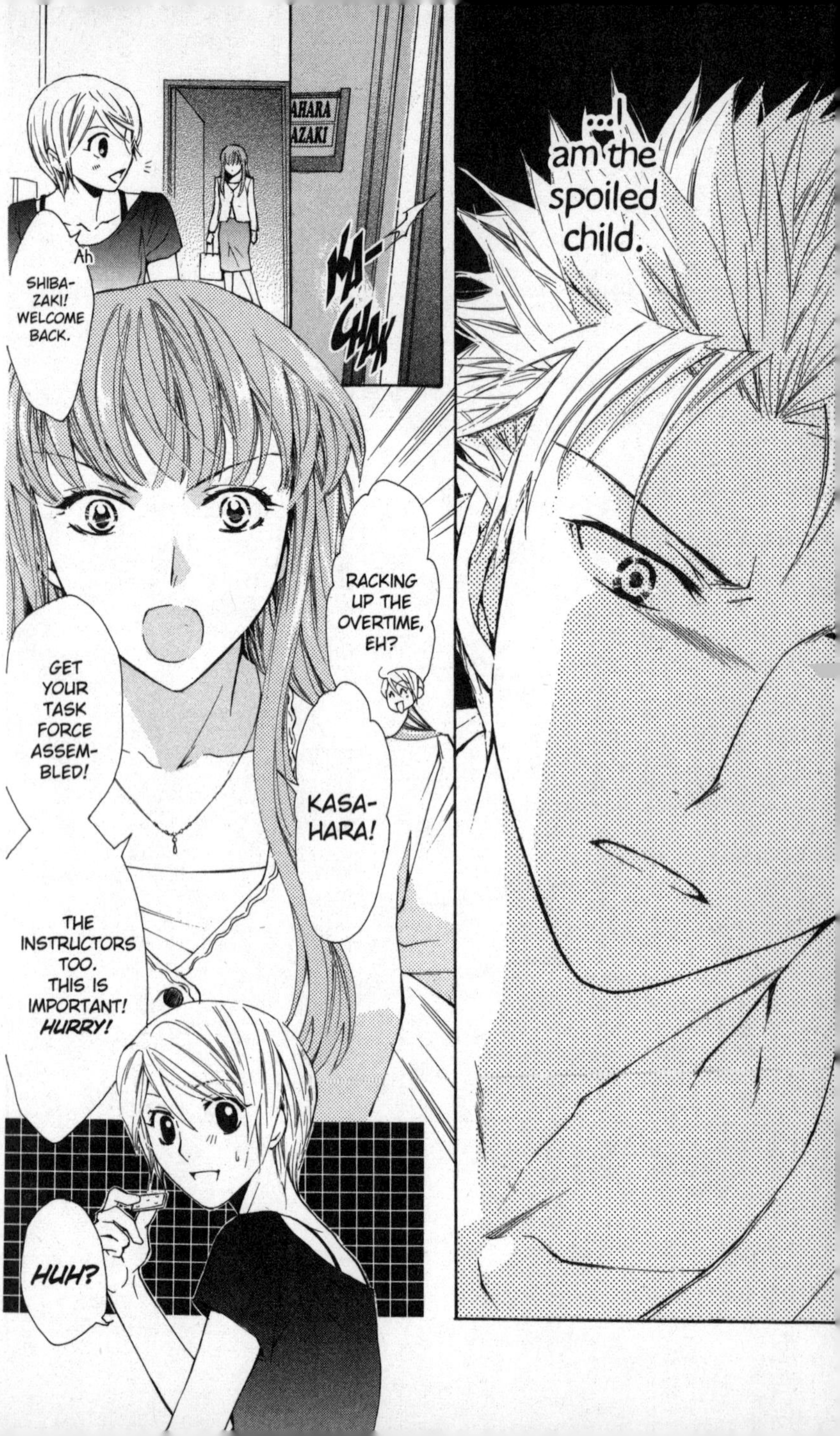
...I am the spoiled child.
KA-CHAK
Ah
SHIBA-ZAKI! WELCOME BACK.
RACKING UP THE OVERTIME, EH?
KASA-HARA!
GET YOUR TASK FORCE ASSEM-BLED!
THE INSTRUCTORS TOO. THIS IS IMPORTANT! *HURRY!*
HUH?

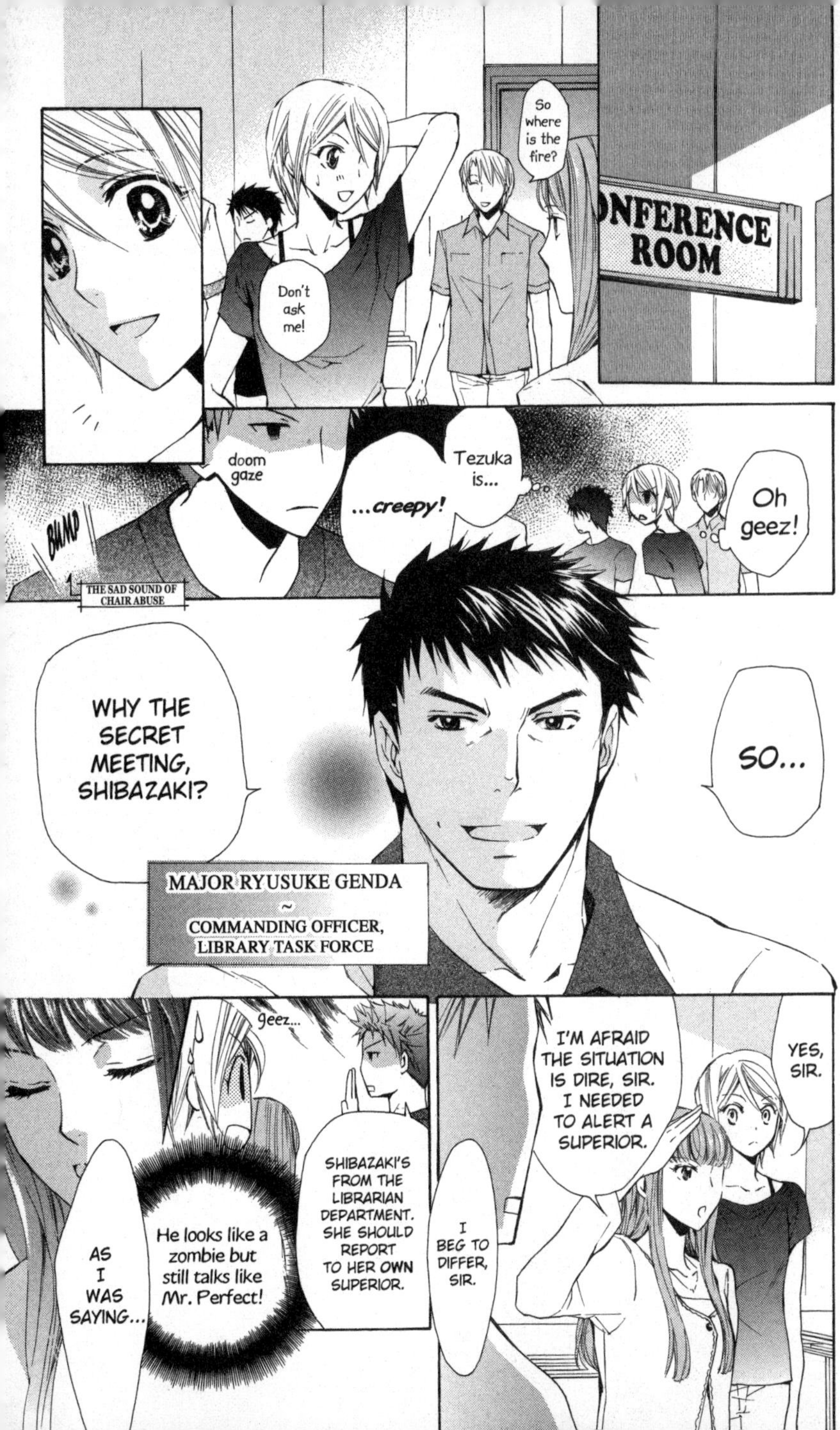
NFERENCE ROOM
So where is the fire?
Don't ask me!
Oh geez!
Tezuka is...
...creepy!
doom gaze
BUMP
THE SAD SOUND OF CHAIR ABUSE
SO...
WHY THE SECRET MEETING, SHIBAZAKI?
MAJOR RYUSUKE GENDA ~ COMMANDING OFFICER, LIBRARY TASK FORCE
YES, SIR.
I'M AFRAID THE SITUATION IS DIRE, SIR. I NEEDED TO ALERT A SUPERIOR.
I BEG TO DIFFER, SIR.
geez...
SHIBAZAKI'S FROM THE LIBRARIAN DEPARTMENT. SHE SHOULD REPORT TO HER OWN SUPERIOR.
He looks like a zombie but still talks like Mr. Perfect!
AS I WAS SAYING...

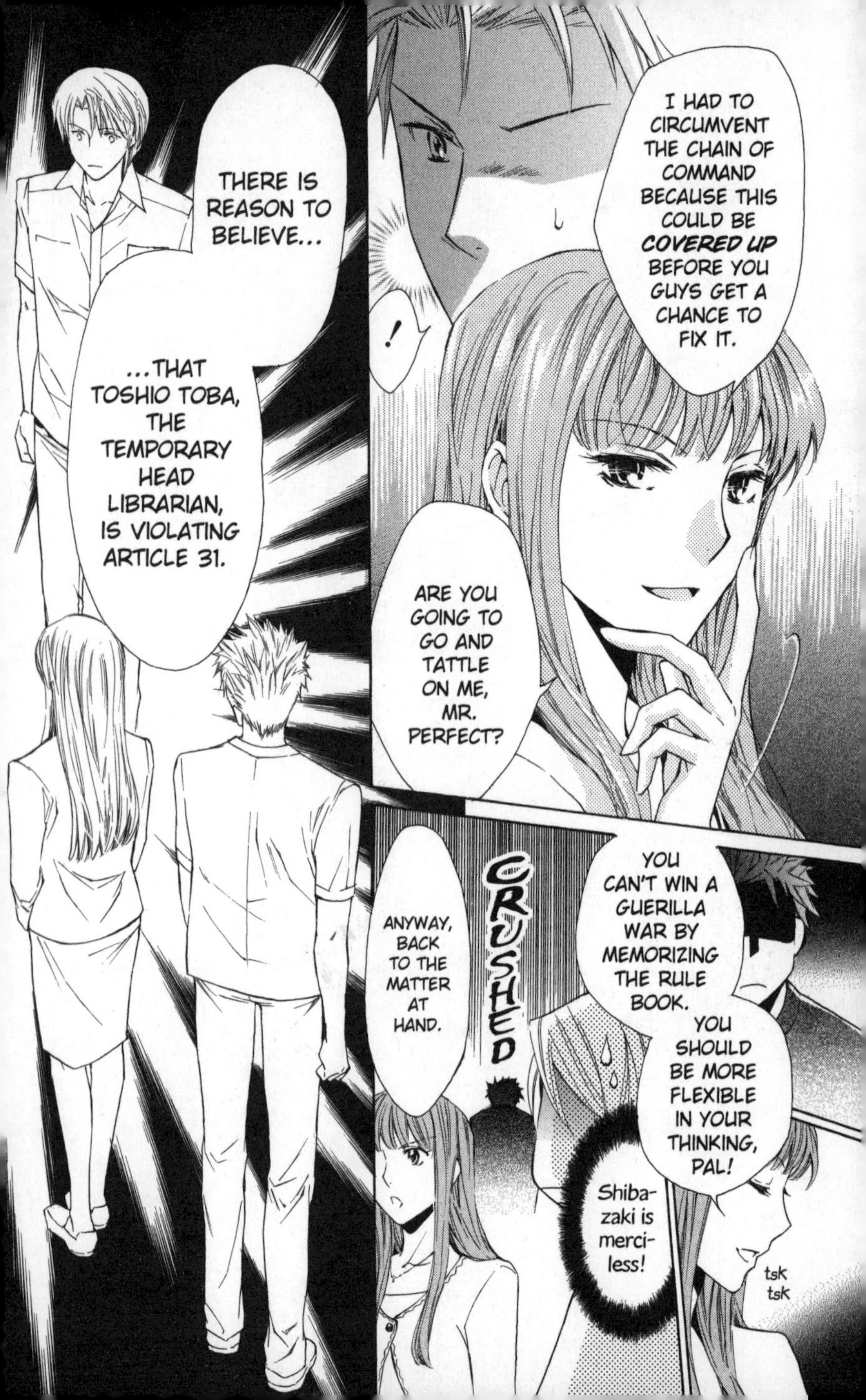
I HAD TO CIRCUMVENT THE CHAIN OF COMMAND BECAUSE THIS COULD BE **COVERED UP** BEFORE YOU GUYS GET A CHANCE TO FIX IT.
!
ARE YOU GOING TO GO AND TATTLE ON ME, MR. PERFECT?
YOU CAN'T WIN A GUERILLA WAR BY MEMORIZING THE RULE BOOK.
YOU SHOULD BE MORE FLEXIBLE IN YOUR THINKING, PAL!
tsk tsk
Shiba-zaki is merci-less!
CRUSHED
ANYWAY, BACK TO THE MATTER AT HAND.
THERE IS REASON TO BELIEVE...
...THAT TOSHIO TOBA, THE TEMPORARY HEAD LIBRARIAN, IS VIOLATING ARTICLE 31.

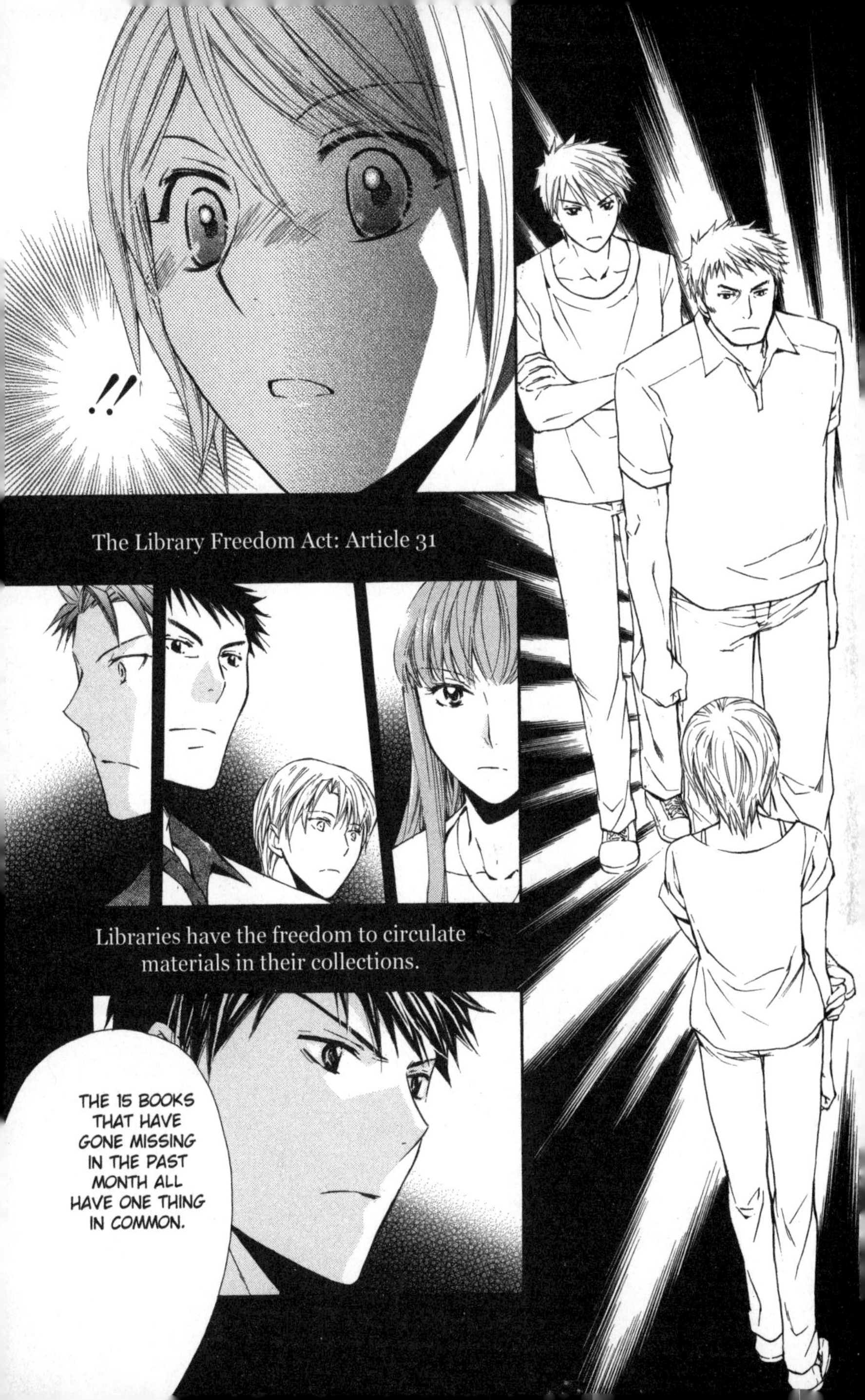
!!
The Library Freedom Act: Article 31
Libraries have the freedom to circulate materials in their collections.
THE 15 BOOKS THAT HAVE GONE MISSING IN THE PAST MONTH ALL HAVE ONE THING IN COMMON.

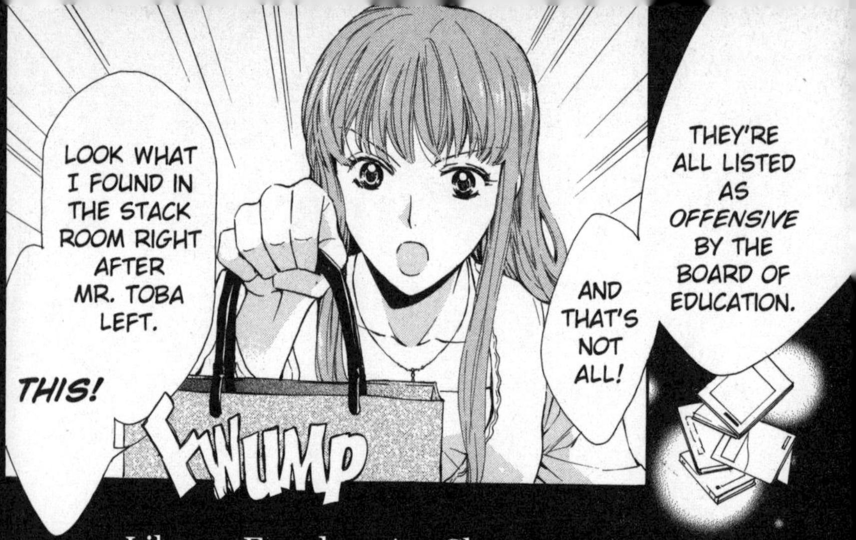
THEY'RE ALL LISTED AS OFFENSIVE BY THE BOARD OF EDUCATION.
AND THAT'S NOT ALL!
LOOK WHAT I FOUND IN THE STACK ROOM RIGHT AFTER MR. TOBA LEFT.
THIS!
FWUMP

Library Freedom Act Chapter 4

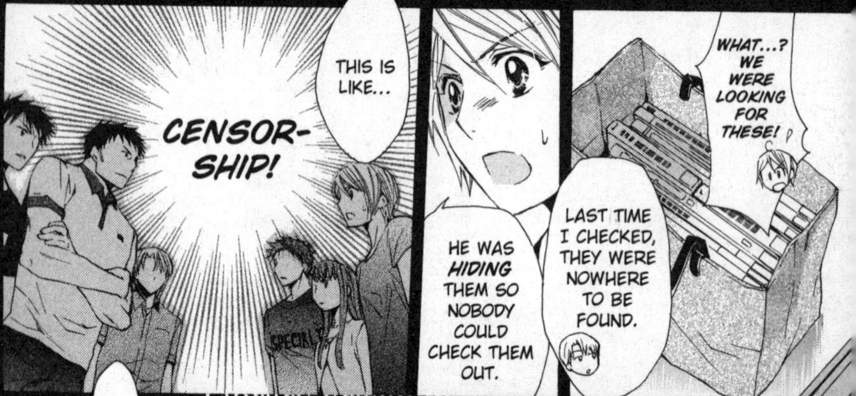
WHAT...? WE WERE LOOKING FOR THESE!
LAST TIME I CHECKED, THEY WERE NOWHERE TO BE FOUND.
HE WAS *HIDING* THEM SO NOBODY COULD CHECK THEM OUT.
THIS IS LIKE...
CENSORSHIP!

Library Freedom Act Chapter 4

Article 30	Libraries have the freedom to acquire their collections.
Article 31	Libraries have the freedom to circulate materials in their collections.
Article 32	Libraries guarantee the privacy of their patrons.
Article 33	Libraries oppose any type of censorship.
Article 34	When libraries are imperiled, librarians will join together to secure their freedom.

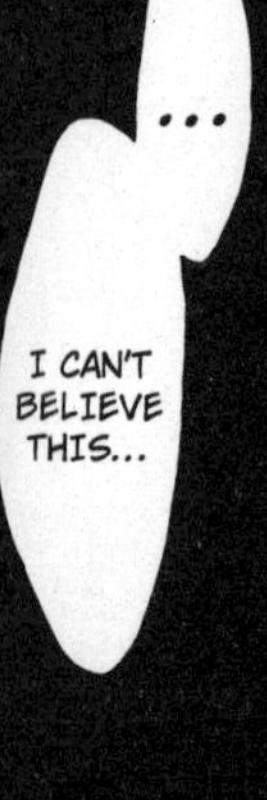
...
I CAN'T BELIEVE THIS...

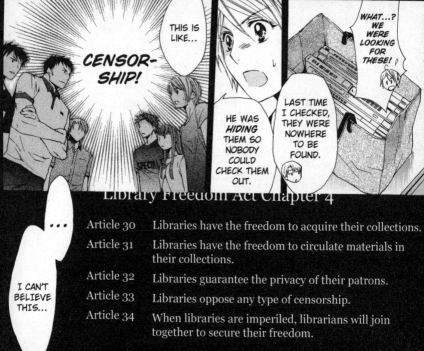

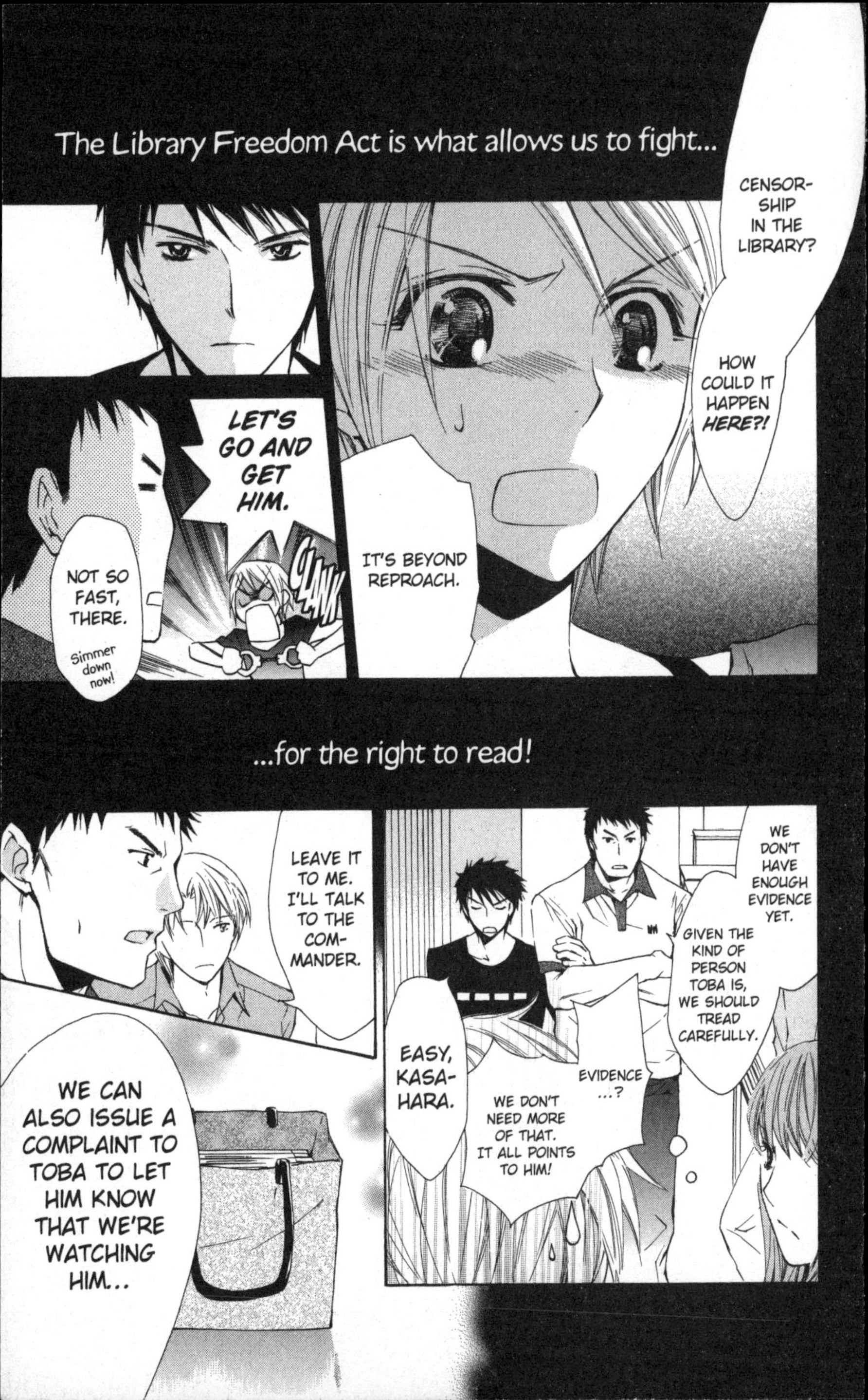
The Library Freedom Act is what allows us to fight...
CENSOR-SHIP IN THE LIBRARY?
HOW COULD IT HAPPEN HERE?!
IT'S BEYOND REPROACH.
LET'S GO AND GET HIM.
CLANK
NOT SO FAST, THERE.
Simmer down now!
...for the right to read!
WE DON'T HAVE ENOUGH EVIDENCE YET.
GIVEN THE KIND OF PERSON TOBA IS, WE SHOULD TREAD CAREFULLY.
EVIDENCE ...?
WE DON'T NEED MORE OF THAT. IT ALL POINTS TO HIM!
EASY, KASA-HARA.
LEAVE IT TO ME. I'LL TALK TO THE COM-MANDER.
WE CAN ALSO ISSUE A COMPLAINT TO TOBA TO LET HIM KNOW THAT WE'RE WATCHING HIM...

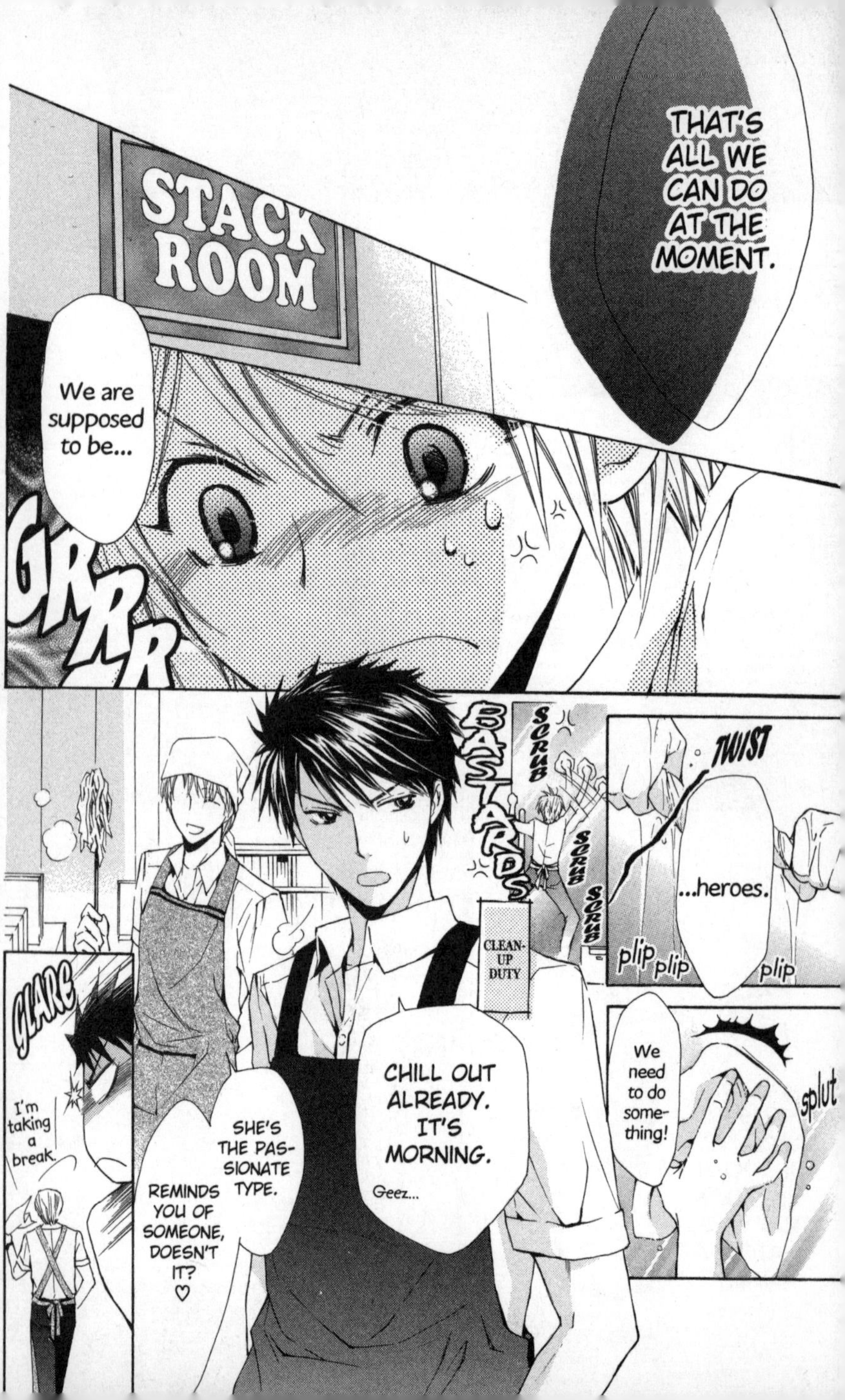
THAT'S ALL WE CAN DO AT THE MOMENT.
STACK ROOM
We are supposed to be...
GRRR
TWIST
...heroes.
plip plip plip
We need to do some-thing!
splut
BASTARDS
SCRUB SCRUB SCRUB
CLEAN-UP DUTY
CHILL OUT ALREADY. IT'S MORNING.
Geez...
SHE'S THE PAS-SIONATE TYPE.
REMINDS YOU OF SOMEONE, DOESN'T IT? ♡
GLARE
I'm taking a break.

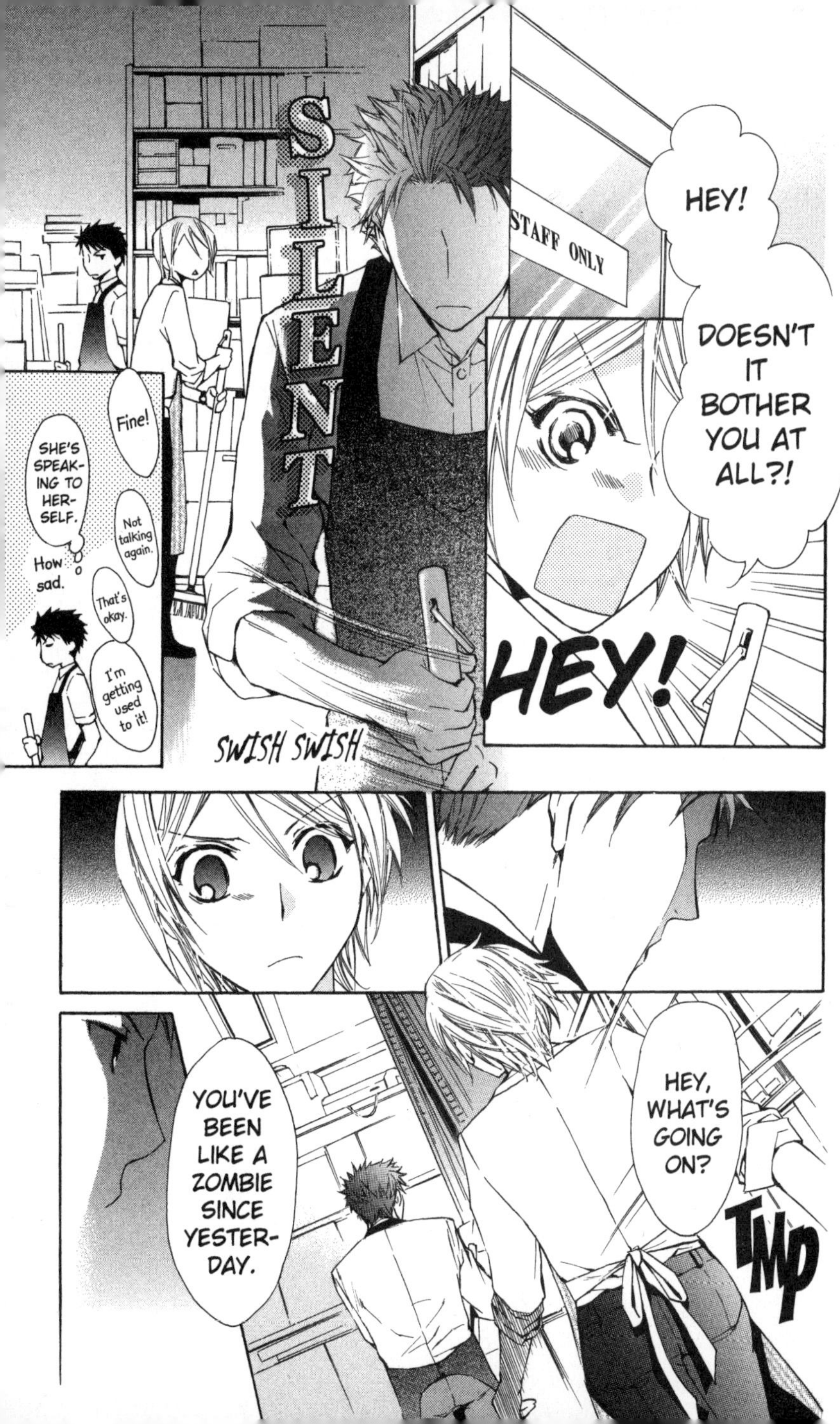
HEY!
DOESN'T IT BOTHER YOU AT ALL?!
HEY!
SILENT
STAFF ONLY
SWISH SWISH
Fine!
SHE'S SPEAKING TO HERSELF.
Not talking again.
How sad.
That's okay.
I'm getting used to it!
HEY, WHAT'S GOING ON?
TMP
YOU'VE BEEN LIKE A ZOMBIE SINCE YESTERDAY.

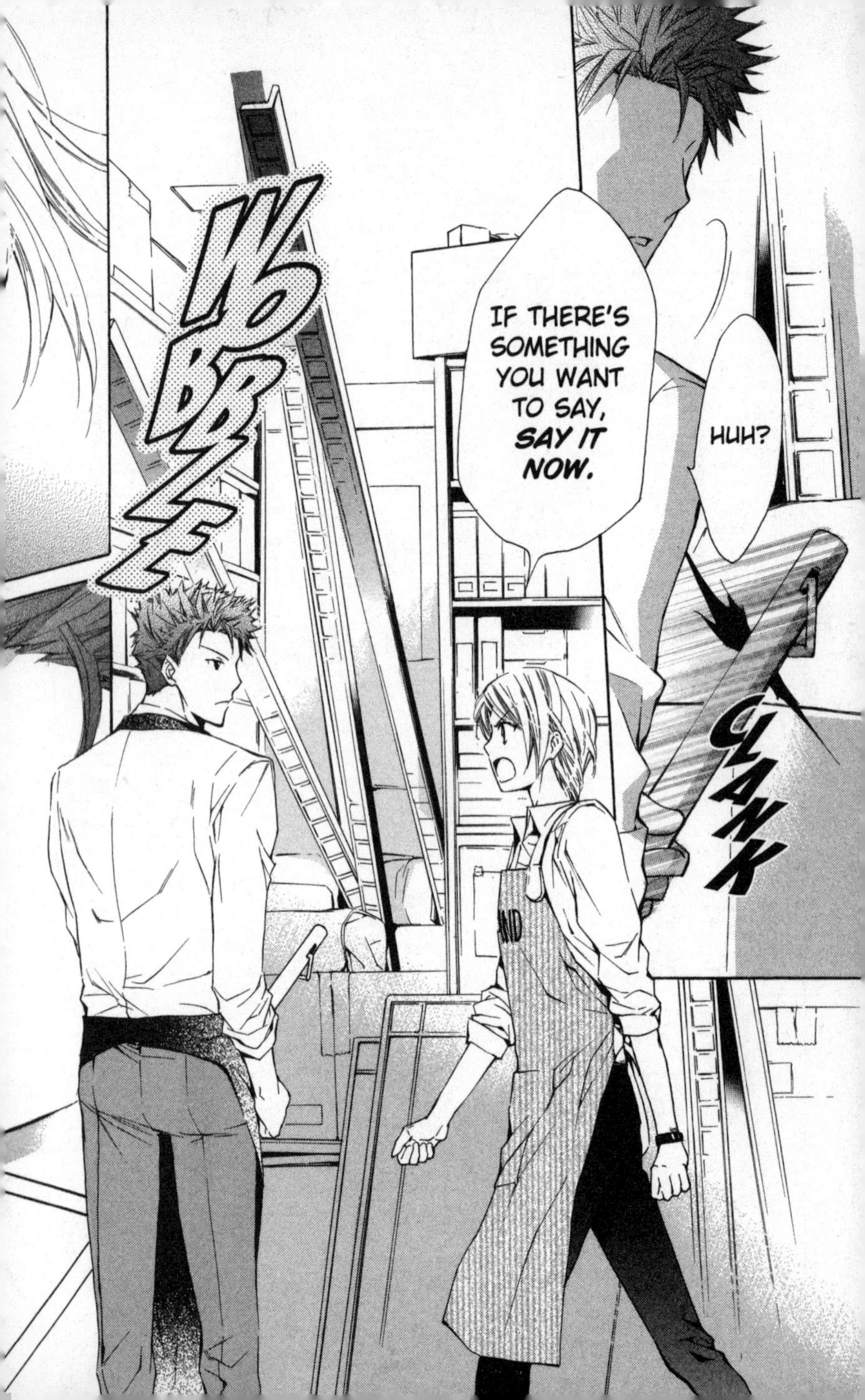

IF THERE'S SOMETHING YOU WANT TO SAY, *SAY IT NOW.*
HUH?
CLANK
WOBBLE

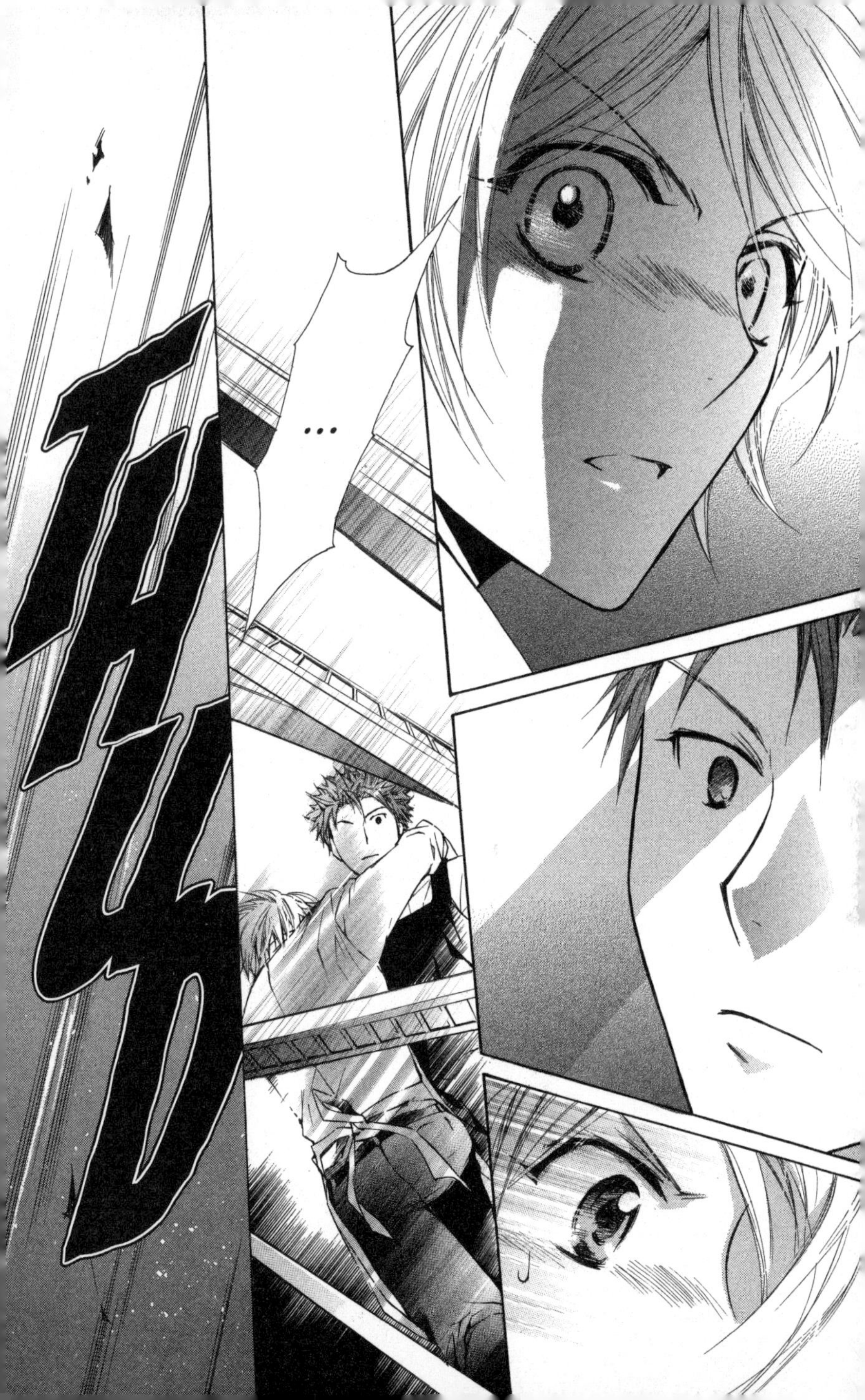
...
THUD

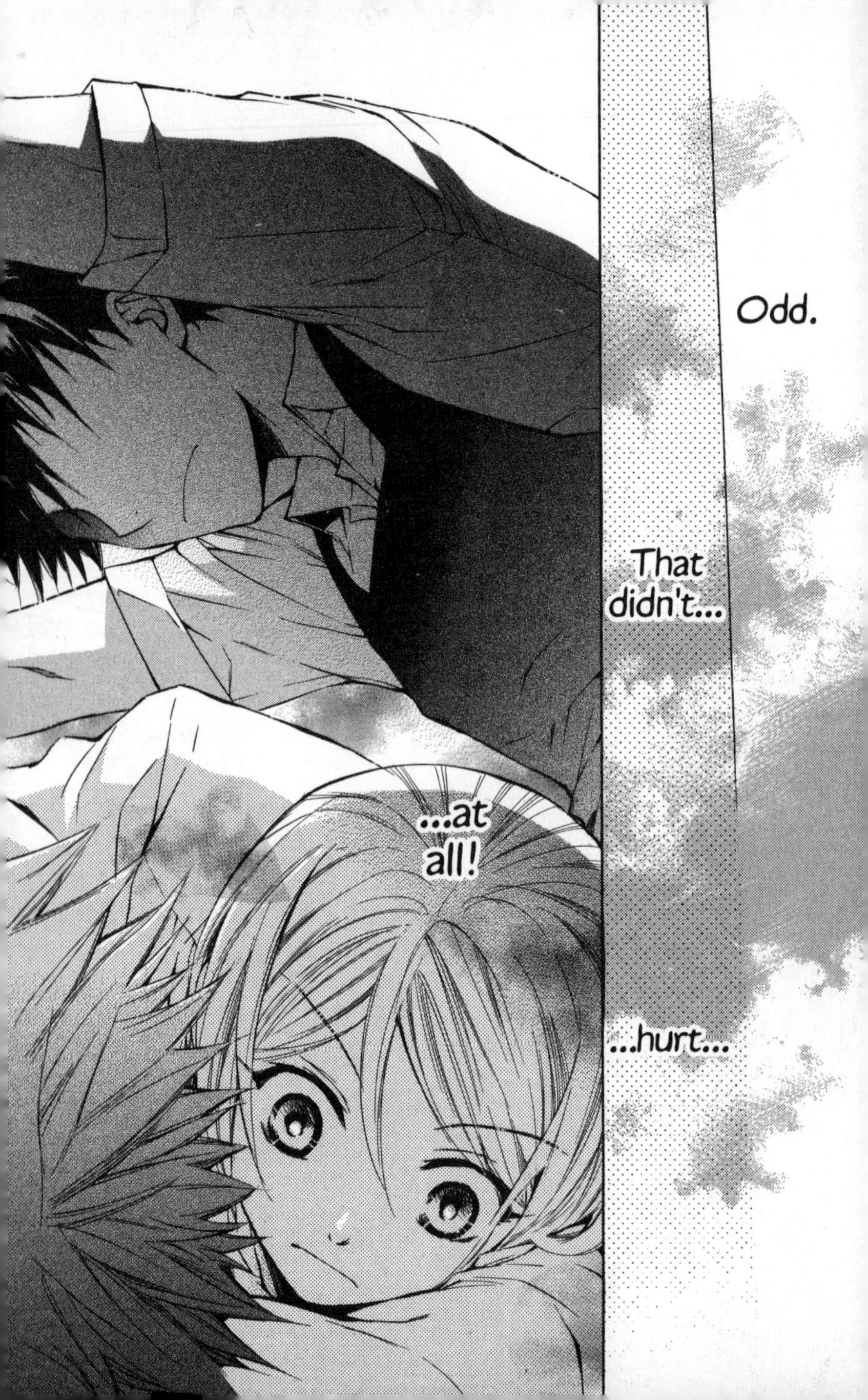
Odd.
That didn't...
...hurt...
...at all!

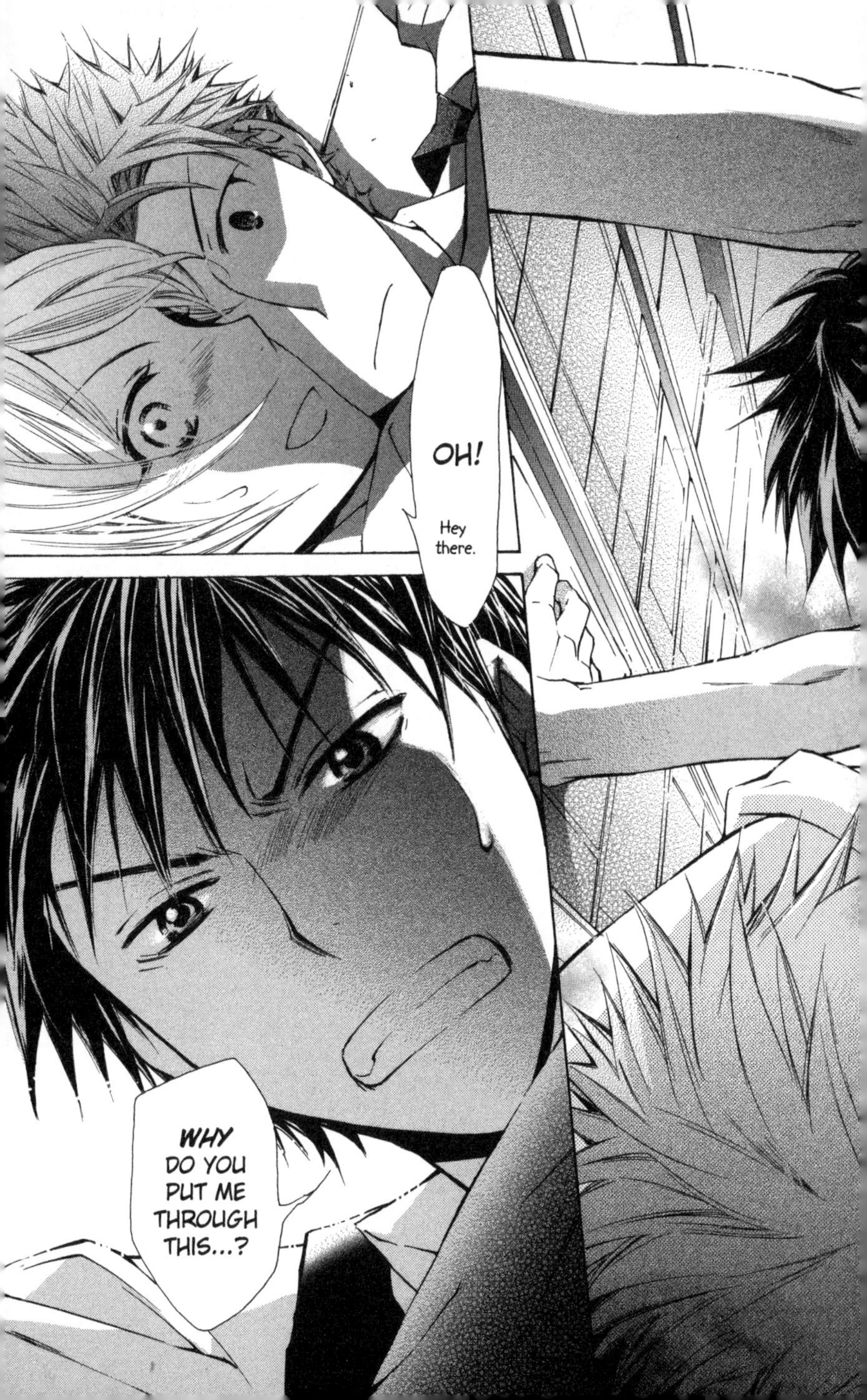
OH!
Hey there.
WHY DO YOU PUT ME THROUGH THIS...?

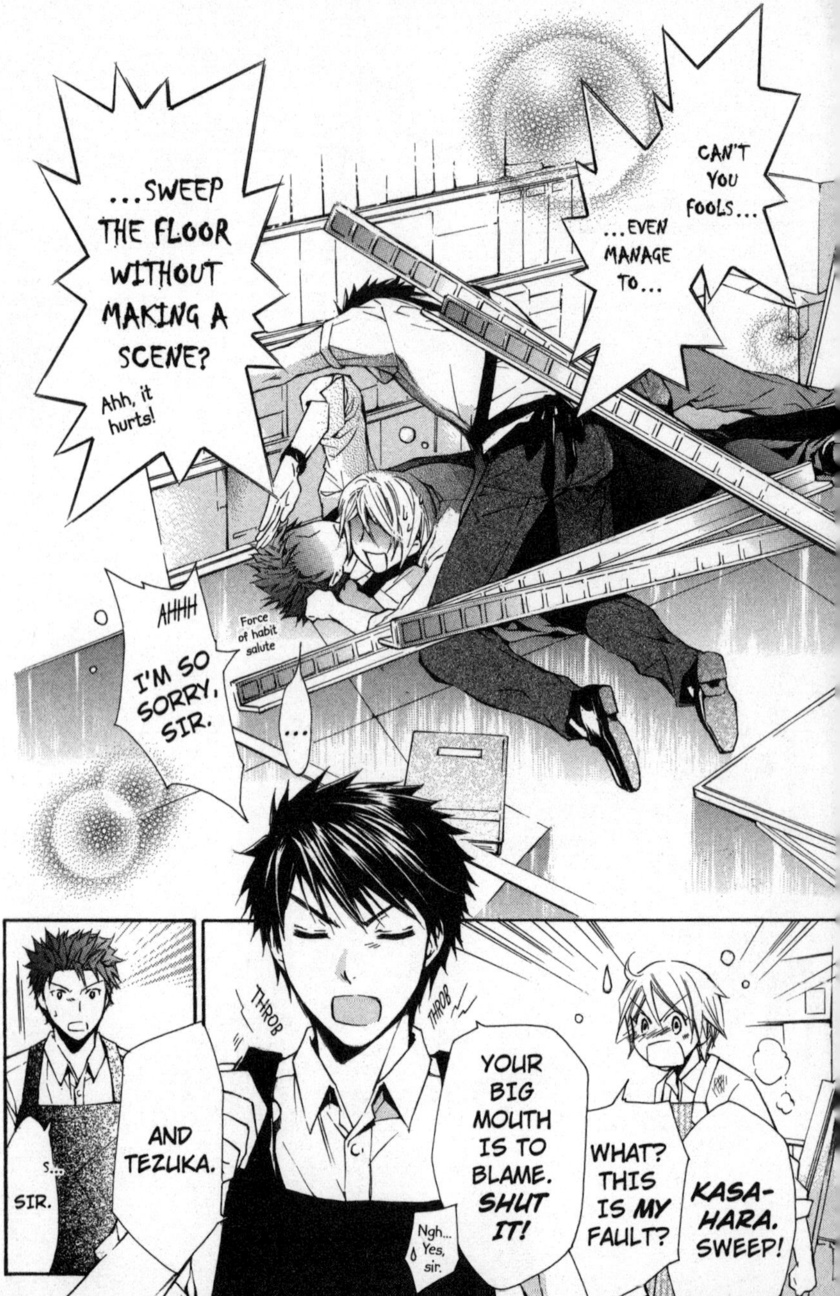
CAN'T YOU FOOLS...
...EVEN MANAGE TO...
...SWEEP THE FLOOR WITHOUT MAKING A SCENE?
Ahh, it hurts!
AHHH
I'M SO SORRY, SIR.
Force of habit salute
...
KASA-HARA. SWEEP!
WHAT? THIS IS MY FAULT?
THROB
THROB
YOUR BIG MOUTH IS TO BLAME. SHUT IT!
Ngh... Yes, sir.
AND TEZUKA.
S... SIR.

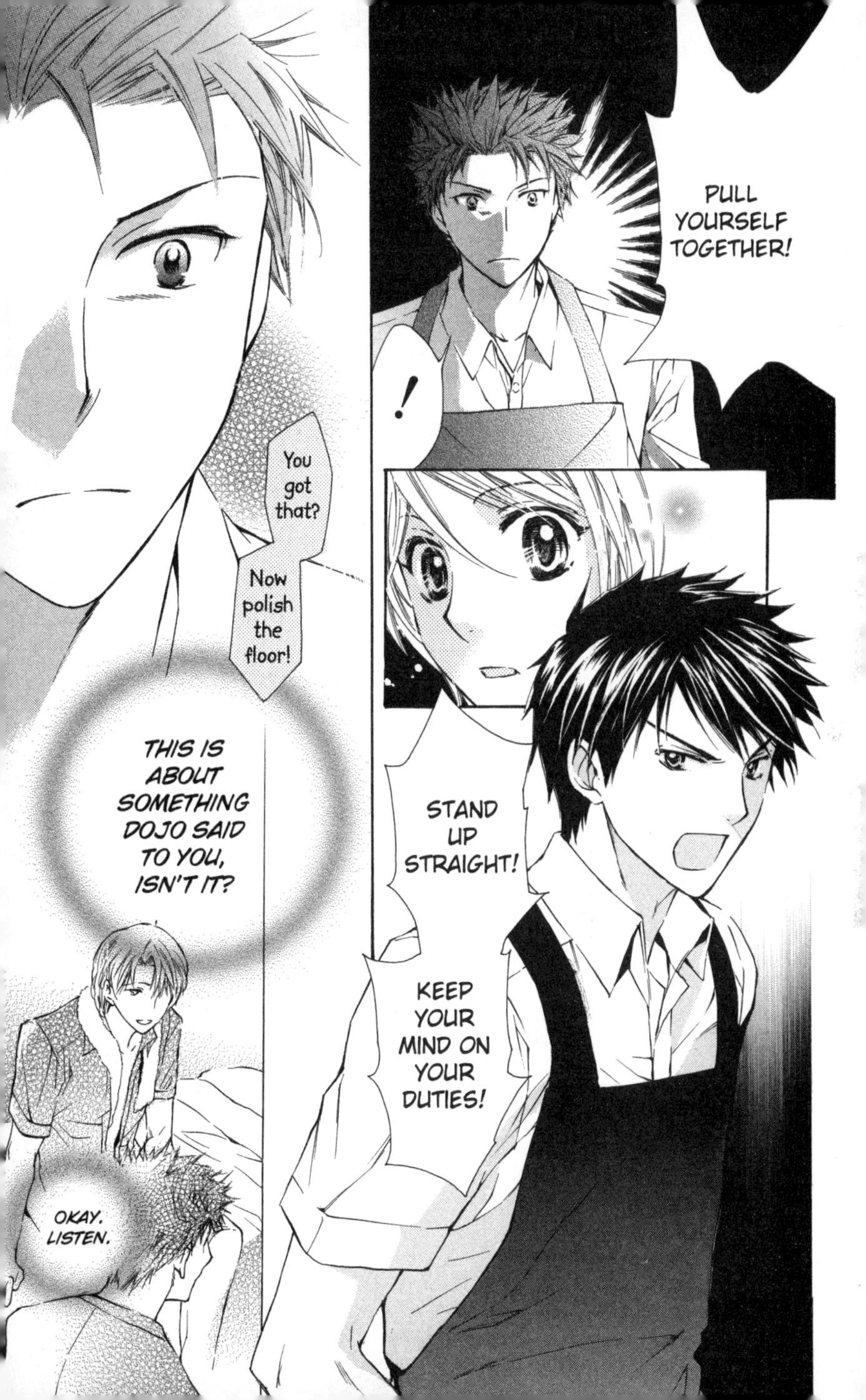
PULL YOURSELF TOGETHER!
!
STAND UP STRAIGHT!
KEEP YOUR MIND ON YOUR DUTIES!
You got that?
Now polish the floor!
THIS IS ABOUT SOMETHING DOJO SAID TO YOU, ISN'T IT?
OKAY. LISTEN.

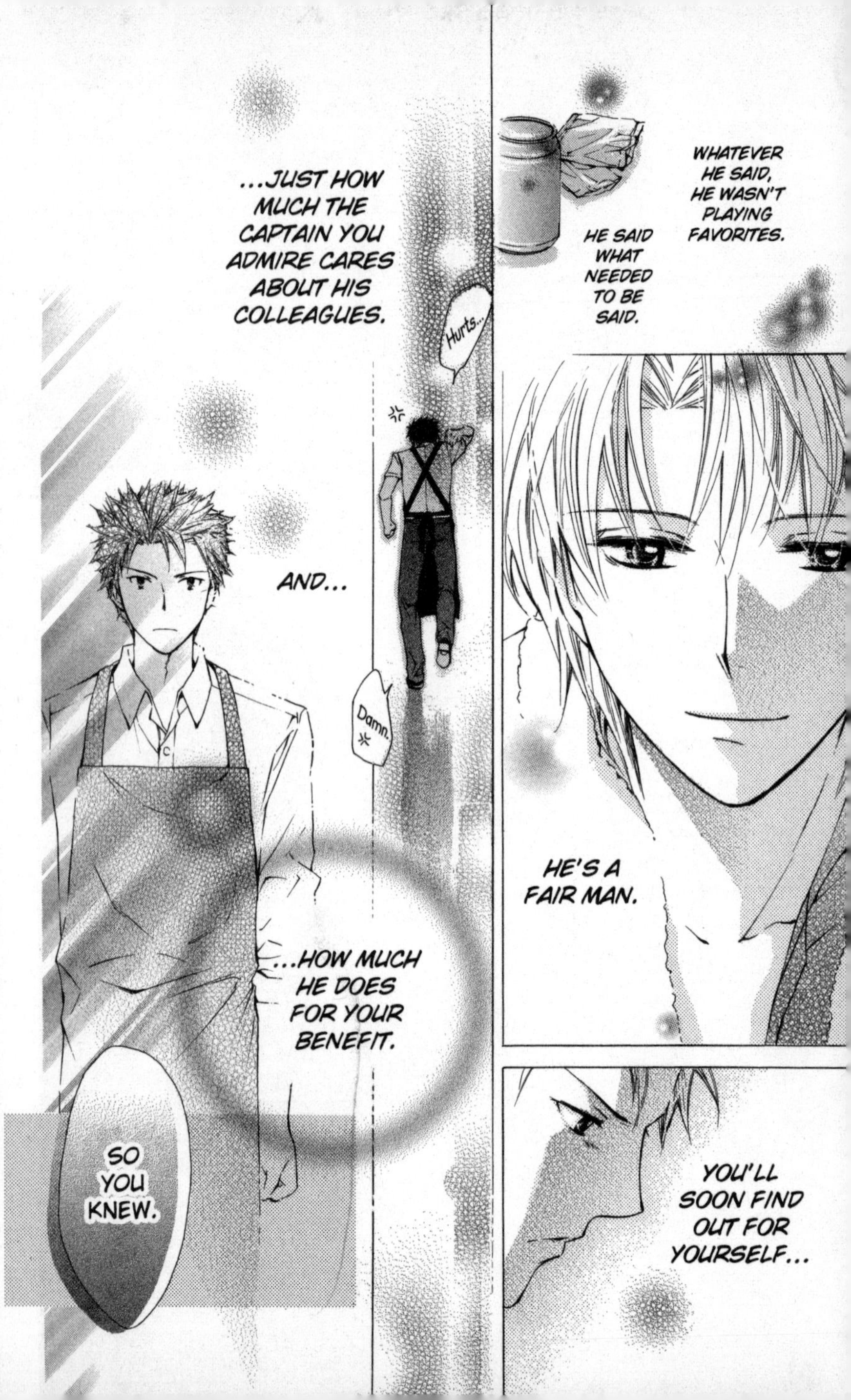
WHATEVER HE SAID, HE WASN'T PLAYING FAVORITES.
HE SAID WHAT NEEDED TO BE SAID.
HE'S A FAIR MAN.
YOU'LL SOON FIND OUT FOR YOURSELF...
...JUST HOW MUCH THE CAPTAIN YOU ADMIRE CARES ABOUT HIS COLLEAGUES.
Hurts...
Damn.
AND...
...HOW MUCH HE DOES FOR YOUR BENEFIT.
SO YOU KNEW.

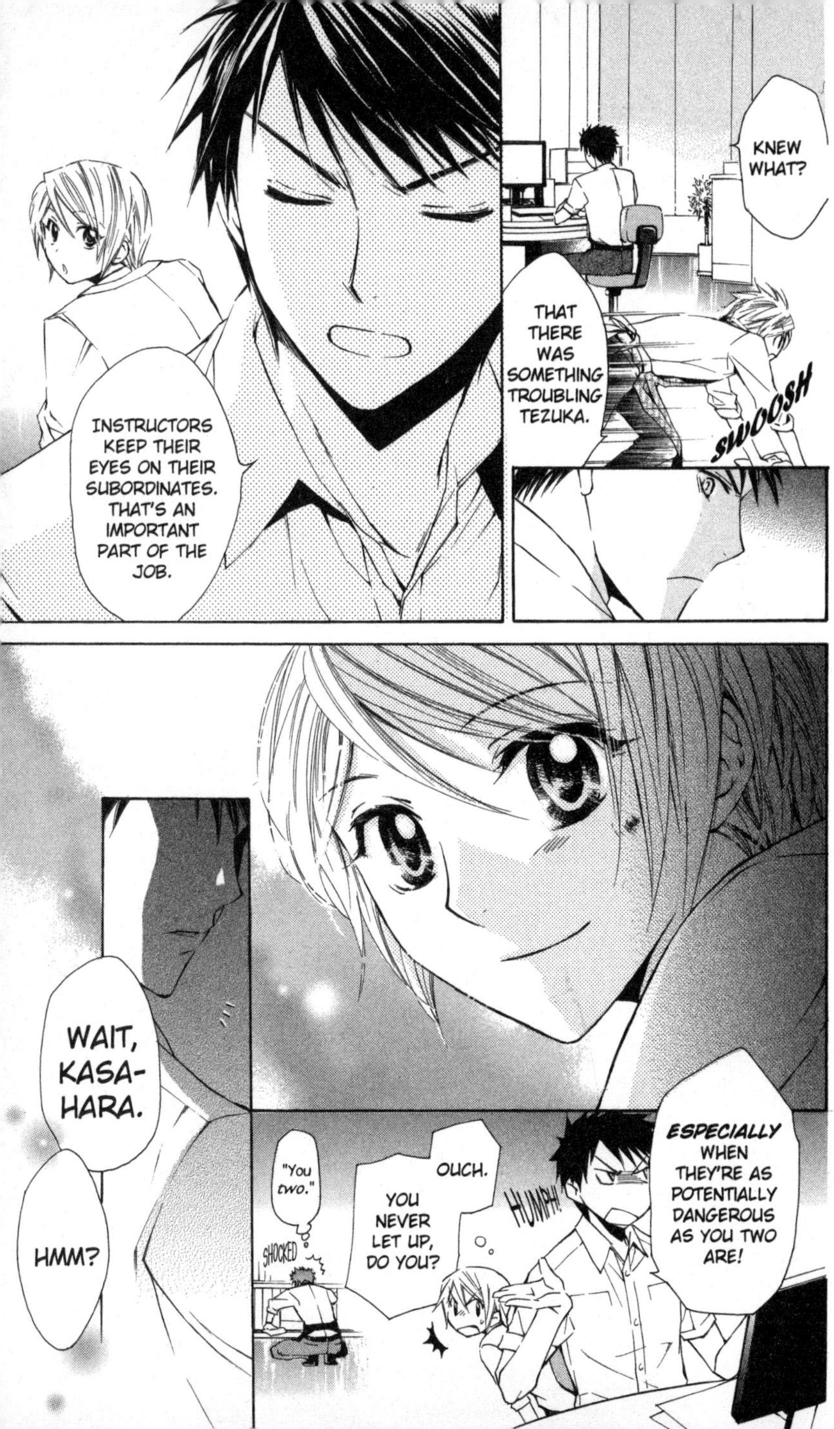
KNEW WHAT?
THAT THERE WAS SOMETHING TROUBLING TEZUKA.
SWOOSH
INSTRUCTORS KEEP THEIR EYES ON THEIR SUBORDINATES. THAT'S AN IMPORTANT PART OF THE JOB.
ESPECIALLY WHEN THEY'RE AS POTENTIALLY DANGEROUS AS YOU TWO ARE!
HUMPH!
OUCH.
YOU NEVER LET UP, DO YOU?
"You two."
SHOCKED
WAIT, KASA-HARA.
HMM?

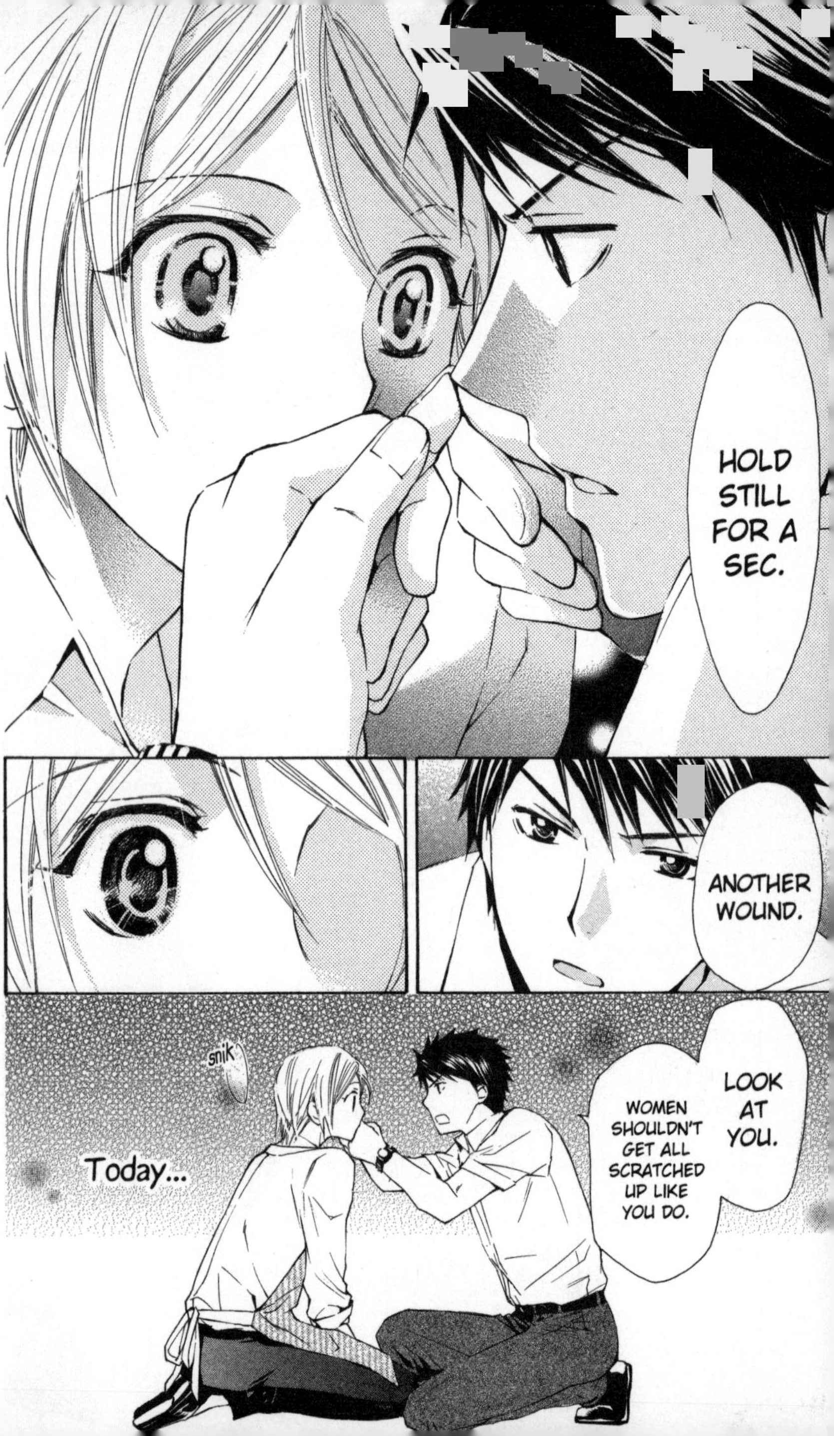
HOLD STILL FOR A SEC.
ANOTHER WOUND.
LOOK AT YOU.
WOMEN SHOULDN'T GET ALL SCRATCHED UP LIKE YOU DO.
snik
Today...

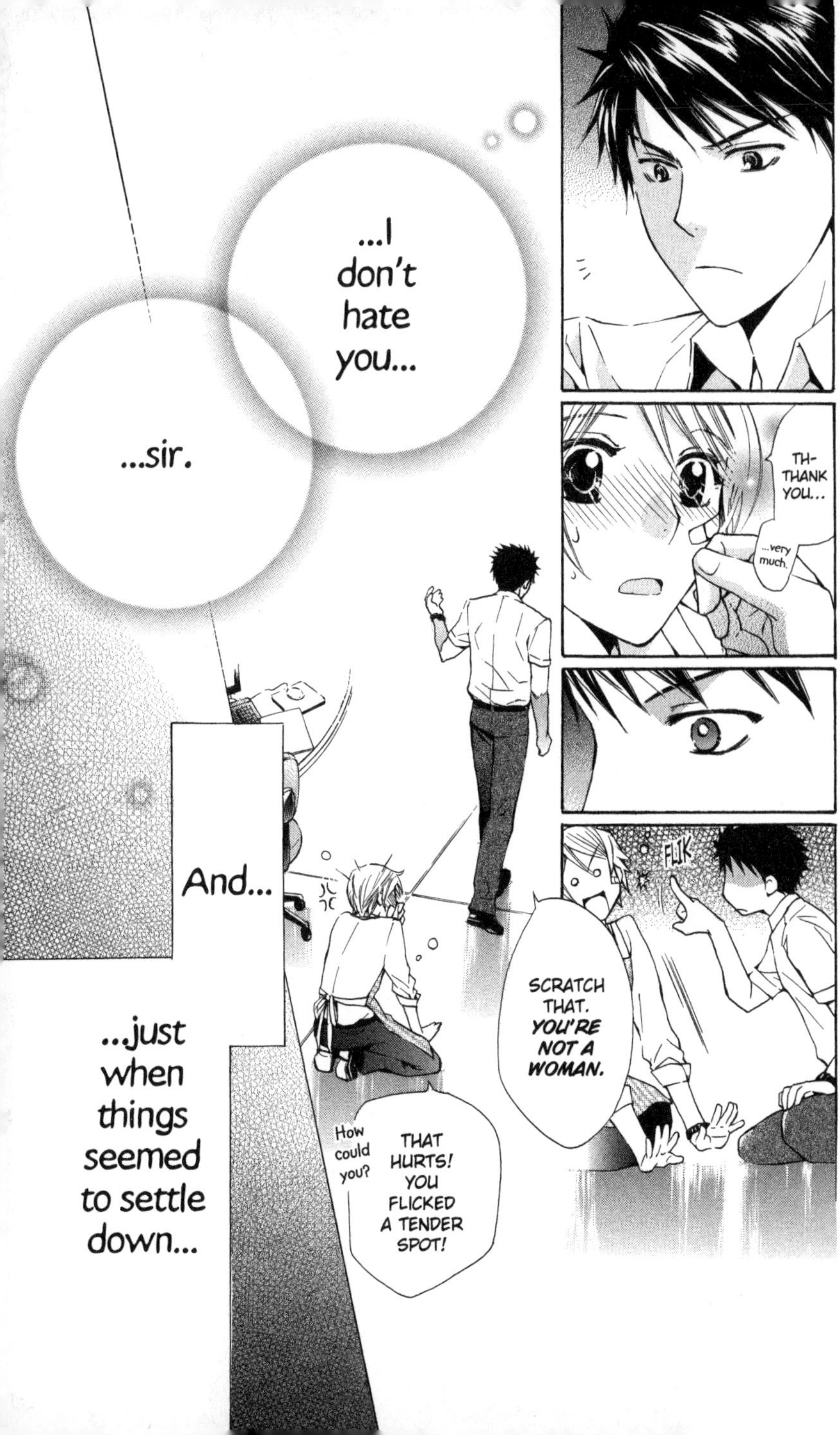
TH-THANK YOU...
...very much.
FLIK
SCRATCH THAT. YOU'RE NOT A WOMAN.
...I don't hate you...
...sir.
And...
...just when things seemed to settle down...
THAT HURTS! YOU FLICKED A TENDER SPOT!
How could you?

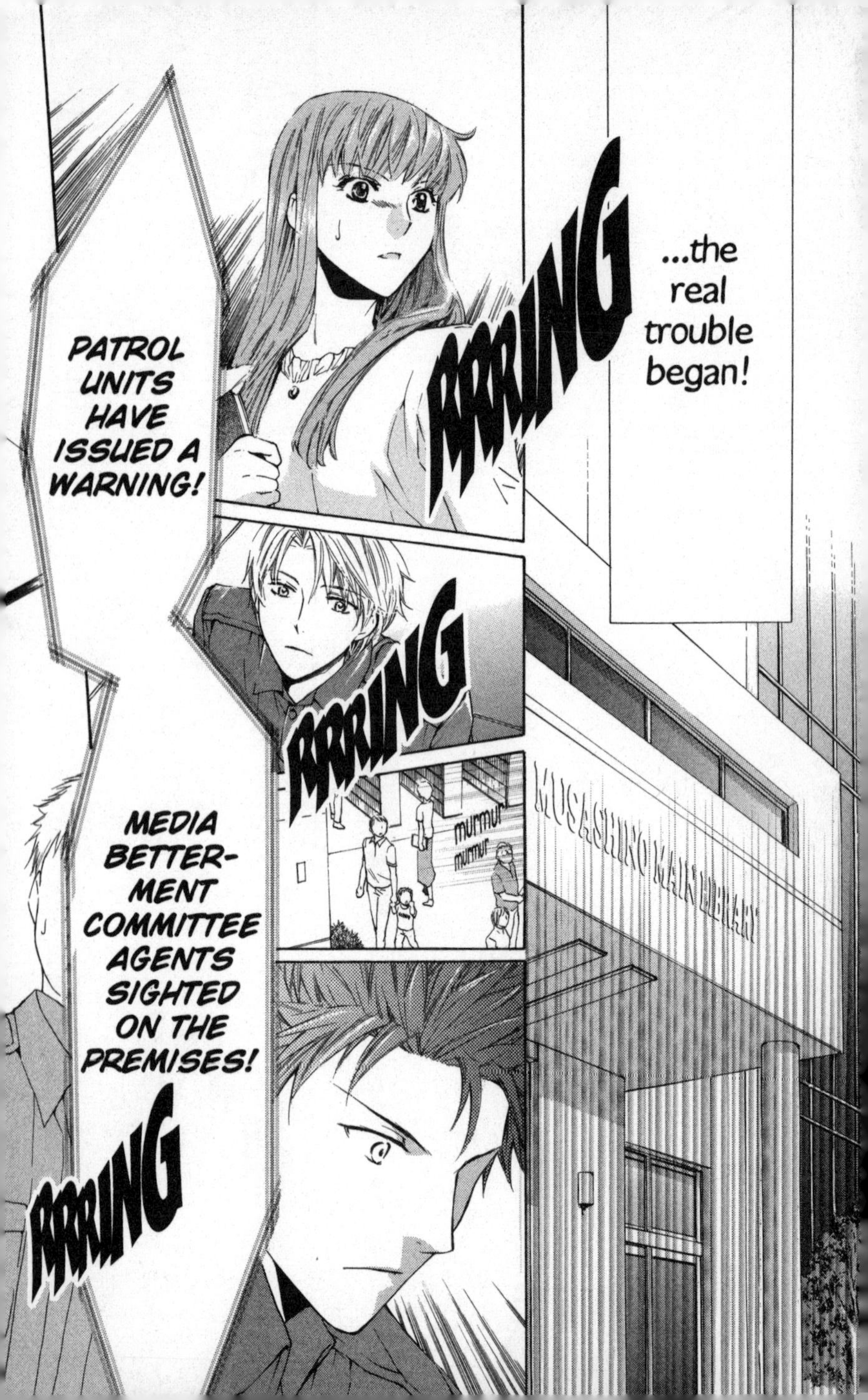
...the real trouble began!
RRRING
PATROL UNITS HAVE ISSUED A WARNING!
RRRING
MUSASHINO MAIN LIBRARY
murmur murmur
MEDIA BETTER-MENT COMMITTEE AGENTS SIGHTED ON THE PREMISES!
RRRING

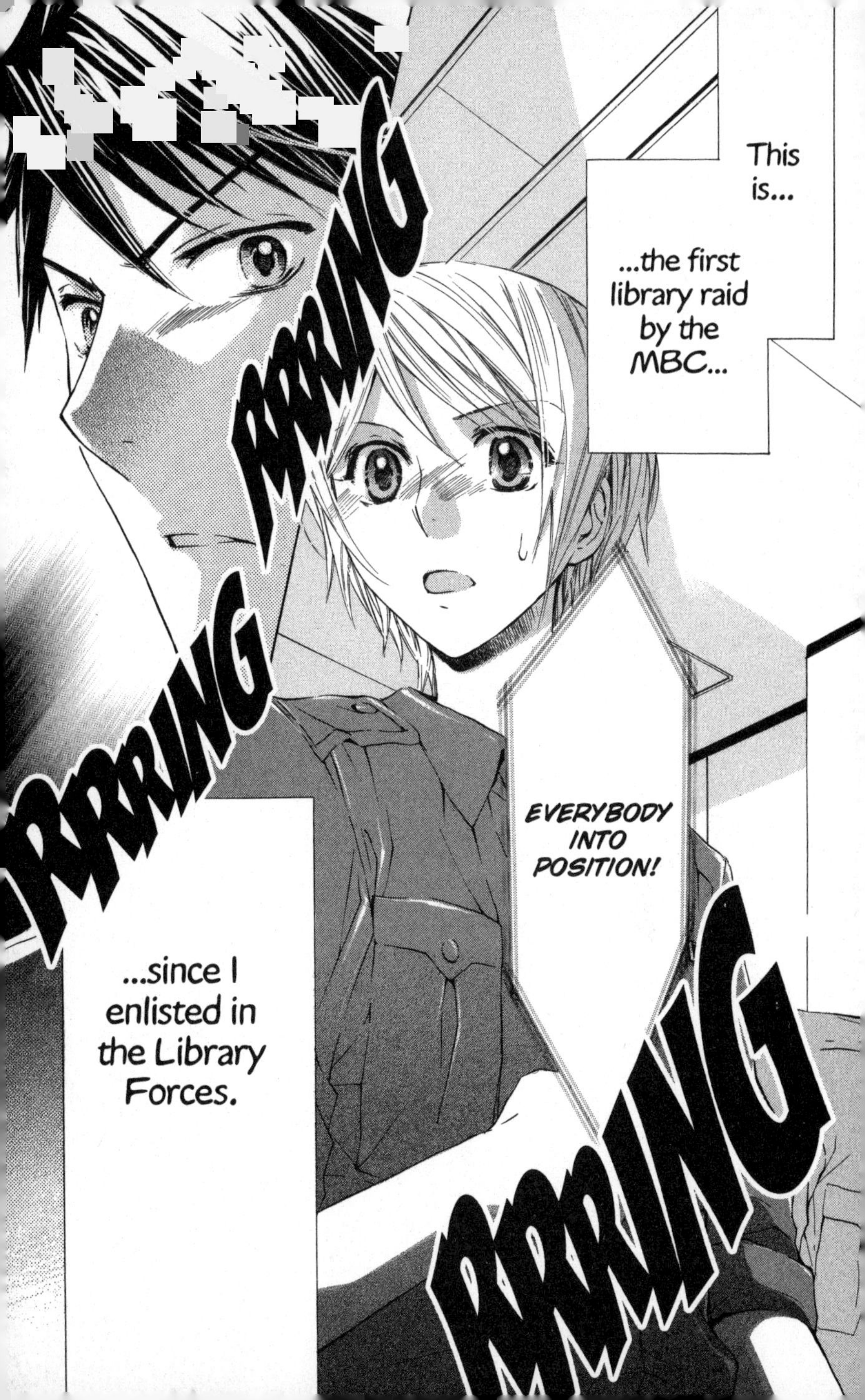

This is...
...the first library raid by the MBC...
RRRING
EVERYBODY INTO POSITION!
RRRING
...since I enlisted in the Library Forces.
RRRING

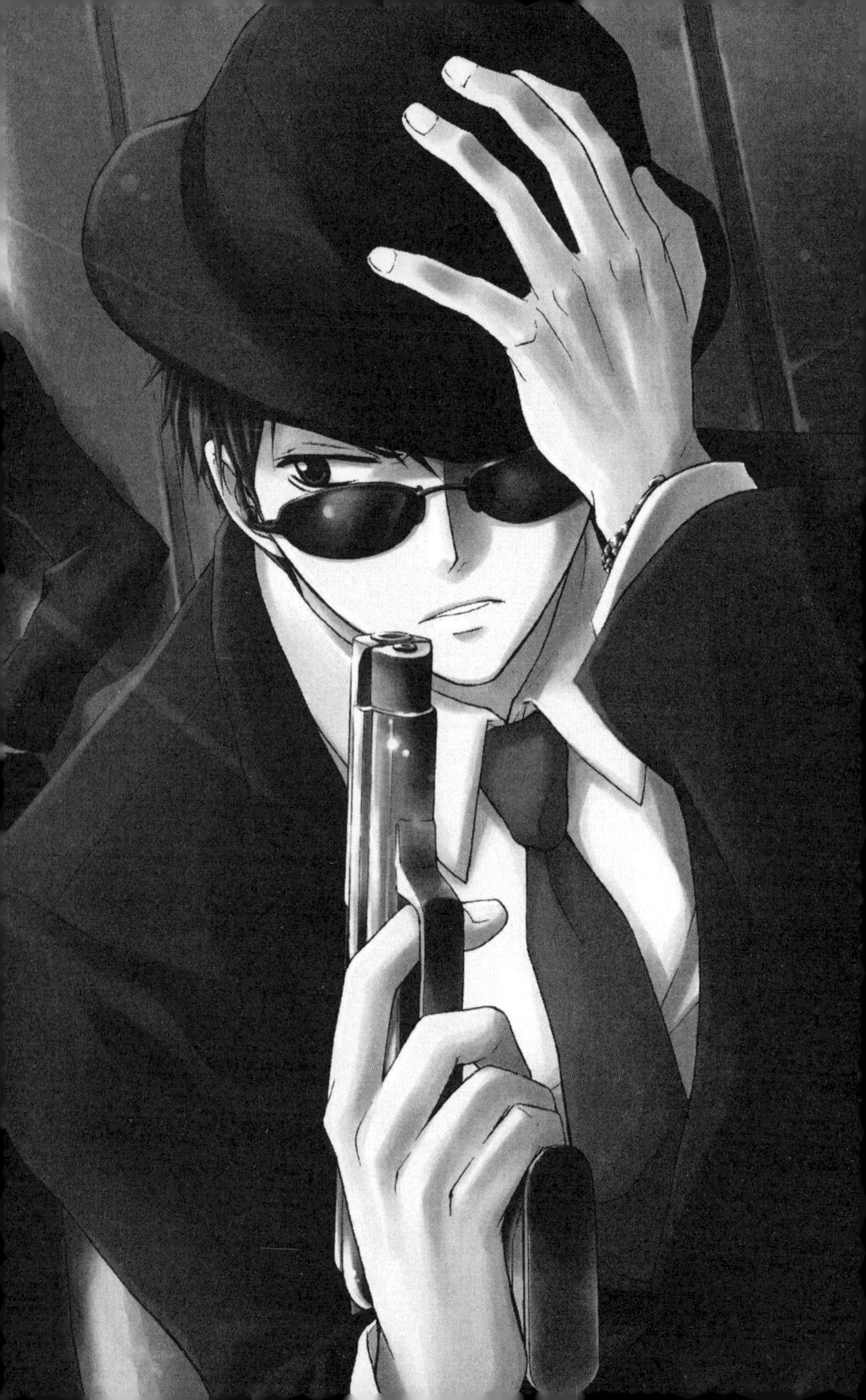

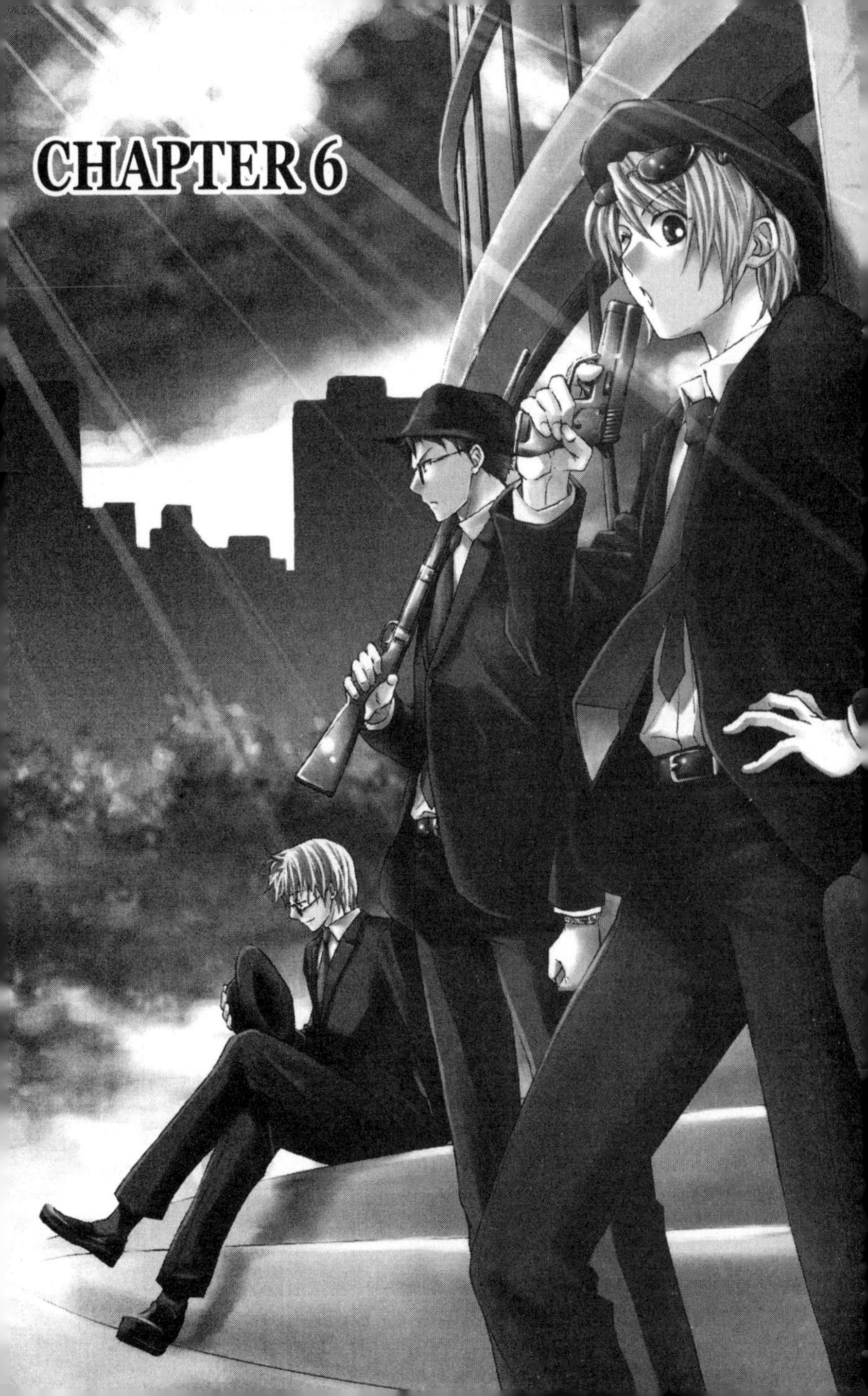
CHAPTER 6

The Absence of Malice Only Makes It Worse!

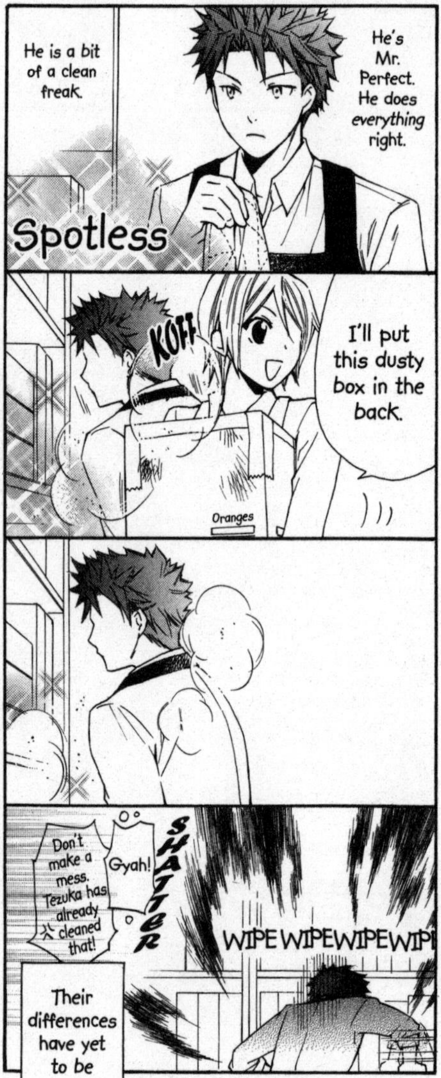
He's Mr. Perfect. He does everything right.
He is a bit of a clean freak.
Spotless
I'll put this dusty box in the back.
KOFF
Oranges
SHATTER
Gyah!
Don't make a mess. Tezuka has already cleaned that!
WIPE WIPE WIPE WIPE
Their differences have yet to be resolved.

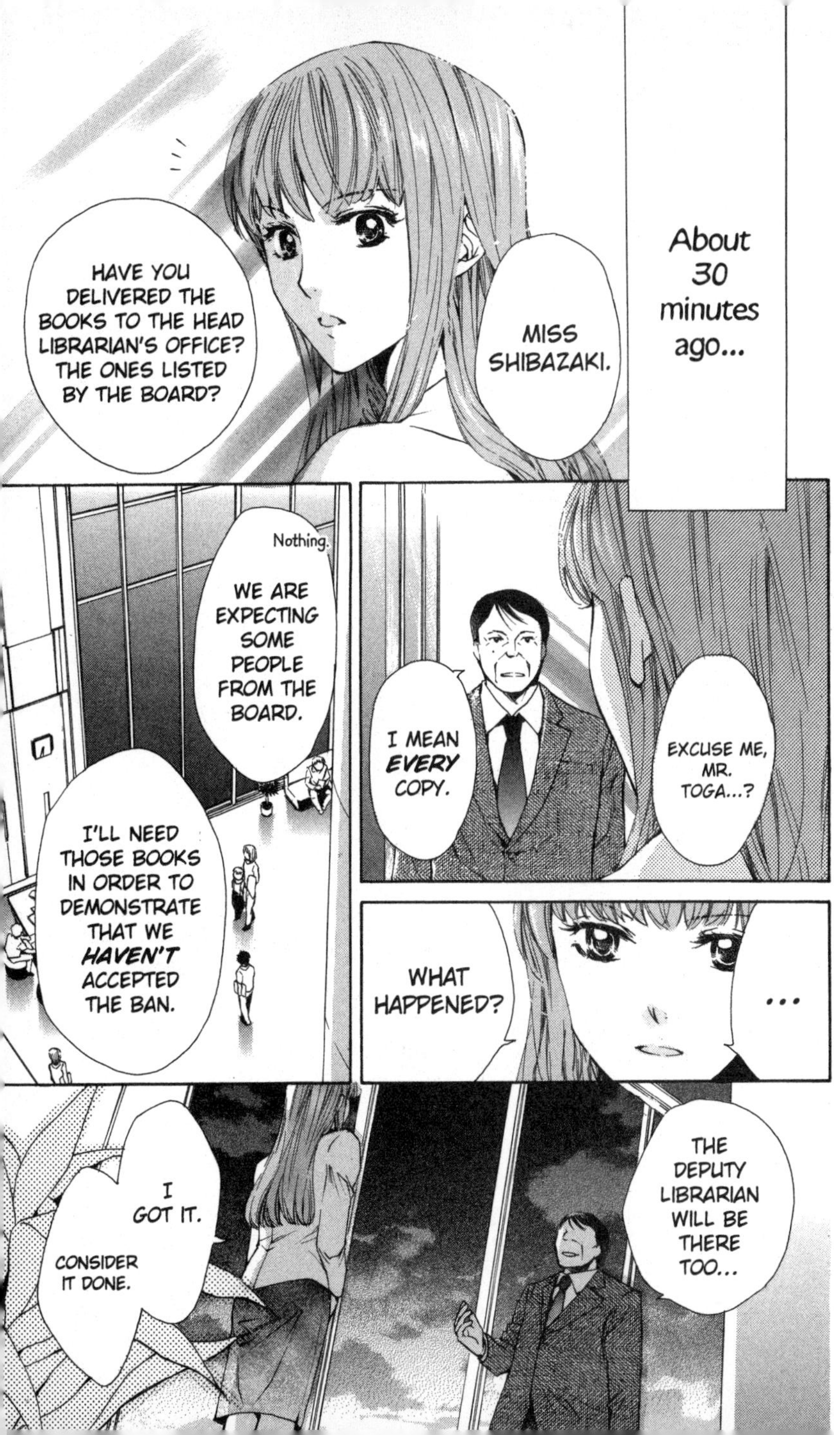
About 30 minutes ago...
MISS SHIBAZAKI.
HAVE YOU DELIVERED THE BOOKS TO THE HEAD LIBRARIAN'S OFFICE? THE ONES LISTED BY THE BOARD?
EXCUSE ME, MR. TOGA...?
I MEAN *EVERY* COPY.
...
WHAT HAPPENED?
Nothing.
WE ARE EXPECTING SOME PEOPLE FROM THE BOARD.
I'LL NEED THOSE BOOKS IN ORDER TO DEMONSTRATE THAT WE *HAVEN'T* ACCEPTED THE BAN.
THE DEPUTY LIBRARIAN WILL BE THERE TOO...
I GOT IT.
CONSIDER IT DONE.

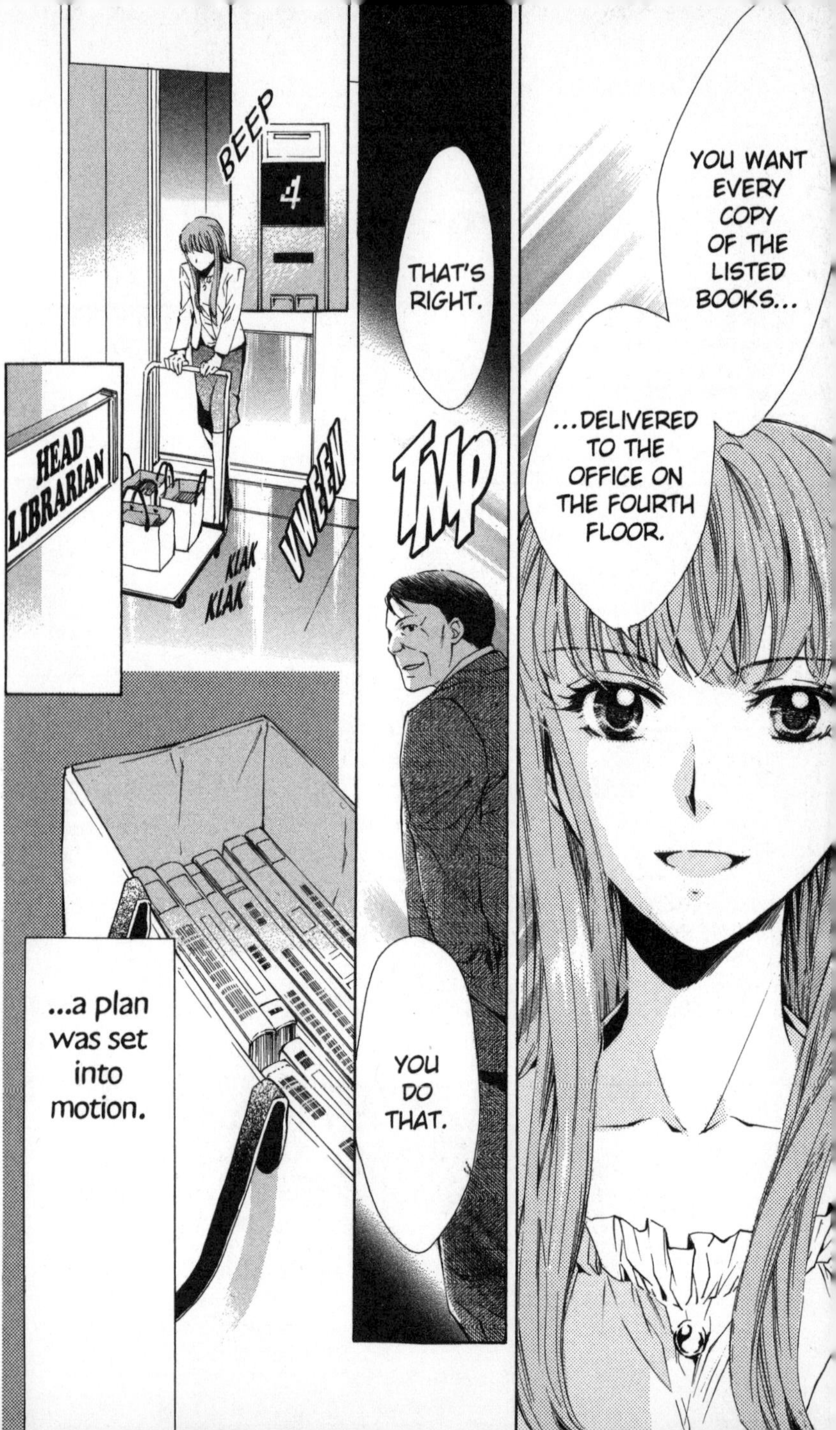
YOU WANT EVERY COPY OF THE LISTED BOOKS...
...DELIVERED TO THE OFFICE ON THE FOURTH FLOOR.
THAT'S RIGHT.
TMP
YOU DO THAT.
BEEP
4
HEAD LIBRARIAN
VWEEN
KLAK KLAK
...a plan was set into motion.

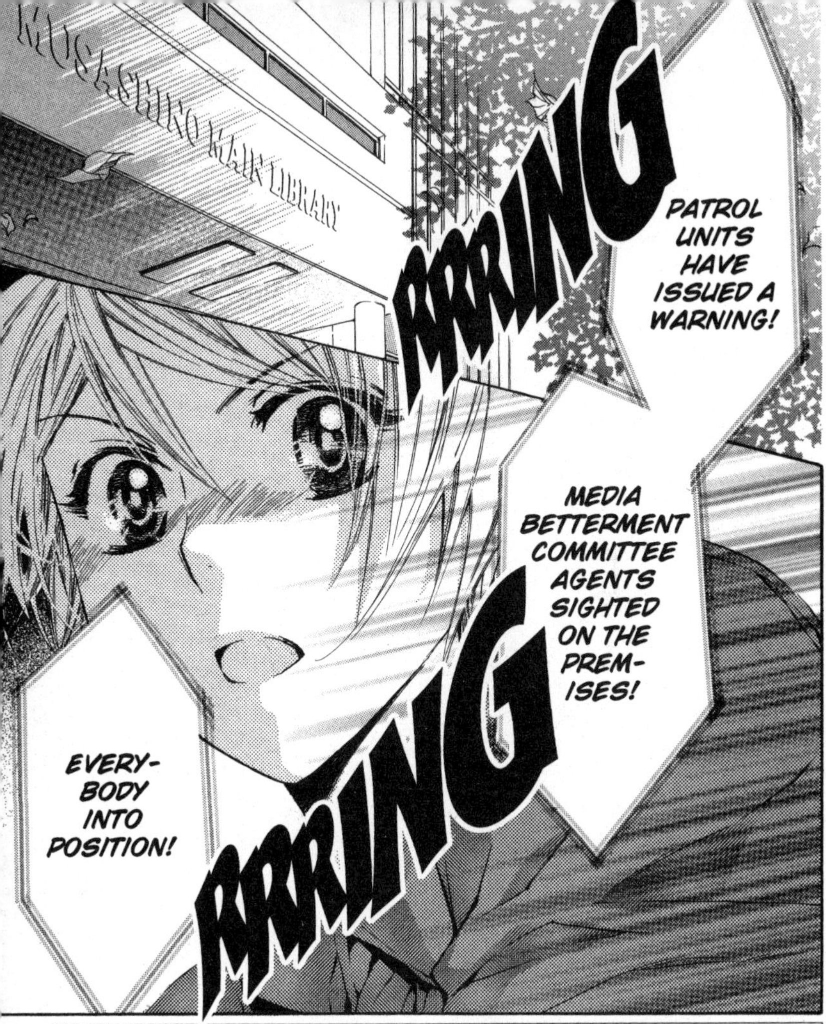
MUSASHINO MAIN LIBRARY
PATROL UNITS HAVE ISSUED A WARNING!
RRRING
MEDIA BETTERMENT COMMITTEE AGENTS SIGHTED ON THE PREM-ISES!
RRRING
EVERY-BODY INTO POSITION!

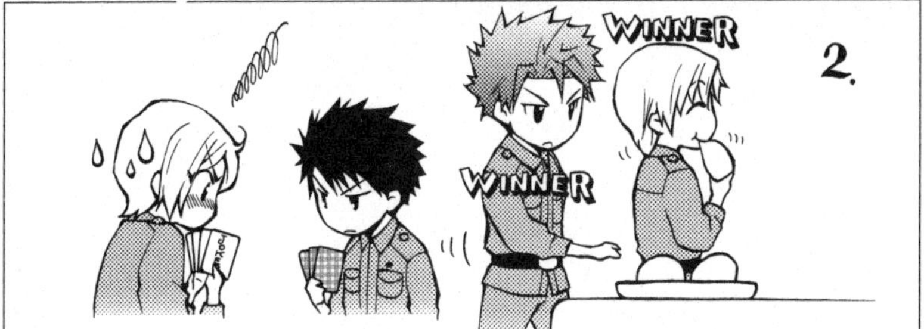
2.
WINNER
WINNER

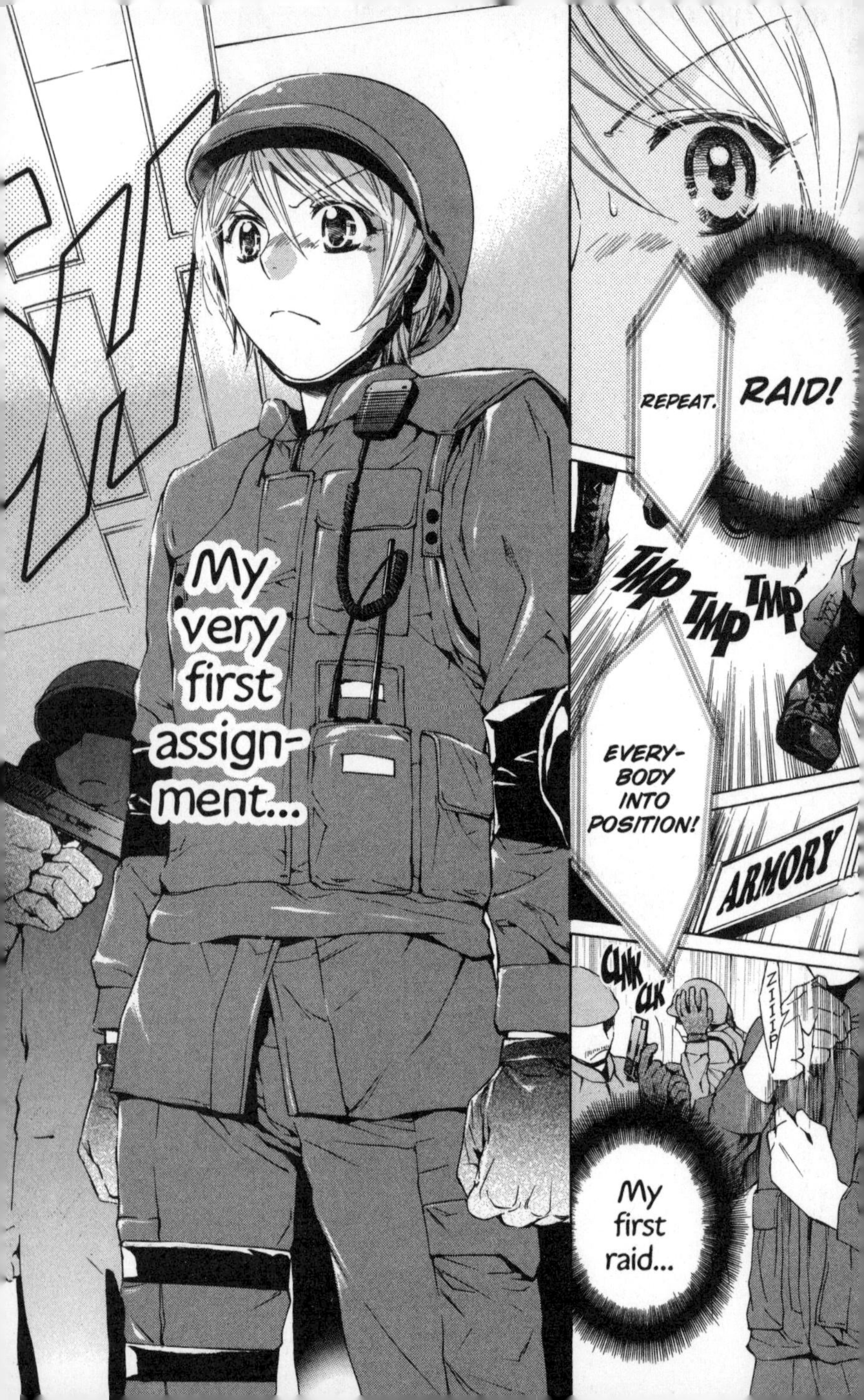
RAID!
REPEAT.
TMP TMP TMP
EVERY-BODY INTO POSITION!
ARMORY
CLNK CLK
ZIIIP
My first raid...
My very first assign-ment...

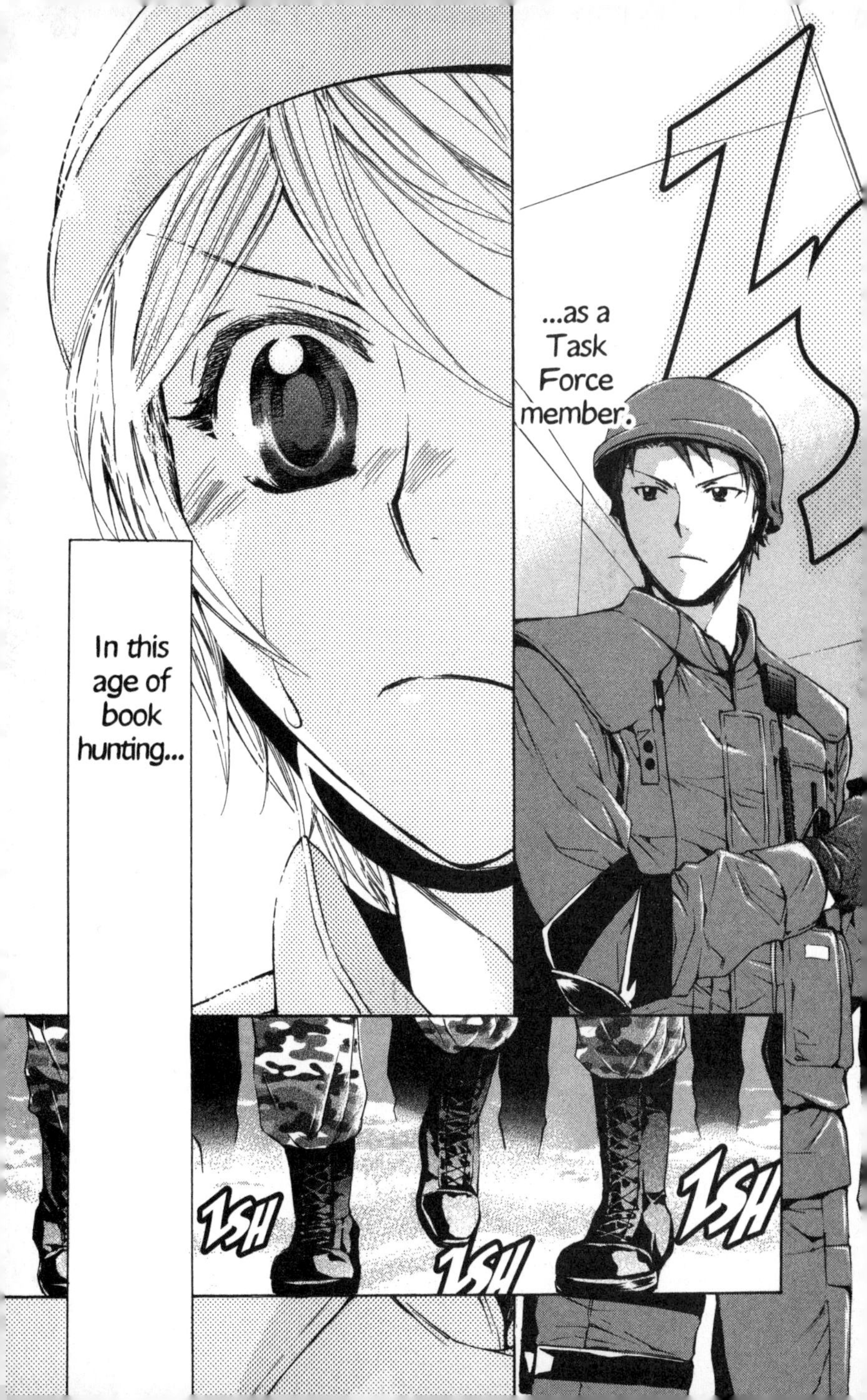
...as a Task Force member.
In this age of book hunting...
ZSH
ZSH
ZSH

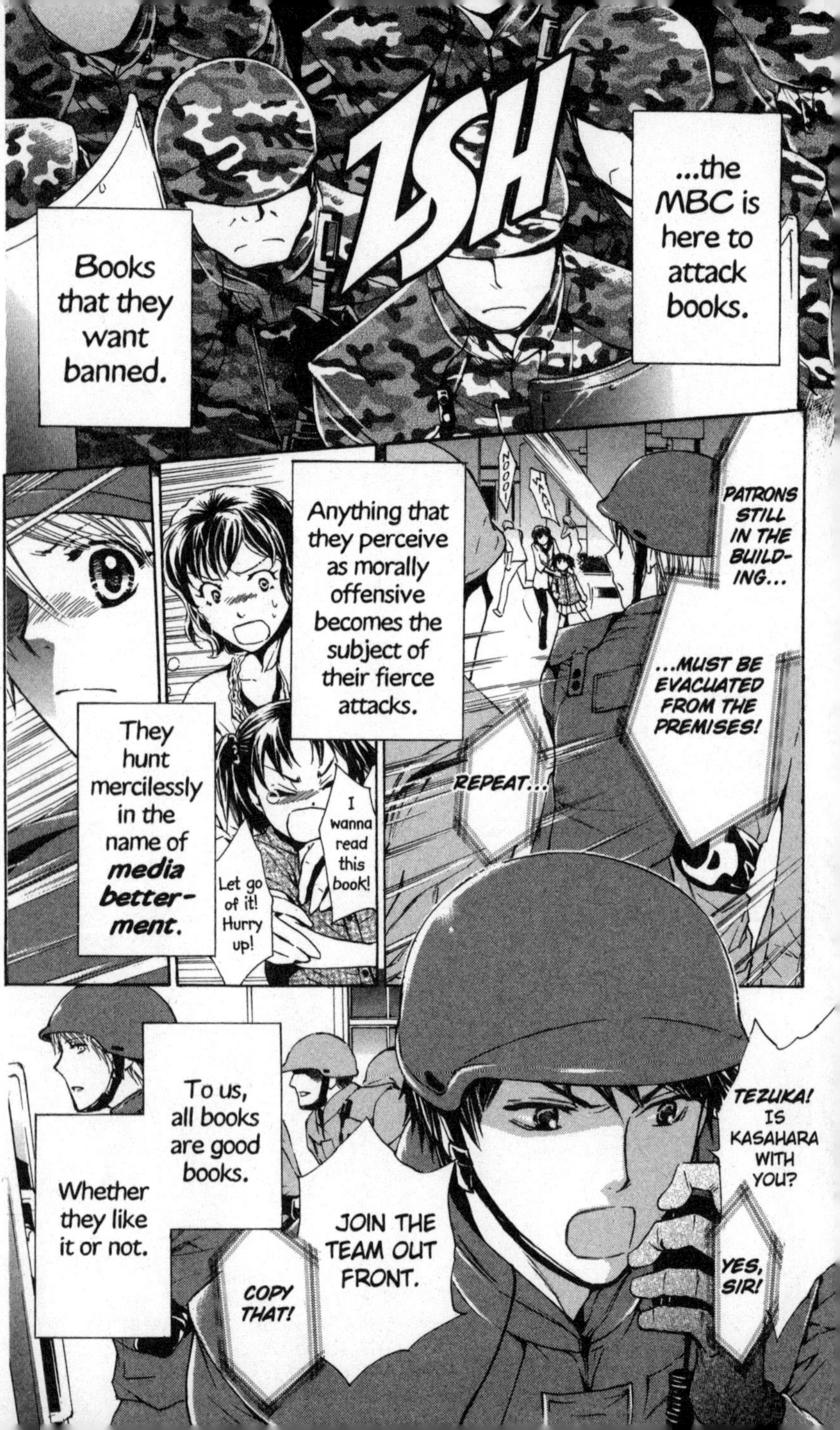
...the MBC is here to attack books.
ZSH
Books that they want banned.
PATRONS STILL IN THE BUILDING...
...MUST BE EVACUATED FROM THE PREMISES!
NOOO!
WAH!
REPEAT...
Anything that they perceive as morally offensive becomes the subject of their fierce attacks.
I wanna read this book!
Let go of it! Hurry up!
They hunt mercilessly in the name of ***media betterment***.
TEZUKA! IS KASAHARA WITH YOU?
YES, SIR!
JOIN THE TEAM OUT FRONT.
COPY THAT!
To us, all books are good books.
Whether they like it or not.

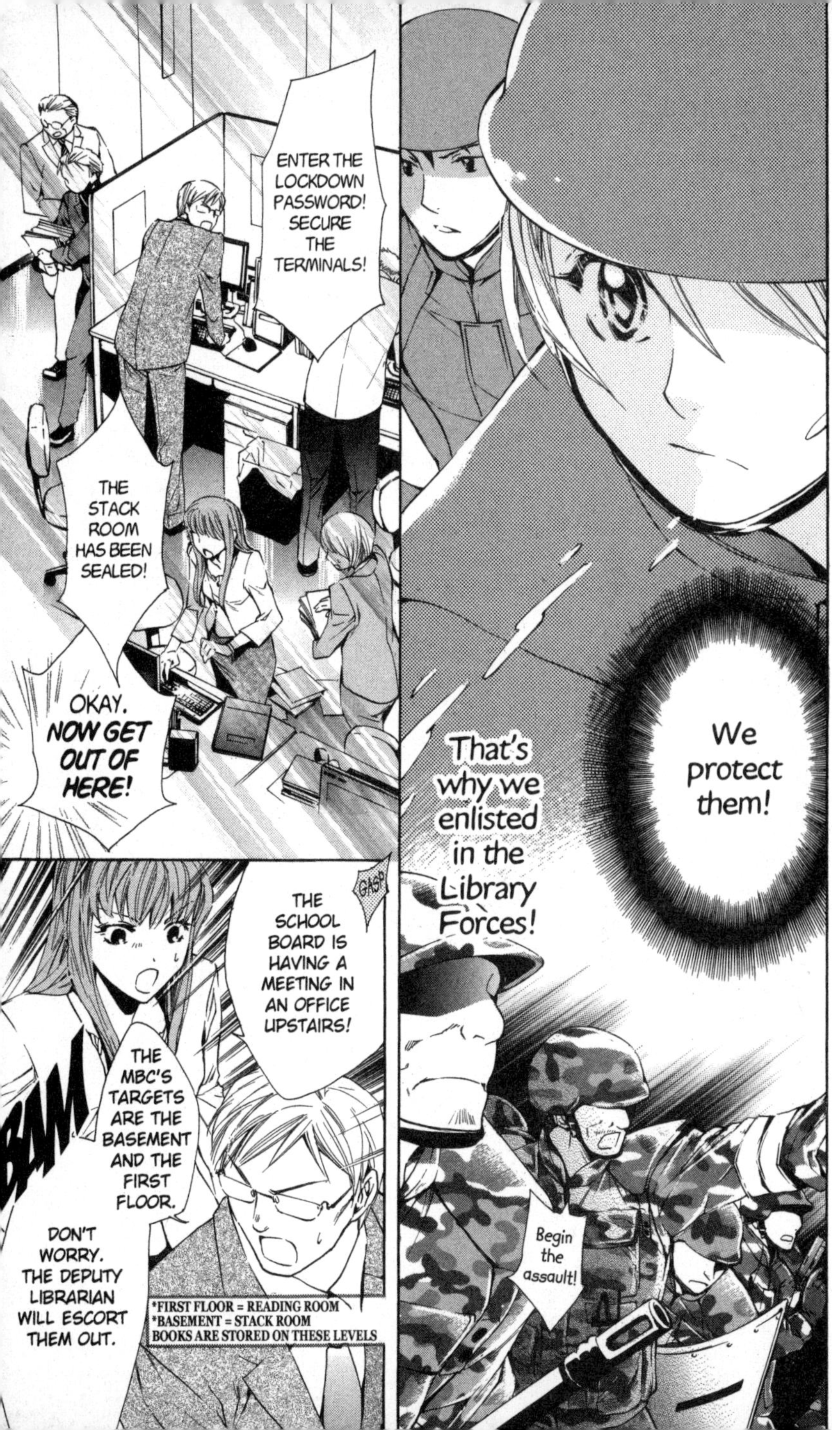
We protect them!
That's why we enlisted in the Library Forces!
Begin the assault!
ENTER THE LOCKDOWN PASSWORD! SECURE THE TERMINALS!
THE STACK ROOM HAS BEEN SEALED!
OKAY. NOW GET OUT OF HERE!
GASP
THE SCHOOL BOARD IS HAVING A MEETING IN AN OFFICE UPSTAIRS!
THE MBC'S TARGETS ARE THE BASEMENT AND THE FIRST FLOOR.
BAM
DON'T WORRY. THE DEPUTY LIBRARIAN WILL ESCORT THEM OUT.
*FIRST FLOOR = READING ROOM
*BASEMENT = STACK ROOM
BOOKS ARE STORED ON THESE LEVELS

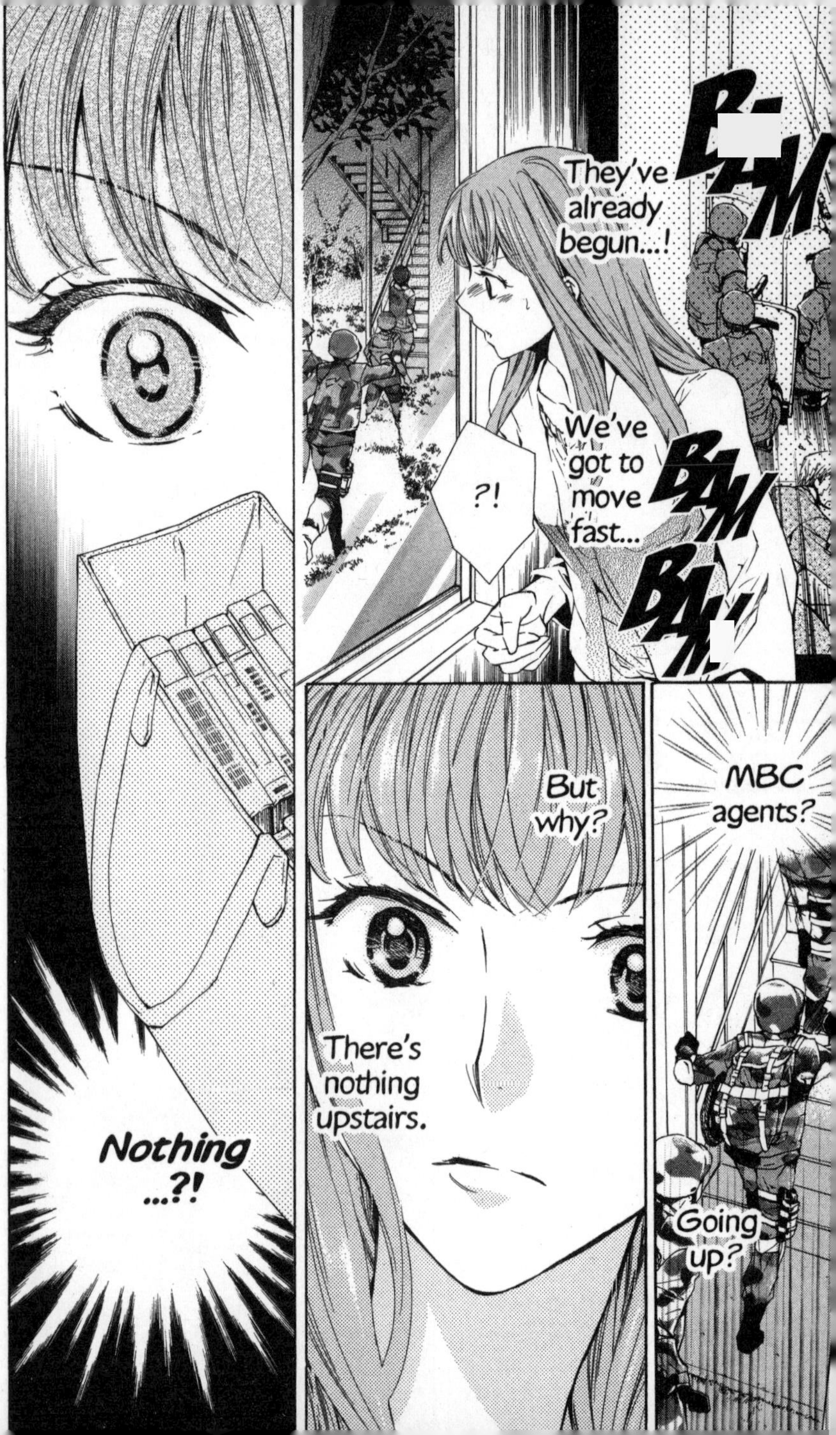
BAM
They've already begun...!
We've got to move fast...
BAM
BAM
?!
MBC agents?
Going up?
But why?
There's nothing upstairs.
Nothing ...?!

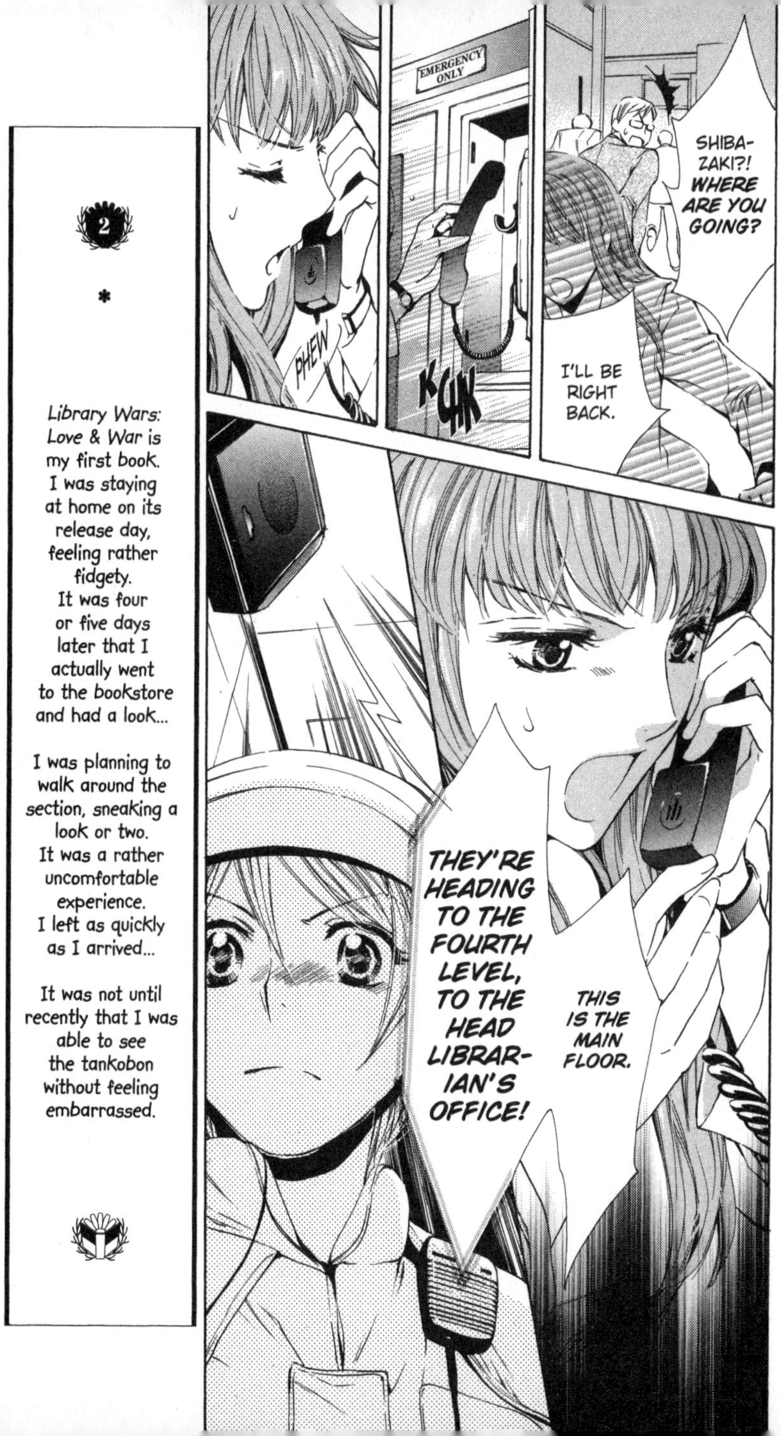
SHIBA-ZAKI?! WHERE ARE YOU GOING?
I'LL BE RIGHT BACK.
EMERGENCY ONLY
KCHK
PHEW
THIS IS THE MAIN FLOOR.
THEY'RE HEADING TO THE FOURTH LEVEL, TO THE HEAD LIBRAR-IAN'S OFFICE!

2

*

Library Wars: Love & War is my first book. I was staying at home on its release day, feeling rather fidgety. It was four or five days later that I actually went to the bookstore and had a look...

I was planning to walk around the section, sneaking a look or two. It was a rather uncomfortable experience. I left as quickly as I arrived...

It was not until recently that I was able to see the tankobon without feeling embarrassed.

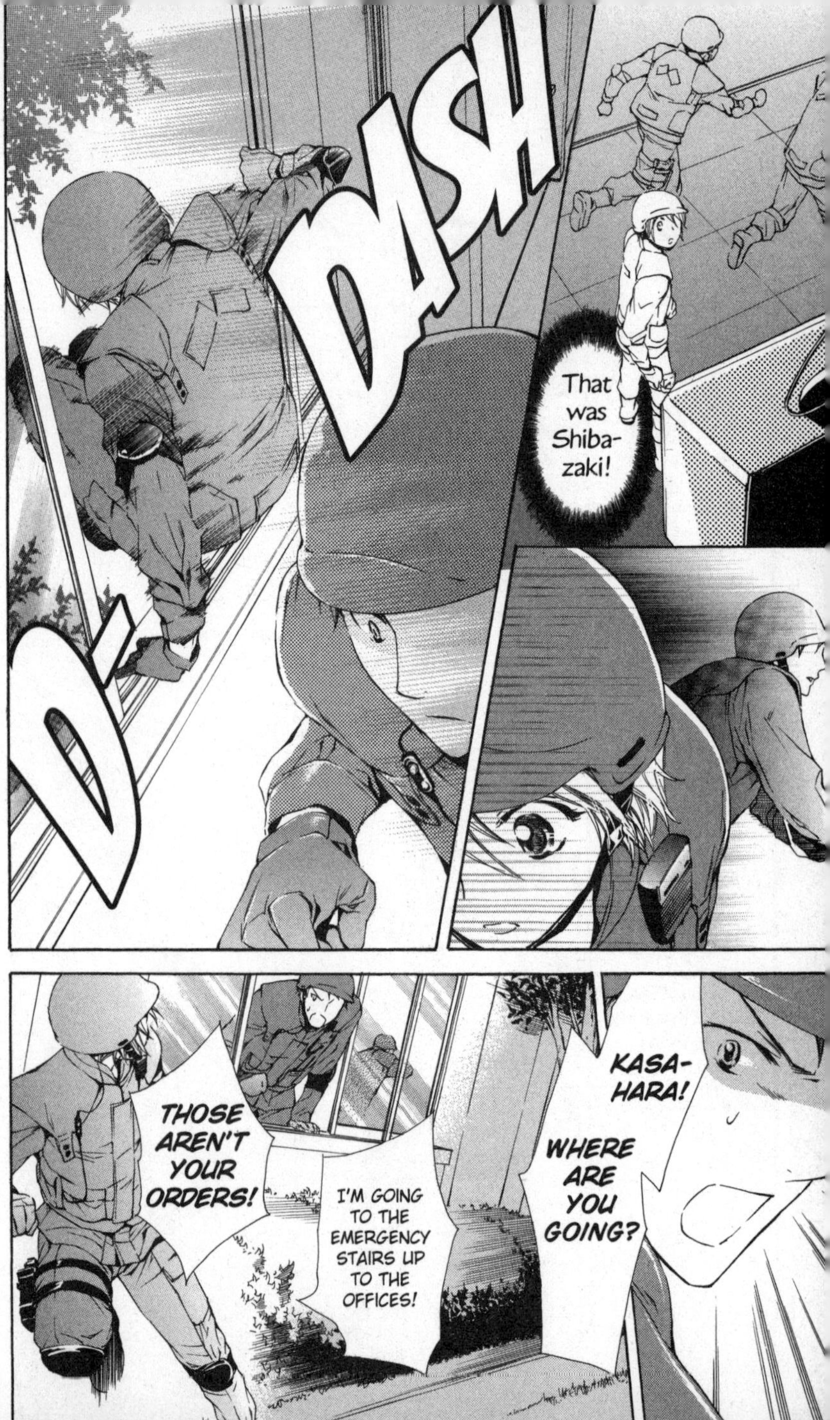
That was Shiba-zaki!
DASH
D
KASA-HARA!
WHERE ARE YOU GOING?
I'M GOING TO THE EMERGENCY STAIRS UP TO THE OFFICES!
THOSE AREN'T YOUR ORDERS!

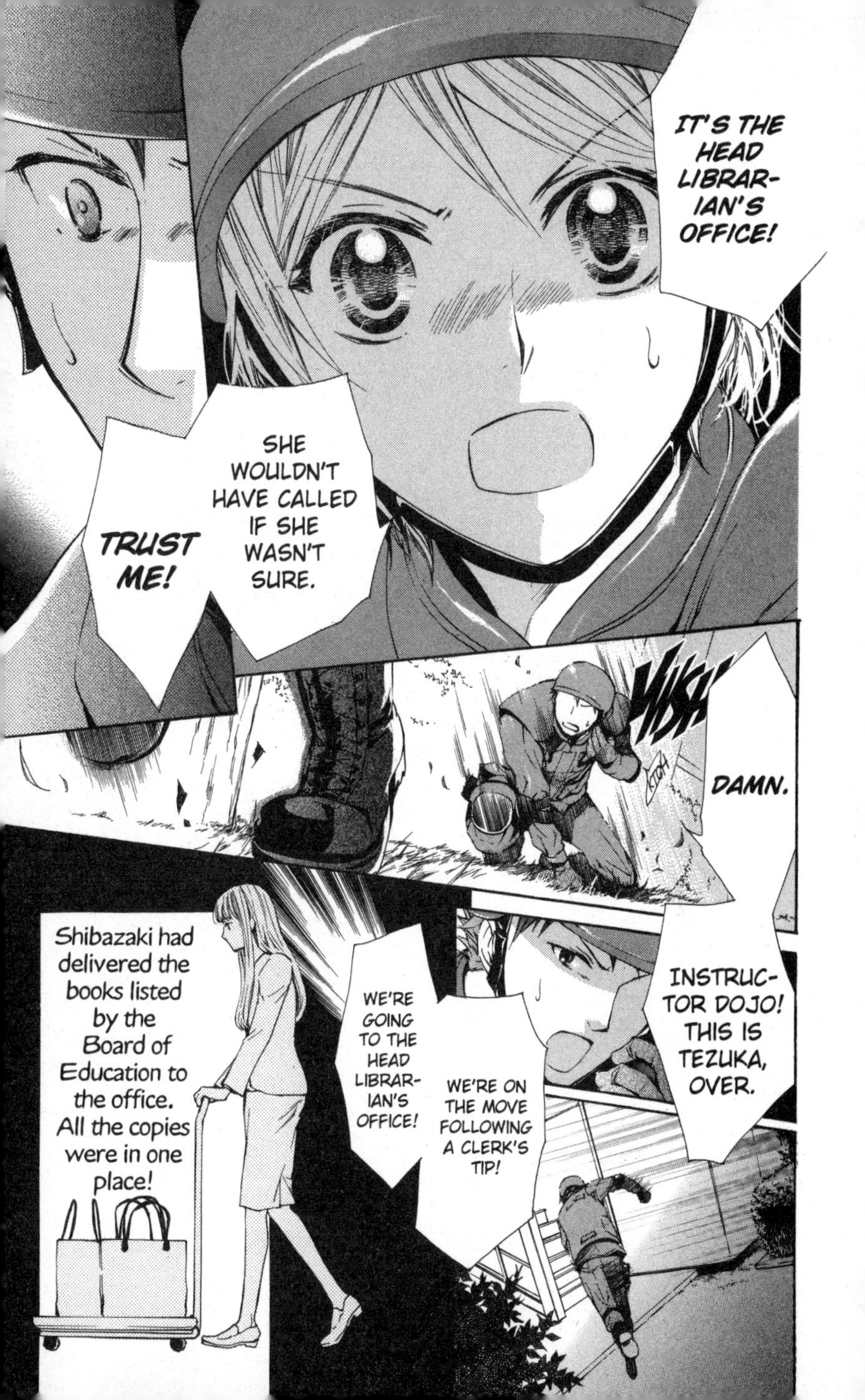
IT'S THE HEAD LIBRARIAN'S OFFICE!
SHE WOULDN'T HAVE CALLED IF SHE WASN'T SURE.
TRUST ME!
DAMN.
INSTRUCTOR DOJO! THIS IS TEZUKA, OVER.
WE'RE ON THE MOVE FOLLOWING A CLERK'S TIP!
WE'RE GOING TO THE HEAD LIBRARIAN'S OFFICE!
Shibazaki had delivered the books listed by the Board of Education to the office. All the copies were in one place!

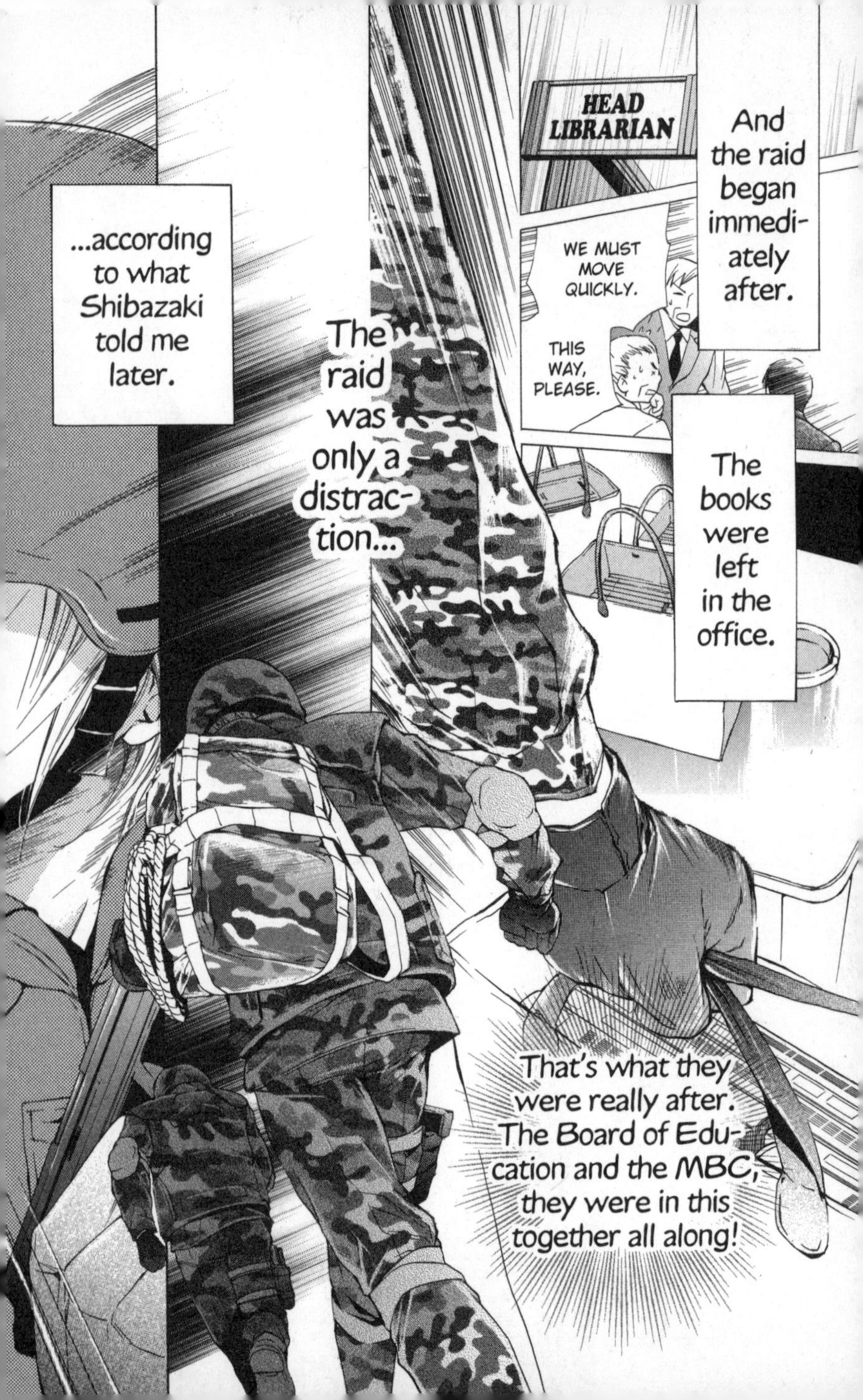

HEAD LIBRARIAN
And the raid began immediately after.
WE MUST MOVE QUICKLY.
THIS WAY, PLEASE.
The books were left in the office.
The raid was only a distraction...
...according to what Shibazaki told me later.
That's what they were really after. The Board of Education and the MBC, they were in this together all along!

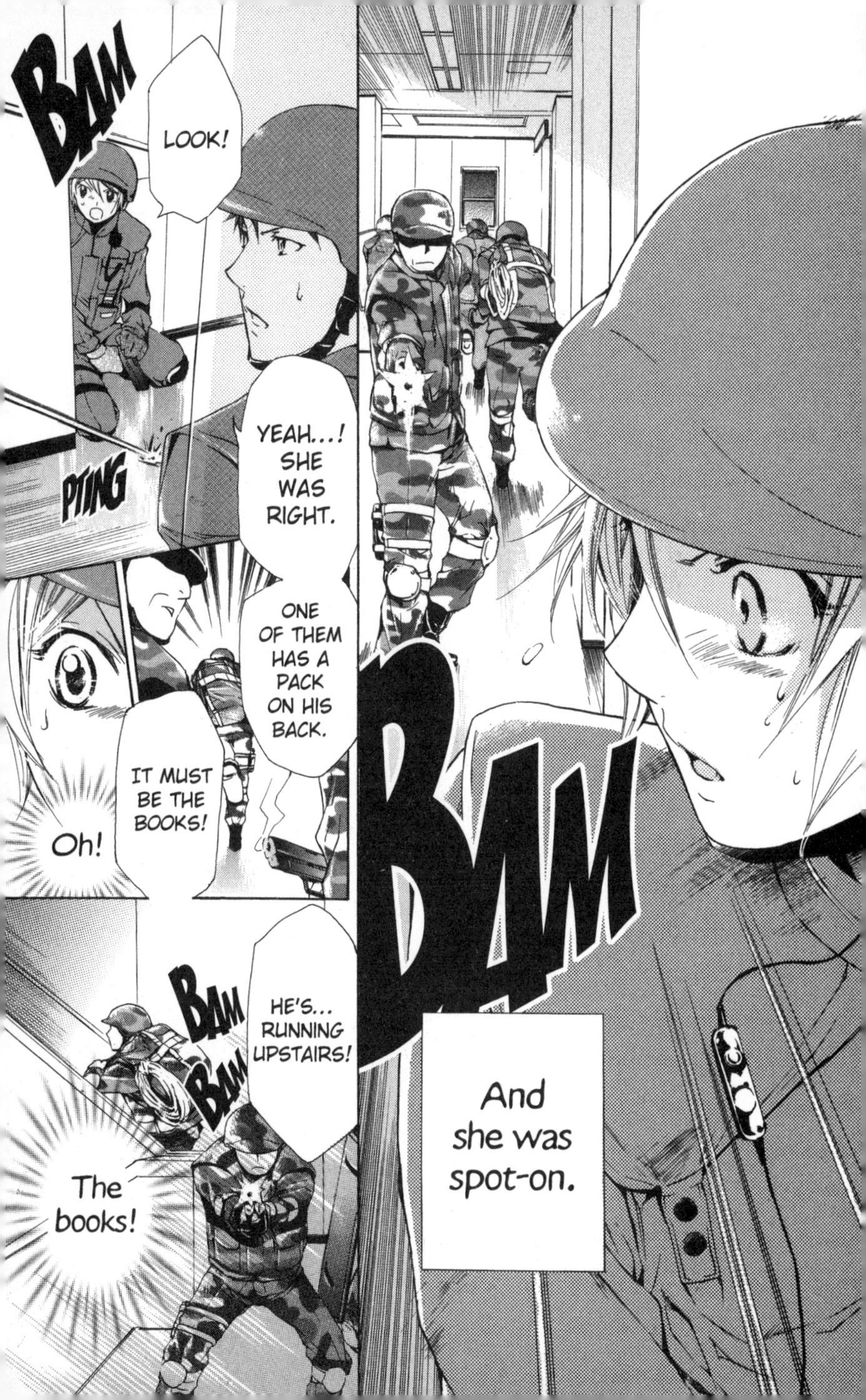
BAM
And she was spot-on.
BAM
LOOK!
YEAH...! SHE WAS RIGHT.
PTING
ONE OF THEM HAS A PACK ON HIS BACK.
IT MUST BE THE BOOKS!
Oh!
HE'S... RUNNING UPSTAIRS!
BAM
BAM
The books!

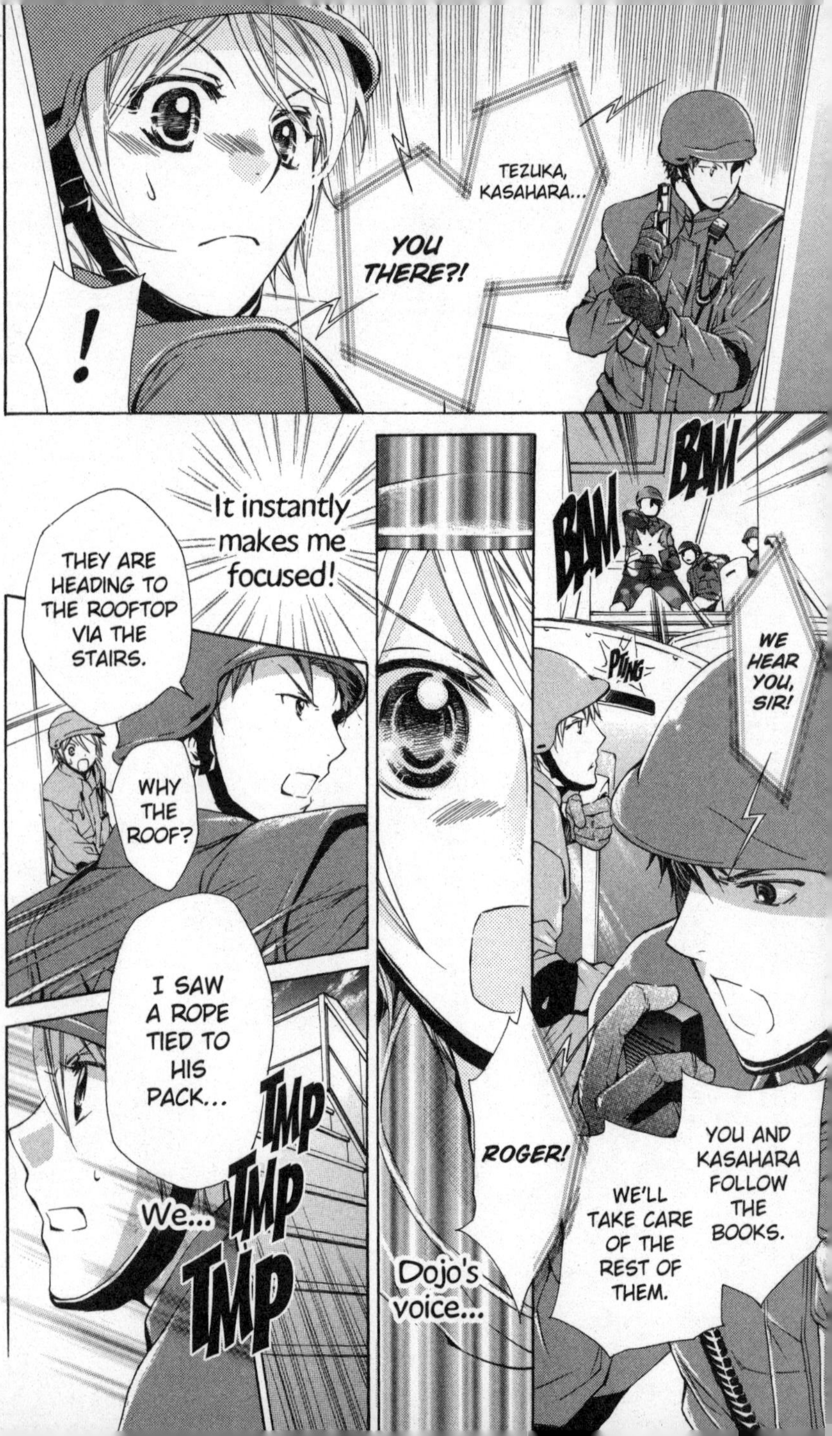

TEZUKA, KASAHARA...
YOU THERE?!
!
BAM
BAM
PTING
WE HEAR YOU, SIR!
YOU AND KASAHARA FOLLOW THE BOOKS.
WE'LL TAKE CARE OF THE REST OF THEM.
ROGER!
Dojo's voice...
It instantly makes me focused!
THEY ARE HEADING TO THE ROOFTOP VIA THE STAIRS.
WHY THE ROOF?
I SAW A ROPE TIED TO HIS PACK...
TMP
TMP
TMP
We...

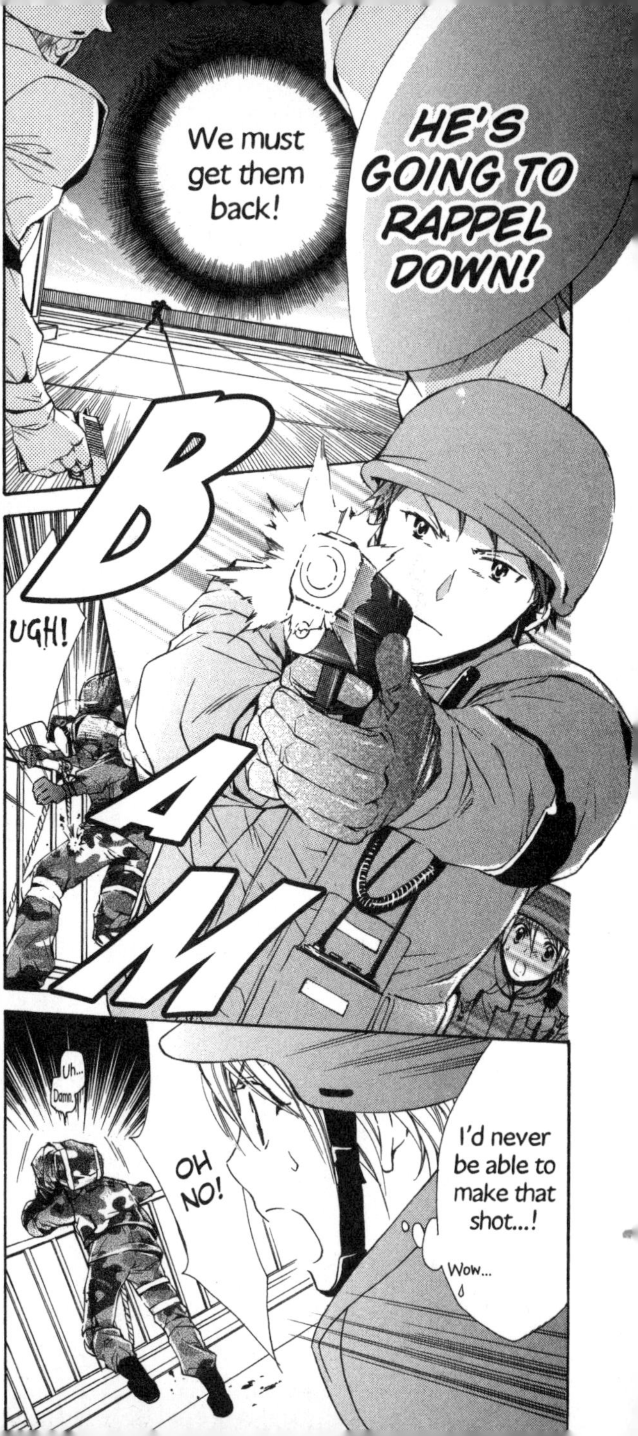
HE'S GOING TO RAPPEL DOWN!
We must get them back!
BAM
UGH!
I'd never be able to make that shot...!
Wow...
OH NO!
Uh...
Damn.

*

There was an autograph session when volume 1 came out. I'm not big on being in front of a crowd, and I was freaking out...!

Later on, people from the publisher told me I was doing fine, but I'm not so sure.

I was a nervous wreck. I was having trouble holding back tears until I got to the third customer because I was so grateful. I was like a jellyfish.

Anyway, it was great being able to see everybody. Thank you so much for coming to see me!

*

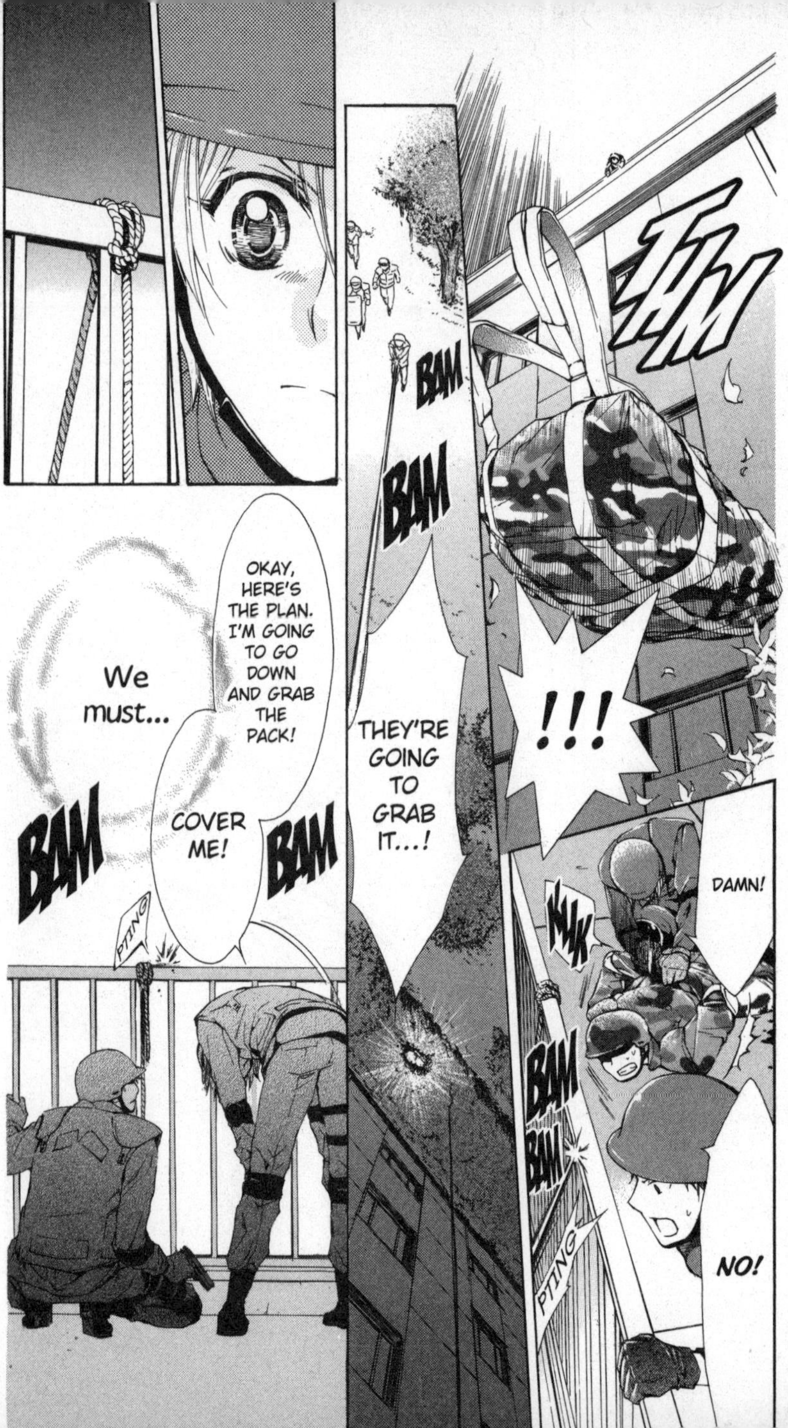
THM
!!!
BAM
BAM
THEY'RE GOING TO GRAB IT...!
DAMN!
NAK
BAM
BAM
PTING
NO!
We must...
OKAY, HERE'S THE PLAN. I'M GOING TO GO DOWN AND GRAB THE PACK!
COVER ME!
BAM
BAM
PTING

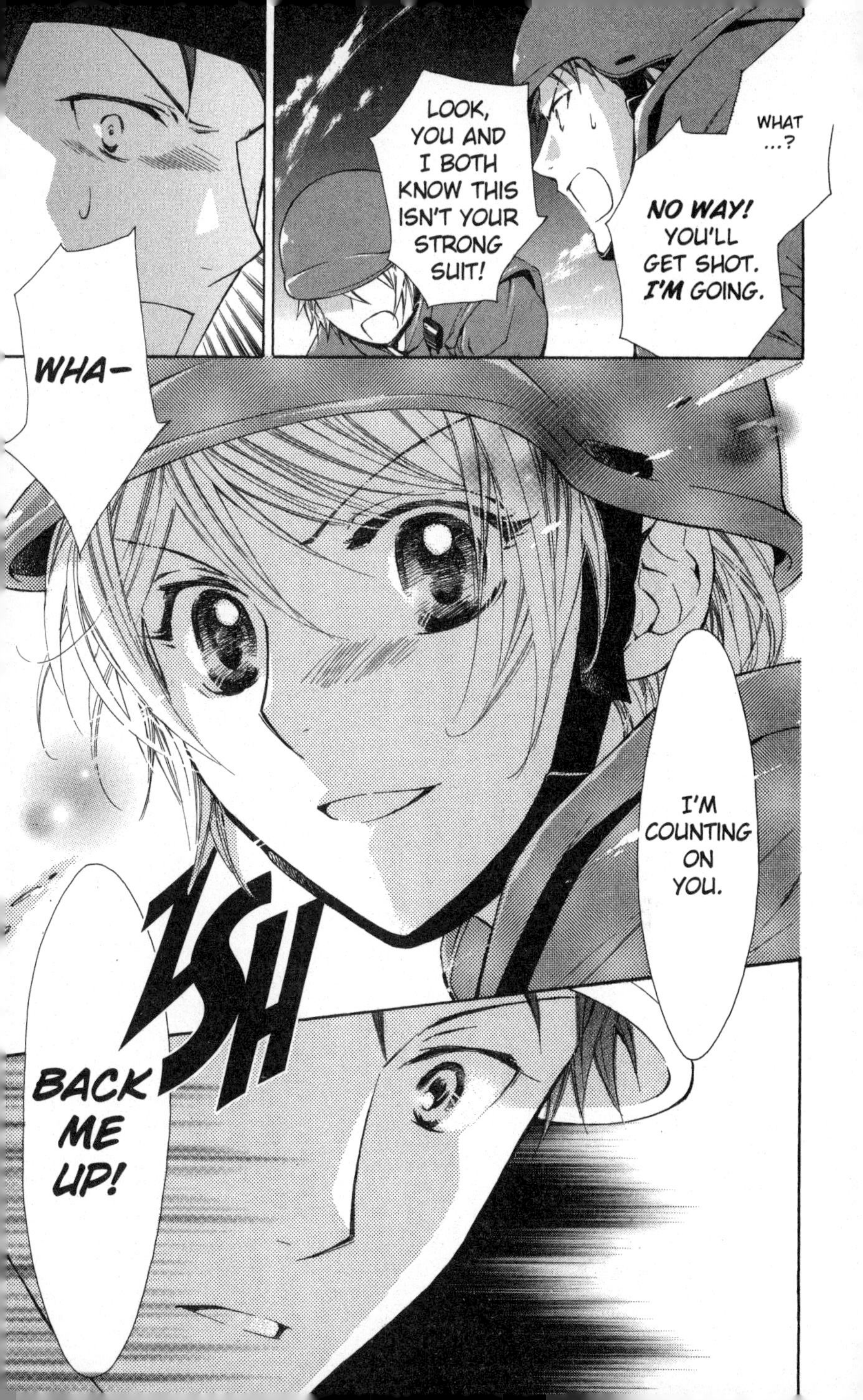
WHAT ...?
NO WAY! YOU'LL GET SHOT. I'M GOING.
LOOK, YOU AND I BOTH KNOW THIS ISN'T YOUR STRONG SUIT!
WHA-
I'M COUNTING ON YOU.
ZSH
BACK ME UP!

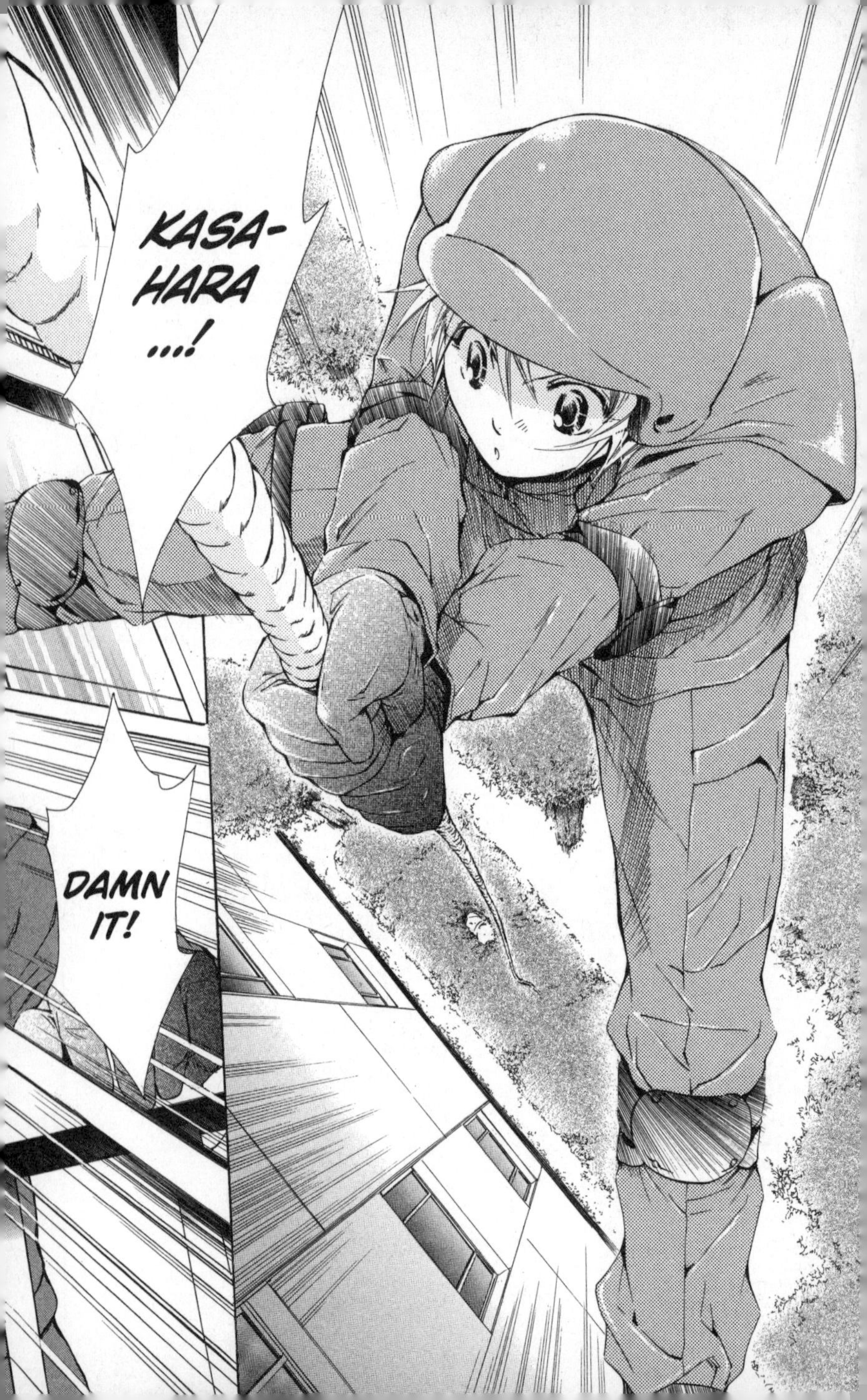
KASA-HARA ...!
DAMN IT!

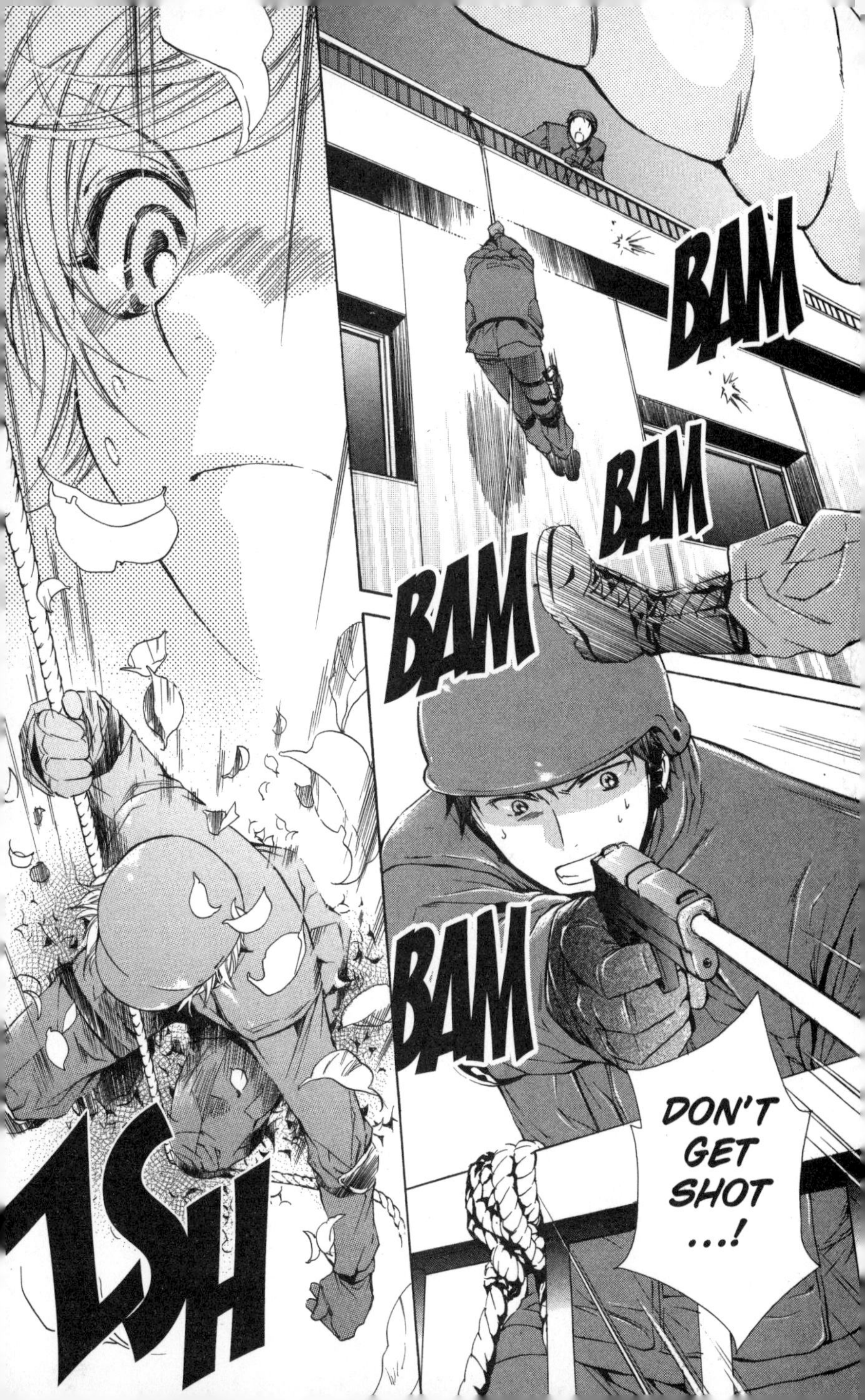
BAM
BAM
BAM
DON'T GET SHOT ...!
BAM
ZSH

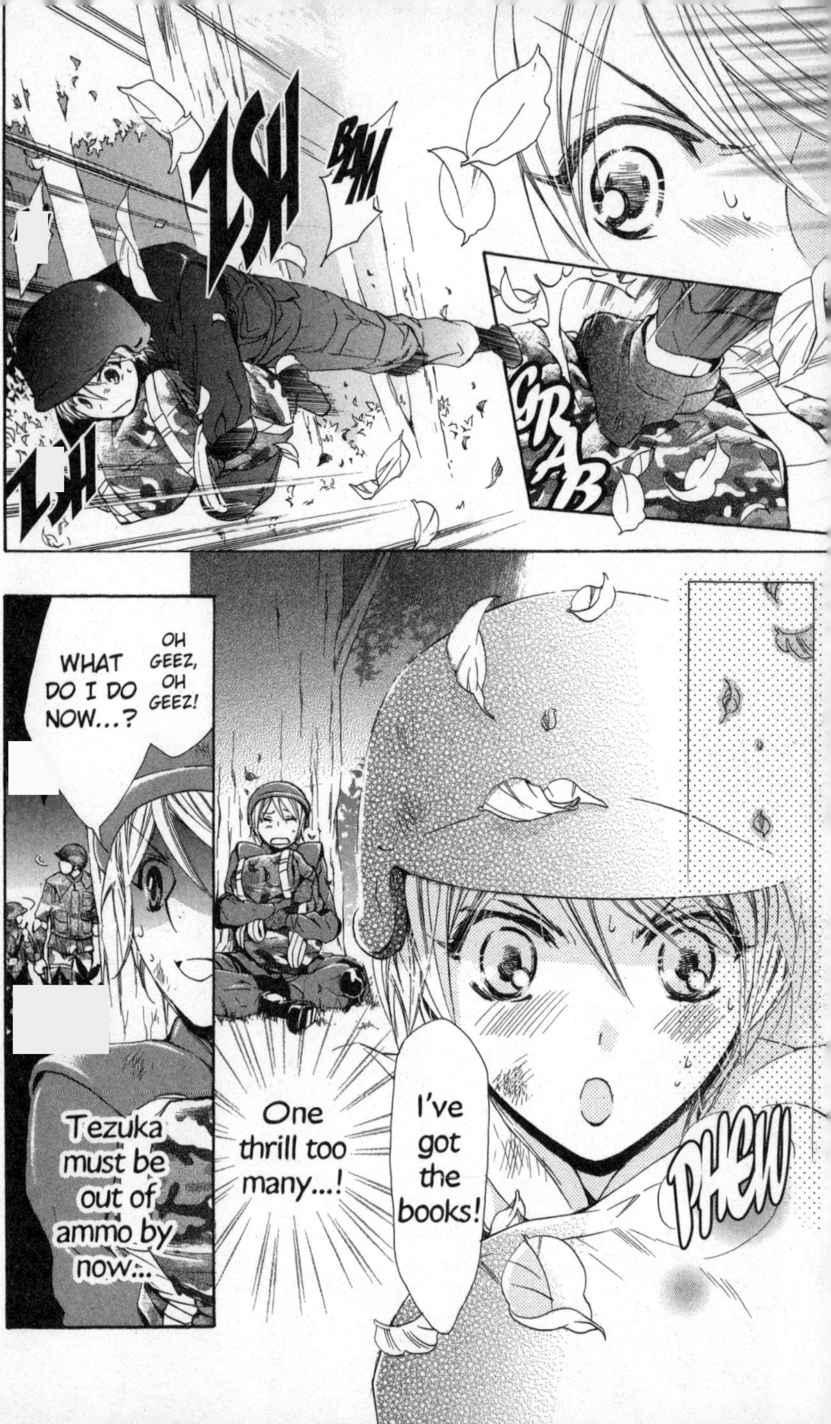
GRAB
ZSH
BAM
ZSH
I've got the books!
PHEW
One thrill too many...!
OH GEEZ, OH GEEZ!
WHAT DO I DO NOW...?
Tezuka must be out of ammo by now...

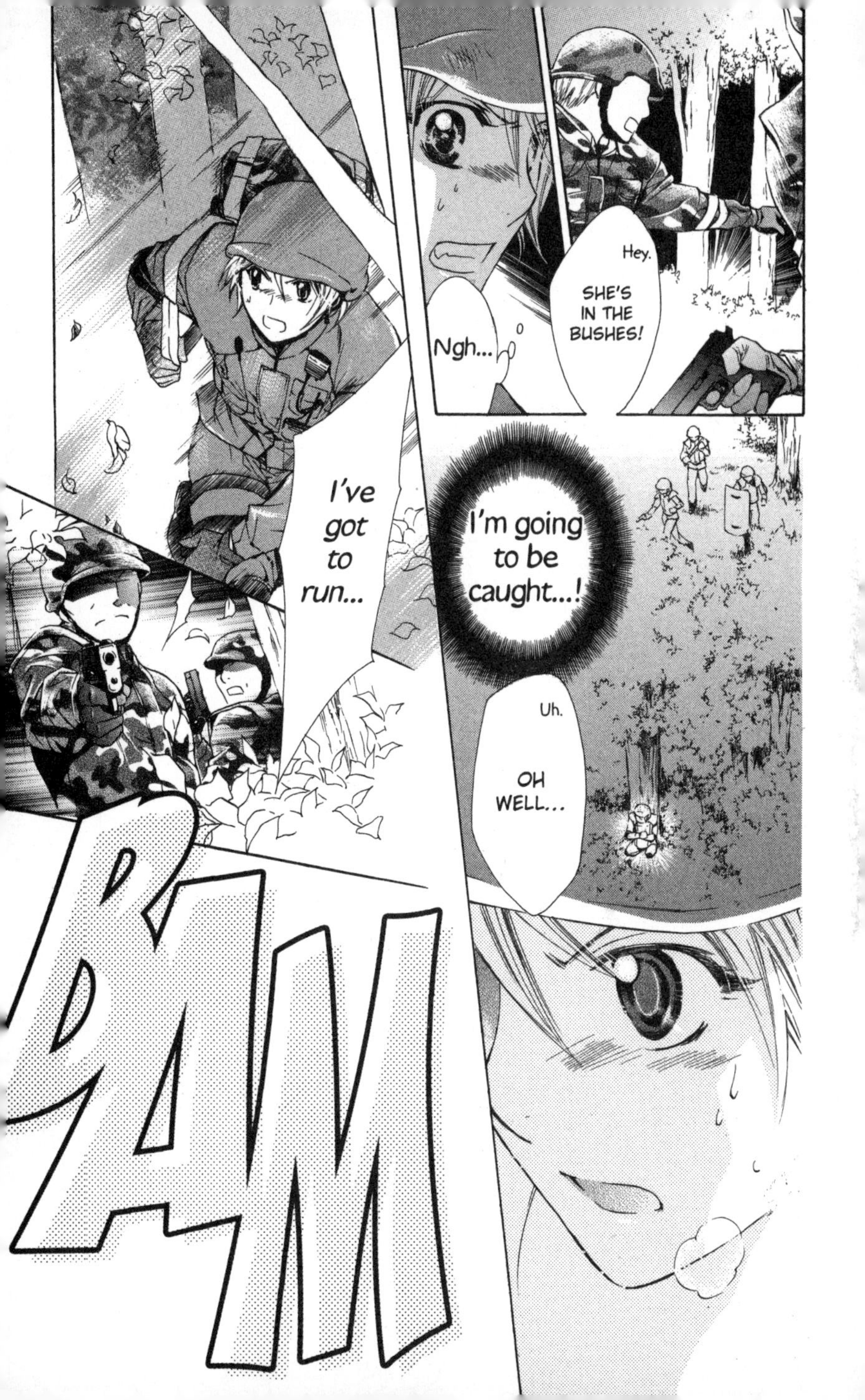

Hey.
SHE'S IN THE BUSHES!
Ngh...
I've got to run...
I'm going to be caught...!
Uh.
OH WELL...
BAM

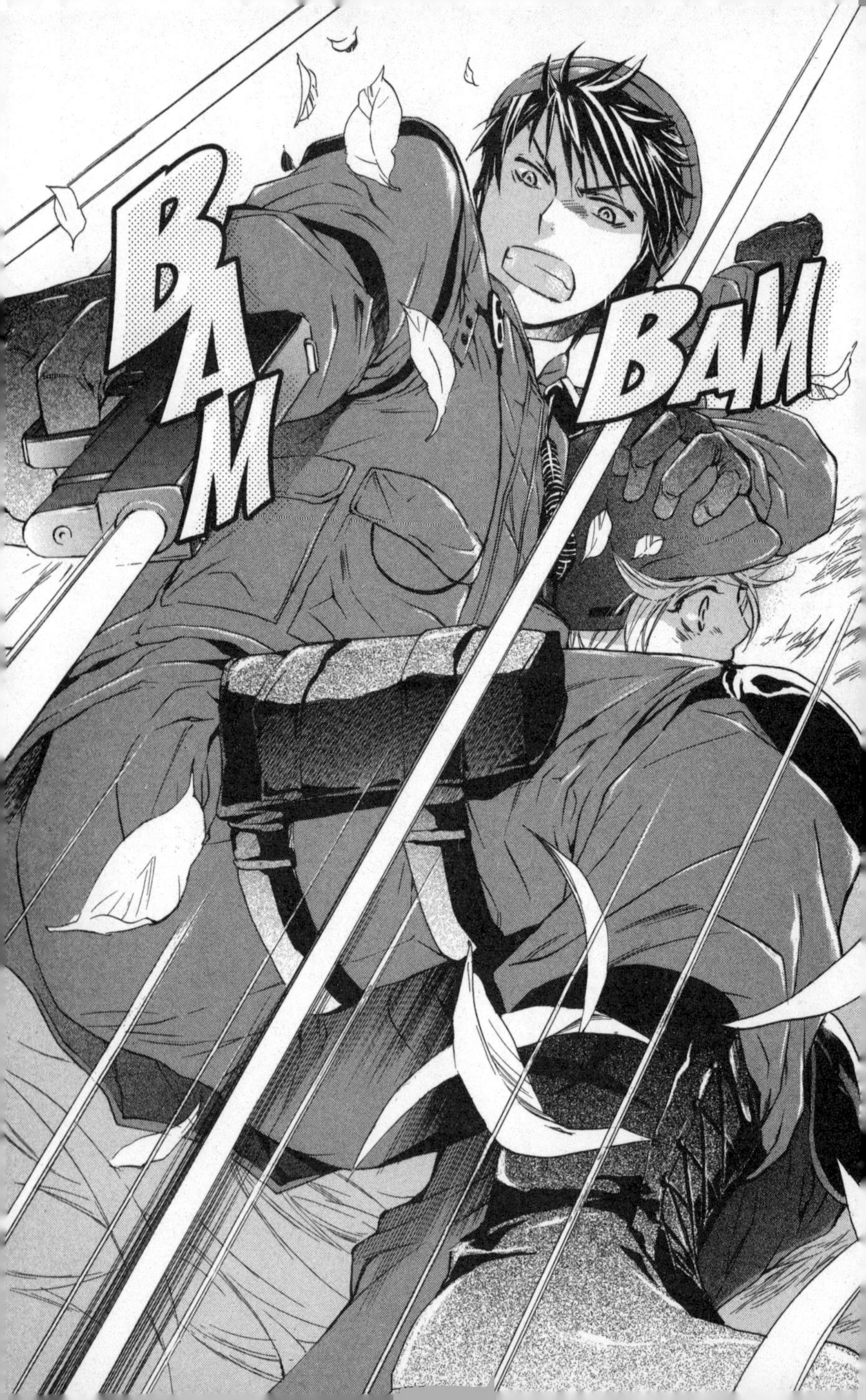
BAM
BAM

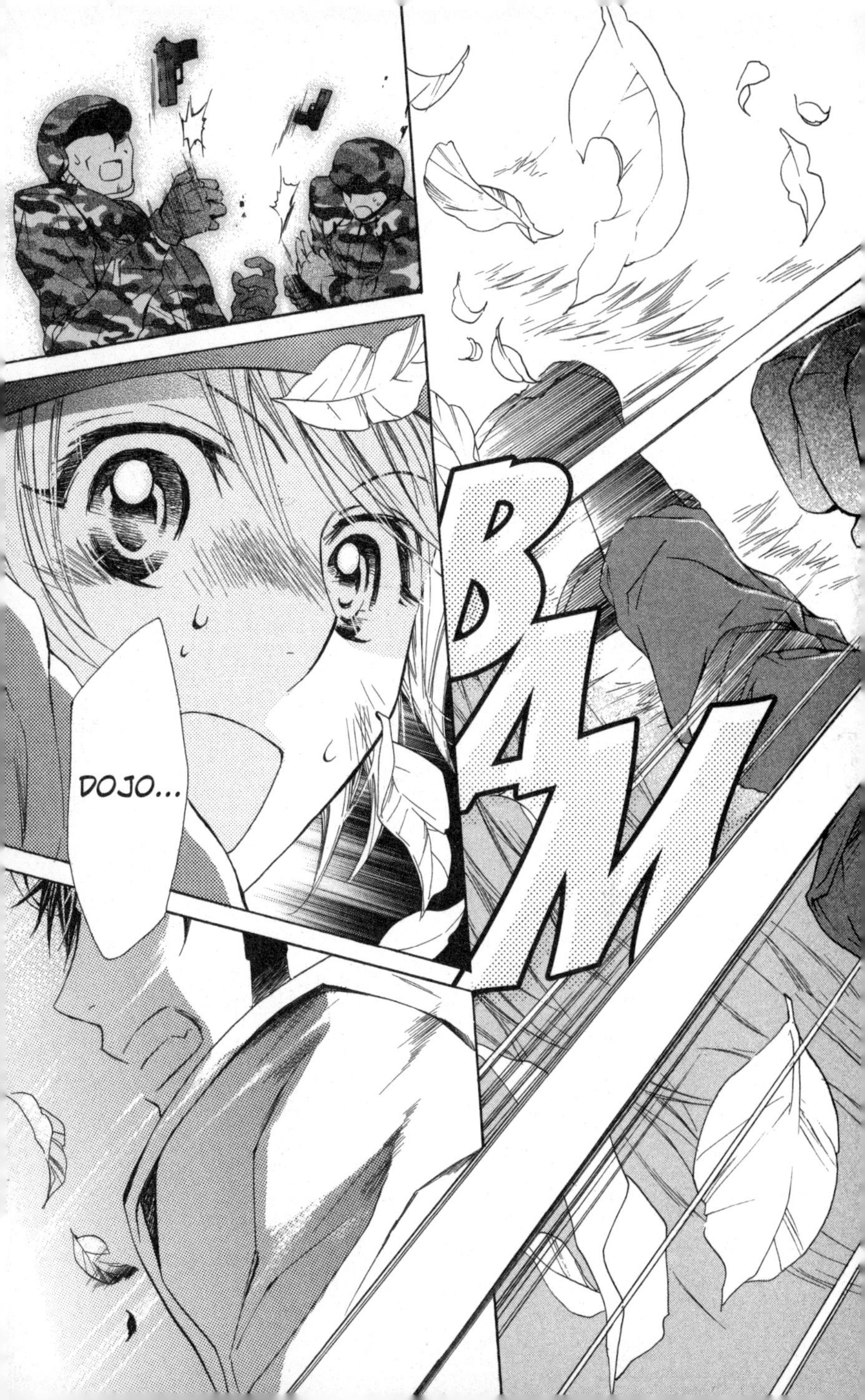
BAM
DOJO...

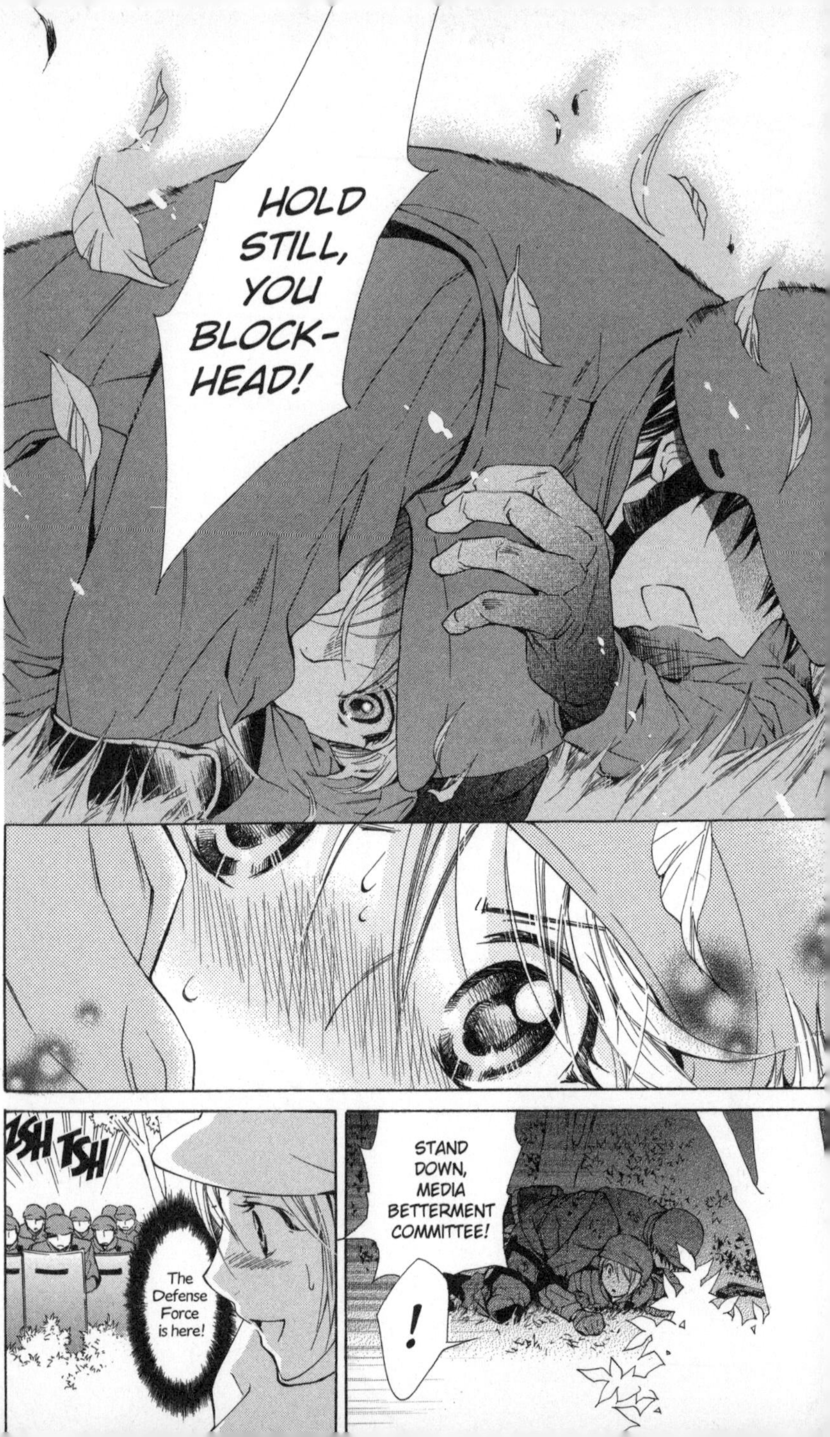
HOLD STILL, YOU BLOCK-HEAD!
STAND DOWN, MEDIA BETTERMENT COMMITTEE!
!
TSH TSH
The Defense Force is here!

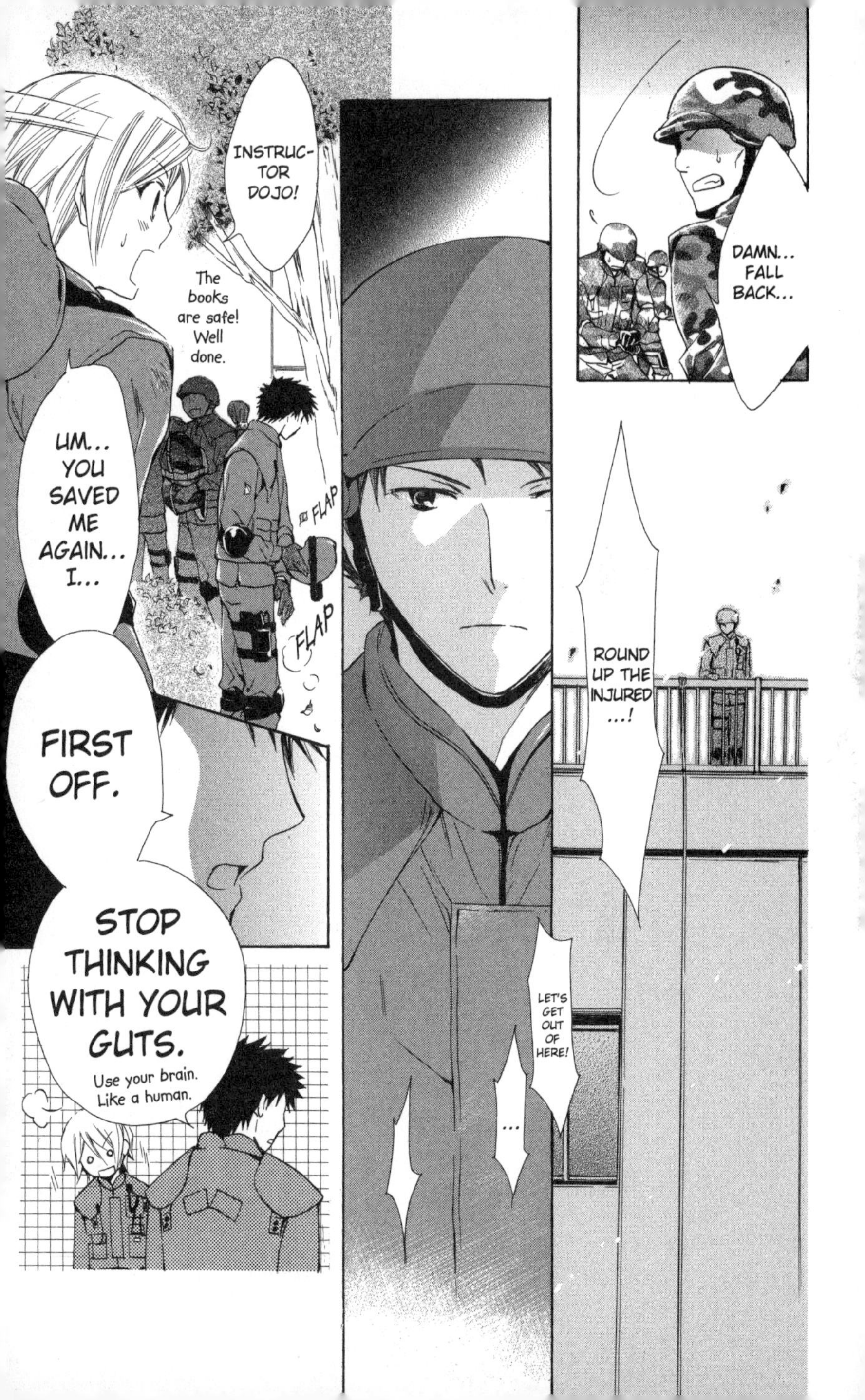
DAMN... FALL BACK...
ROUND UP THE INJURED ...!
LET'S GET OUT OF HERE!
...
INSTRUCTOR DOJO!
The books are safe! Well done.
UM... YOU SAVED ME AGAIN... I...
FLAP
FLAP
FIRST OFF.
STOP THINKING WITH YOUR GUTS.
Use your brain. Like a human.

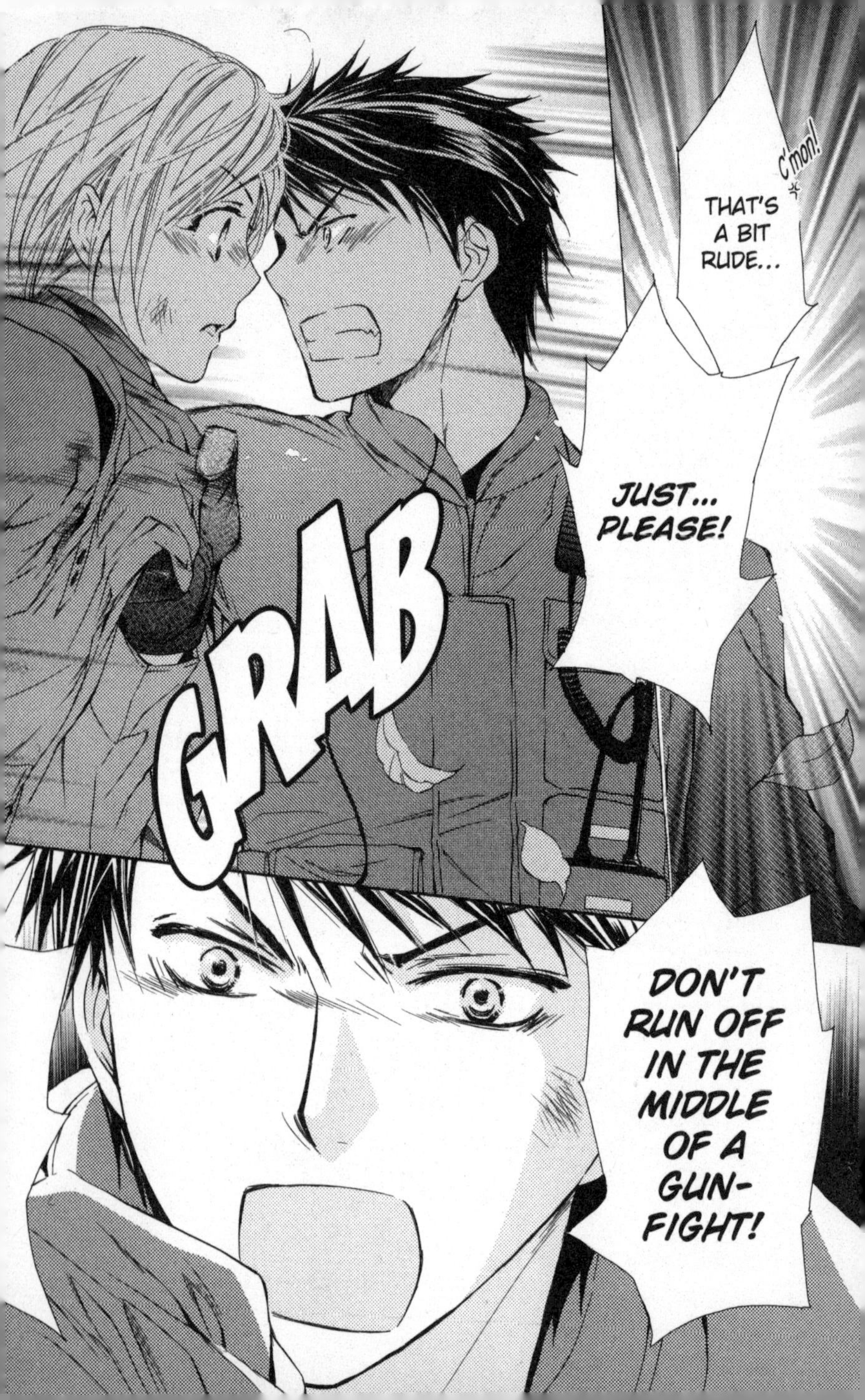
THAT'S A BIT RUDE...
C'mon!
JUST... PLEASE!
GRAB
DON'T RUN OFF IN THE MIDDLE OF A GUN-FIGHT!

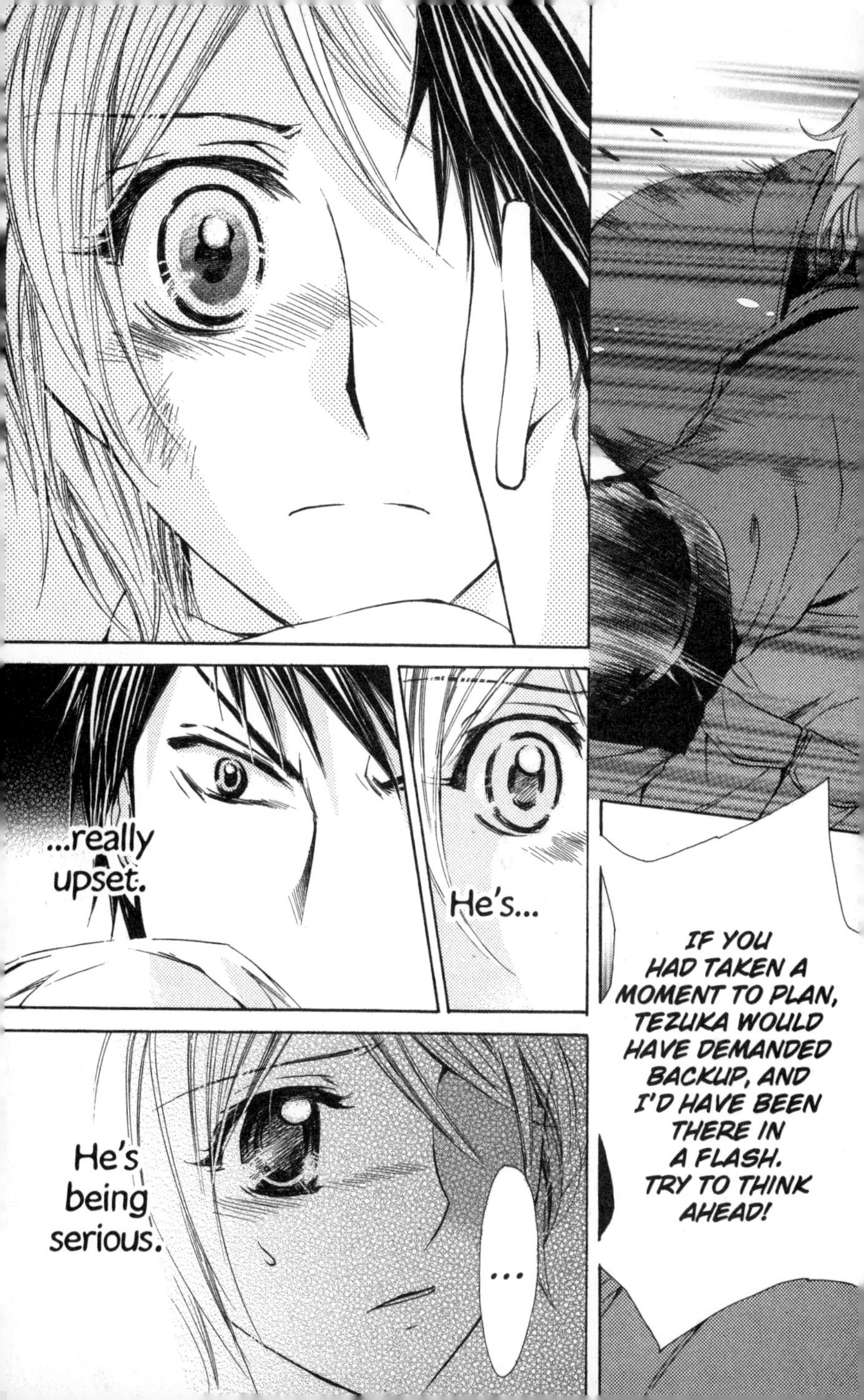
IF YOU HAD TAKEN A MOMENT TO PLAN, TEZUKA WOULD HAVE DEMANDED BACKUP, AND I'D HAVE BEEN THERE IN A FLASH. TRY TO THINK AHEAD!
He's...
...really upset.
...
He's being serious.

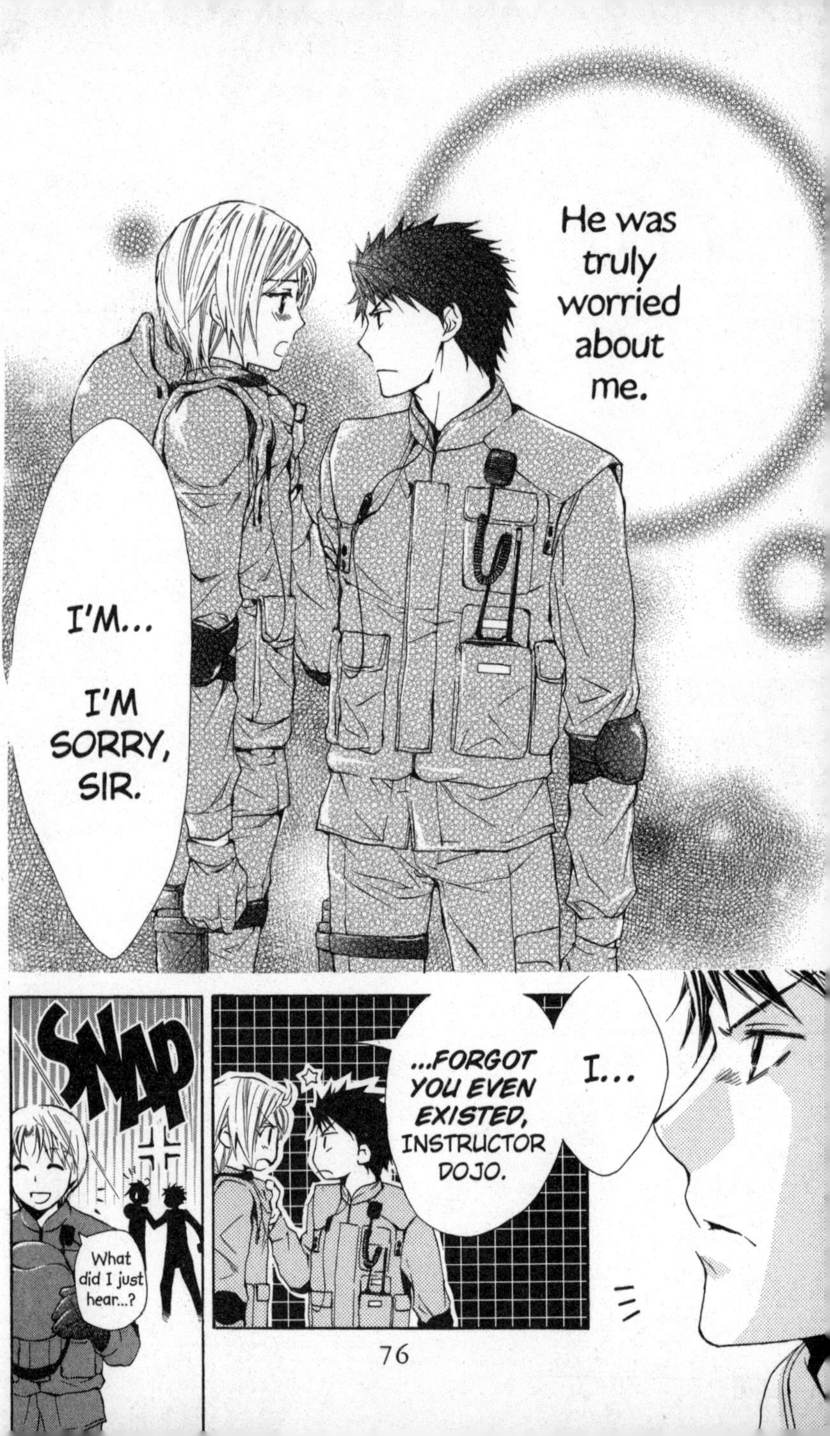
He was truly worried about me.
I'M...
I'M SORRY, SIR.
I...
...FORGOT YOU EVEN EXISTED, INSTRUCTOR DOJO.
SNAP
What did I just hear...?

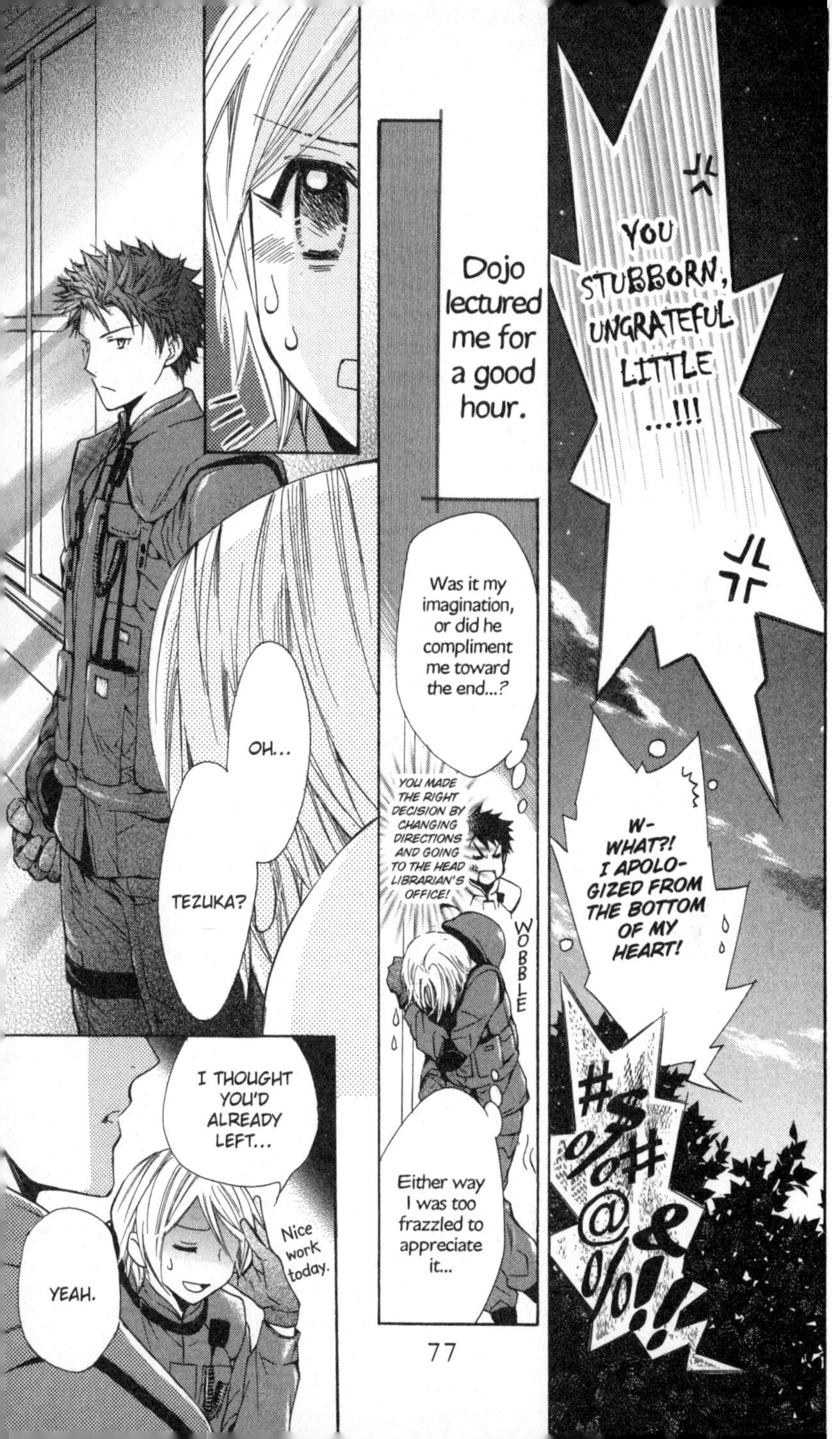
YOU STUBBORN, UNGRATEFUL LITTLE ...!!!
W- WHAT?! I APOLOGIZED FROM THE BOTTOM OF MY HEART!
#$%#@&%!!
Dojo lectured me for a good hour.
Was it my imagination, or did he compliment me toward the end...?
YOU MADE THE RIGHT DECISION BY CHANGING DIRECTIONS AND GOING TO THE HEAD LIBRARIAN'S OFFICE!
WOBBLE
Either way I was too frazzled to appreciate it...
OH...
TEZUKA?
I THOUGHT YOU'D ALREADY LEFT...
Nice work today.
YEAH.

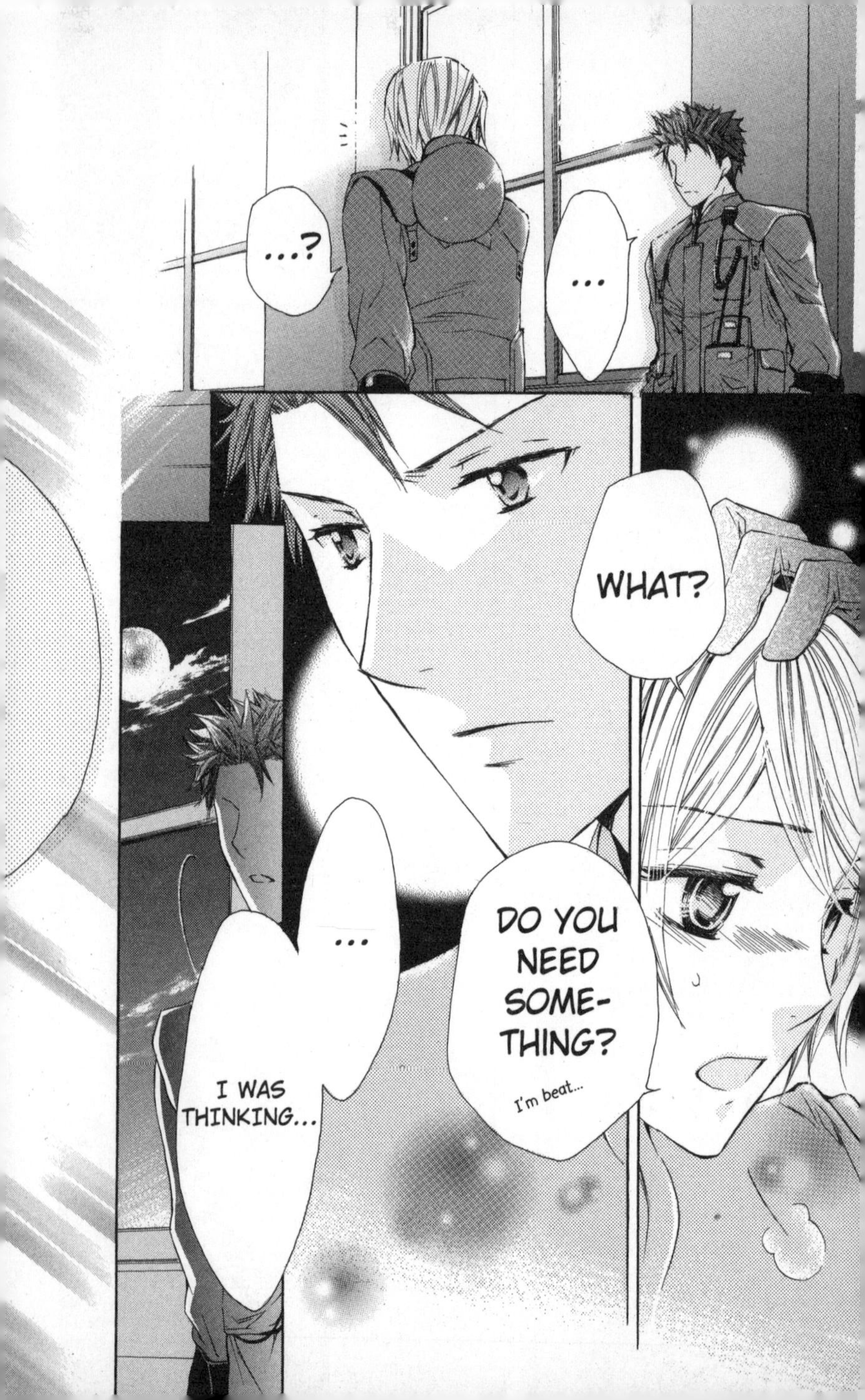
...
...?
WHAT?
DO YOU NEED SOMETHING?
I'm beat...
...
I WAS THINKING...

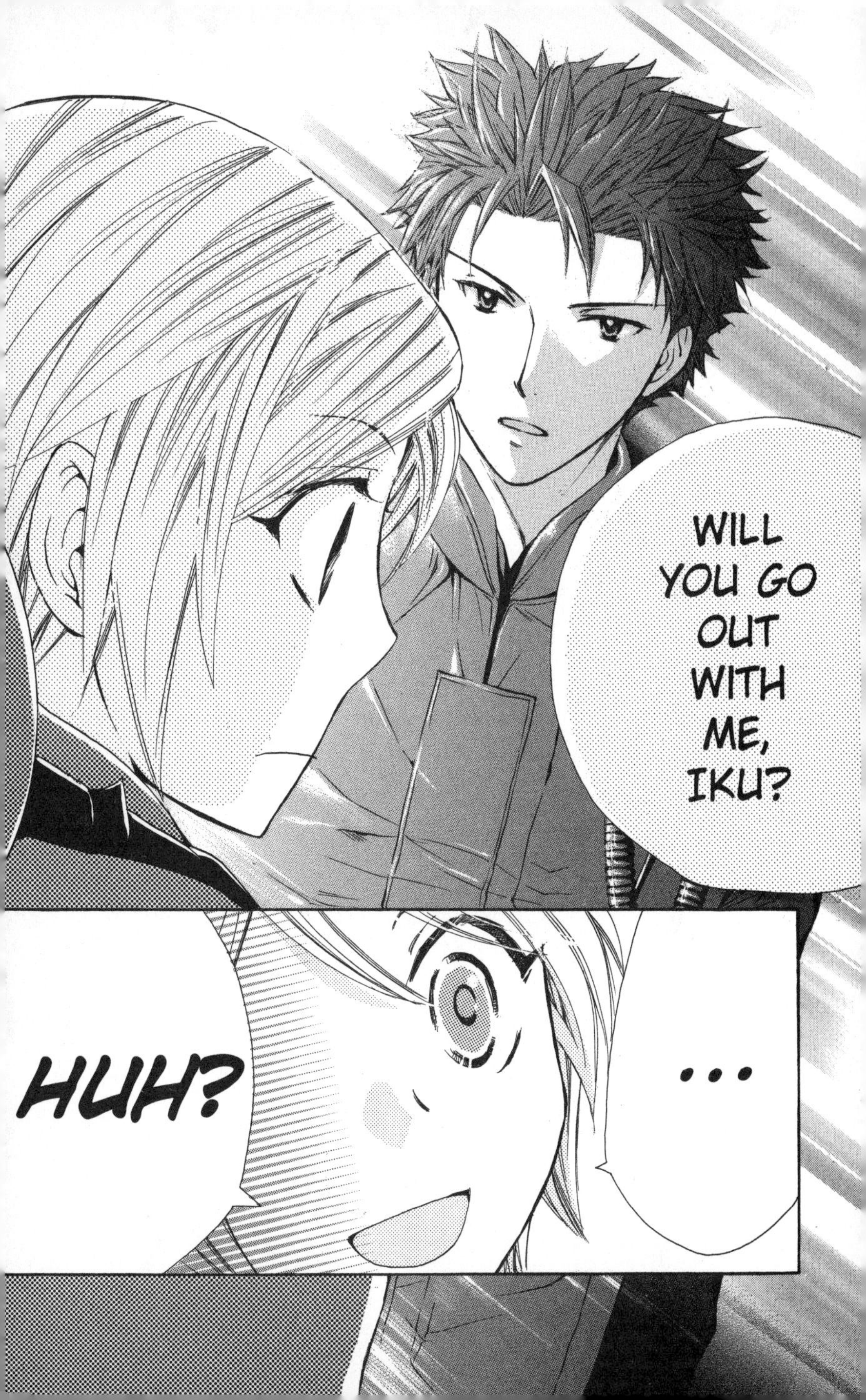
WILL YOU GO OUT WITH ME, IKU?
...
HUH?

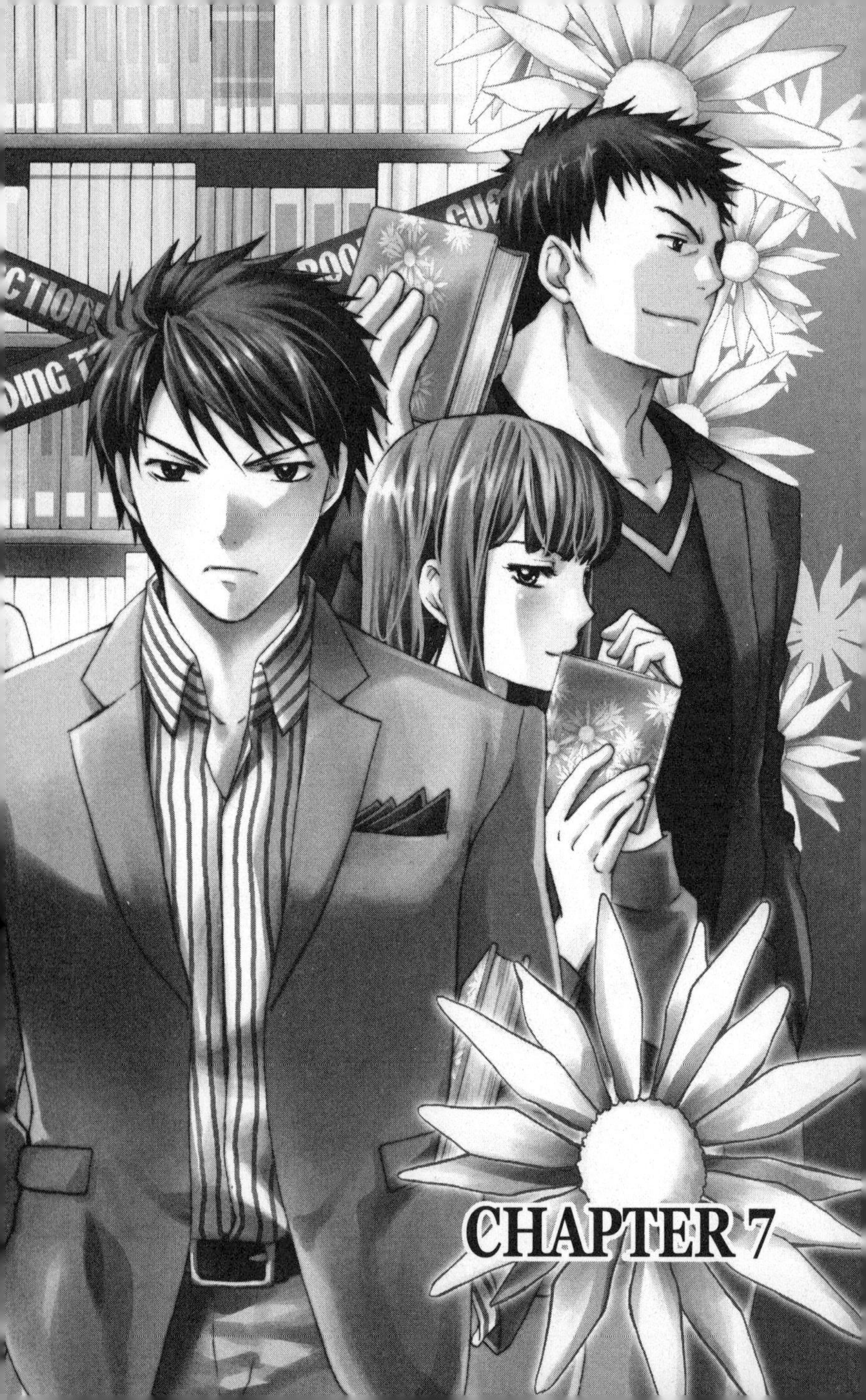
CHAPTER 7

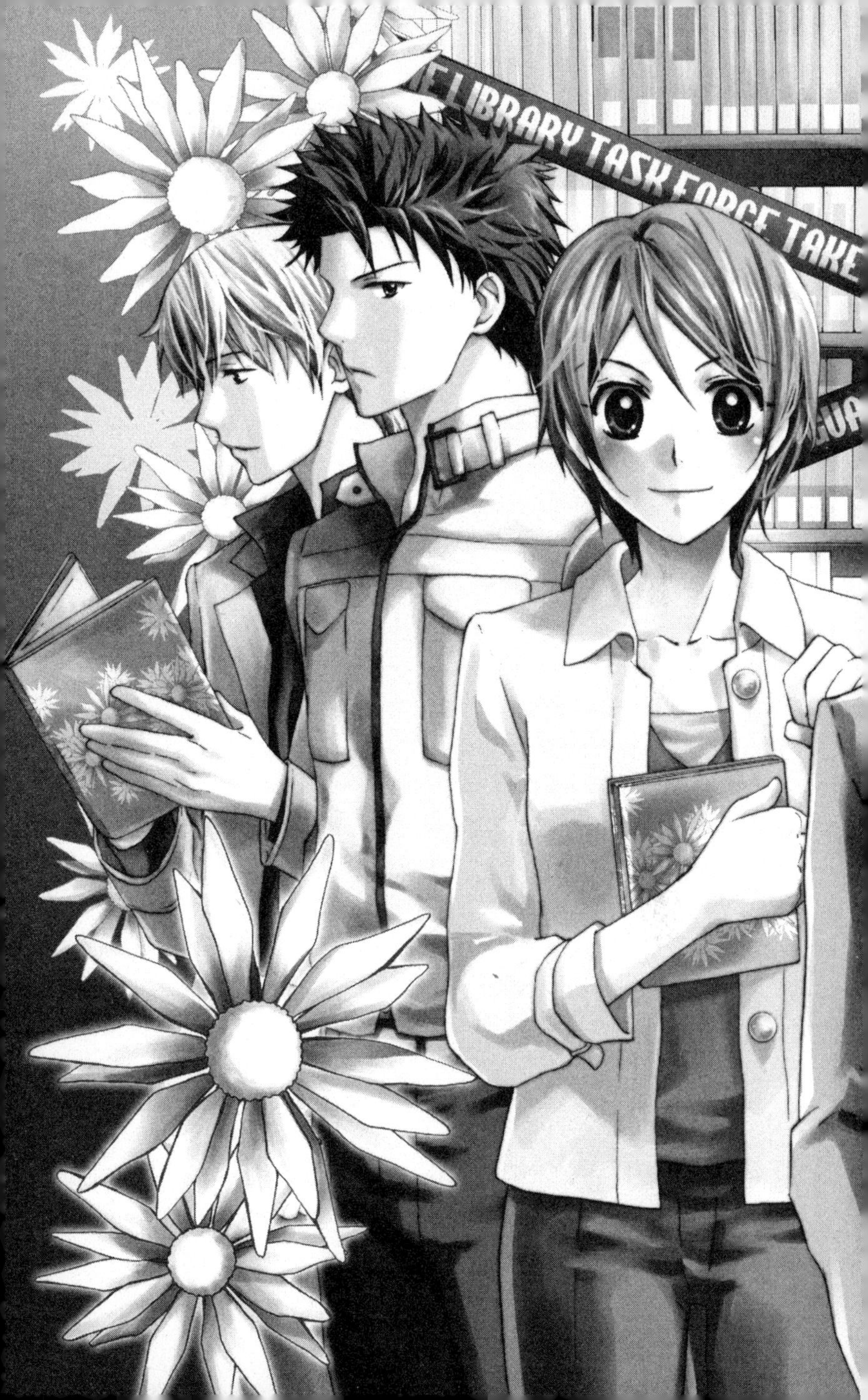
LIBRARY TASK FORCE TAKE

Komaki Discusses the Tender Moment:
"Hold Still, You Blockhead"

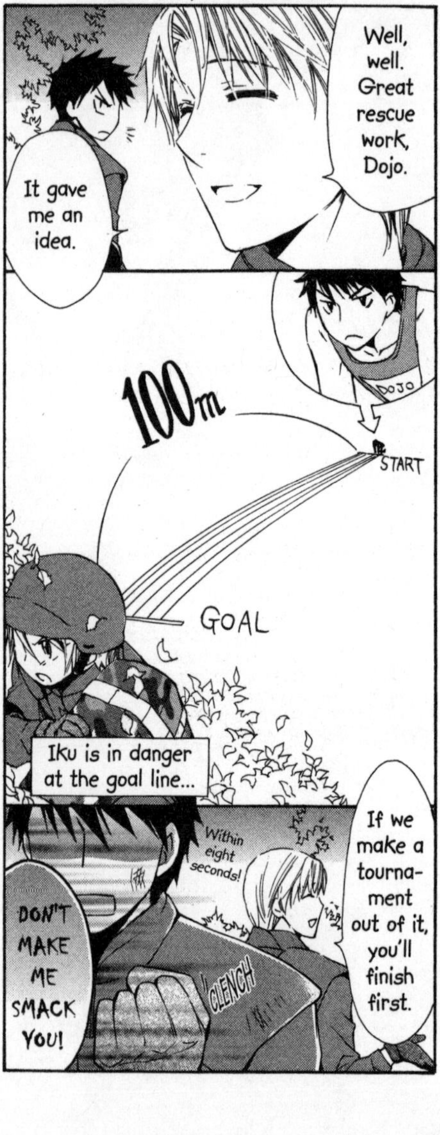
Well, well. Great rescue work, Dojo.
It gave me an idea.
DOJO
100m
START
GOAL
Iku is in danger at the goal line...
If we make a tourna-ment out of it, you'll finish first.
Within eight seconds!
CLENCH
DON'T MAKE ME SMACK YOU!

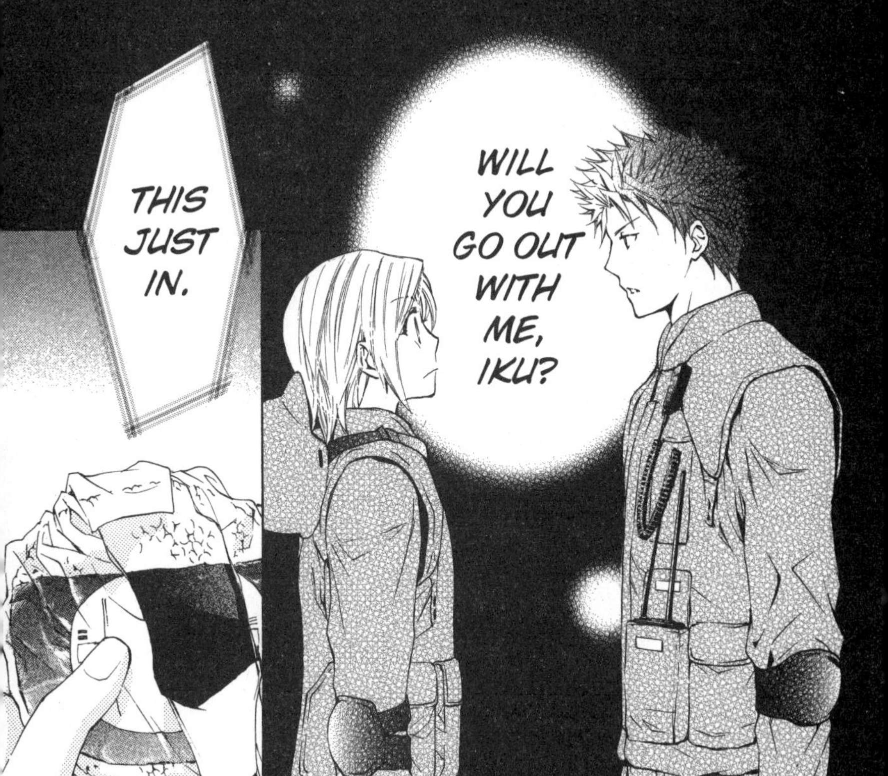
WILL YOU GO OUT WITH ME, IKU?
THIS JUST IN.
RIP
RIP

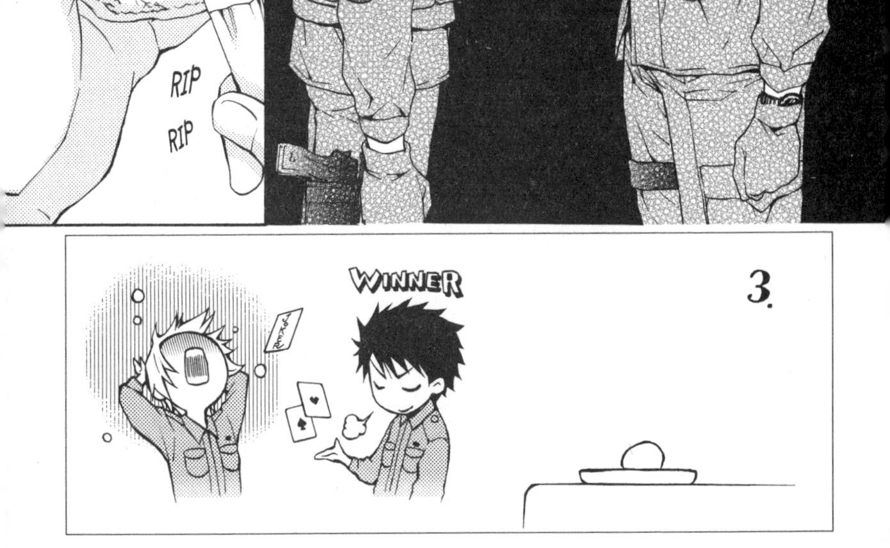
3.
WINNER

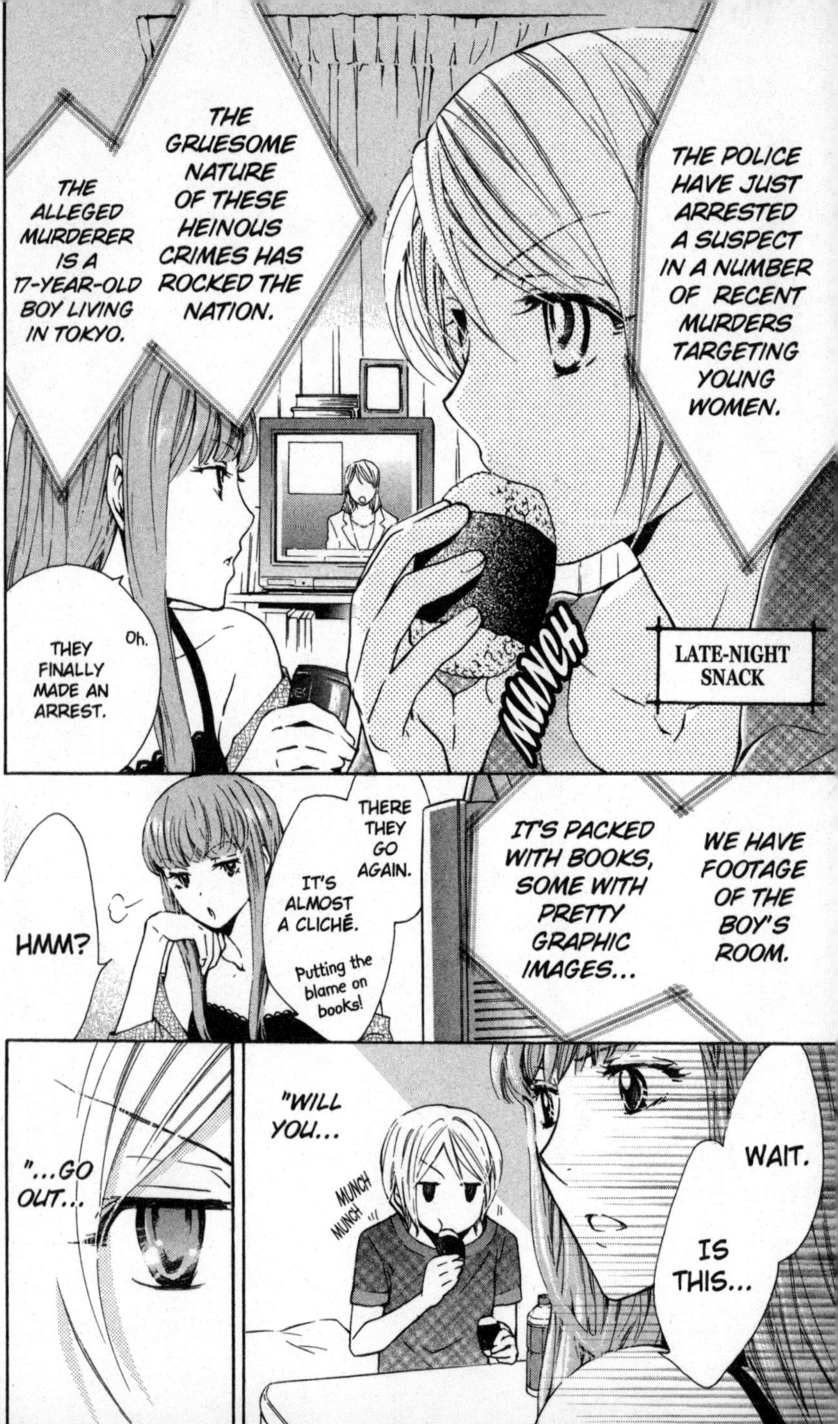
THE POLICE HAVE JUST ARRESTED A SUSPECT IN A NUMBER OF RECENT MURDERS TARGETING YOUNG WOMEN.
THE GRUESOME NATURE OF THESE HEINOUS CRIMES HAS ROCKED THE NATION.
THE ALLEGED MURDERER IS A 17-YEAR-OLD BOY LIVING IN TOKYO.
LATE-NIGHT SNACK
MUNCH
Oh.
THEY FINALLY MADE AN ARREST.
WE HAVE FOOTAGE OF THE BOY'S ROOM.
IT'S PACKED WITH BOOKS, SOME WITH PRETTY GRAPHIC IMAGES...
THERE THEY GO AGAIN.
IT'S ALMOST A CLICHÉ.
Putting the blame on books!
HMM?
WAIT.
IS THIS...
"WILL YOU...
MUNCH MUNCH
"...GO OUT...

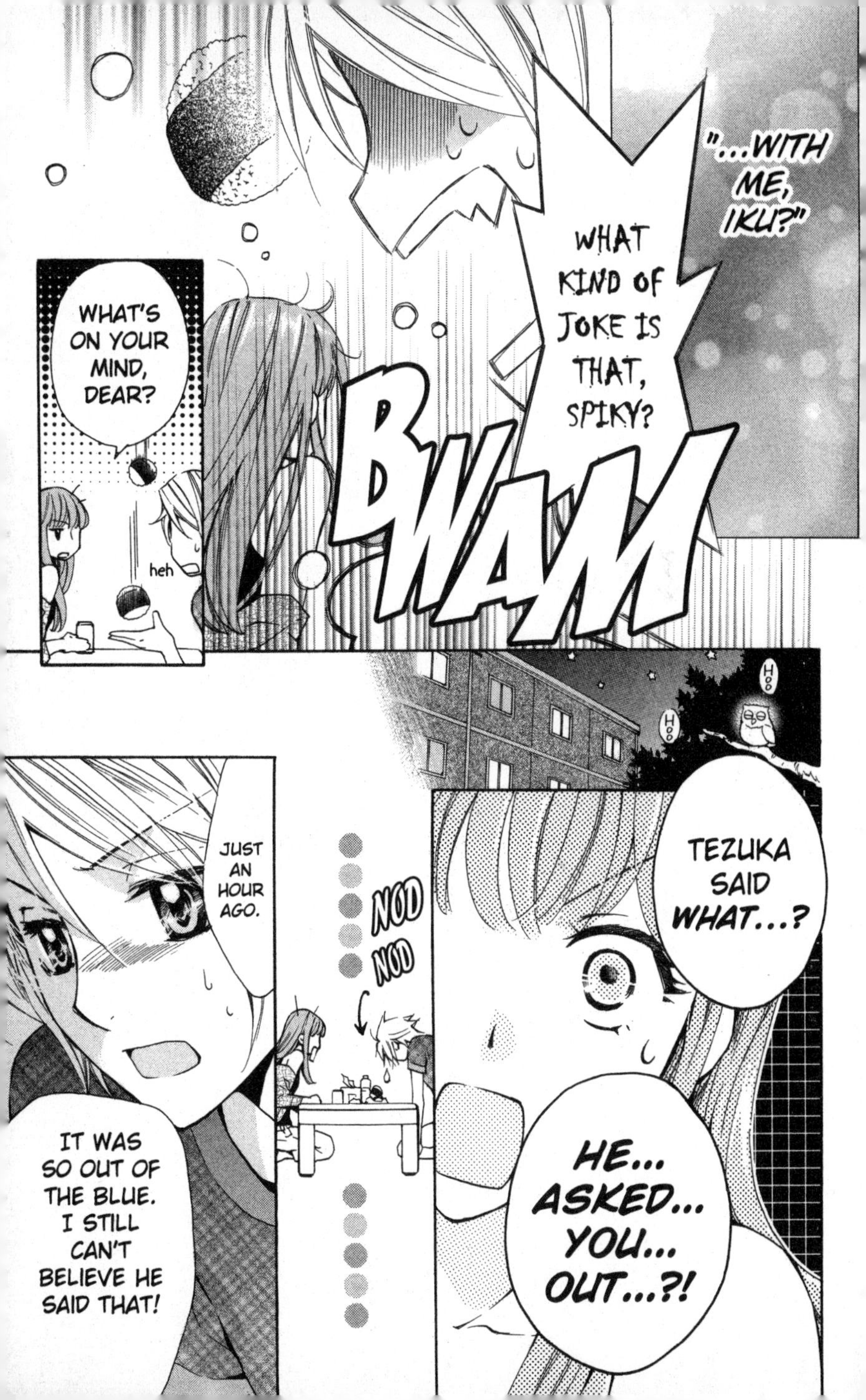
"...WITH ME, IKU?"
WHAT KIND OF JOKE IS THAT, SPIKY?
BWAM
WHAT'S ON YOUR MIND, DEAR?
heh
Hoo
Hoo
TEZUKA SAID WHAT...?
HE... ASKED... YOU... OUT...?!
NOD NOD
JUST AN HOUR AGO.
IT WAS SO OUT OF THE BLUE. I STILL CAN'T BELIEVE HE SAID THAT!

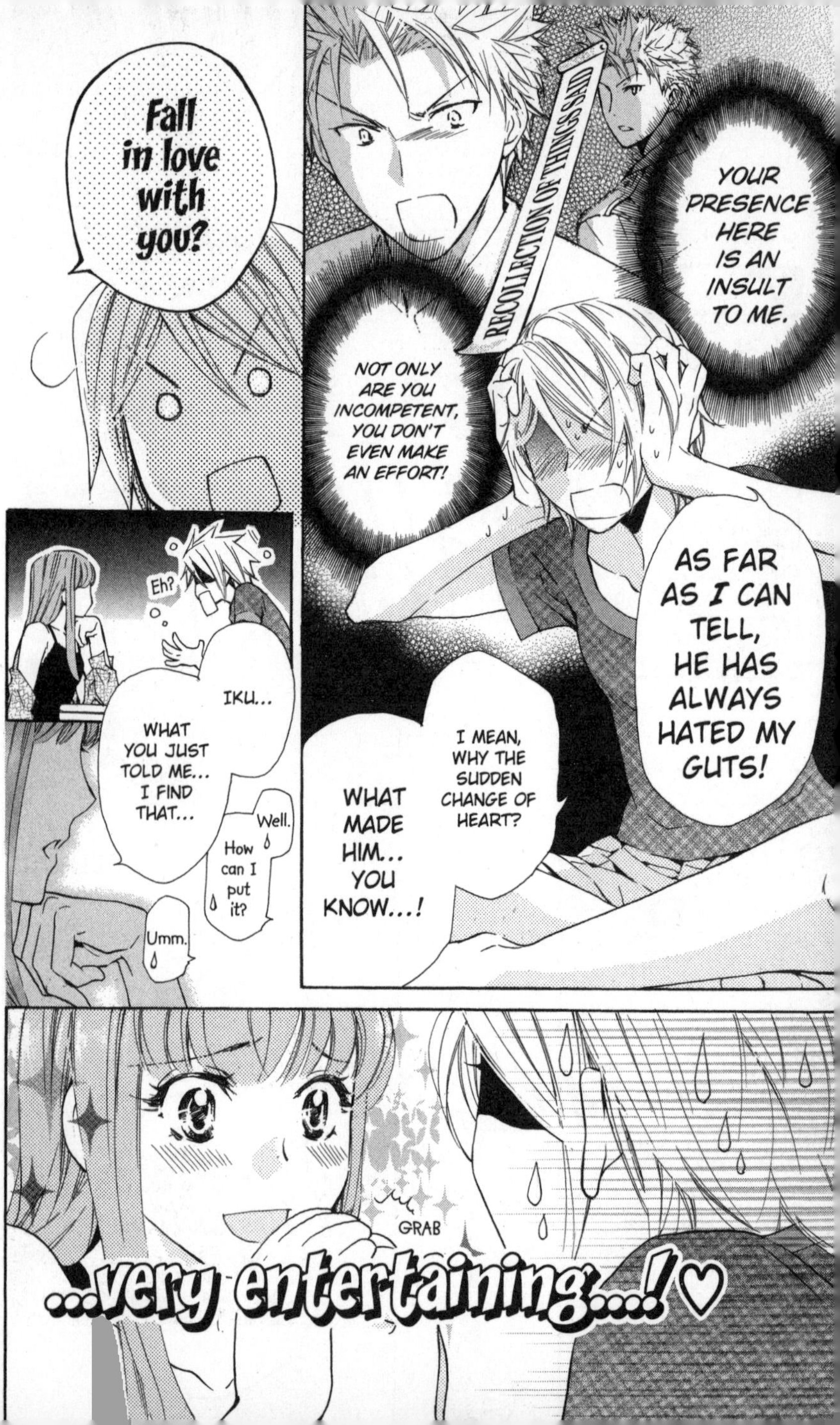
RECOLLECTION OF THINGS SAID
YOUR PRESENCE HERE IS AN INSULT TO ME.
NOT ONLY ARE YOU INCOMPETENT, YOU DON'T EVEN MAKE AN EFFORT!
AS FAR AS I CAN TELL, HE HAS ALWAYS HATED MY GUTS!
I MEAN, WHY THE SUDDEN CHANGE OF HEART?
WHAT MADE HIM... YOU KNOW...!
Fall in love with you?
Eh?
IKU...
WHAT YOU JUST TOLD ME... I FIND THAT...
Well.
How can I put it?
Umm.
GRAB
...very entertaining...!♥

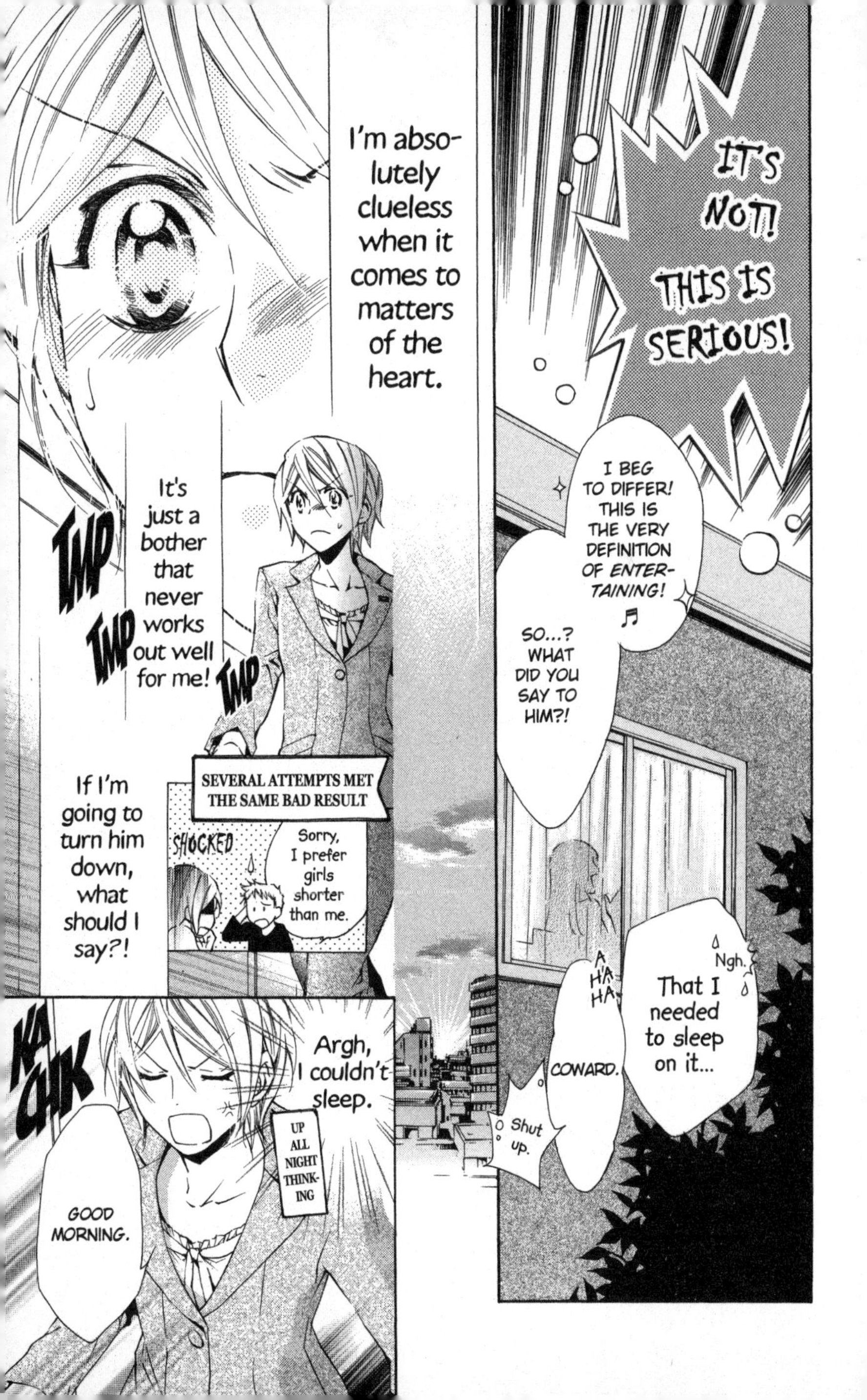
IT'S NOT! THIS IS SERIOUS!
I BEG TO DIFFER! THIS IS THE VERY DEFINITION OF *ENTERTAINING!* ♫
SO...? WHAT DID YOU SAY TO HIM?!
That I needed to sleep on it...
Ngh.
AHAHAHA
COWARD.
Shut up.
I'm absolutely clueless when it comes to matters of the heart.
It's just a bother that never works out well for me!
TMP
TMP
TMP
SEVERAL ATTEMPTS MET THE SAME BAD RESULT
Sorry, I prefer girls shorter than me.
SHOCKED
If I'm going to turn him down, what should I say?!
Argh, I couldn't sleep.
UP ALL NIGHT THINKING
GOOD MORNING.
KA CHIK

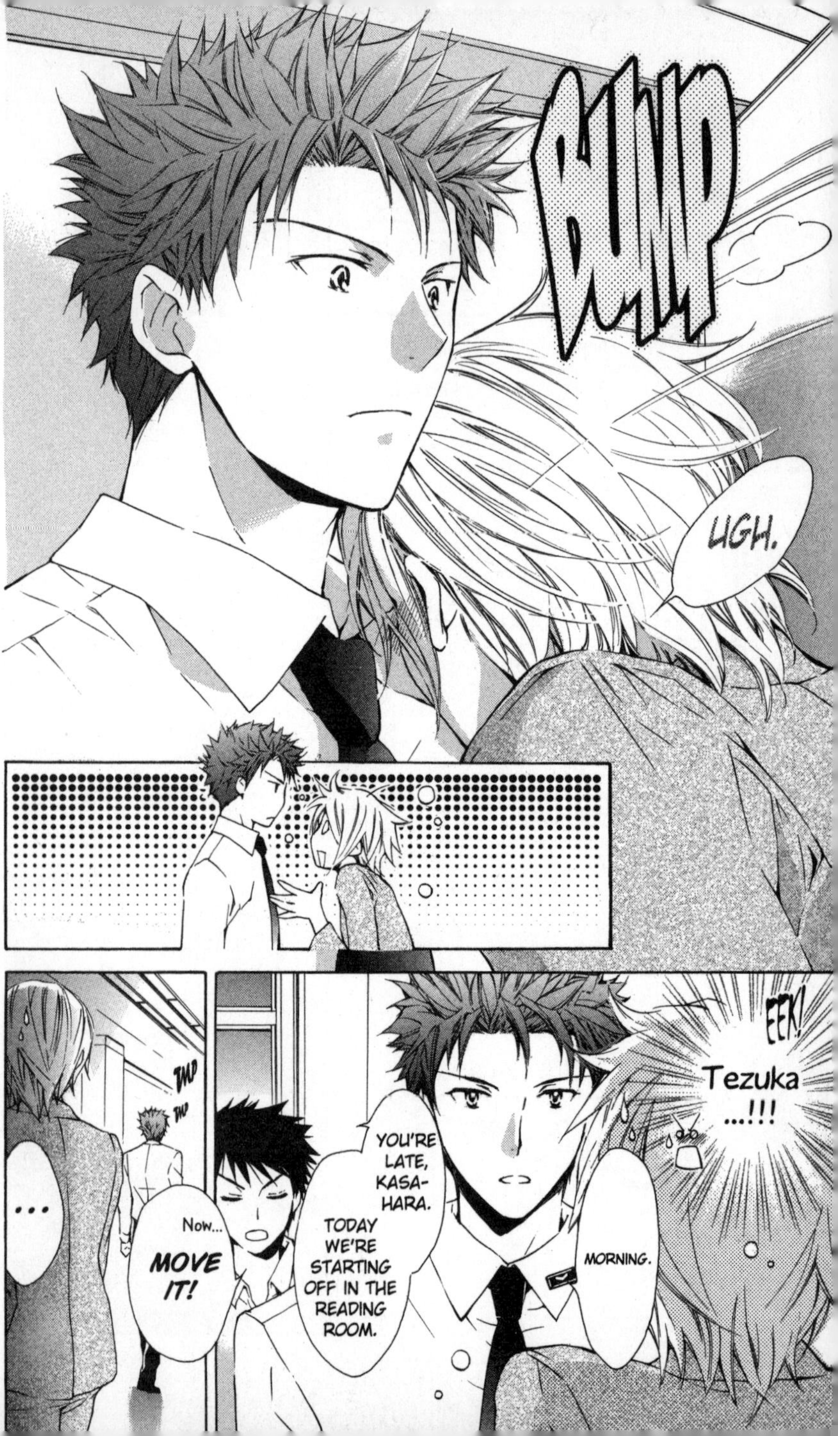
BUMP
UGH.
EEK!
Tezuka ...!!!
MORNING.
YOU'RE LATE, KASAHARA.
TODAY WE'RE STARTING OFF IN THE READING ROOM.
Now... MOVE IT!
TMP TMP
...

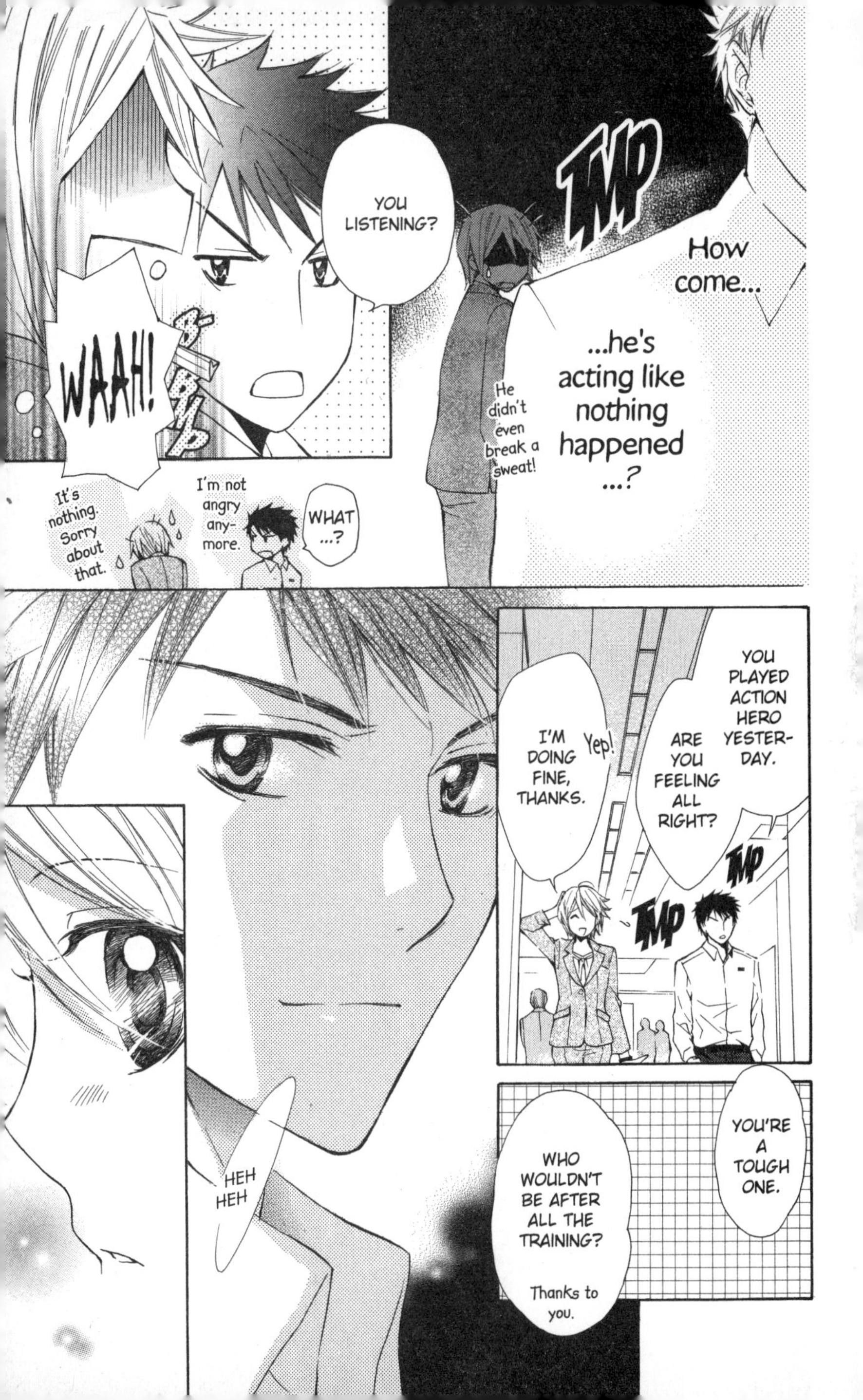
TMP
How come...
...he's acting like nothing happened ...?
He didn't even break a sweat!
YOU LISTENING?
WAAH!
WHAT ...?
I'm not angry any- more.
It's nothing. Sorry about that.
YOU PLAYED ACTION HERO YESTER- DAY.
ARE YOU FEELING ALL RIGHT?
Yep!
I'M DOING FINE, THANKS.
TMP
TMP
YOU'RE A TOUGH ONE.
WHO WOULDN'T BE AFTER ALL THE TRAINING?
Thanks to you.
HEH HEH

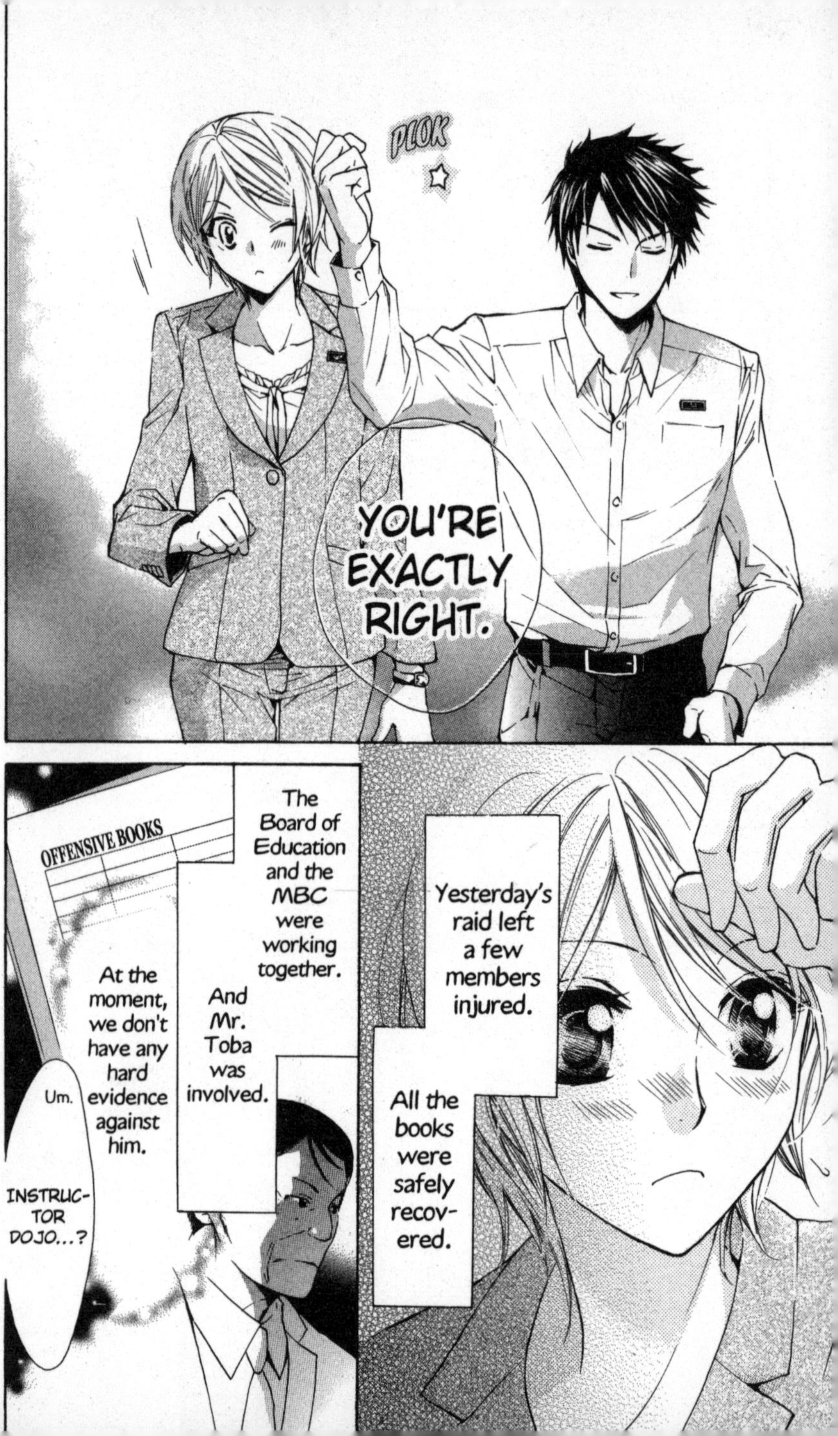
PLOK
YOU'RE EXACTLY RIGHT.
Yesterday's raid left a few members injured.
All the books were safely recovered.
The Board of Education and the MBC were working together.
OFFENSIVE BOOKS
And Mr. Toba was involved.
At the moment, we don't have any hard evidence against him.
Um.
INSTRUC-TOR DOJO...?

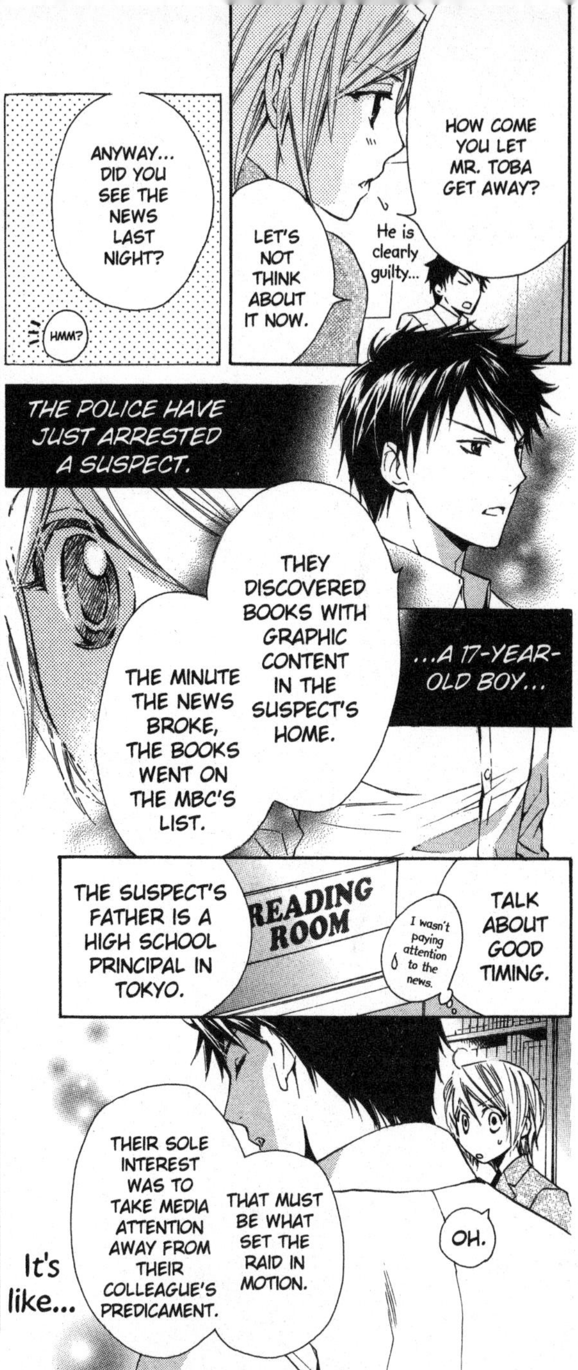
HOW COME YOU LET MR. TOBA GET AWAY?
He is clearly guilty...
LET'S NOT THINK ABOUT IT NOW.
ANYWAY... DID YOU SEE THE NEWS LAST NIGHT?
HMM?
THE POLICE HAVE JUST ARRESTED A SUSPECT.
...A 17-YEAR-OLD BOY...
THEY DISCOVERED BOOKS WITH GRAPHIC CONTENT IN THE SUSPECT'S HOME.
THE MINUTE THE NEWS BROKE, THE BOOKS WENT ON THE MBC'S LIST.
TALK ABOUT GOOD TIMING.
I wasn't paying attention to the news.
READING ROOM
THE SUSPECT'S FATHER IS A HIGH SCHOOL PRINCIPAL IN TOKYO.
OH.
THAT MUST BE WHAT SET THE RAID IN MOTION.
THEIR SOLE INTEREST WAS TO TAKE MEDIA ATTENTION AWAY FROM THEIR COLLEAGUE'S PREDICAMENT.
It's like...

4

*

I was invited to observe a recording session for the animated version of *Library Wars*. I asked my editor for this opportunity because it would be the chance of a lifetime for me. It was wonderful watching the professional actors! They weren't just blessed with beautiful voices, they were drop-dead gorgeous...!

It was a great day for me. Thanks so much!

They're doing a great job, and it was very inspirational.

I love the anime version too.

*

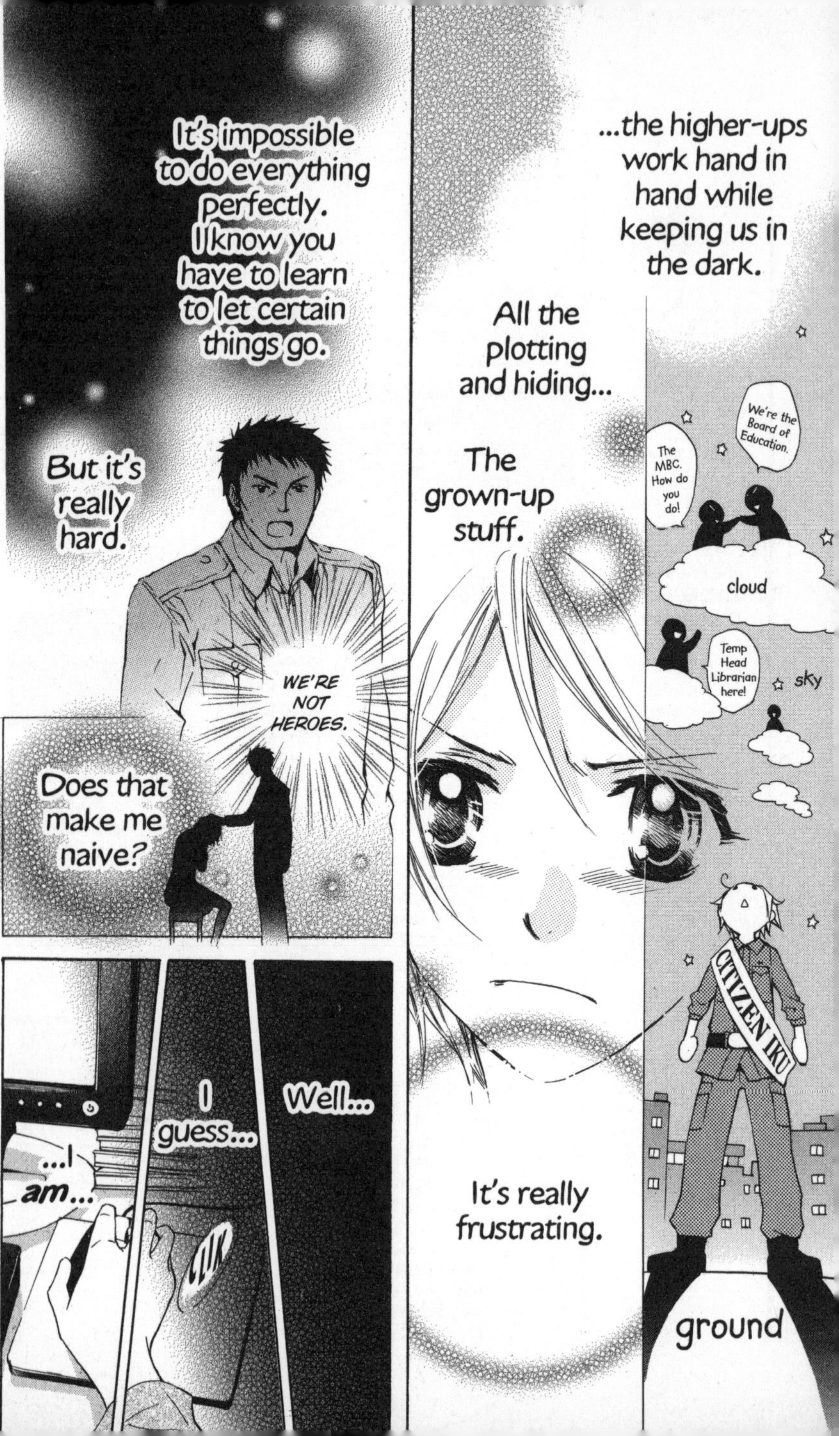
...the higher-ups work hand in hand while keeping us in the dark.
We're the Board of Education.
The MBC. How do you do!
cloud
Temp Head Librarian here!
sky
CITIZEN IKU
ground
All the plotting and hiding...
The grown-up stuff.
It's really frustrating.
It's impossible to do everything perfectly. I know you have to learn to let certain things go.
But it's really hard.
WE'RE NOT HEROES.
Does that make me naive?
Well...
I guess...
...I am...
CLIK

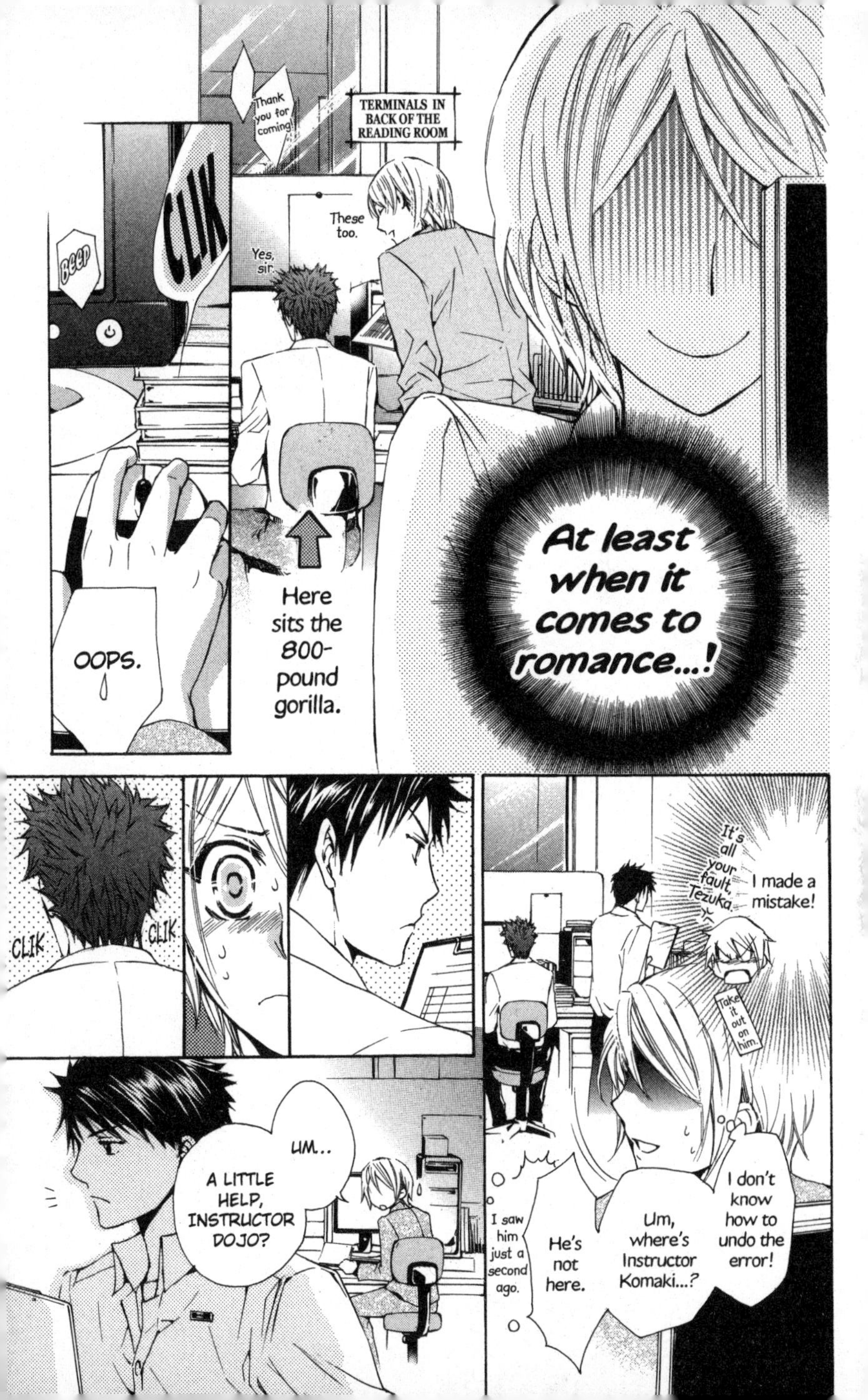
At least when it comes to romance...!
TERMINALS IN BACK OF THE READING ROOM
Thank you for coming!
These too.
Yes, sir.
Here sits the 800-pound gorilla.
CLIK
BEEP
OOPS.
I made a mistake!
It's all your fault, Tezuka!
Take it out on him.
I don't know how to undo the error!
Um, where's Instructor Komaki...?
He's not here.
I saw him just a second ago.
CLIK
CLIK
UM...
A LITTLE HELP, INSTRUCTOR DOJO?

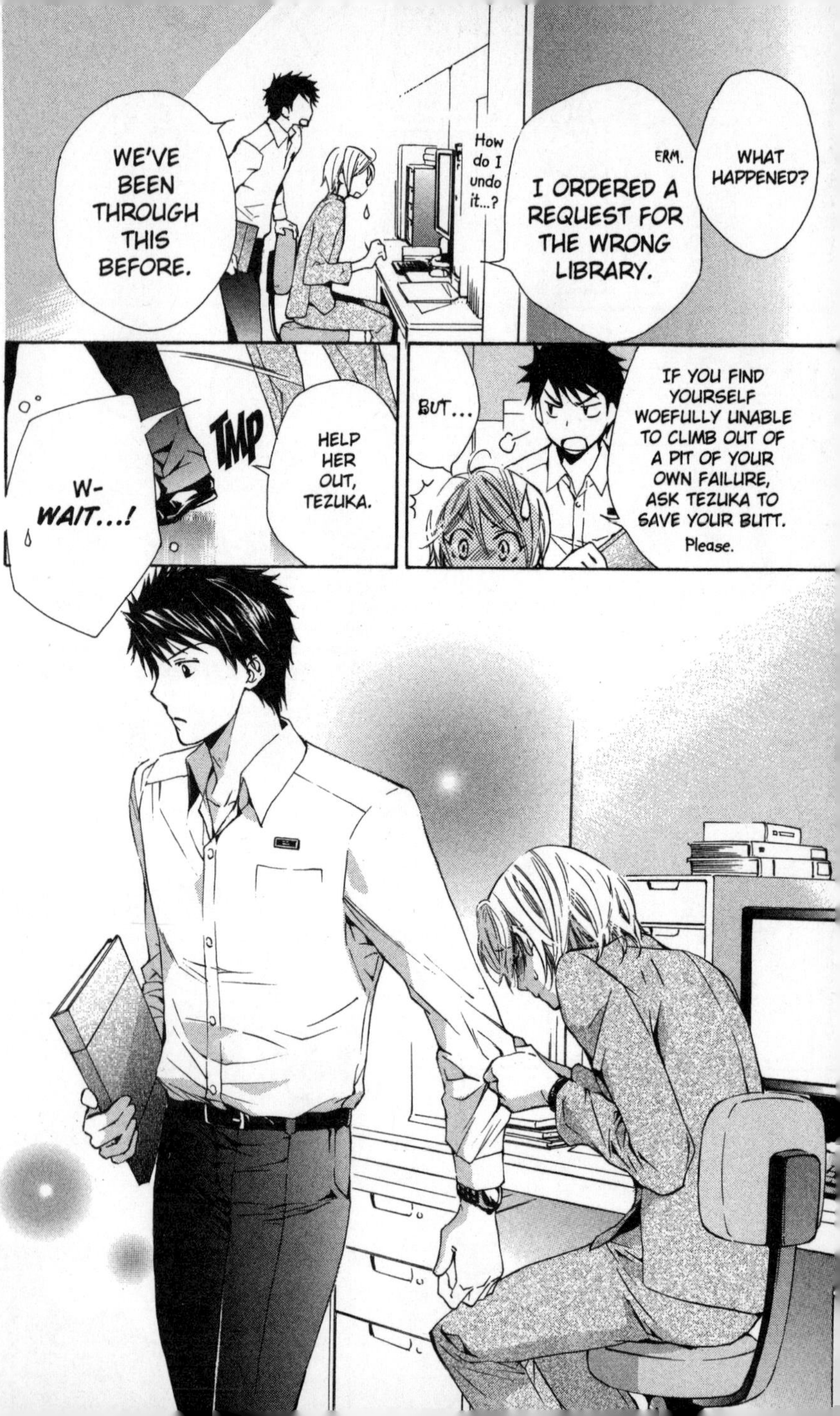
WHAT HAPPENED?
ERM.
I ORDERED A REQUEST FOR THE WRONG LIBRARY.
How do I undo it...?
WE'VE BEEN THROUGH THIS BEFORE.
IF YOU FIND YOURSELF WOEFULLY UNABLE TO CLIMB OUT OF A PIT OF YOUR OWN FAILURE, ASK TEZUKA TO SAVE YOUR BUTT.
Please.
BUT...
HELP HER OUT, TEZUKA.
TMP
W- WAIT...!

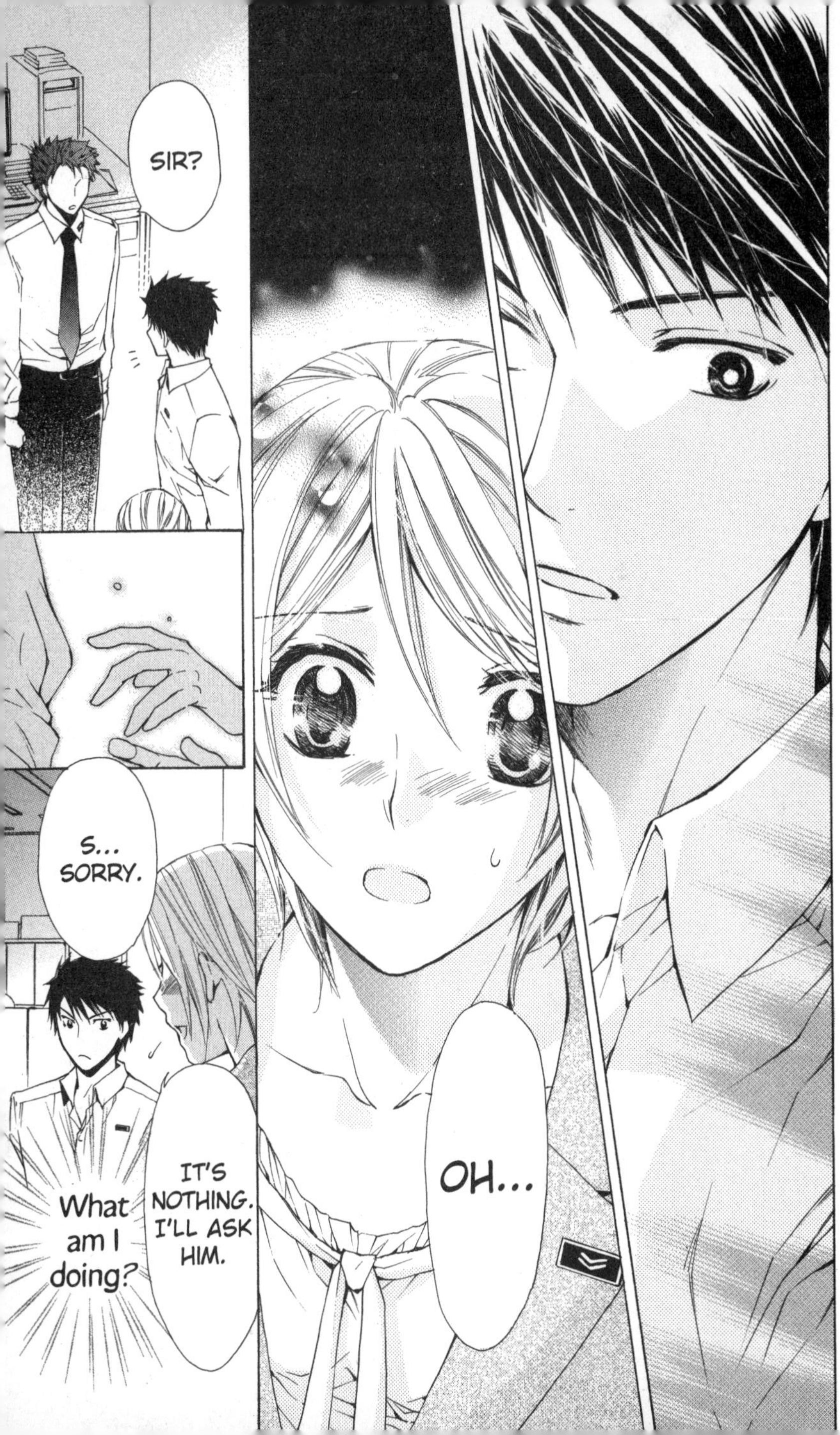
OH...
SIR?
S... SORRY.
IT'S NOTHING. I'LL ASK HIM.
What am I doing?

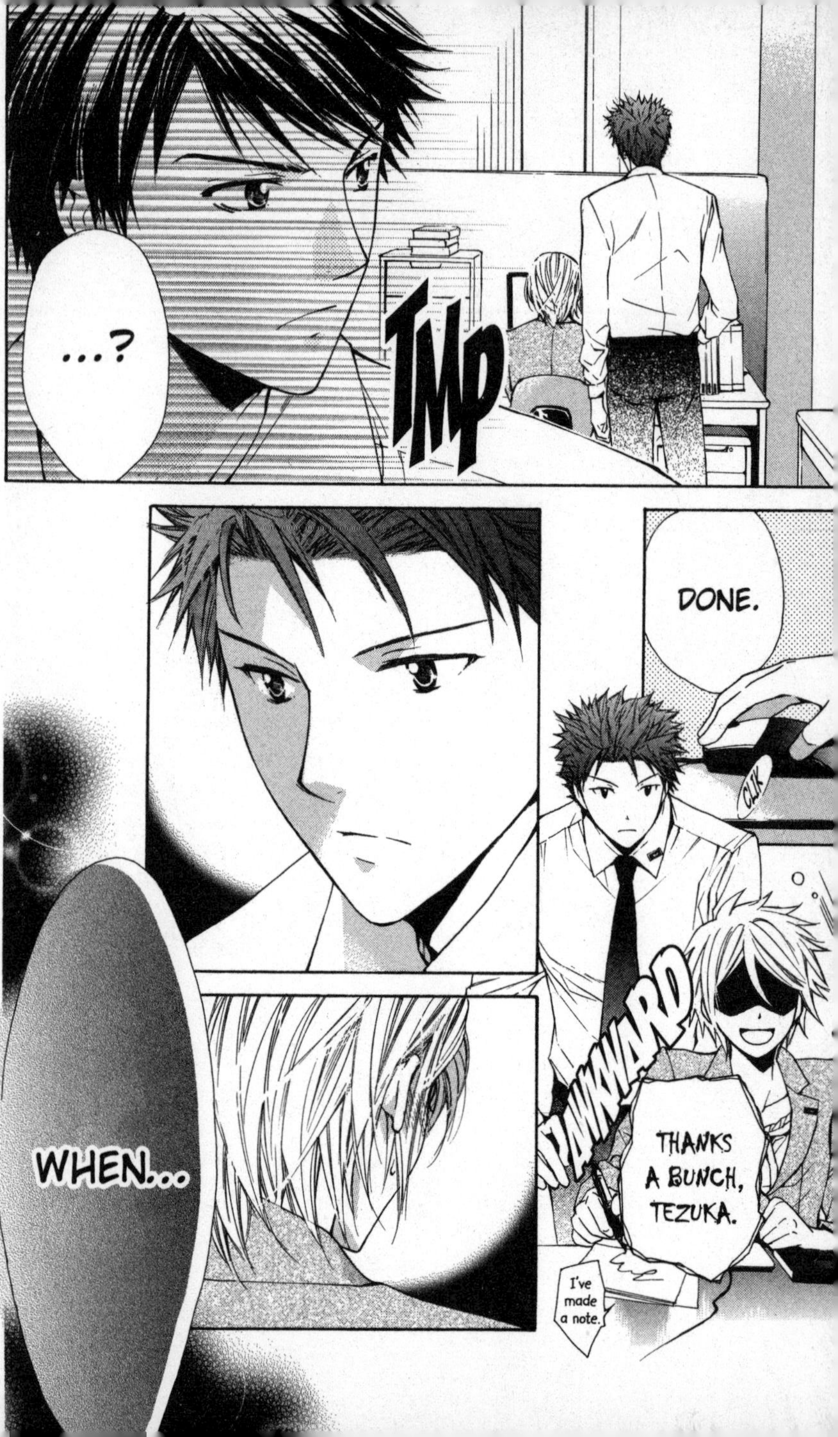
TMP
...?
DONE.
CLIK
AWKWARD
THANKS A BUNCH, TEZUKA.
I've made a note.
WHEN...

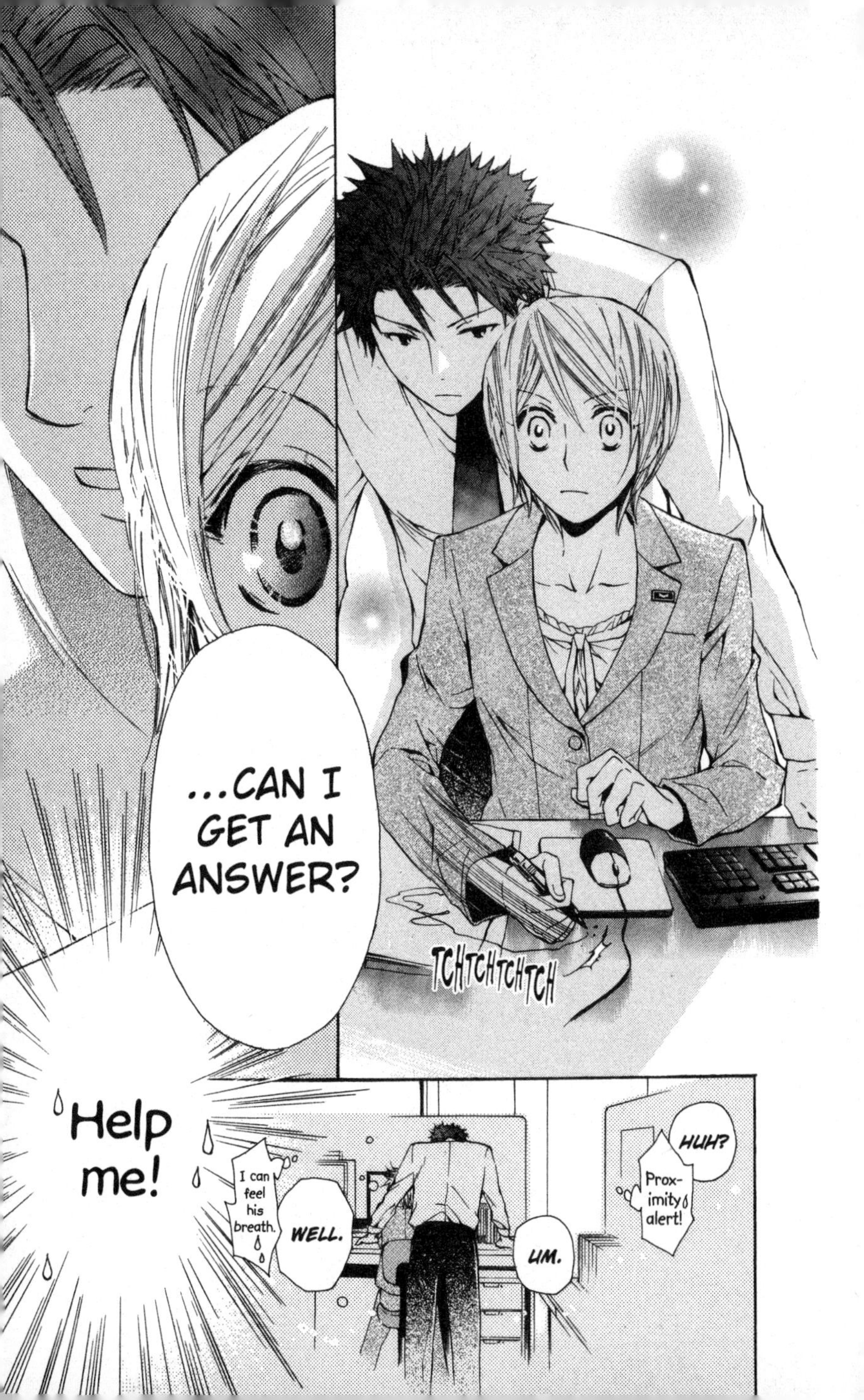
TCHTCHTCHTCH
...CAN I GET AN ANSWER?
HUH?
Prox-imity alert!
UM.
WELL.
I can feel his breath.
Help me!

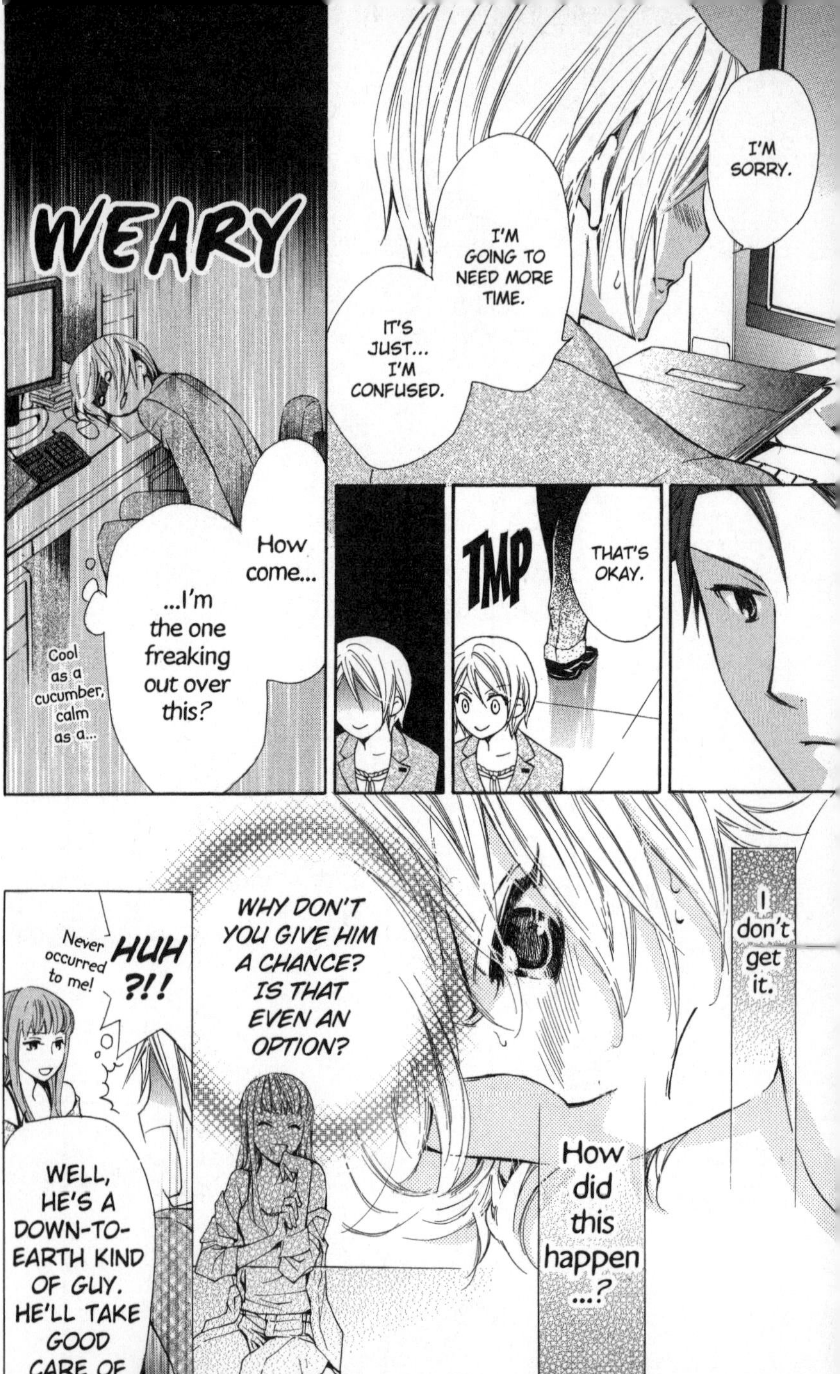
I'M SORRY.
I'M GOING TO NEED MORE TIME.
IT'S JUST... I'M CONFUSED.
TMP
THAT'S OKAY.
WEARY
How come...
...I'm the one freaking out over this?
Cool as a cucumber, calm as a...
I don't get it.
How did this happen ...?
WHY DON'T YOU GIVE HIM A CHANCE? IS THAT EVEN AN OPTION?
HUH ?!!
Never occurred to me!
WELL, HE'S A DOWN-TO-EARTH KIND OF GUY. HE'LL TAKE GOOD CARE OF YOU.

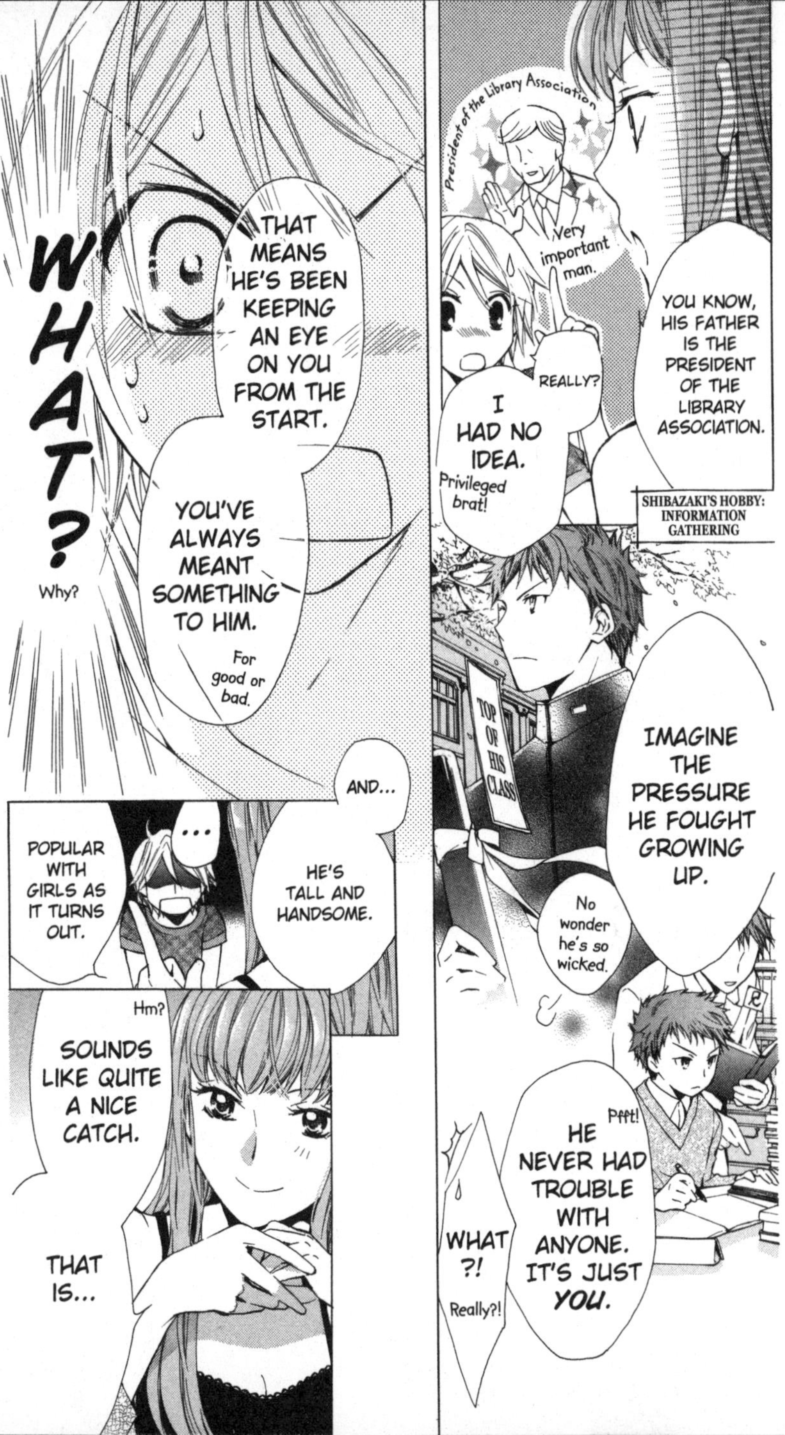
President of the Library Association
Very important man.
YOU KNOW, HIS FATHER IS THE PRESIDENT OF THE LIBRARY ASSOCIATION.
REALLY?
I HAD NO IDEA.
Privileged brat!
SHIBAZAKI'S HOBBY: INFORMATION GATHERING
TOP OF HIS CLASS
IMAGINE THE PRESSURE HE FOUGHT GROWING UP.
No wonder he's so wicked.
Pffft!
HE NEVER HAD TROUBLE WITH ANYONE. IT'S JUST *YOU*.
WHAT?!
Really?!
THAT MEANS HE'S BEEN KEEPING AN EYE ON YOU FROM THE START.
YOU'VE ALWAYS MEANT SOMETHING TO HIM.
For good or bad.
WHAT?
Why?
AND...
HE'S TALL AND HANDSOME.
...
POPULAR WITH GIRLS AS IT TURNS OUT.
Hm?
SOUNDS LIKE QUITE A NICE CATCH.
THAT IS...

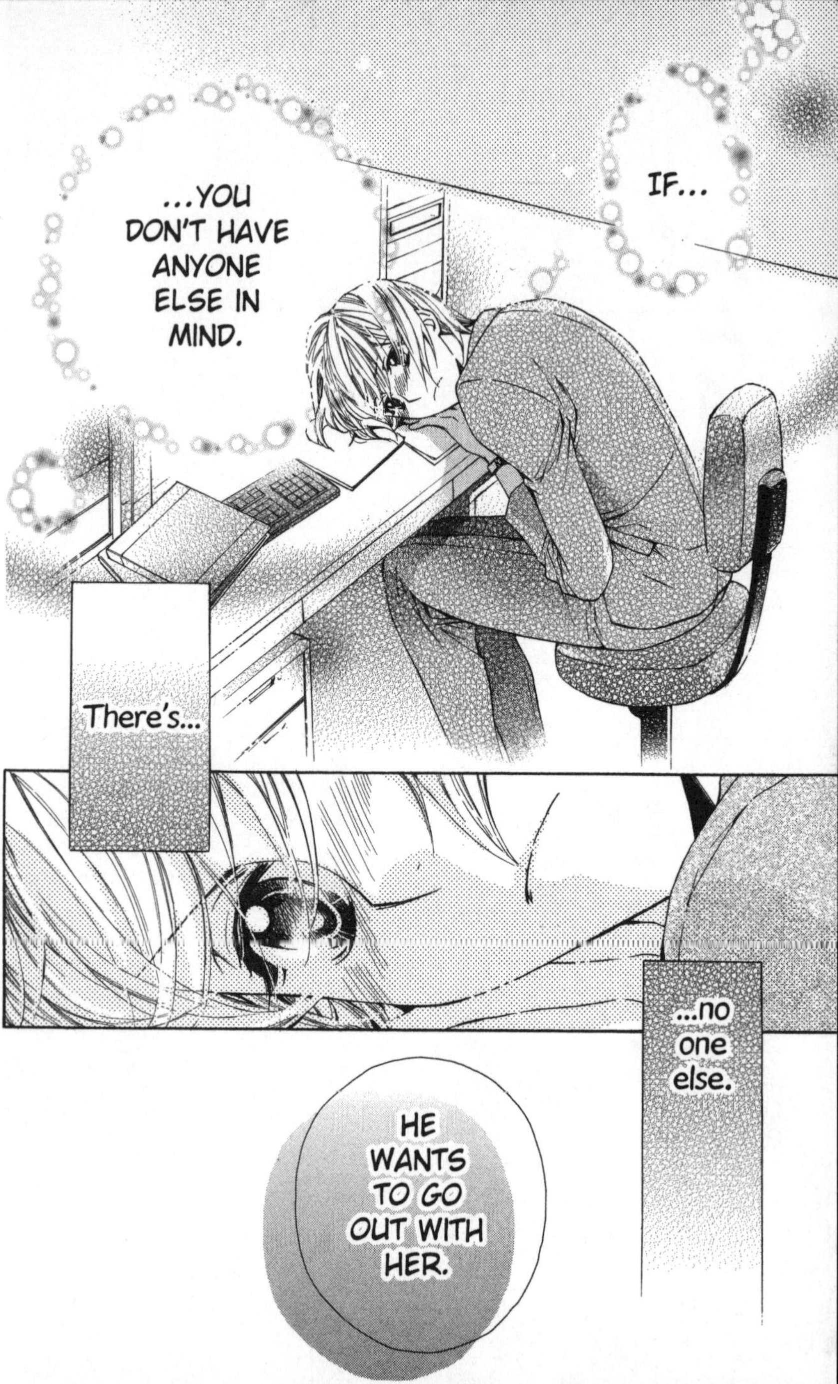
IF...
...YOU DON'T HAVE ANYONE ELSE IN MIND.
There's...
...no one else.
HE WANTS TO GO OUT WITH HER.

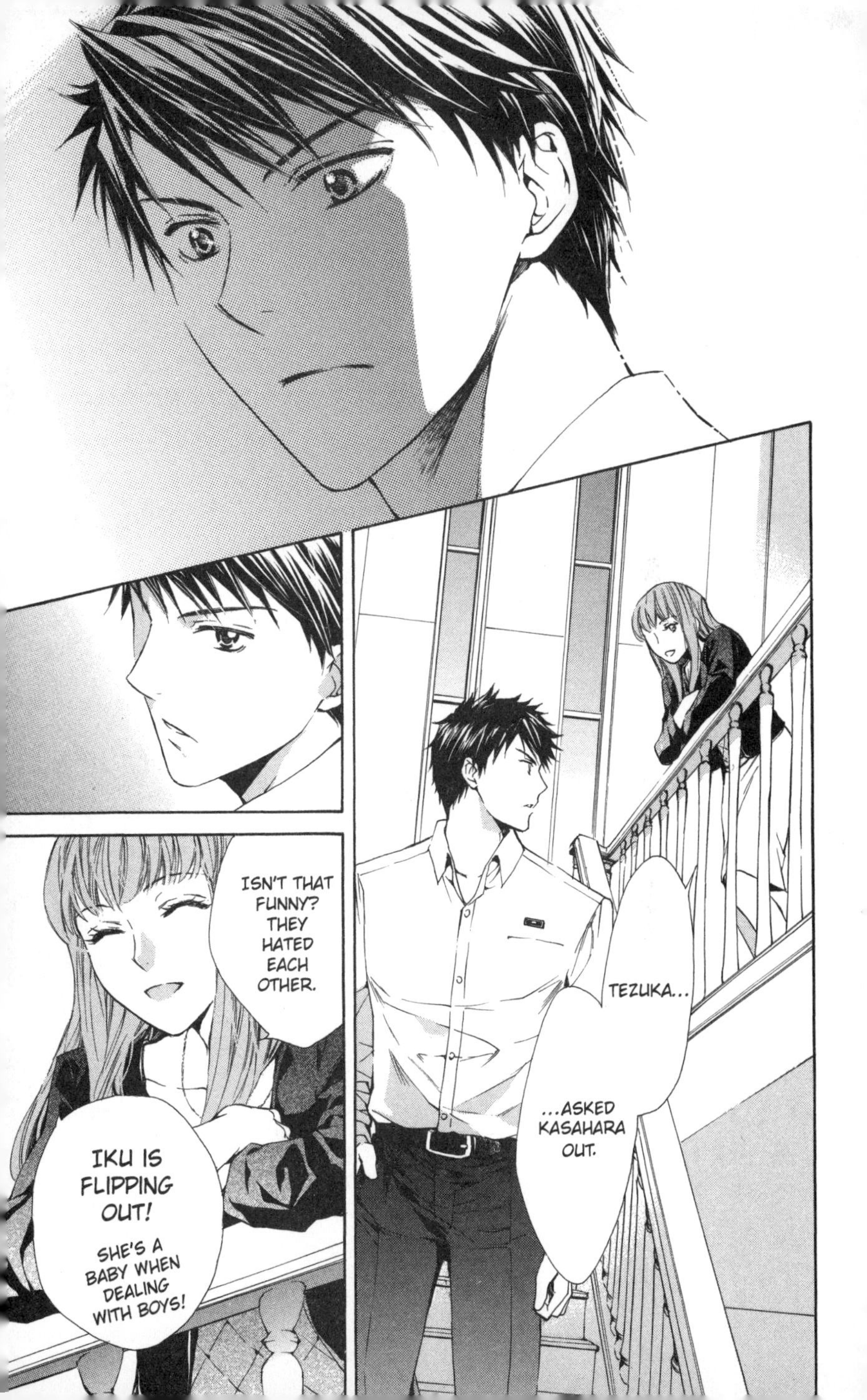
TEZUKA...
...ASKED KASAHARA OUT.
ISN'T THAT FUNNY? THEY HATED EACH OTHER.
IKU IS FLIPPING OUT!
SHE'S A BABY WHEN DEALING WITH BOYS!

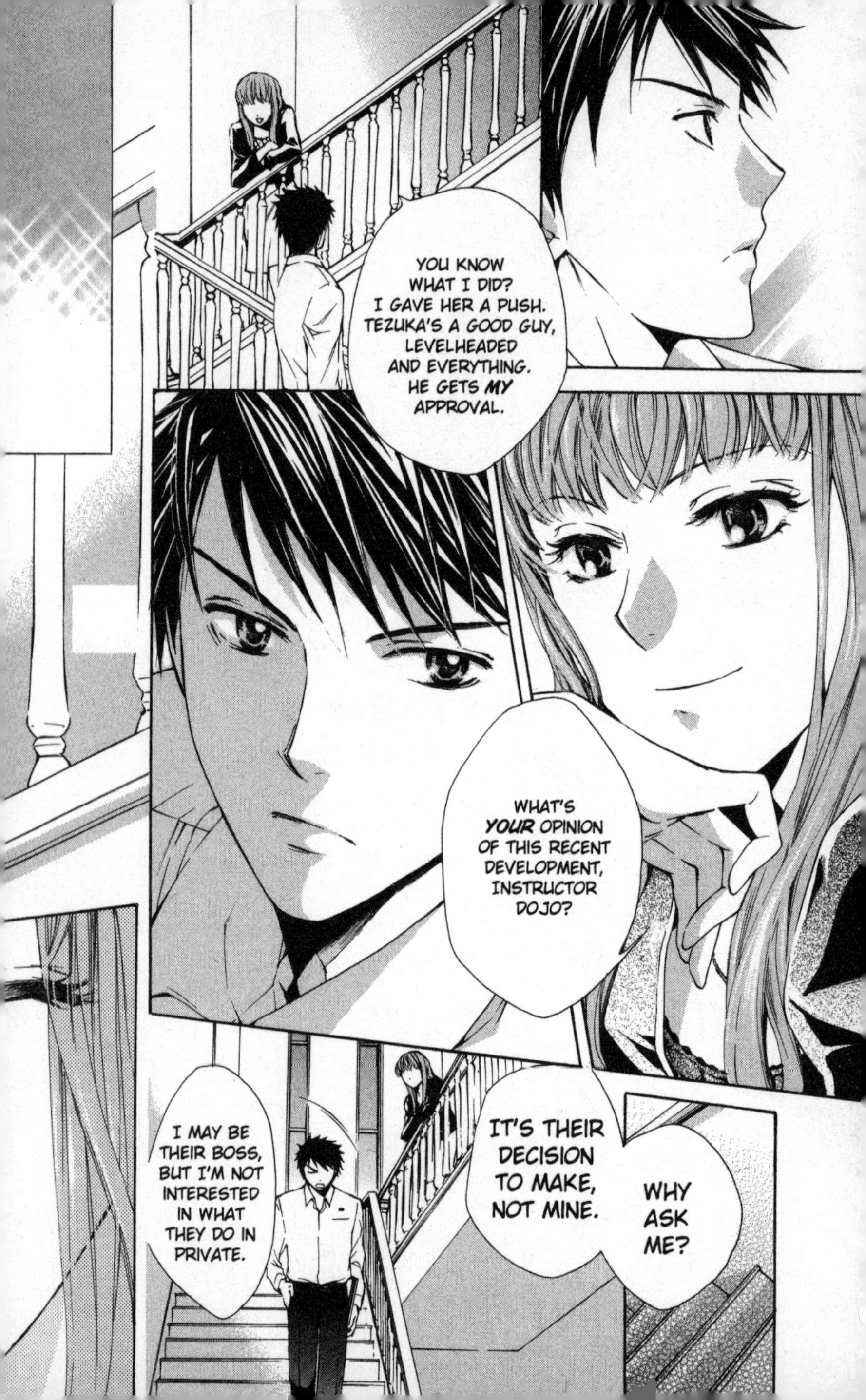
YOU KNOW WHAT I DID? I GAVE HER A PUSH. TEZUKA'S A GOOD GUY, LEVELHEADED AND EVERYTHING. HE GETS *MY* APPROVAL.
WHAT'S ***YOUR*** OPINION OF THIS RECENT DEVELOPMENT, INSTRUCTOR DOJO?
WHY ASK ME?
IT'S THEIR DECISION TO MAKE, NOT MINE.
I MAY BE THEIR BOSS, BUT I'M NOT INTERESTED IN WHAT THEY DO IN PRIVATE.

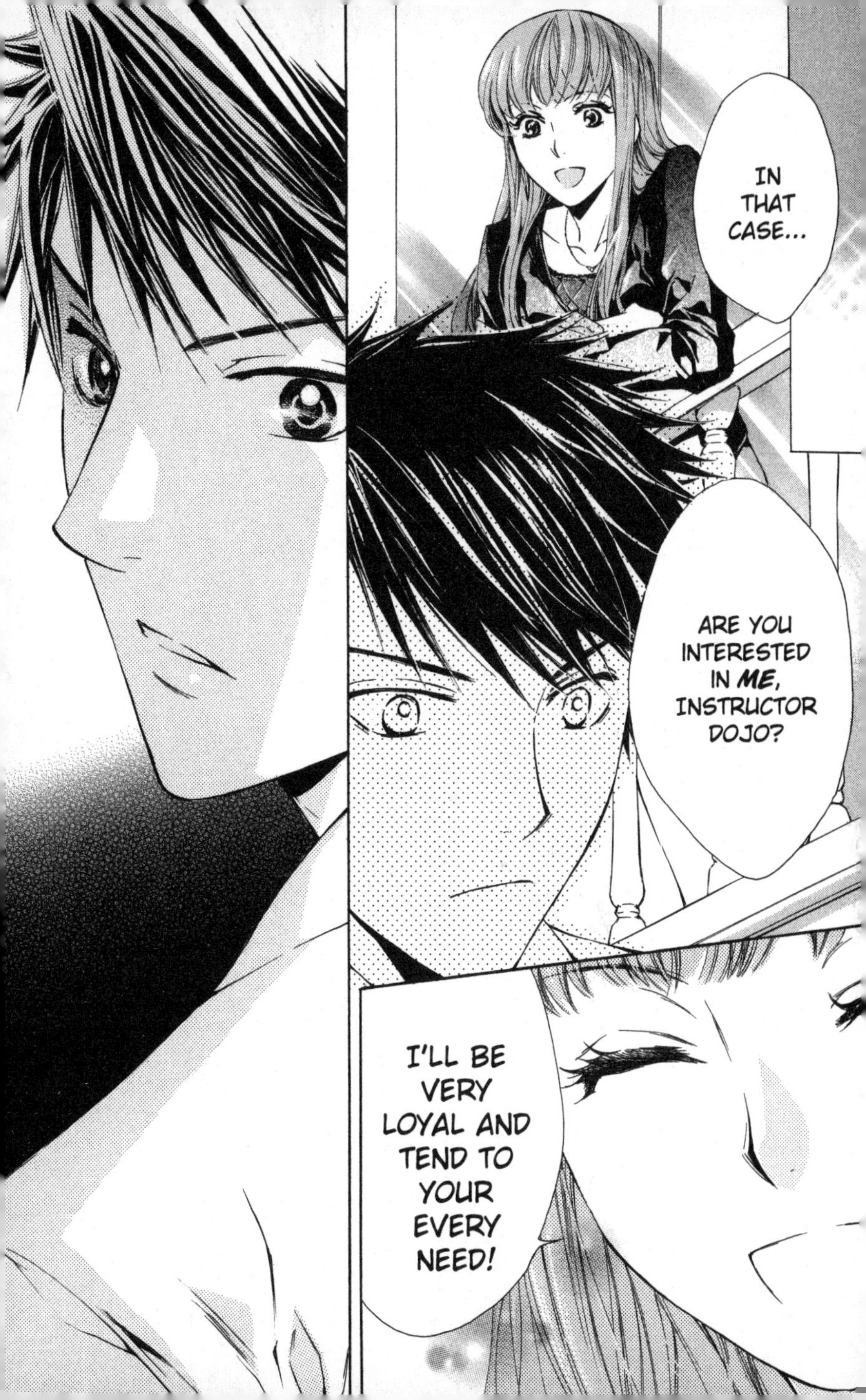
IN THAT CASE...
ARE YOU INTERESTED IN *ME*, INSTRUCTOR DOJO?
I'LL BE VERY LOYAL AND TEND TO YOUR EVERY NEED!

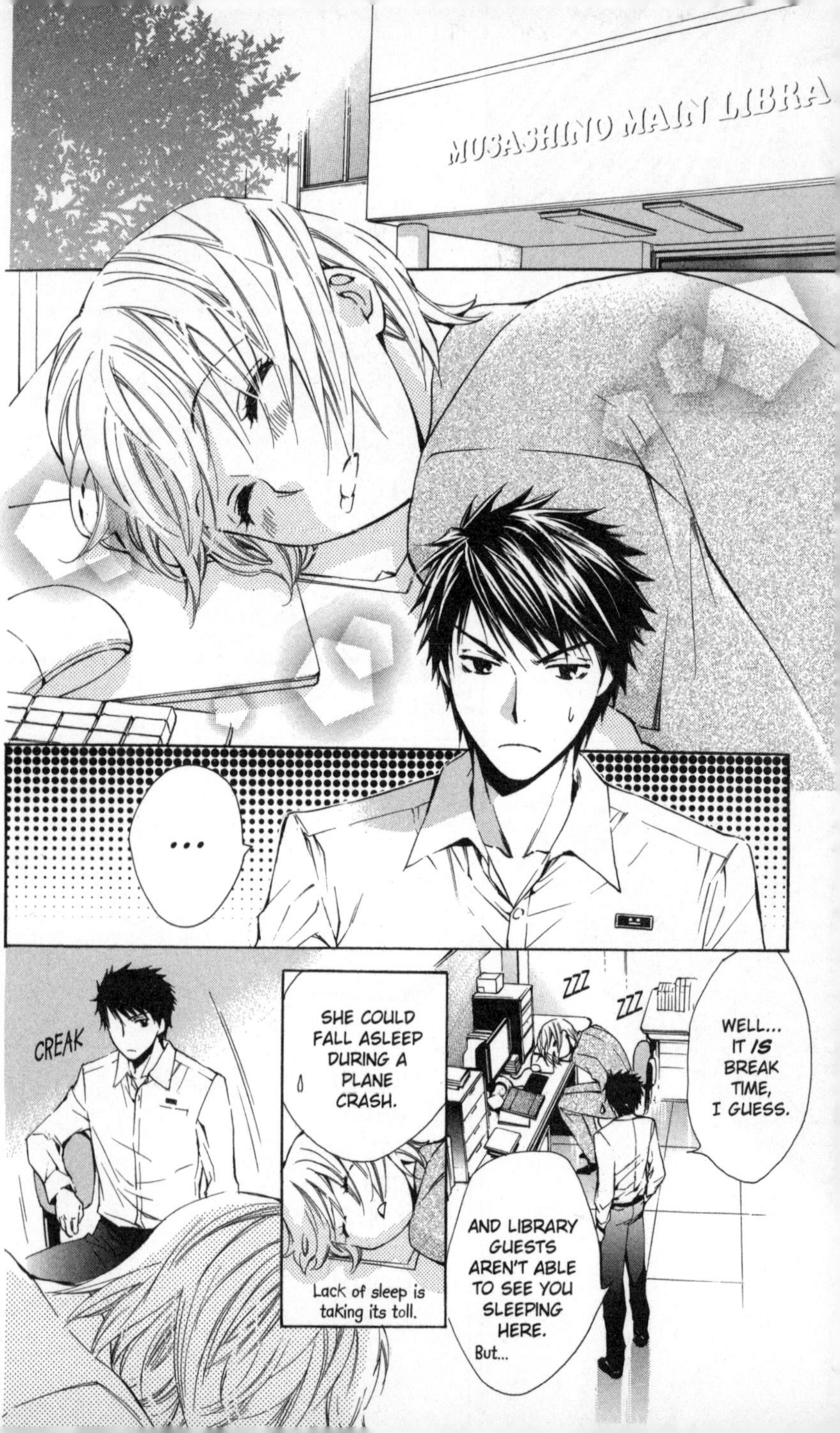
MUSASHINO MAIN LIBRA
...
ZZZ
ZZZ
WELL... IT *IS* BREAK TIME, I GUESS.
AND LIBRARY GUESTS AREN'T ABLE TO SEE YOU SLEEPING HERE.
But...
SHE COULD FALL ASLEEP DURING A PLANE CRASH.
Lack of sleep is taking its toll.
CREAK

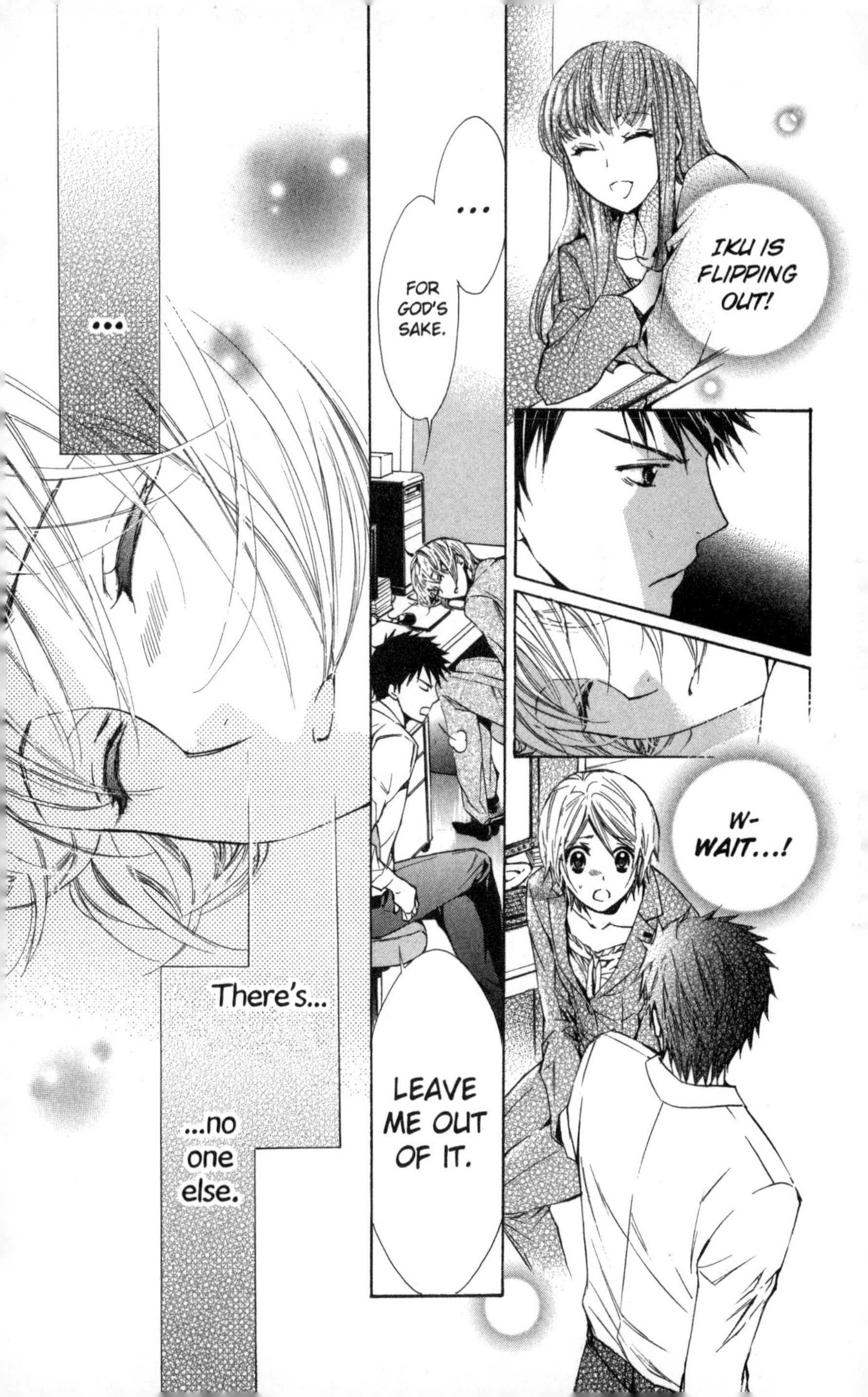
IKU IS FLIPPING OUT!
W-WAIT...!
...
FOR GOD'S SAKE.
LEAVE ME OUT OF IT.
...
There's...
...no one else.

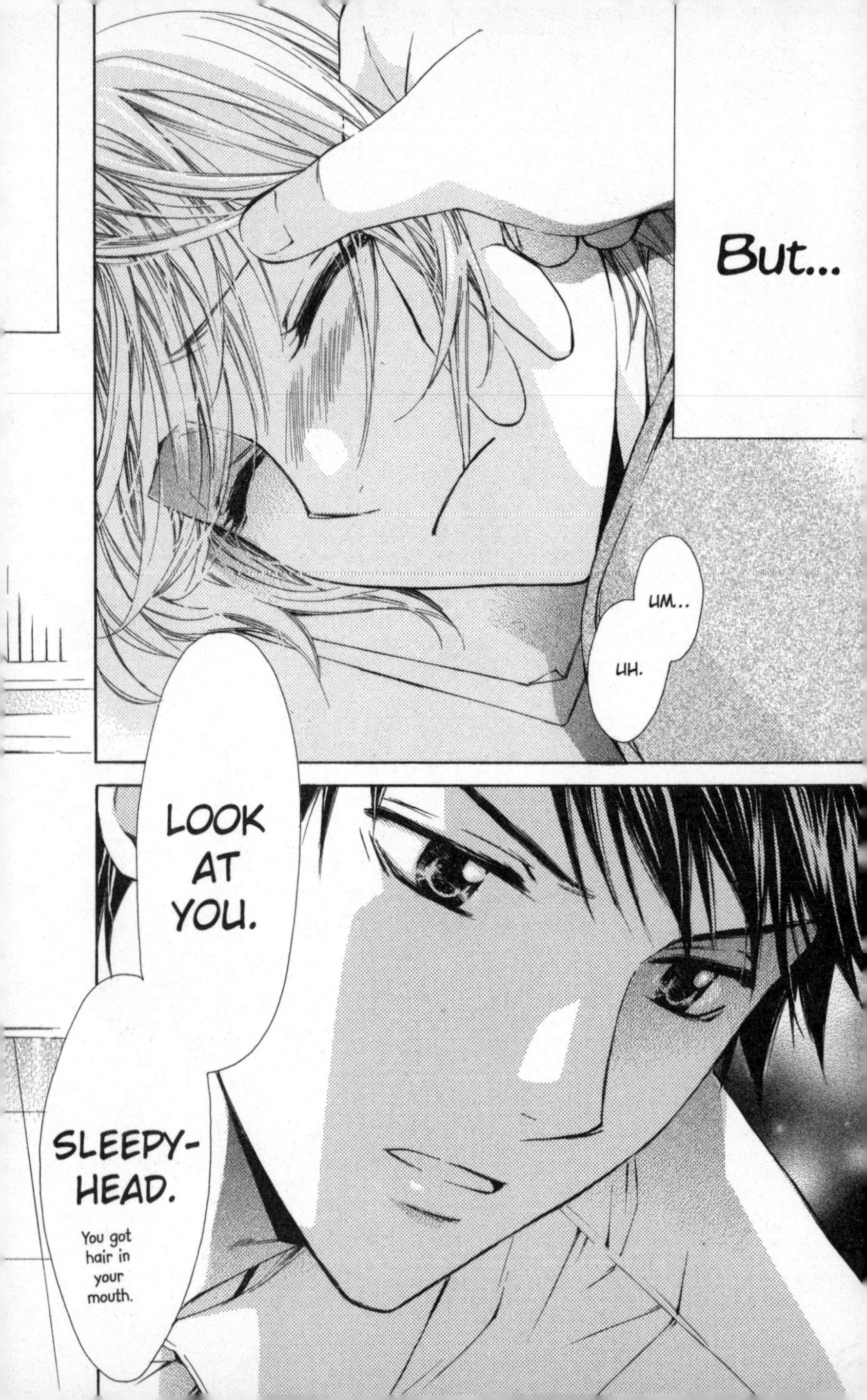
But...
UM.. UH.
LOOK AT YOU.
SLEEPY-HEAD.
You got hair in your mouth.

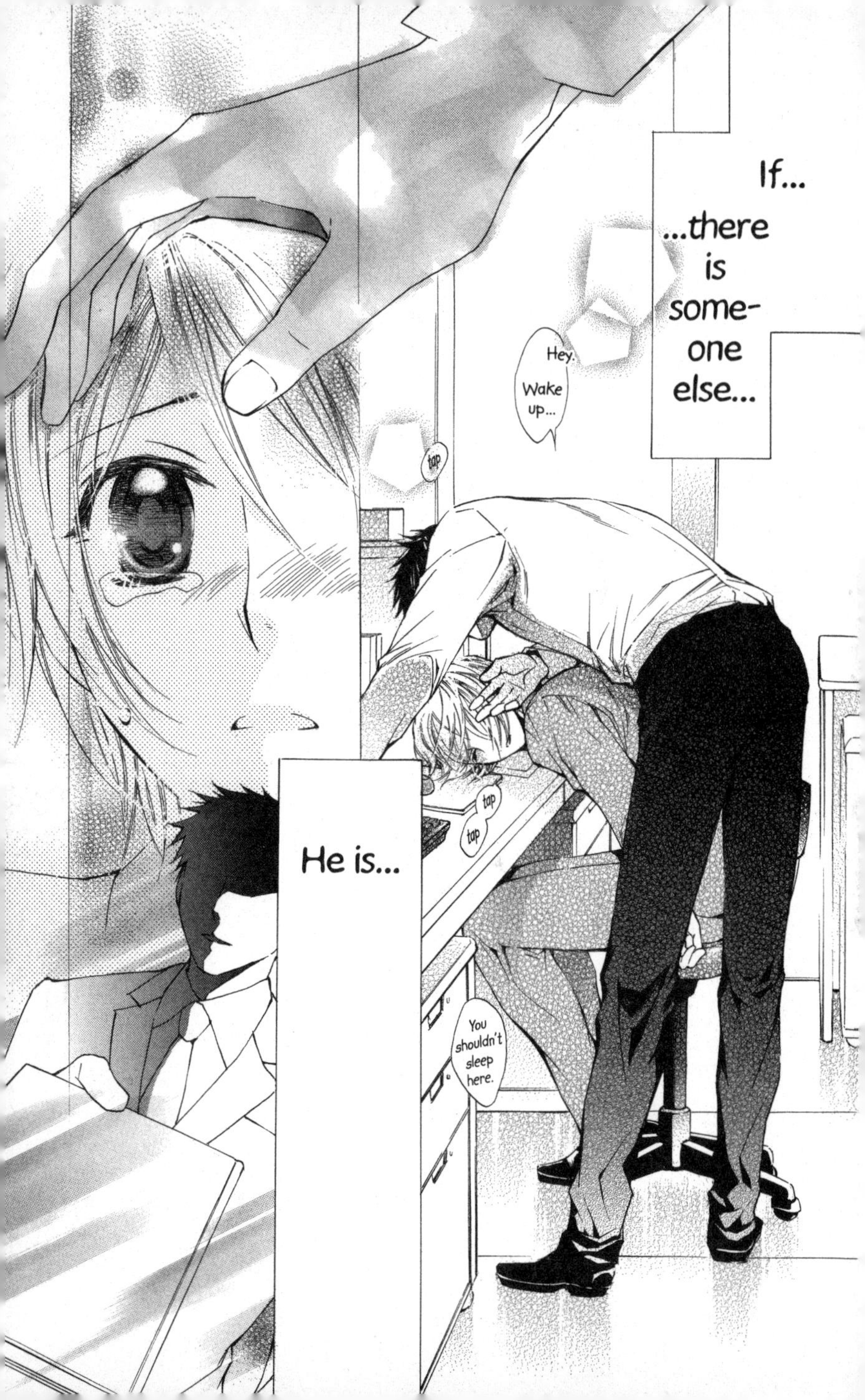
If...
...there is some-one else...
Hey. Wake up...
tap
tap
tap
You shouldn't sleep here.
He is...

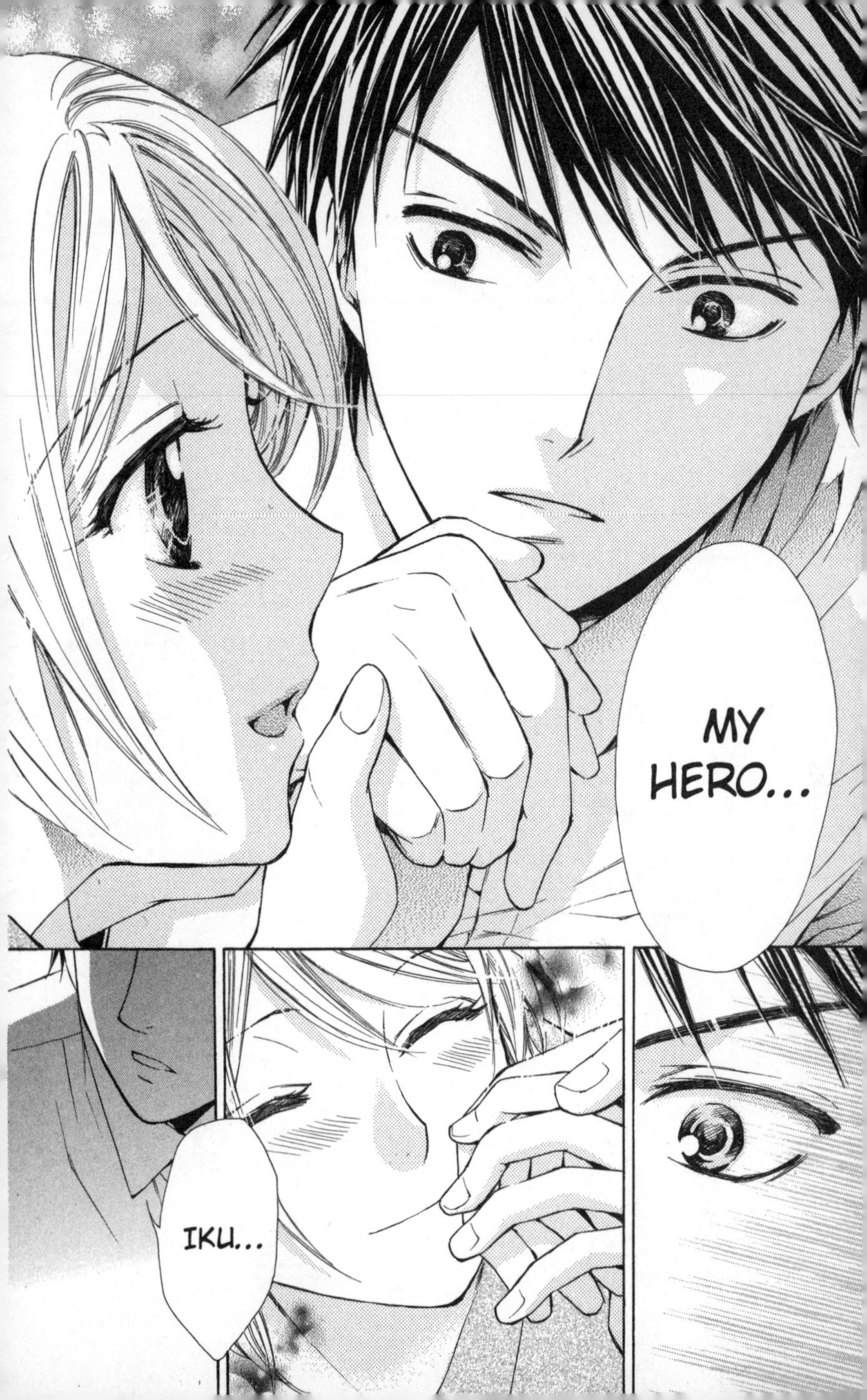
MY HERO...
IKU...

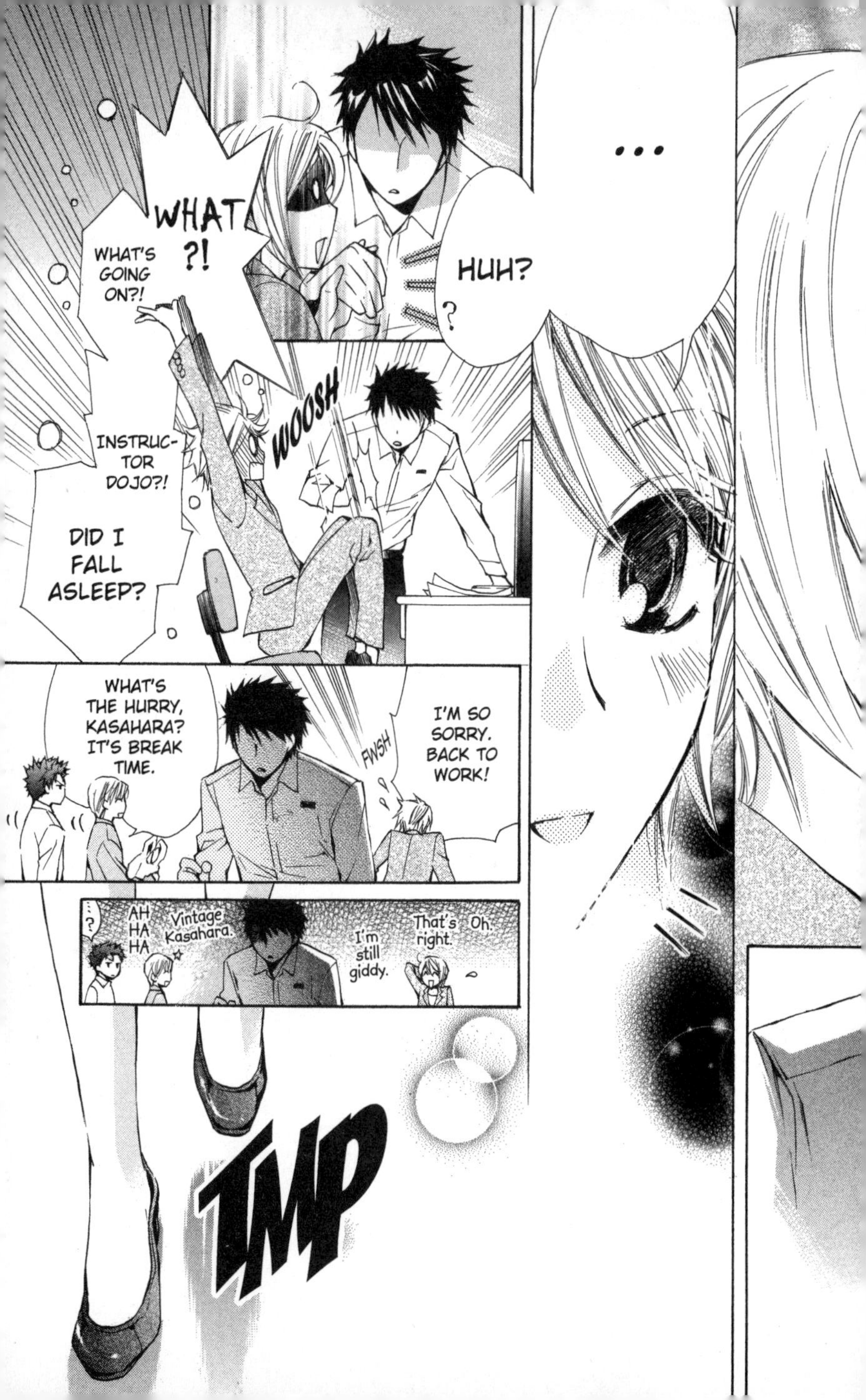
...
HUH?
?
WHAT?!
WHAT'S GOING ON?!
WOOSH
INSTRUCTOR DOJO?!
DID I FALL ASLEEP?
I'M SO SORRY. BACK TO WORK!
FWSH
WHAT'S THE HURRY, KASAHARA? IT'S BREAK TIME.
Oh.
That's right.
I'm still giddy.
Vintage Kasahara.
AH HA HA
...?
TMP

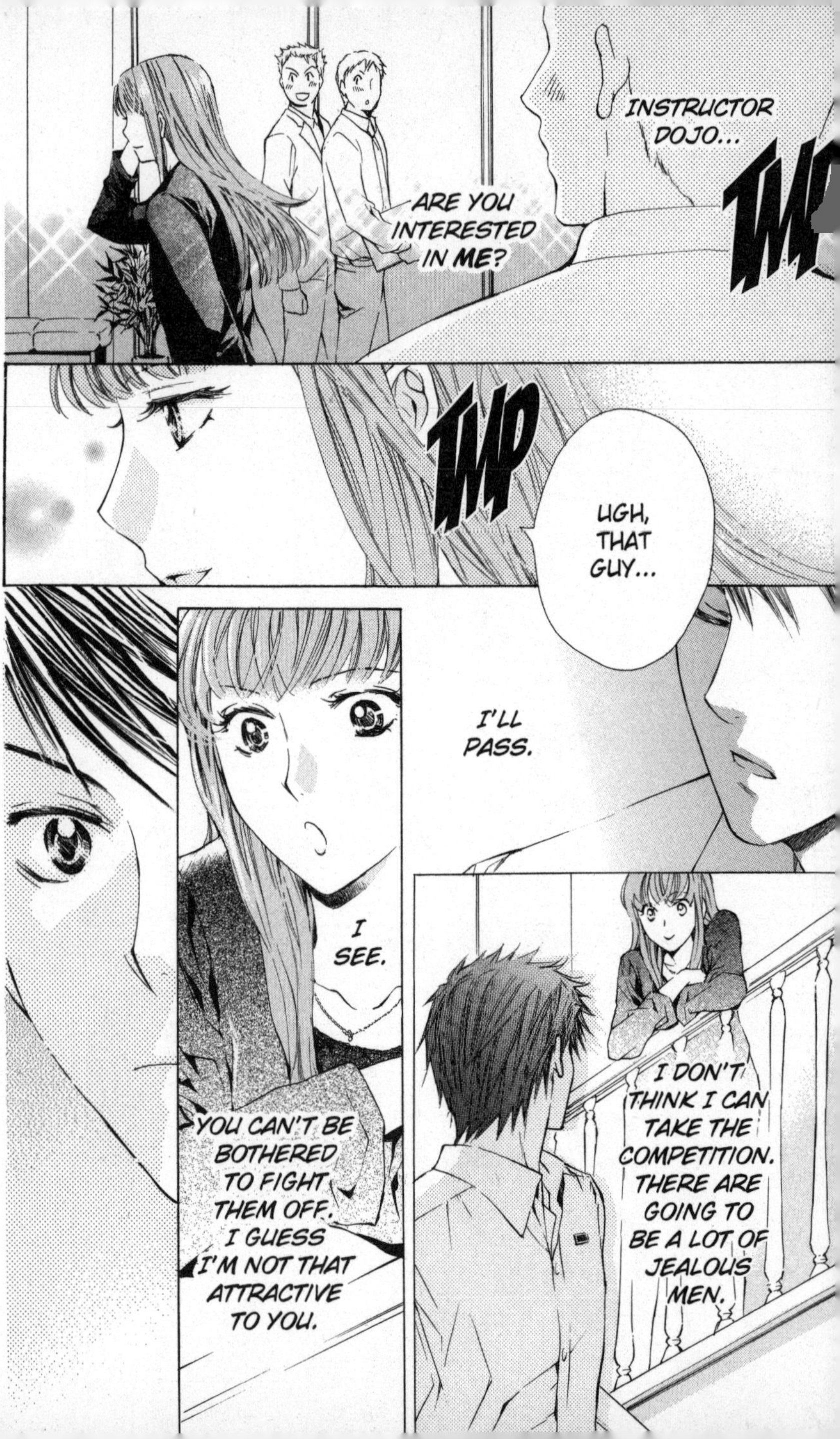
INSTRUCTOR DOJO...
TMP
ARE YOU INTERESTED IN ME?
UGH, THAT GUY...
TMP
I'LL PASS.
I DON'T THINK I CAN TAKE THE COMPETITION. THERE ARE GOING TO BE A LOT OF JEALOUS MEN.
I SEE.
YOU CAN'T BE BOTHERED TO FIGHT THEM OFF. I GUESS I'M NOT THAT ATTRACTIVE TO YOU.

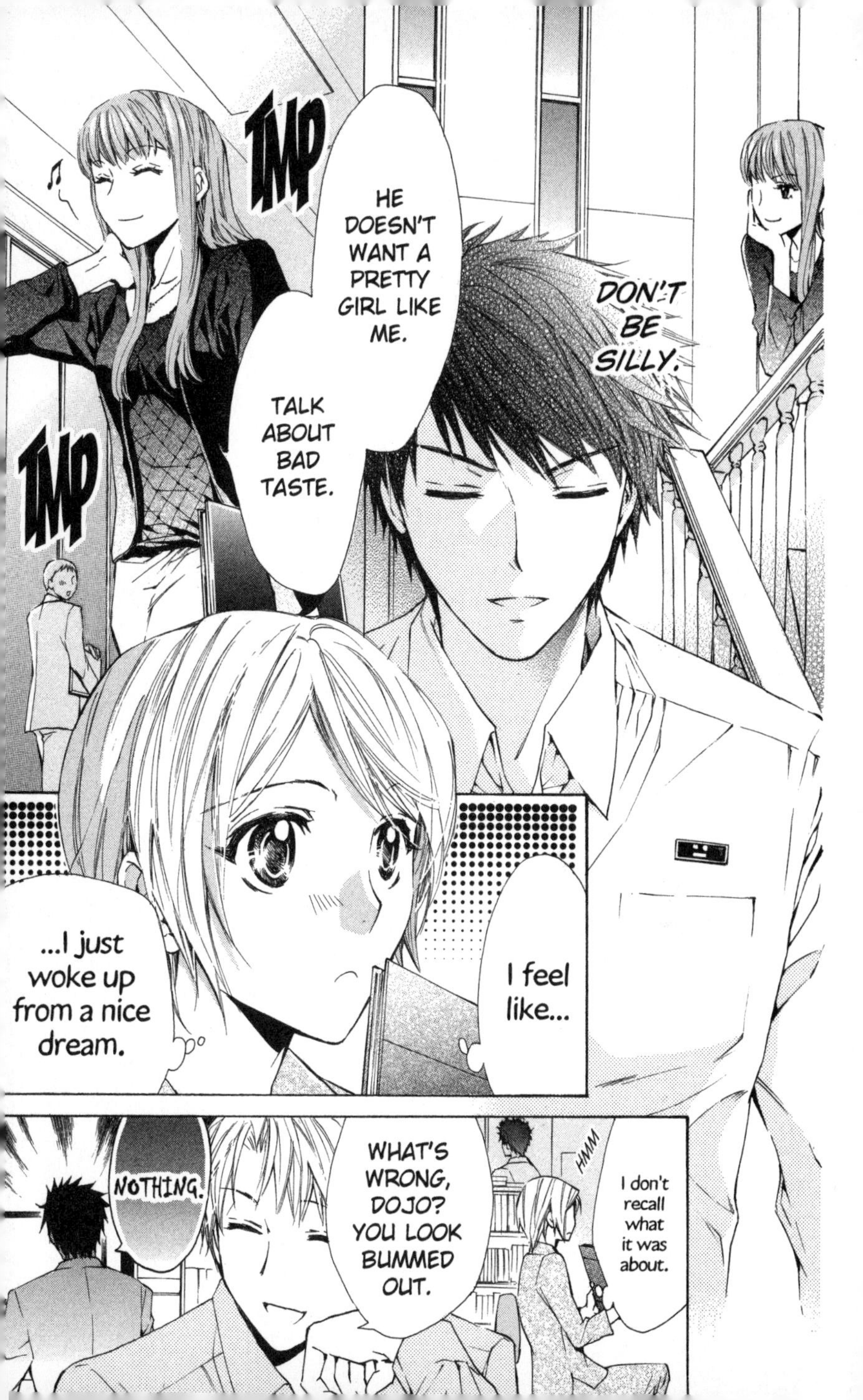

DON'T BE SILLY.
TMP
HE DOESN'T WANT A PRETTY GIRL LIKE ME.
TALK ABOUT BAD TASTE.
TMP
I feel like...
...I just woke up from a nice dream.
I don't recall what it was about.
HMM
WHAT'S WRONG, DOJO? YOU LOOK BUMMED OUT.
NOTHING.

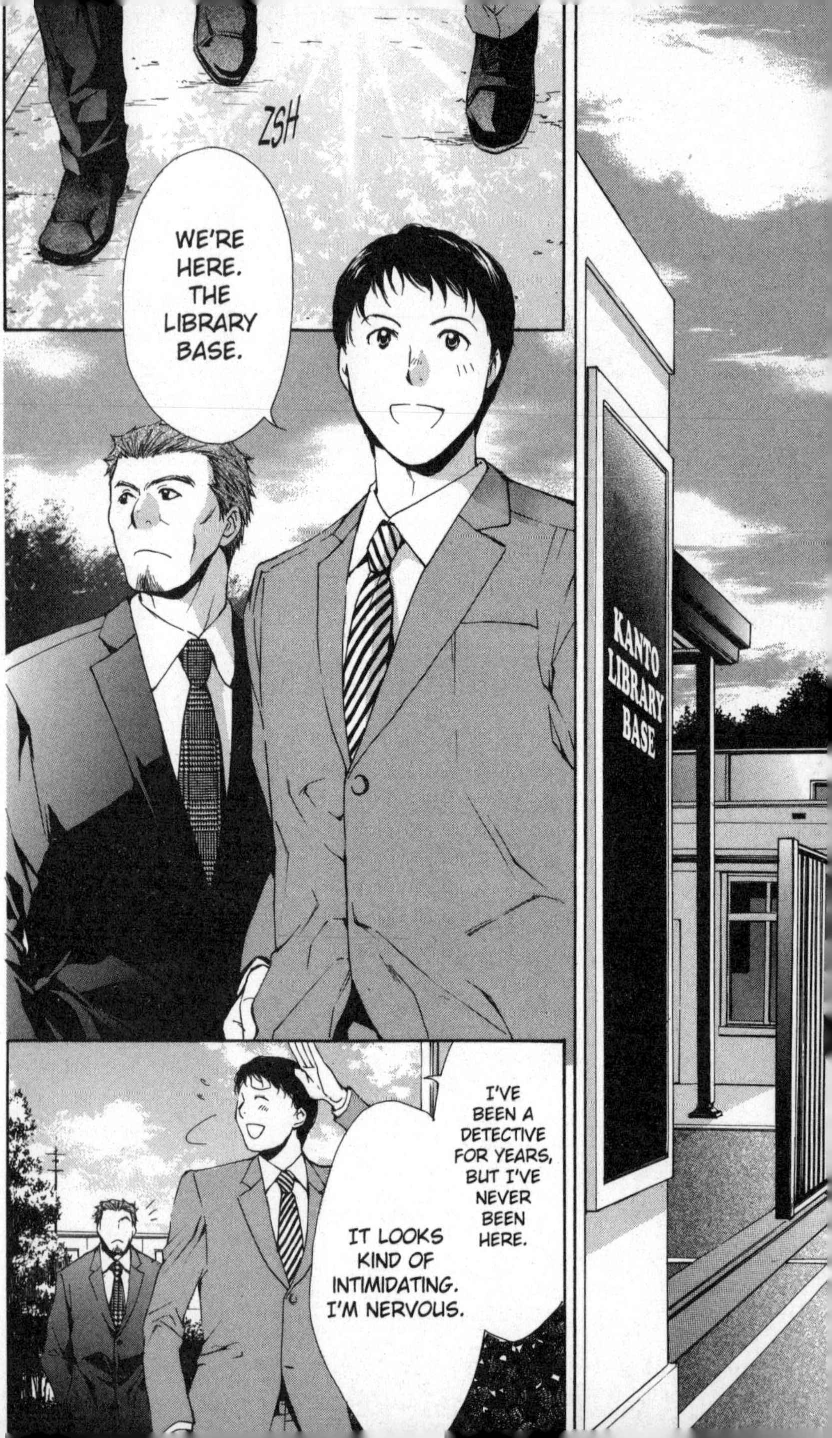
KANTO LIBRARY BASE
ZSH
WE'RE HERE. THE LIBRARY BASE.
I'VE BEEN A DETECTIVE FOR YEARS, BUT I'VE NEVER BEEN HERE.
IT LOOKS KIND OF INTIMIDATING. I'M NERVOUS.

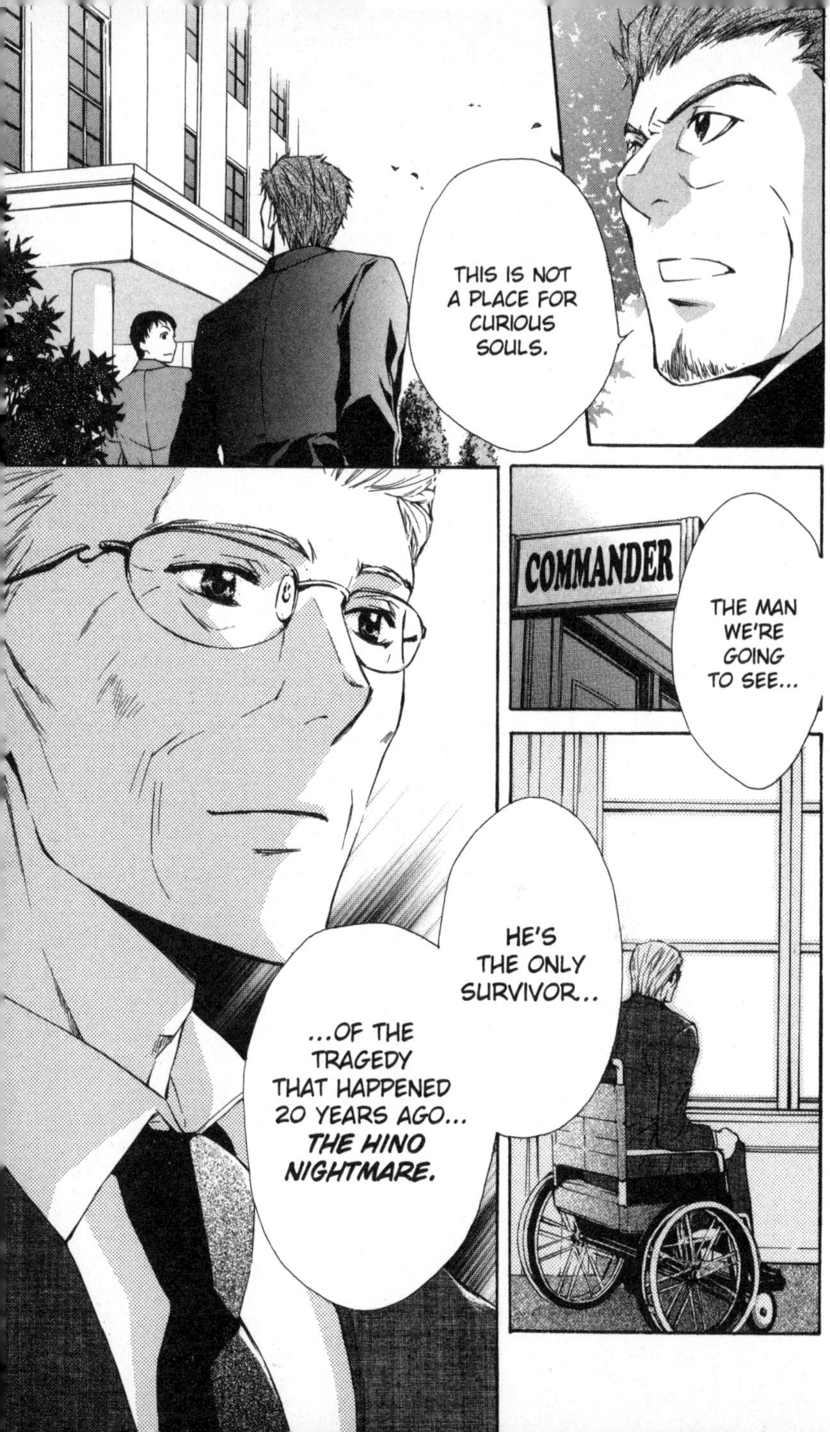
THIS IS NOT A PLACE FOR CURIOUS SOULS.
COMMANDER
THE MAN WE'RE GOING TO SEE...
HE'S THE ONLY SURVIVOR...
...OF THE TRAGEDY THAT HAPPENED 20 YEARS AGO... *THE HINO NIGHTMARE.*

LEGIBILITY ISN'T EVEN THE PROBLEM

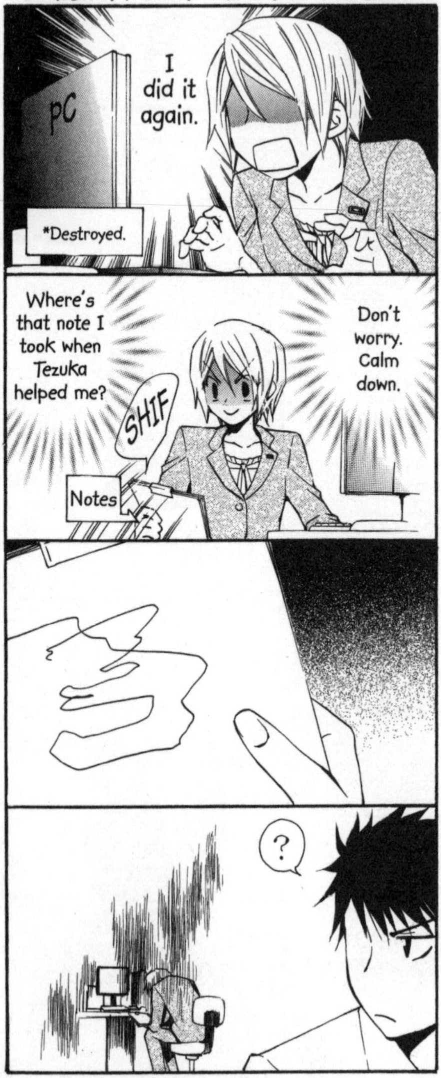
I did it again.
pC
*Destroyed.
Don't worry. Calm down.
Where's that note I took when Tezuka helped me?
SHIF
Notes
?

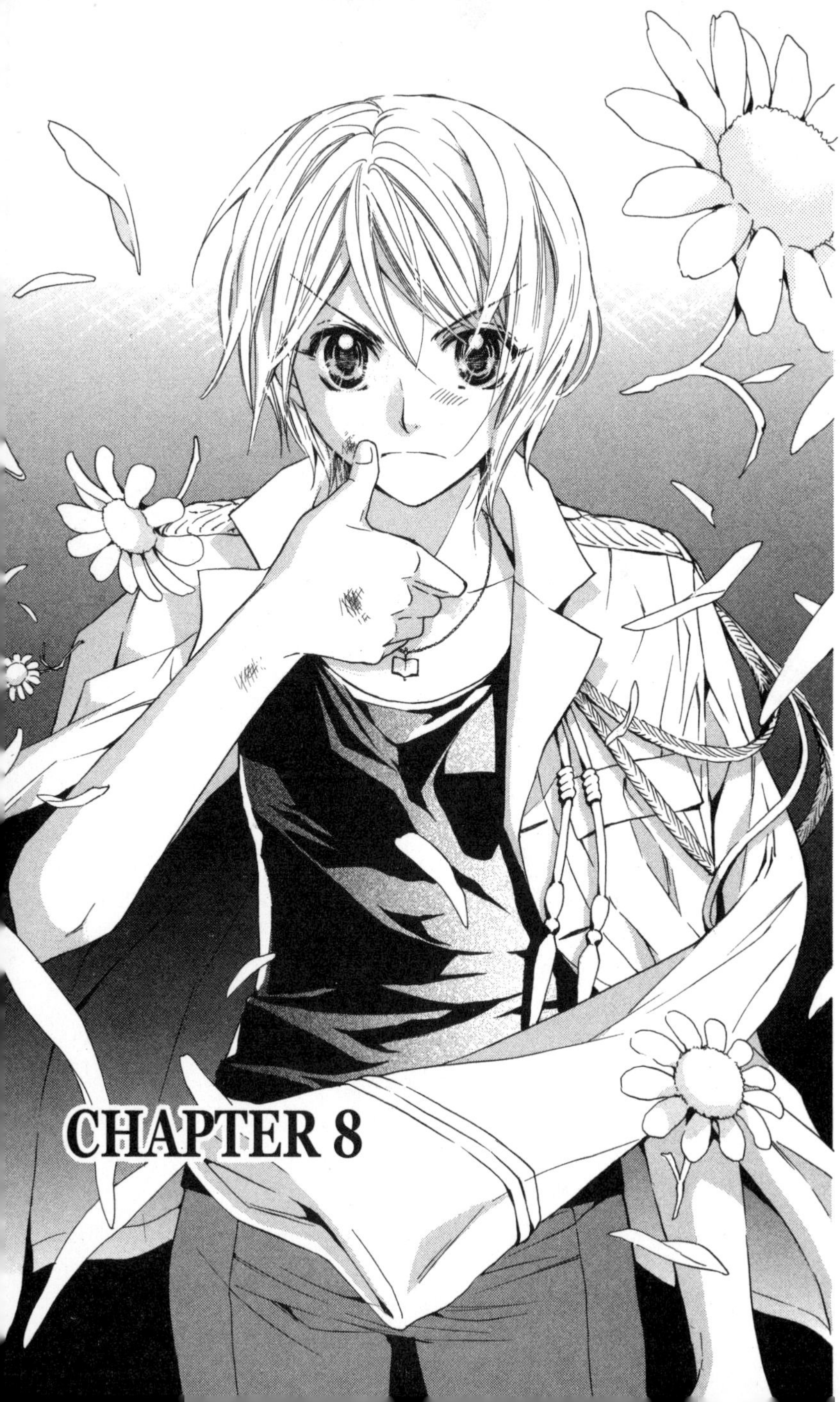
CHAPTER 8

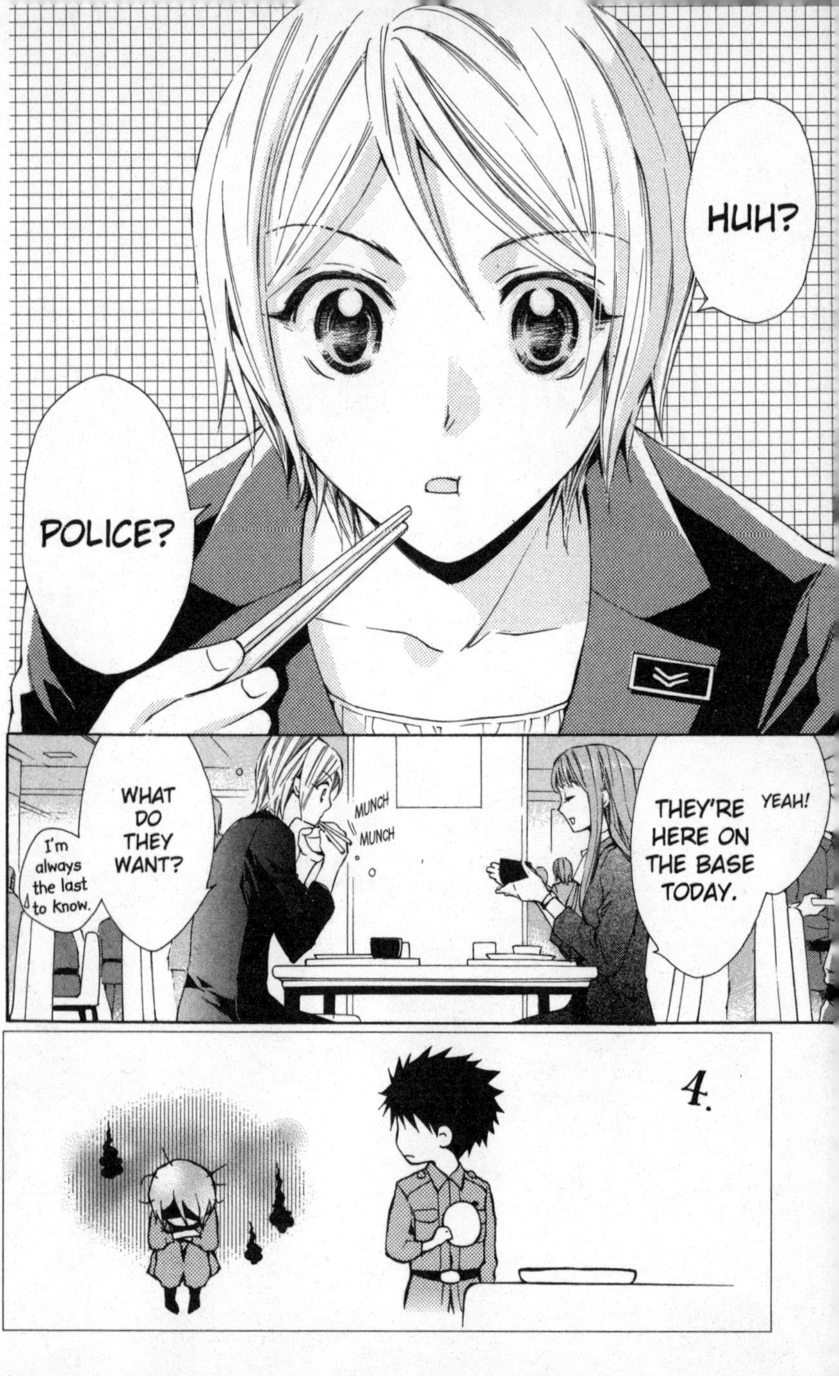
HUH?
POLICE?
YEAH!
THEY'RE HERE ON THE BASE TODAY.
MUNCH
MUNCH
WHAT DO THEY WANT?
I'm always the last to know.
4.

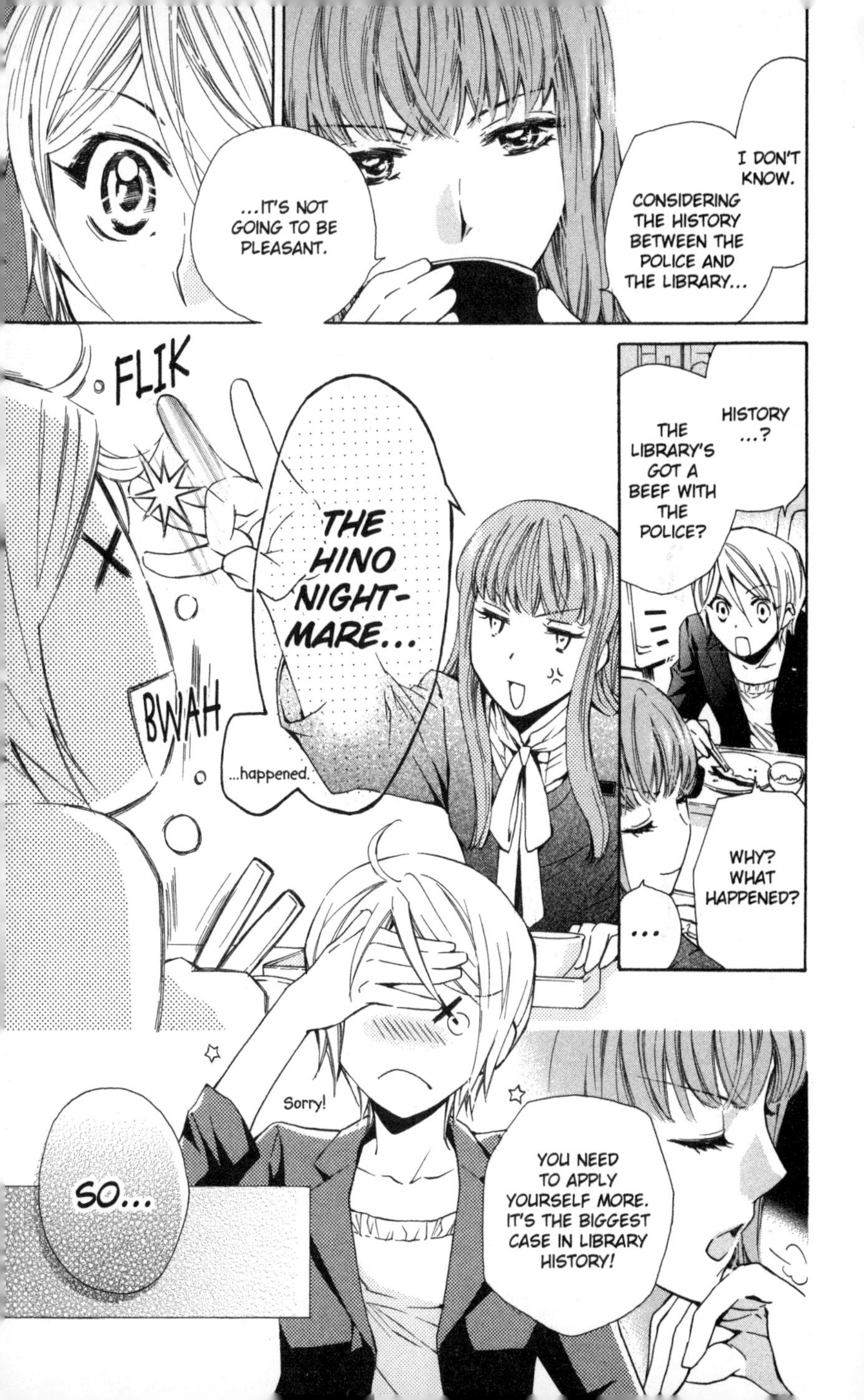
I DON'T KNOW.
CONSIDERING THE HISTORY BETWEEN THE POLICE AND THE LIBRARY...
...IT'S NOT GOING TO BE PLEASANT.
HISTORY ...?
THE LIBRARY'S GOT A BEEF WITH THE POLICE?
WHY? WHAT HAPPENED?
...
THE HINO NIGHT-MARE...
FLIK
...happened.
BWAH
Sorry!
YOU NEED TO APPLY YOURSELF MORE. IT'S THE BIGGEST CASE IN LIBRARY HISTORY!
SO...

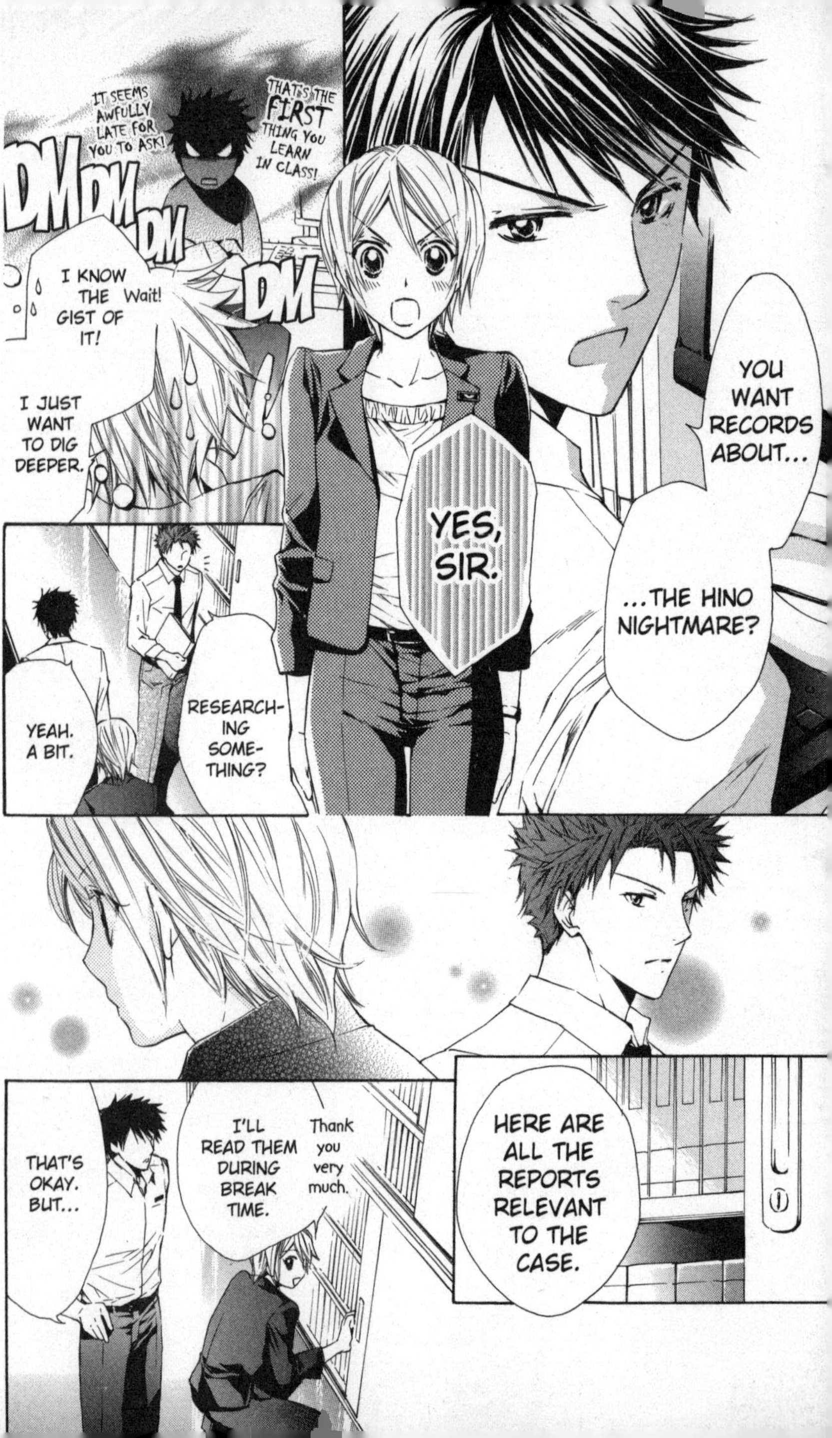
YOU WANT RECORDS ABOUT...
...THE HINO NIGHTMARE?
YES, SIR.
THAT'S THE FIRST THING YOU LEARN IN CLASS!
IT SEEMS AWFULLY LATE FOR YOU TO ASK!
DM DM DM DM
DM
Wait!
I KNOW THE GIST OF IT!
I JUST WANT TO DIG DEEPER.
RESEARCHING SOMETHING?
YEAH. A BIT.
HERE ARE ALL THE REPORTS RELEVANT TO THE CASE.
Thank you very much.
I'LL READ THEM DURING BREAK TIME.
THAT'S OKAY. BUT...

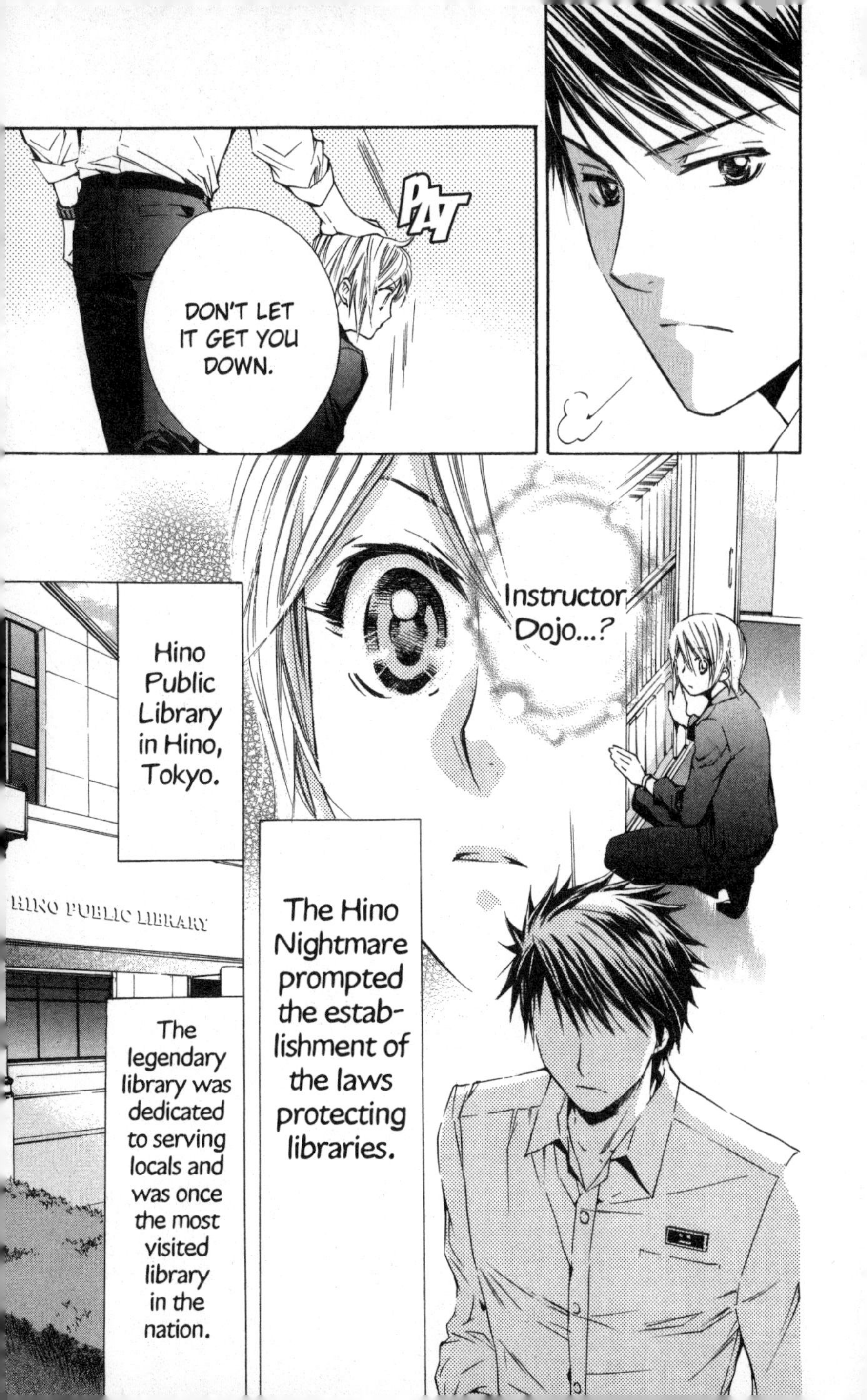
PAT
DON'T LET IT GET YOU DOWN.
Instructor Dojo...?
Hino Public Library in Hino, Tokyo.
HINO PUBLIC LIBRARY
The legendary library was dedicated to serving locals and was once the most visited library in the nation.
The Hino Nightmare prompted the establishment of the laws protecting libraries.

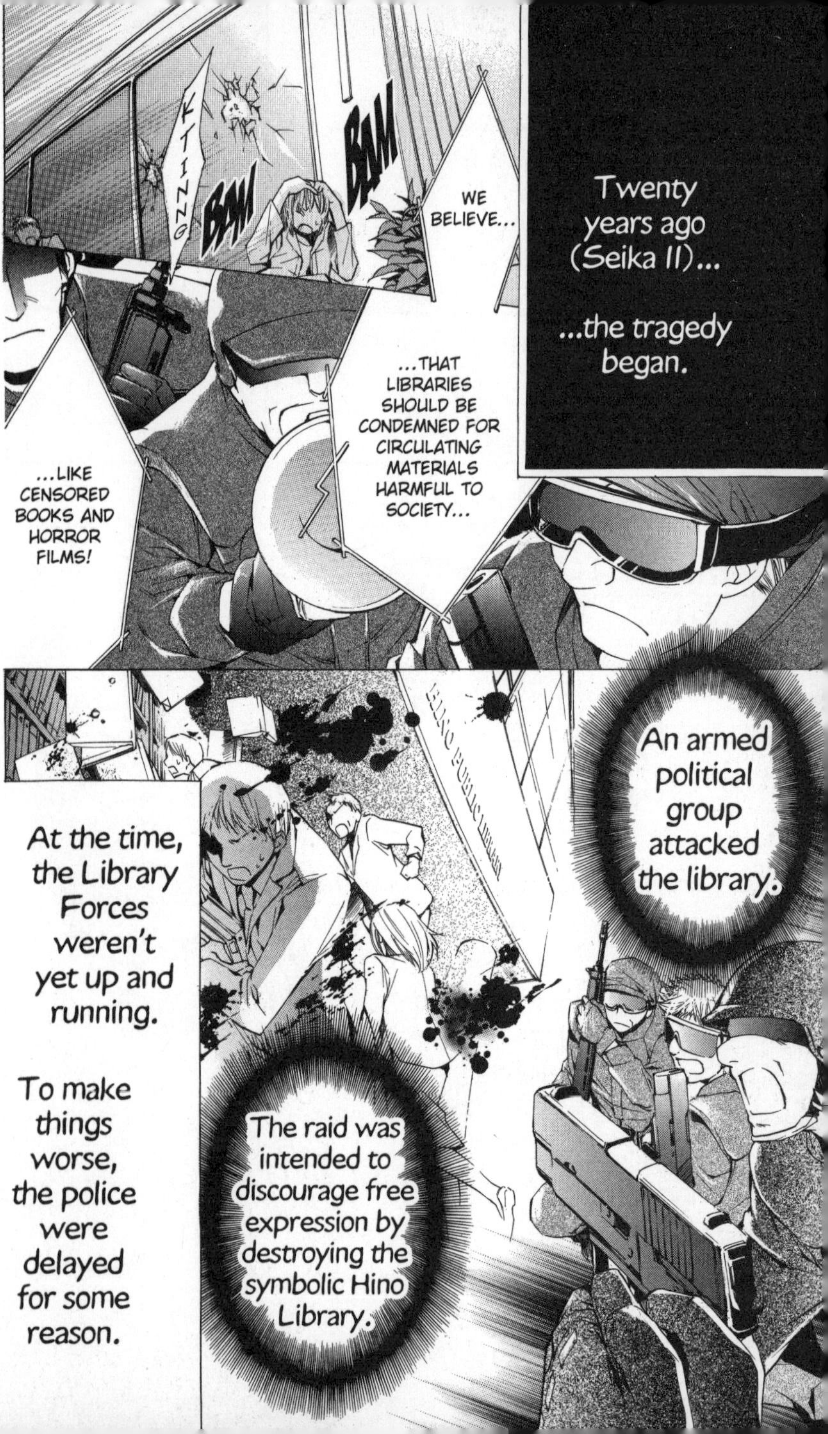

Twenty years ago (Seika II)...
...the tragedy began.
WE BELIEVE...
BAM
BAM
KTING
...THAT LIBRARIES SHOULD BE CONDEMNED FOR CIRCULATING MATERIALS HARMFUL TO SOCIETY...
...LIKE CENSORED BOOKS AND HORROR FILMS!
An armed political group attacked the library.
HINO PUBLIC LIBRARY
The raid was intended to discourage free expression by destroying the symbolic Hino Library.
At the time, the Library Forces weren't yet up and running.
To make things worse, the police were delayed for some reason.

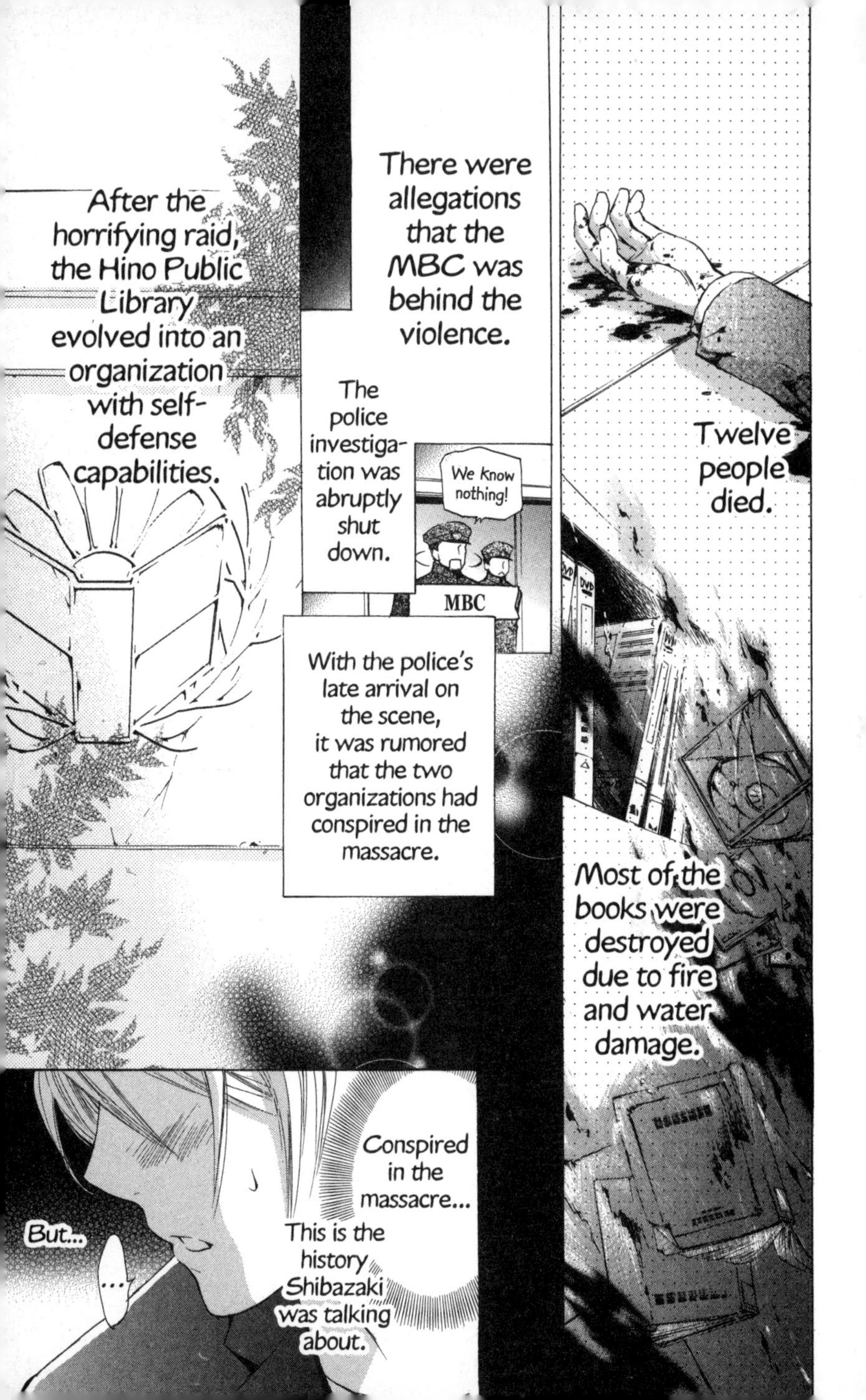

Twelve people died.
Most of the books were destroyed due to fire and water damage.
There were allegations that the MBC was behind the violence.
The police investigation was abruptly shut down.
We know nothing!
MBC
After the horrifying raid, the Hino Public Library evolved into an organization with self-defense capabilities.
With the police's late arrival on the scene, it was rumored that the two organizations had conspired in the massacre.
Conspired in the massacre...
This is the history Shibazaki was talking about.
But...
...

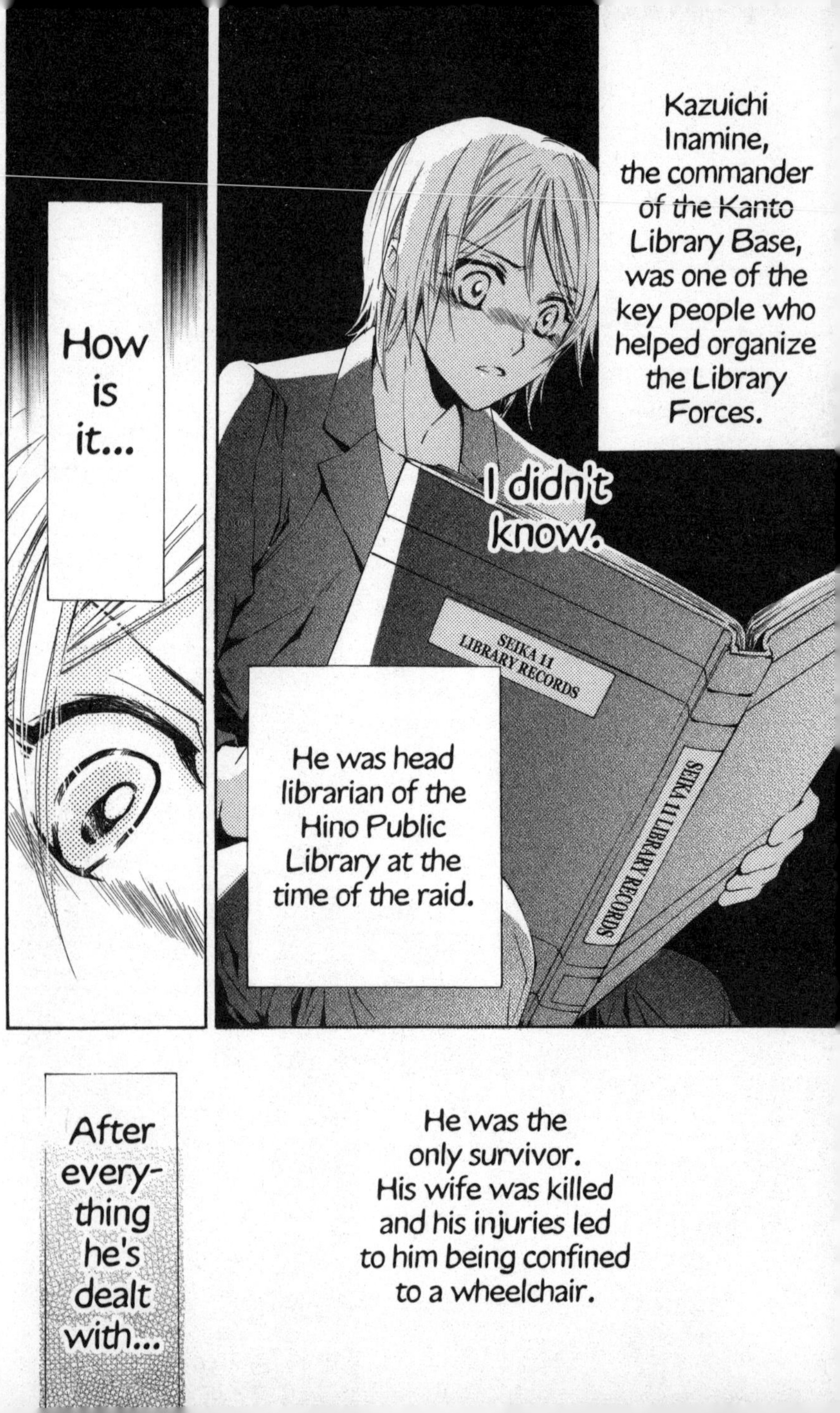
Kazuichi Inamine, the commander of the Kanto Library Base, was one of the key people who helped organize the Library Forces.
I didn't know.
SEIKA 11 LIBRARY RECORDS
SEIKA 11 LIBRARY RECORDS
He was head librarian of the Hino Public Library at the time of the raid.
How is it...
He was the only survivor. His wife was killed and his injuries led to him being confined to a wheelchair.
After every-thing he's dealt with...

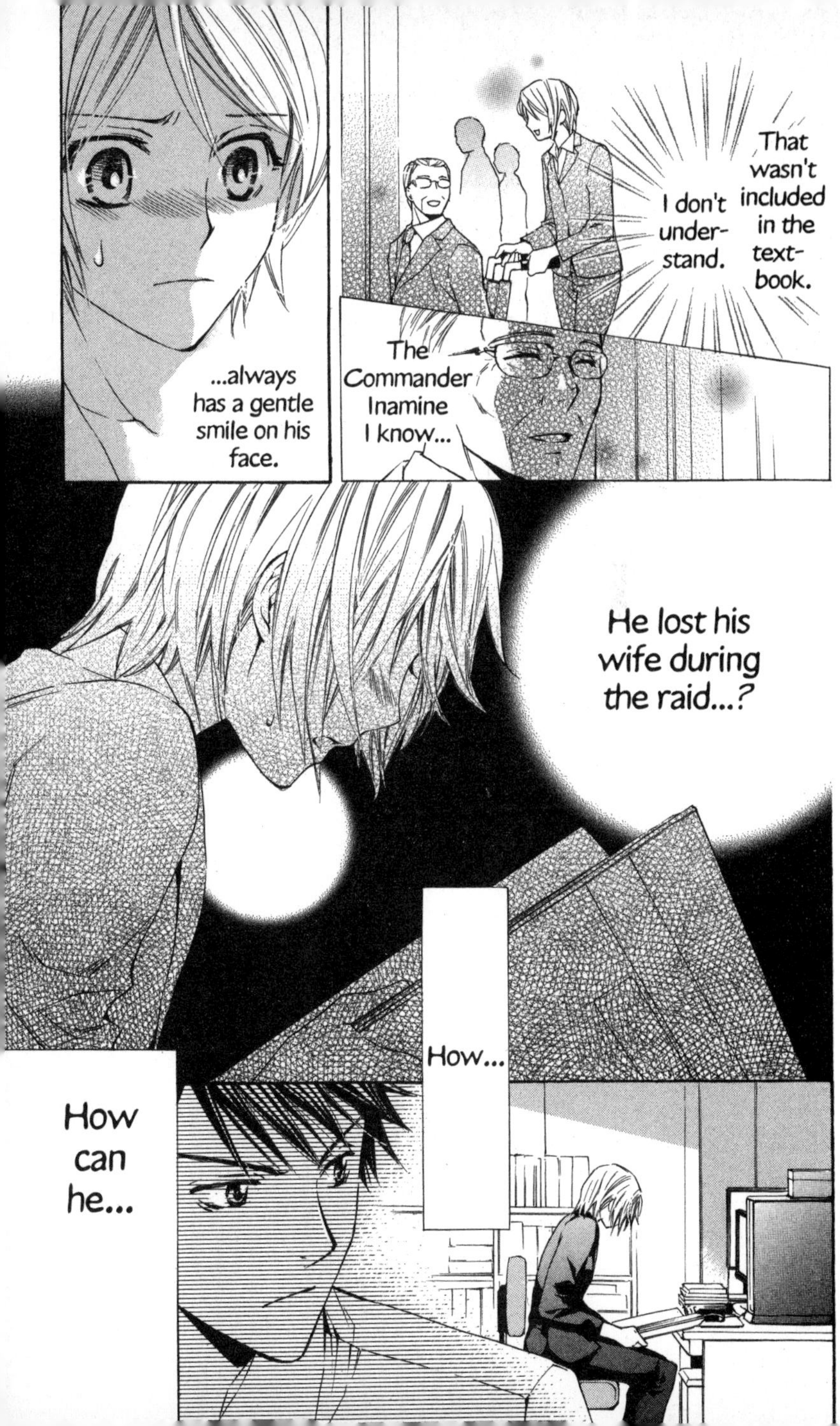
That wasn't included in the text-book.
I don't under-stand.
The Commander Inamine I know...
...always has a gentle smile on his face.
He lost his wife during the raid...?
How...
How can he...

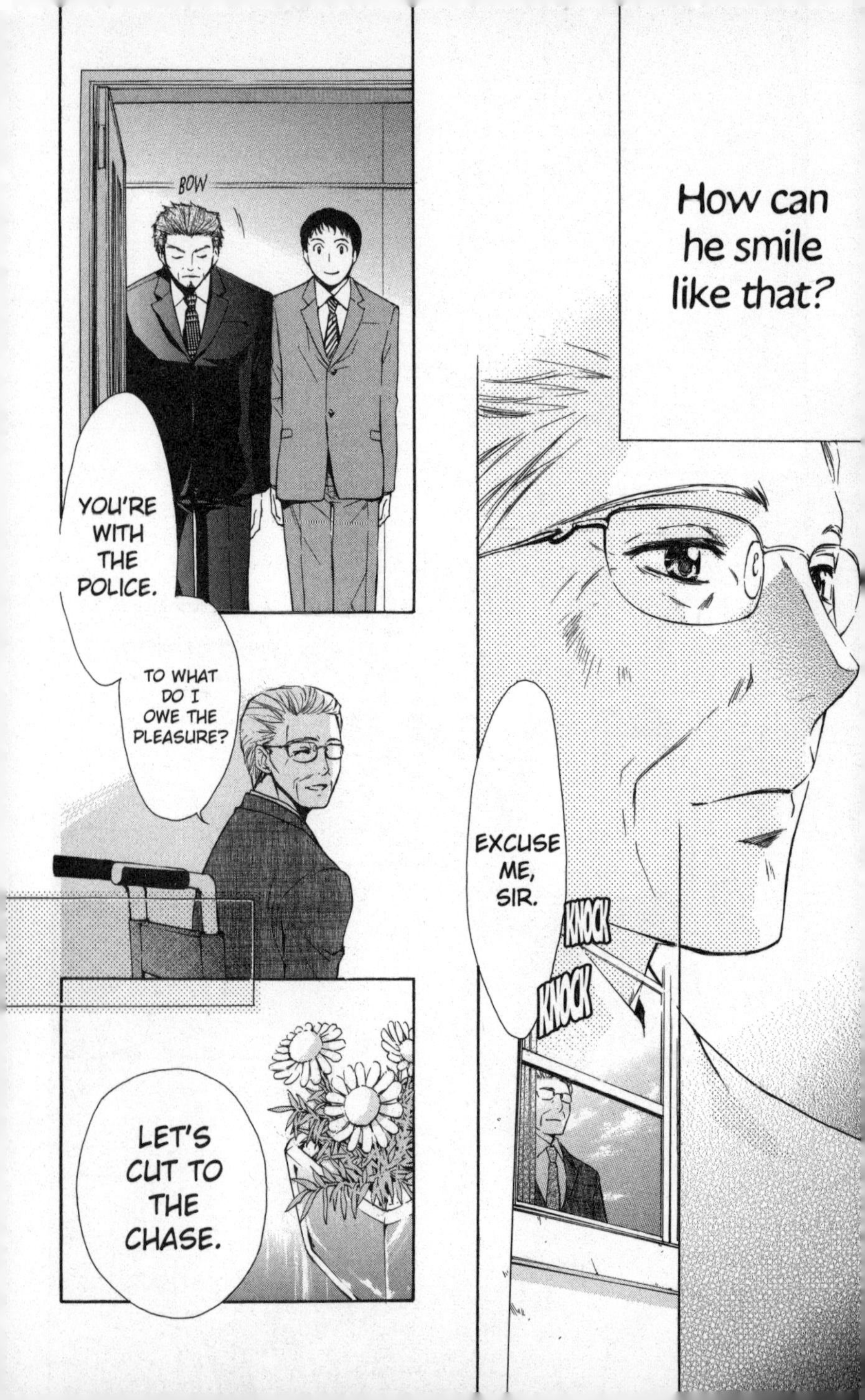
How can he smile like that?
KNOCK
KNOCK
EXCUSE ME, SIR.
BOW
YOU'RE WITH THE POLICE.
TO WHAT DO I OWE THE PLEASURE?
LET'S CUT TO THE CHASE.

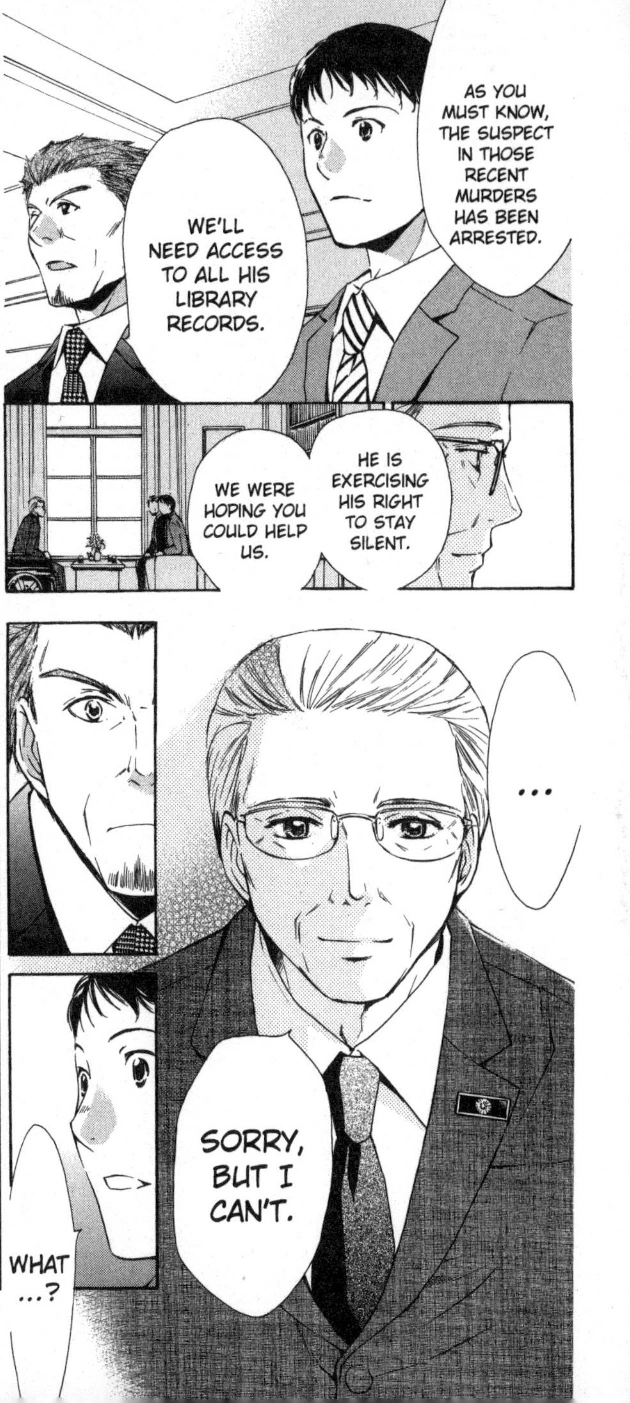
AS YOU MUST KNOW, THE SUSPECT IN THOSE RECENT MURDERS HAS BEEN ARRESTED.
WE'LL NEED ACCESS TO ALL HIS LIBRARY RECORDS.
HE IS EXERCISING HIS RIGHT TO STAY SILENT.
WE WERE HOPING YOU COULD HELP US.
...
SORRY, BUT I CAN'T.
WHAT ...?

5

Friends of mine planned a surprise party for me to celebrate the publication of the first volume.

A couple of them took me out and brought me to a place filled with lots of other people waiting for me. They had me totally fooled!

There was this huge cake! (I wish I could show it to you...!) It was delightful. Later, the same friends surprised me with another present. They're a lot of fun. It's nice to have friends like them.

Thank you for always being there for me.

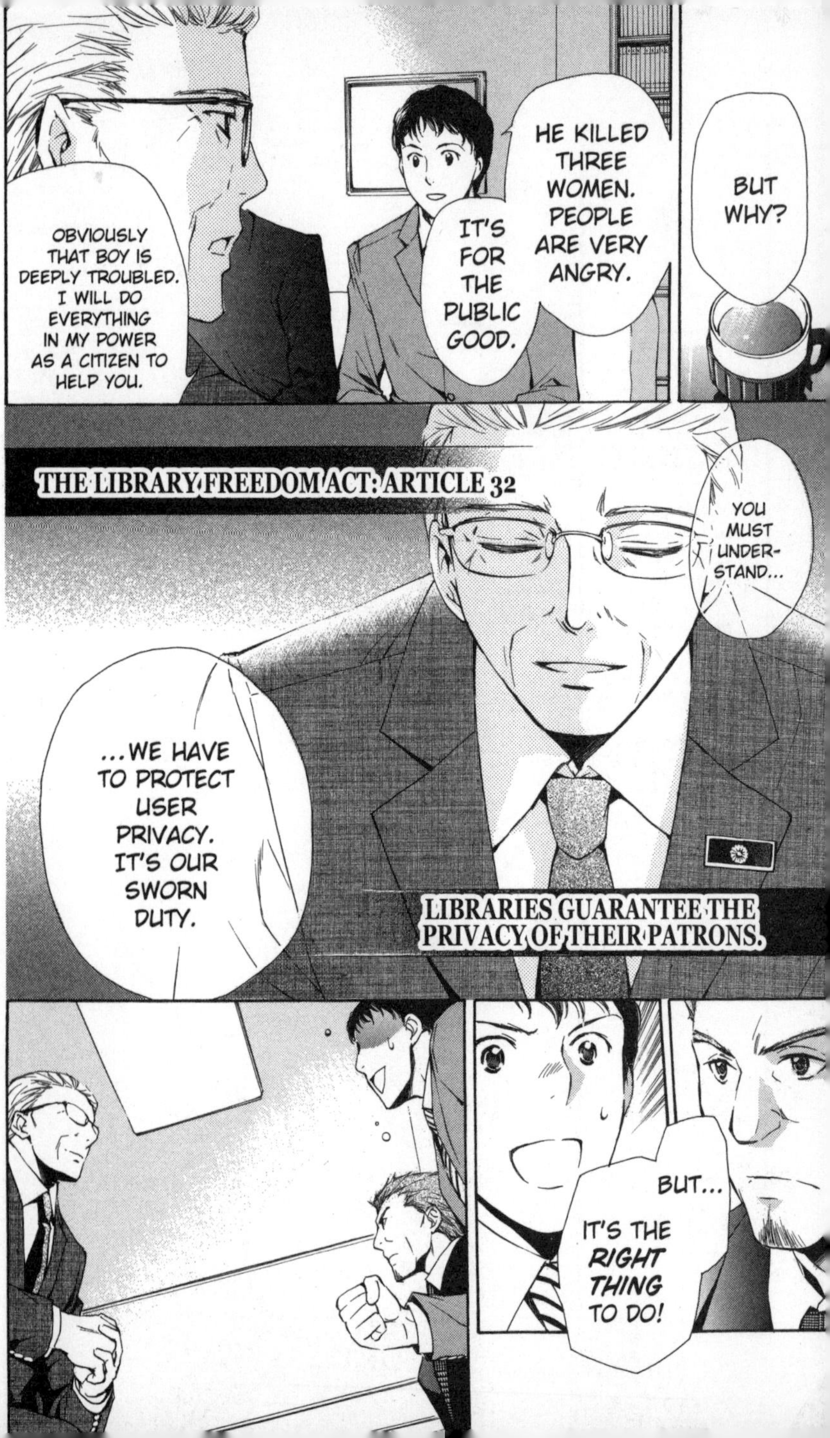
BUT WHY?
HE KILLED THREE WOMEN. PEOPLE ARE VERY ANGRY.
IT'S FOR THE PUBLIC GOOD.
OBVIOUSLY THAT BOY IS DEEPLY TROUBLED. I WILL DO EVERYTHING IN MY POWER AS A CITIZEN TO HELP YOU.
THE LIBRARY FREEDOM ACT: ARTICLE 32
YOU MUST UNDER-STAND...
...WE HAVE TO PROTECT USER PRIVACY. IT'S OUR SWORN DUTY.
LIBRARIES GUARANTEE THE PRIVACY OF THEIR PATRONS.
BUT... IT'S THE *RIGHT THING* TO DO!

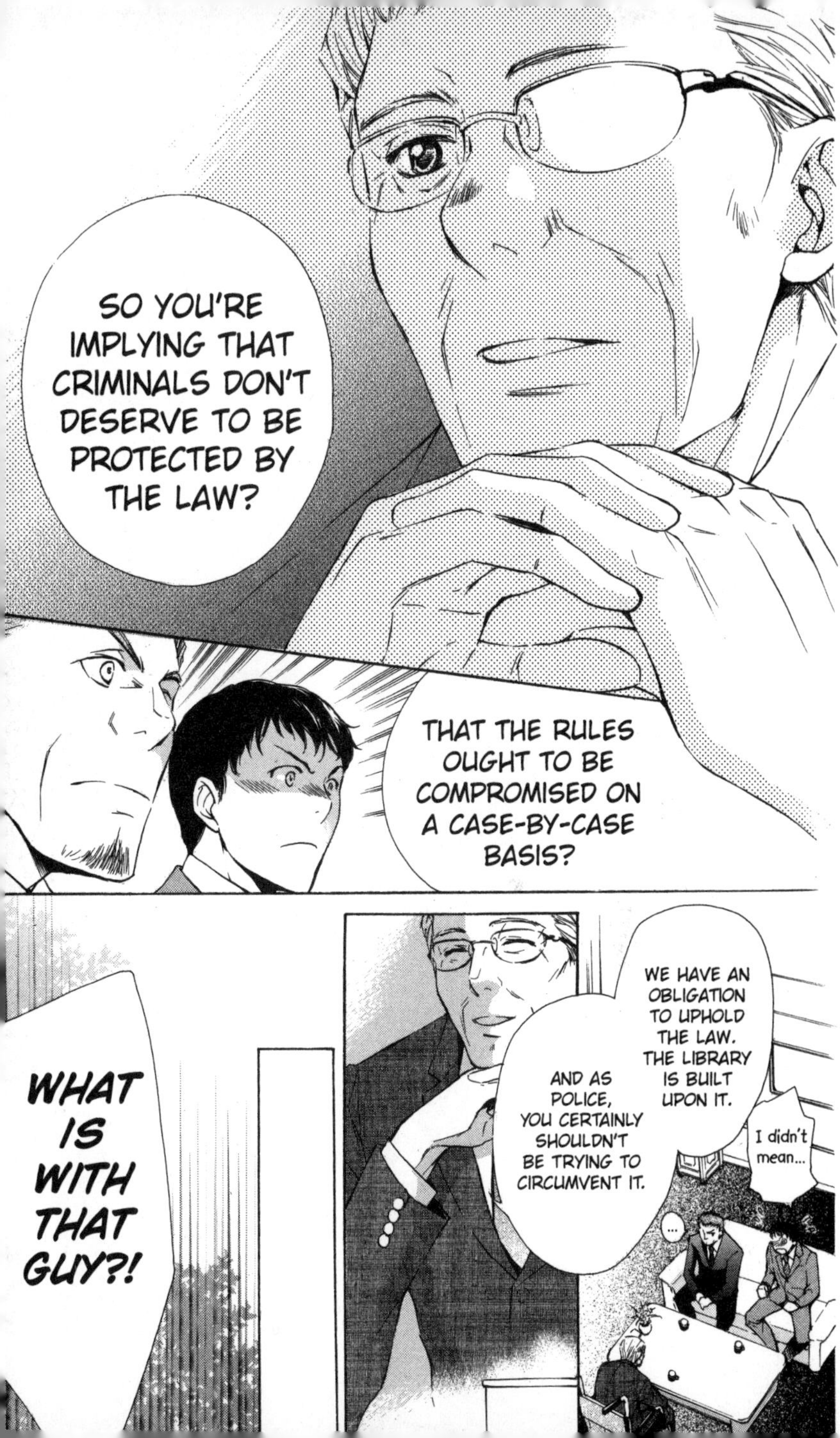
SO YOU'RE IMPLYING THAT CRIMINALS DON'T DESERVE TO BE PROTECTED BY THE LAW?
THAT THE RULES OUGHT TO BE COMPROMISED ON A CASE-BY-CASE BASIS?
WE HAVE AN OBLIGATION TO UPHOLD THE LAW. THE LIBRARY IS BUILT UPON IT.
AND AS POLICE, YOU CERTAINLY SHOULDN'T BE TRYING TO CIRCUMVENT IT.
I didn't mean...
...
WHAT IS WITH THAT GUY?!

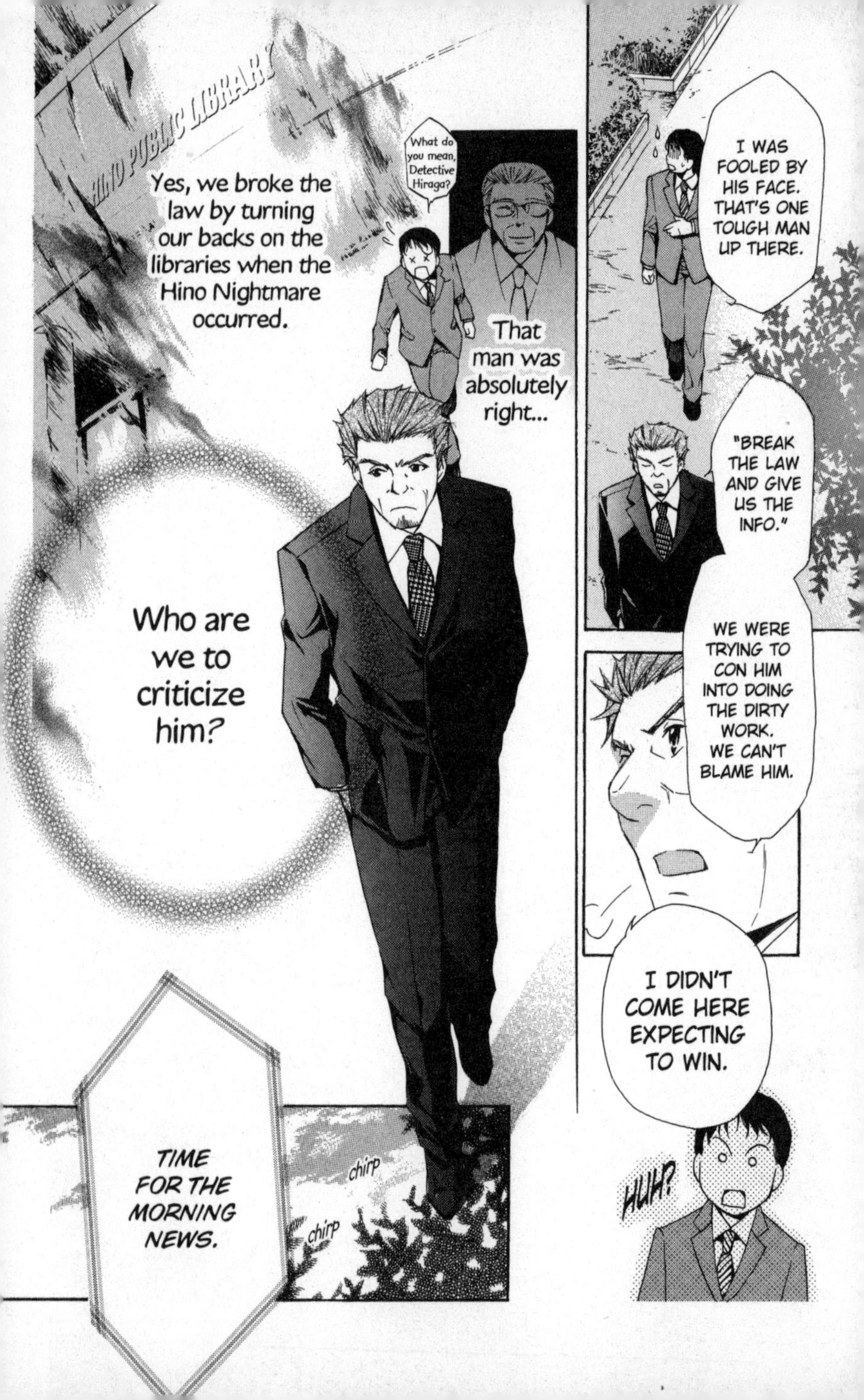
I WAS FOOLED BY HIS FACE. THAT'S ONE TOUGH MAN UP THERE.
"BREAK THE LAW AND GIVE US THE INFO."
WE WERE TRYING TO CON HIM INTO DOING THE DIRTY WORK. WE CAN'T BLAME HIM.
I DIDN'T COME HERE EXPECTING TO WIN.
HUH?
HINO PUBLIC LIBRARY
What do you mean, Detective Hiraga?
That man was absolutely right...
Yes, we broke the law by turning our backs on the libraries when the Hino Nightmare occurred.
Who are we to criticize him?
TIME FOR THE MORNING NEWS.
chirp
chirp

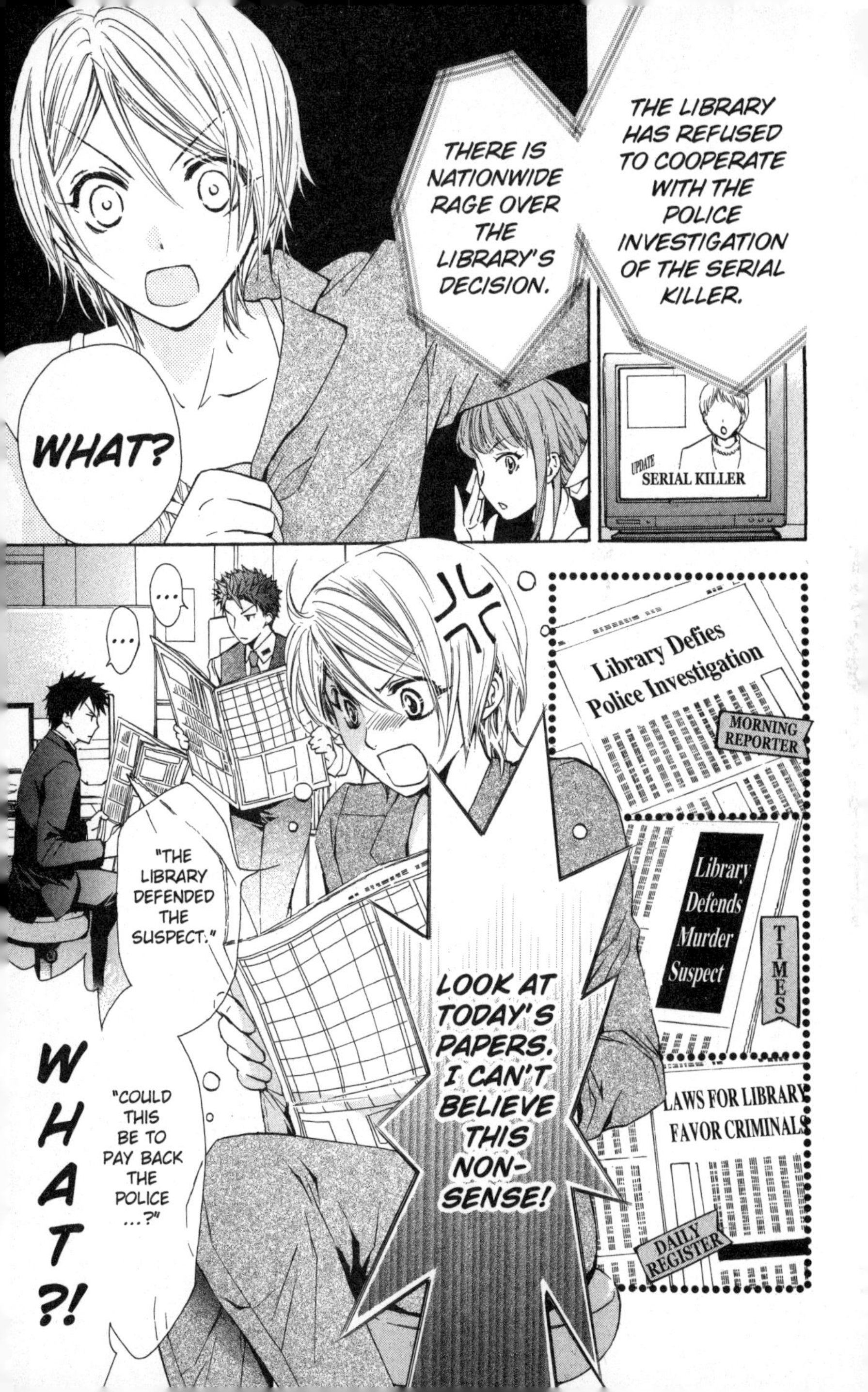

THE LIBRARY HAS REFUSED TO COOPERATE WITH THE POLICE INVESTIGATION OF THE SERIAL KILLER.
UPDATE
SERIAL KILLER
THERE IS NATIONWIDE RAGE OVER THE LIBRARY'S DECISION.
WHAT?
Library Defies Police Investigation
MORNING REPORTER
...
...
Library Defends Murder Suspect
TIMES
LOOK AT TODAY'S PAPERS. I CAN'T BELIEVE THIS NON-SENSE!
LAWS FOR LIBRARY FAVOR CRIMINALS
DAILY REGISTER
"THE LIBRARY DEFENDED THE SUSPECT."
"COULD THIS BE TO PAY BACK THE POLICE ...?"
WHAT?!

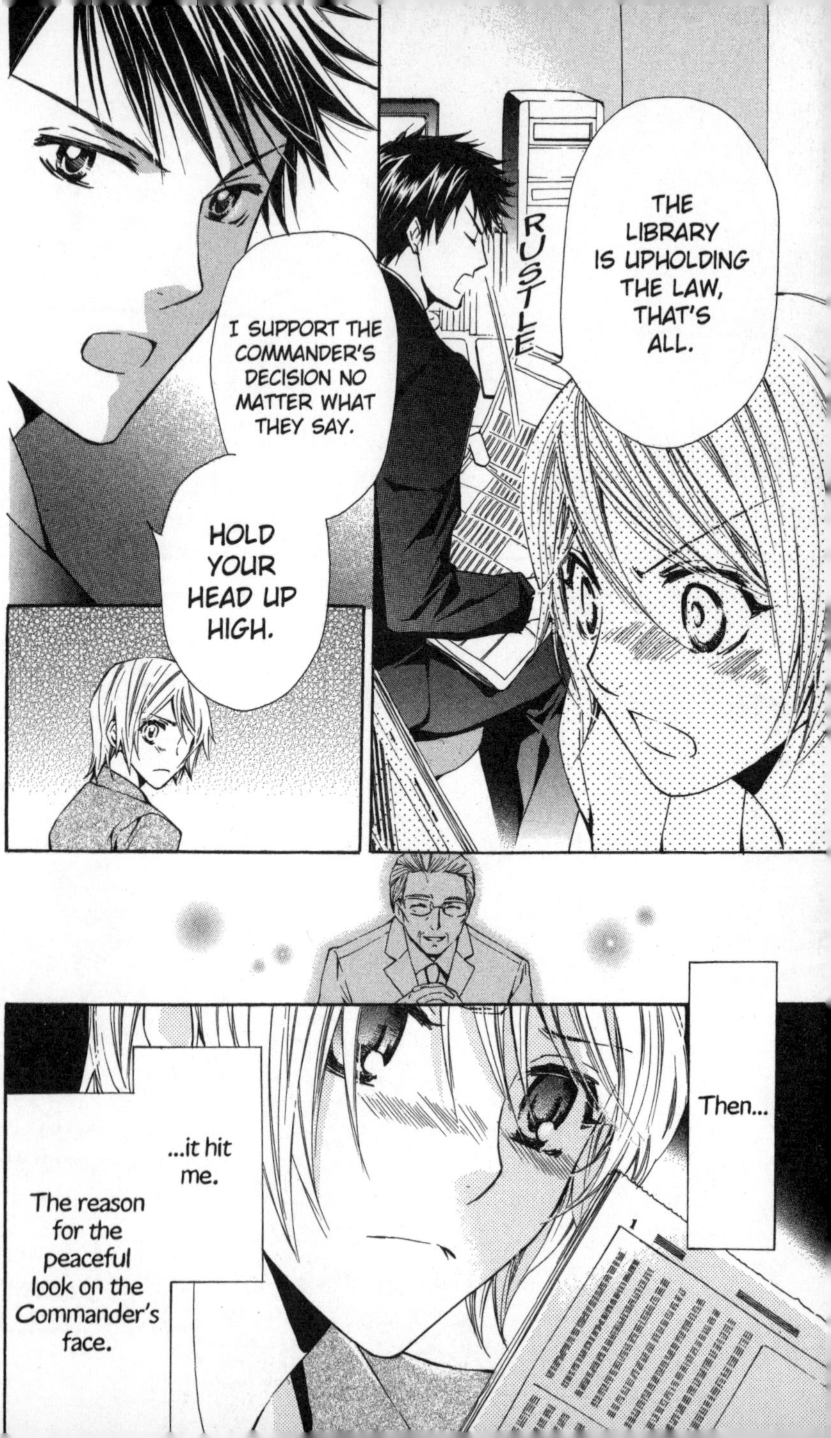
THE LIBRARY IS UPHOLDING THE LAW, THAT'S ALL.
RUSTLE
I SUPPORT THE COMMANDER'S DECISION NO MATTER WHAT THEY SAY.
HOLD YOUR HEAD UP HIGH.
Then...
...it hit me.
The reason for the peaceful look on the Commander's face.

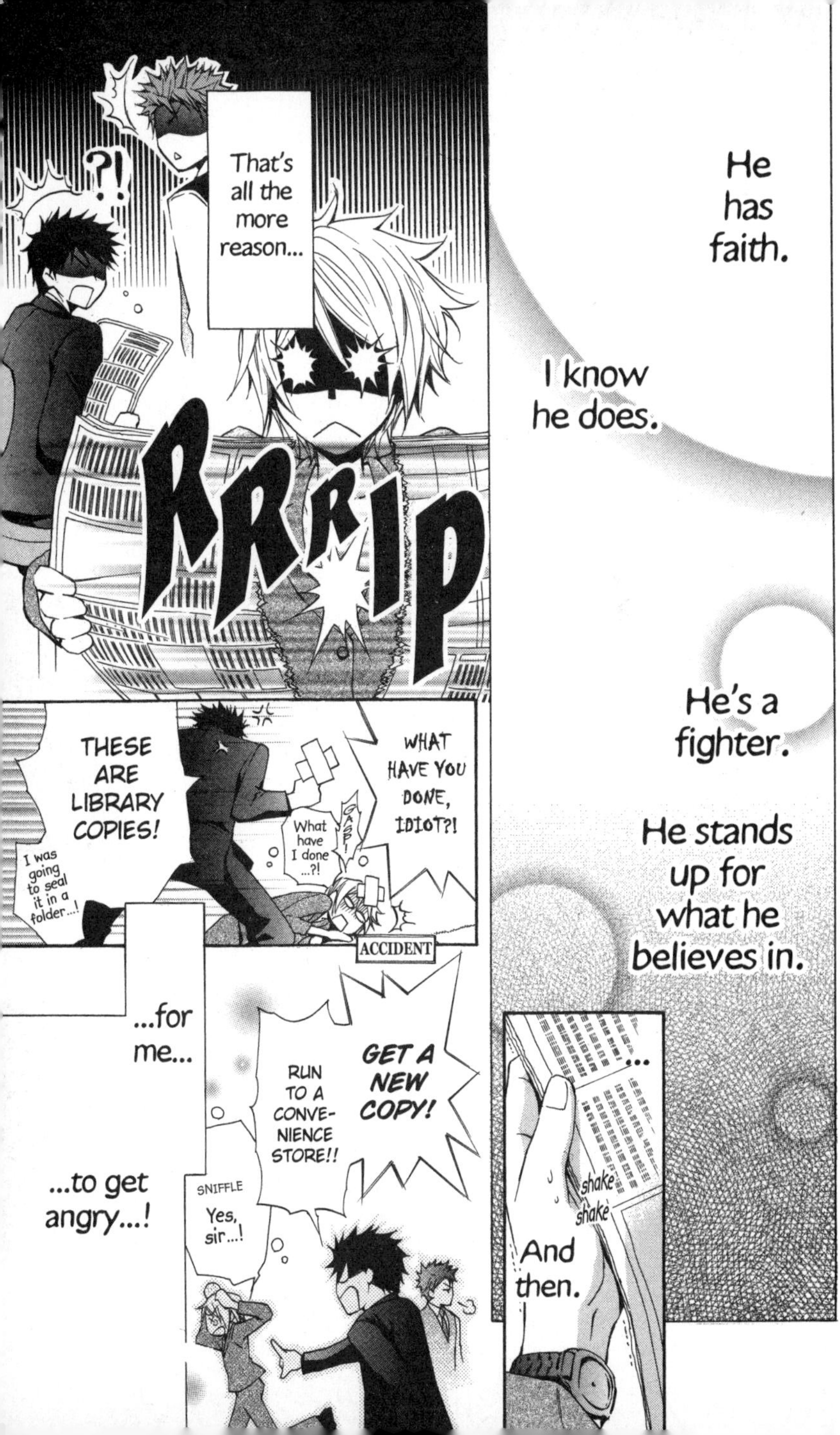
He has faith.
I know he does.
He's a fighter.
He stands up for what he believes in.
...
shake shake
And then.
That's all the more reason...
?!
RRRIP
WHAT HAVE YOU DONE, IDIOT?!
GASP!
What have I done ...?!
THESE ARE LIBRARY COPIES!
I was going to seal it in a folder...!
ACCIDENT
...for me...
GET A NEW COPY!
RUN TO A CONVENIENCE STORE!!
SNIFFLE
Yes, sir...!
...to get angry...!

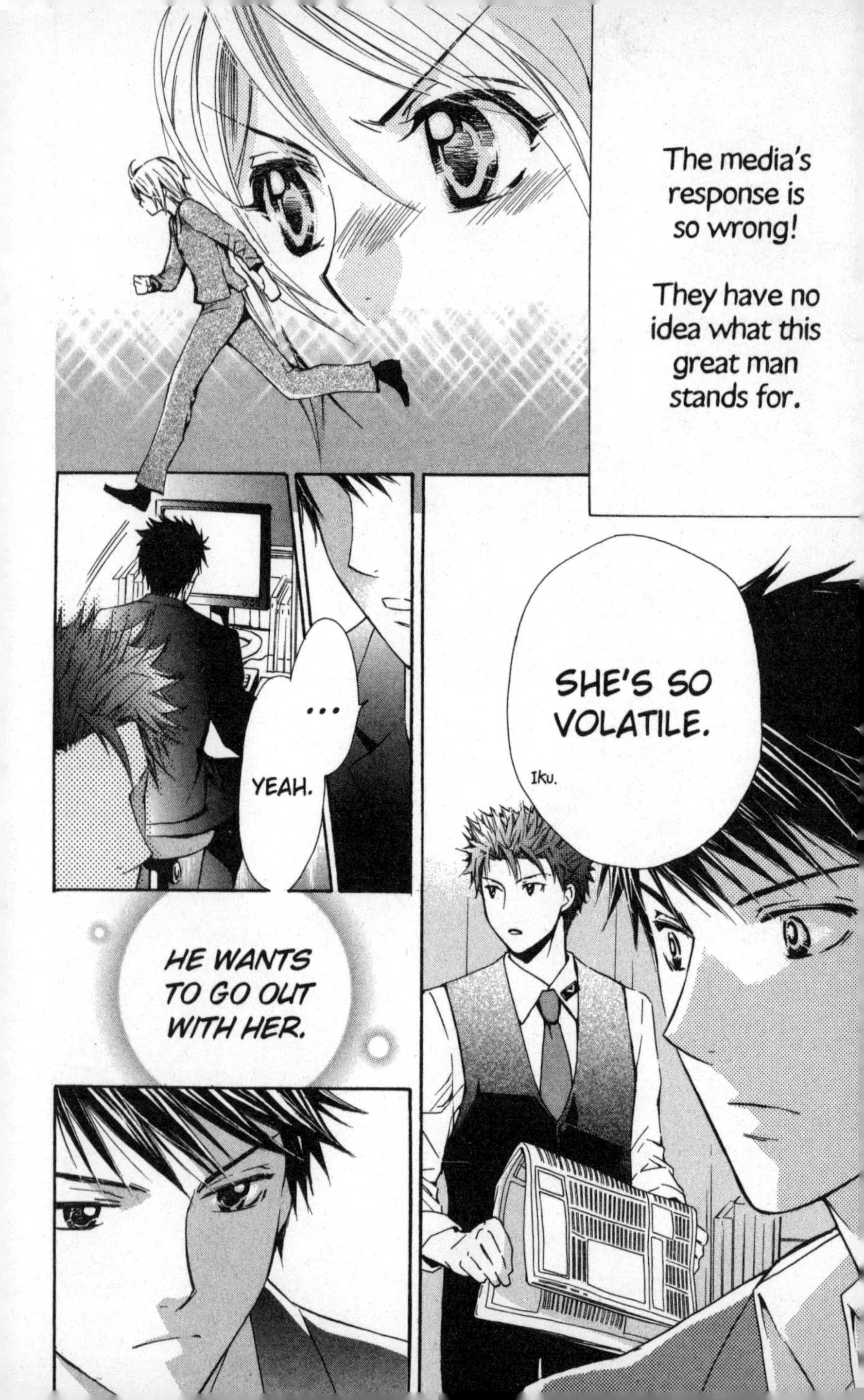
The media's response is so wrong!
They have no idea what this great man stands for.
SHE'S SO VOLATILE.
IKU.
... YEAH.
HE WANTS TO GO OUT WITH HER.

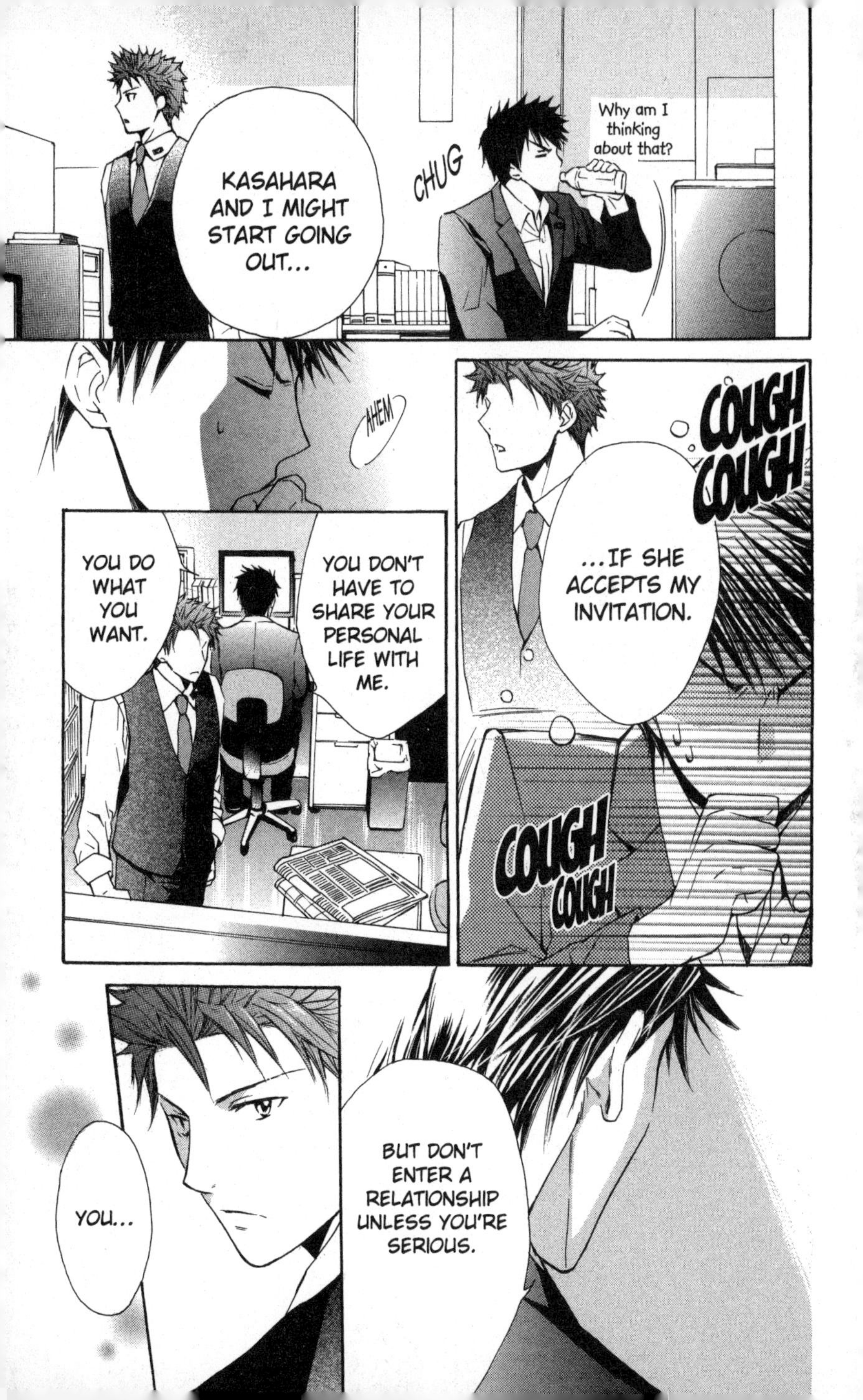
Why am I thinking about that?
CHUG
KASAHARA AND I MIGHT START GOING OUT...
COUGH COUGH
...IF SHE ACCEPTS MY INVITATION.
COUGH COUGH
AHEM
YOU DON'T HAVE TO SHARE YOUR PERSONAL LIFE WITH ME.
YOU DO WHAT YOU WANT.
BUT DON'T ENTER A RELATIONSHIP UNLESS YOU'RE SERIOUS.
YOU...

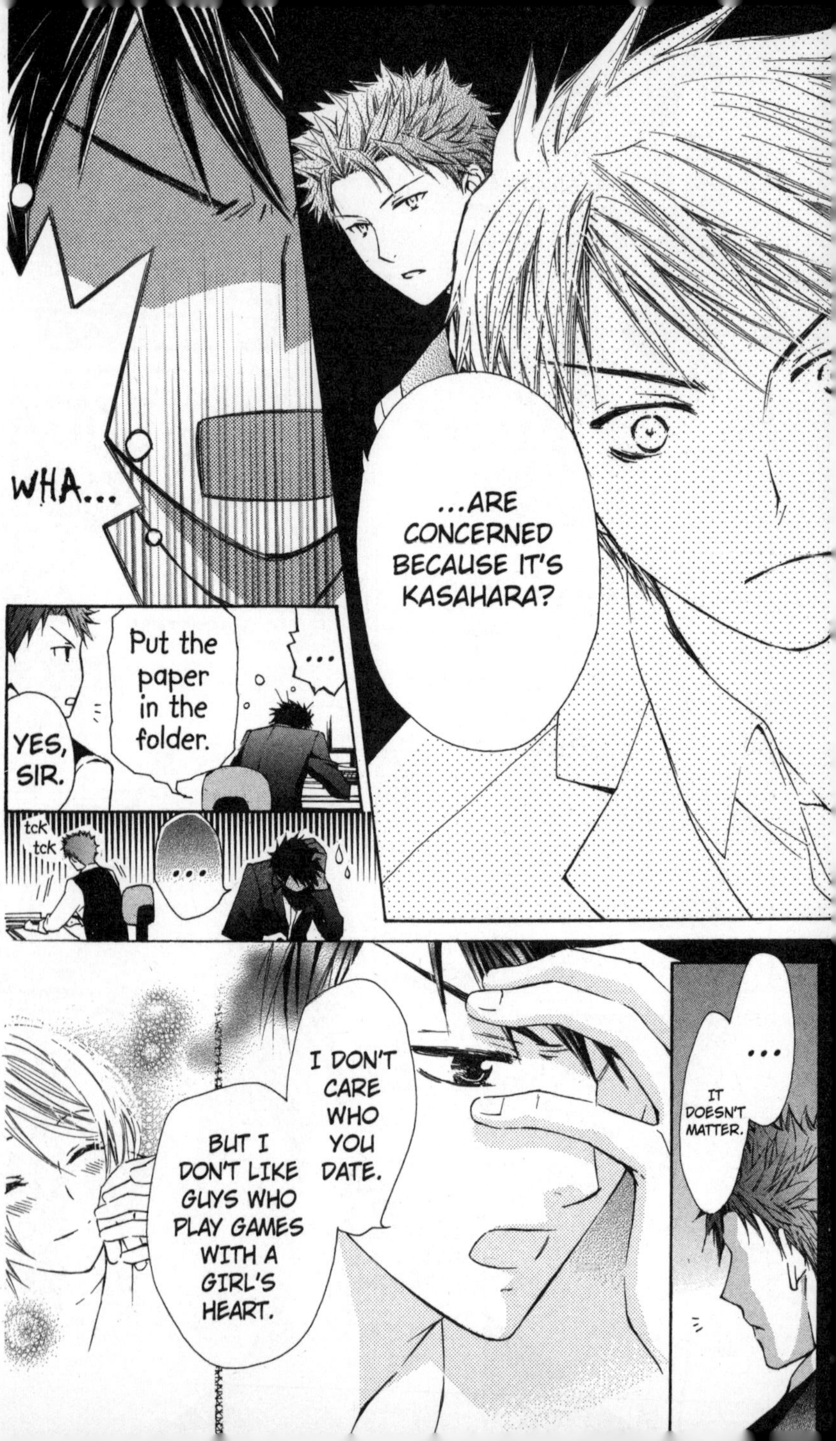

...ARE CONCERNED BECAUSE IT'S KASAHARA?
WHA...
...
Put the paper in the folder.
YES, SIR.
...
tck tck
...
IT DOESN'T MATTER.
I DON'T CARE WHO YOU DATE.
BUT I DON'T LIKE GUYS WHO PLAY GAMES WITH A GIRL'S HEART.

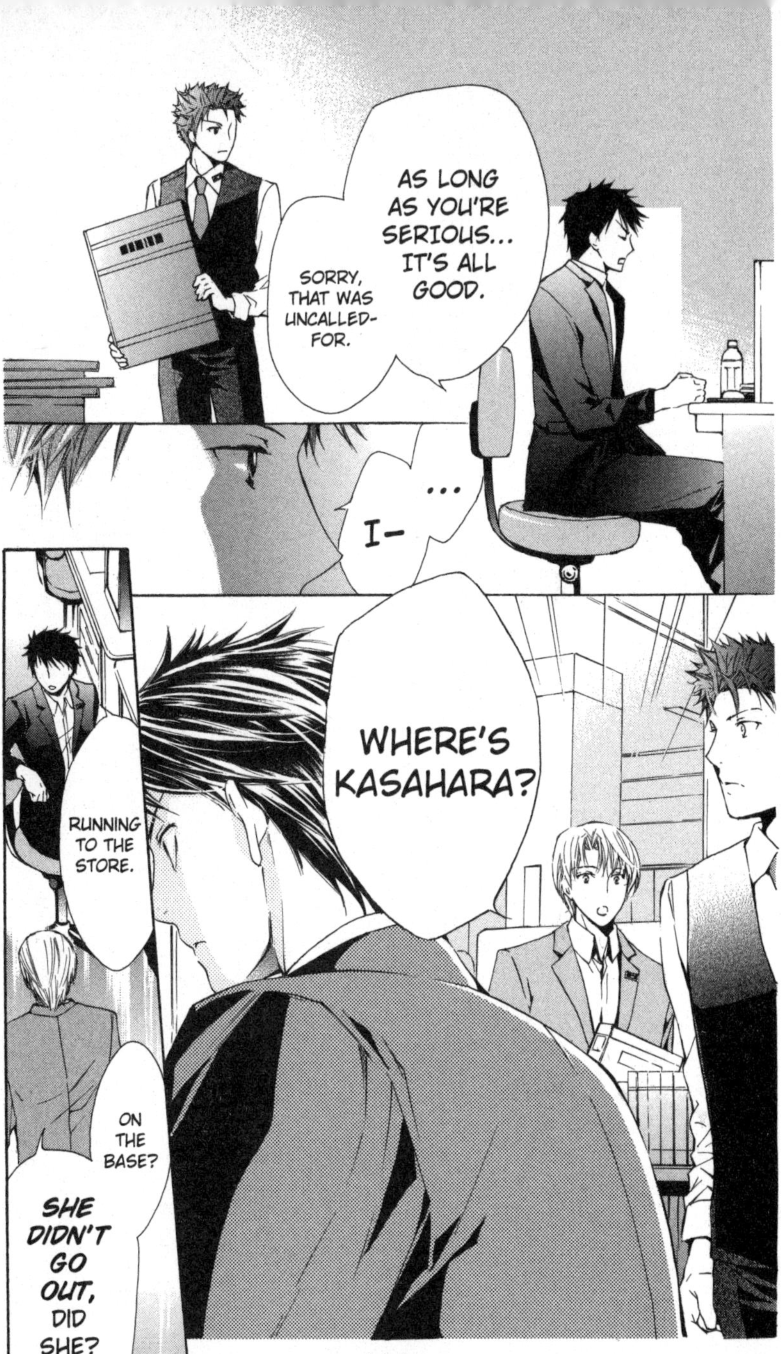
AS LONG AS YOU'RE SERIOUS... IT'S ALL GOOD.
SORRY, THAT WAS UNCALLED-FOR.
...
I-
WHERE'S KASAHARA?
RUNNING TO THE STORE.
ON THE BASE?
SHE DIDN'T GO OUT, DID SHE?

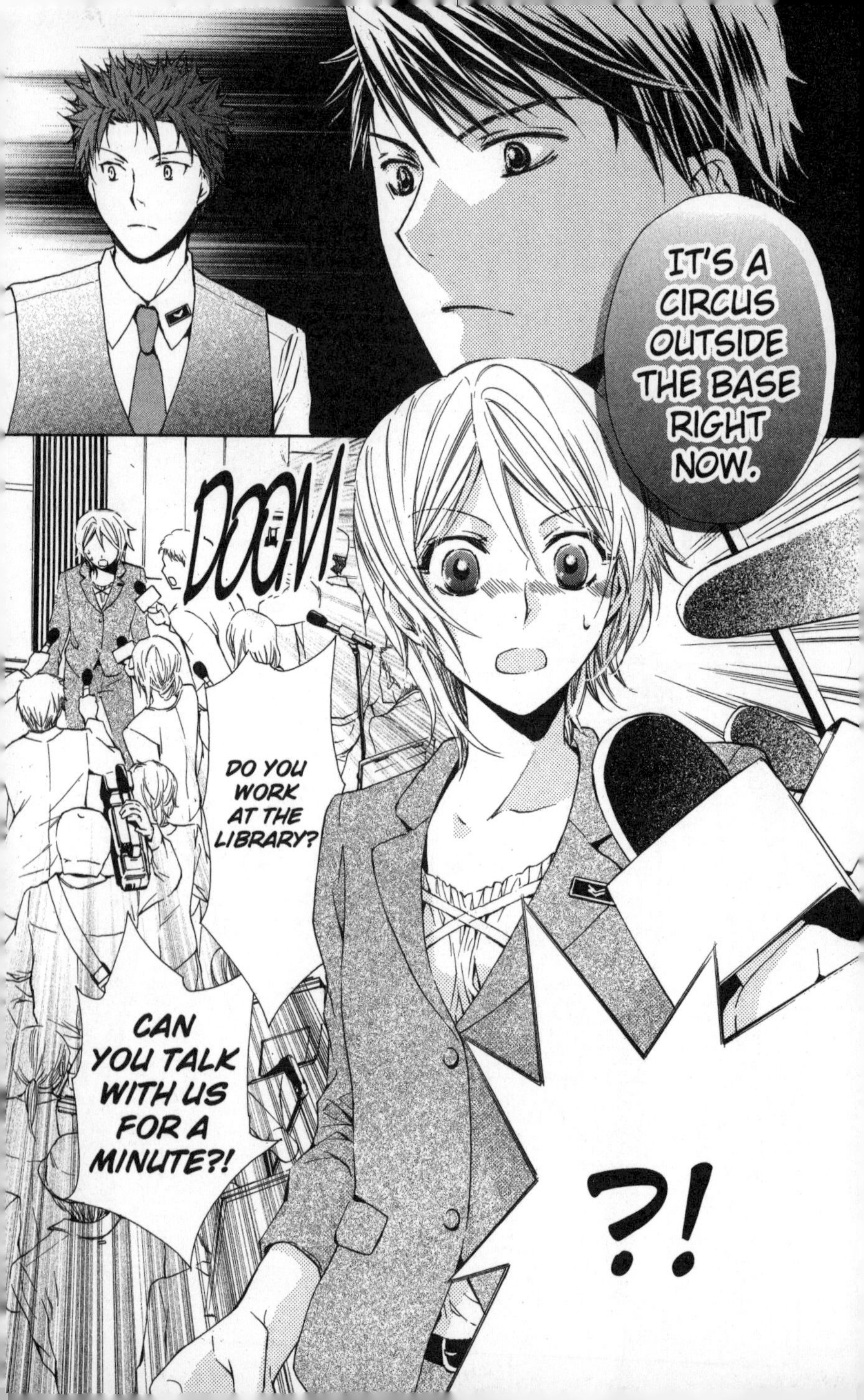
IT'S A CIRCUS OUTSIDE THE BASE RIGHT NOW.
DOOM
DO YOU WORK AT THE LIBRARY?
CAN YOU TALK WITH US FOR A MINUTE?!
?!

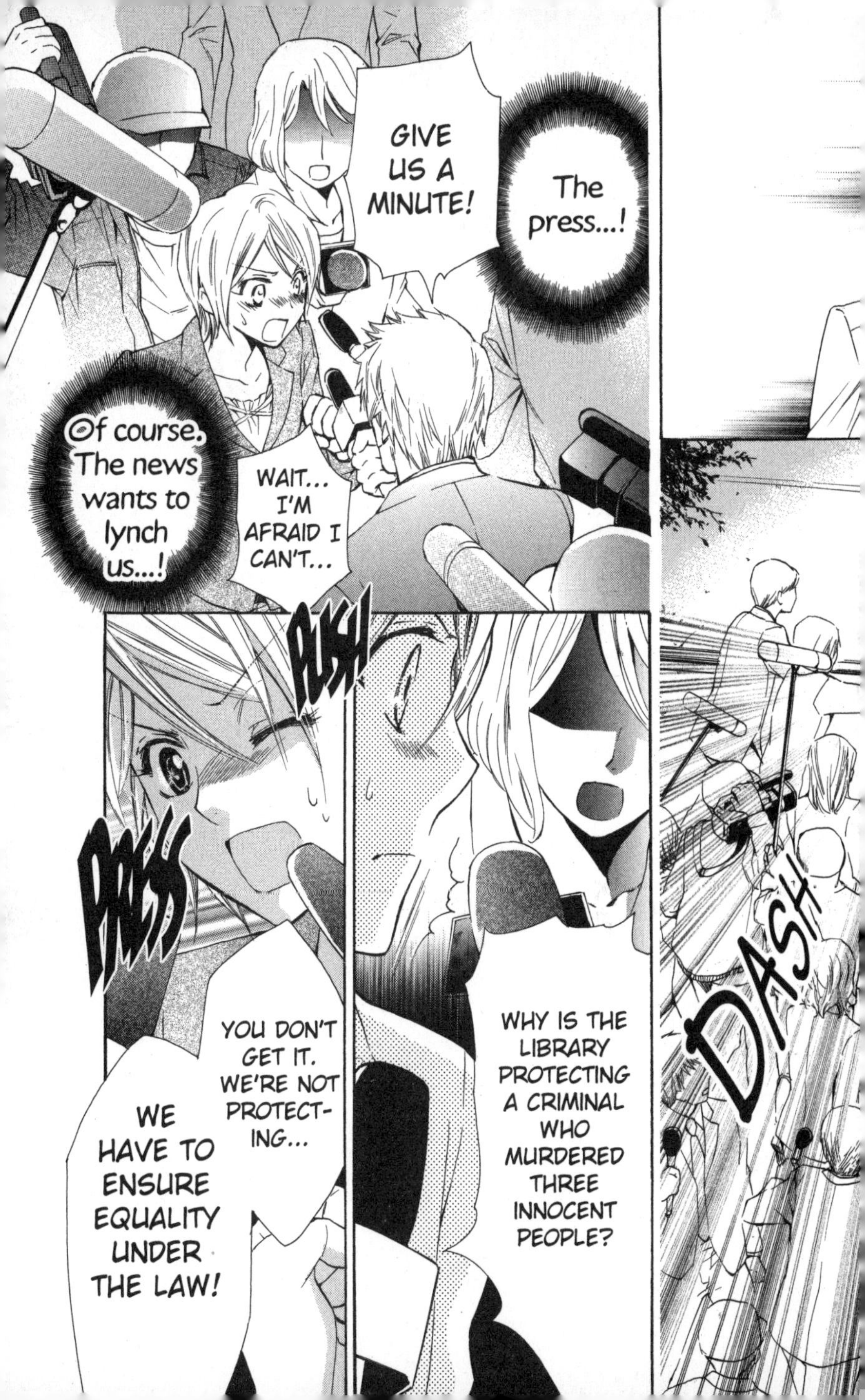
DASH
The press...!
GIVE US A MINUTE!
WAIT... I'M AFRAID I CAN'T...
Of course. The news wants to lynch us...!
PUSH
WHY IS THE LIBRARY PROTECTING A CRIMINAL WHO MURDERED THREE INNOCENT PEOPLE?
PRESS
YOU DON'T GET IT. WE'RE NOT PROTECT-ING...
WE HAVE TO ENSURE EQUALITY UNDER THE LAW!

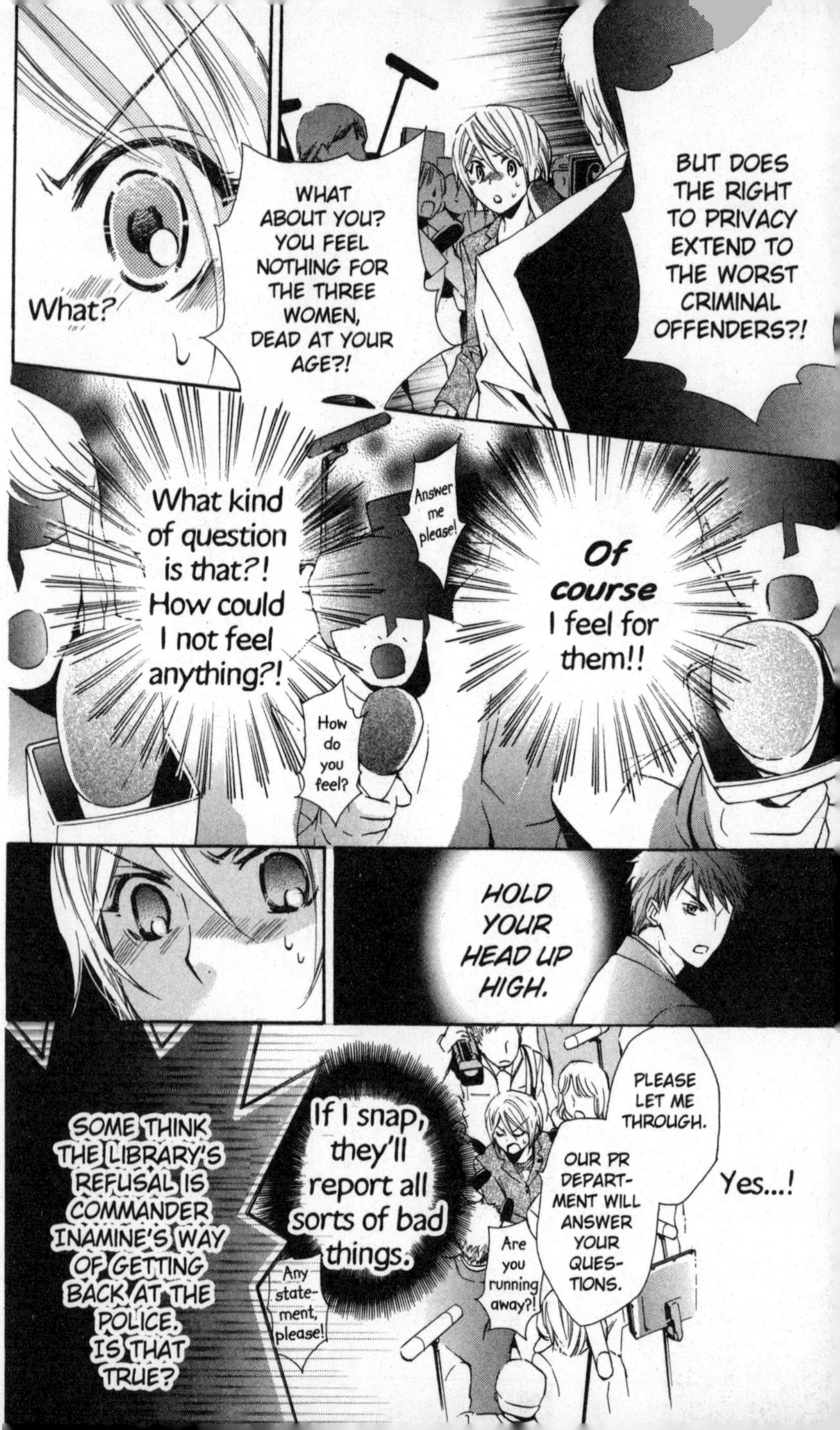
BUT DOES THE RIGHT TO PRIVACY EXTEND TO THE WORST CRIMINAL OFFENDERS?!
WHAT ABOUT YOU? YOU FEEL NOTHING FOR THE THREE WOMEN, DEAD AT YOUR AGE?!
What?
Answer me please!
Of course I feel for them!!
What kind of question is that?! How could I not feel anything?!
How do you feel?
HOLD YOUR HEAD UP HIGH.
Yes...!
PLEASE LET ME THROUGH.
OUR PR DEPARTMENT WILL ANSWER YOUR QUESTIONS.
Are you running away?!
If I snap, they'll report all sorts of bad things.
Any statement, please!
SOME THINK THE LIBRARY'S REFUSAL IS COMMANDER INAMINE'S WAY OF GETTING BACK AT THE POLICE. IS THAT TRUE?

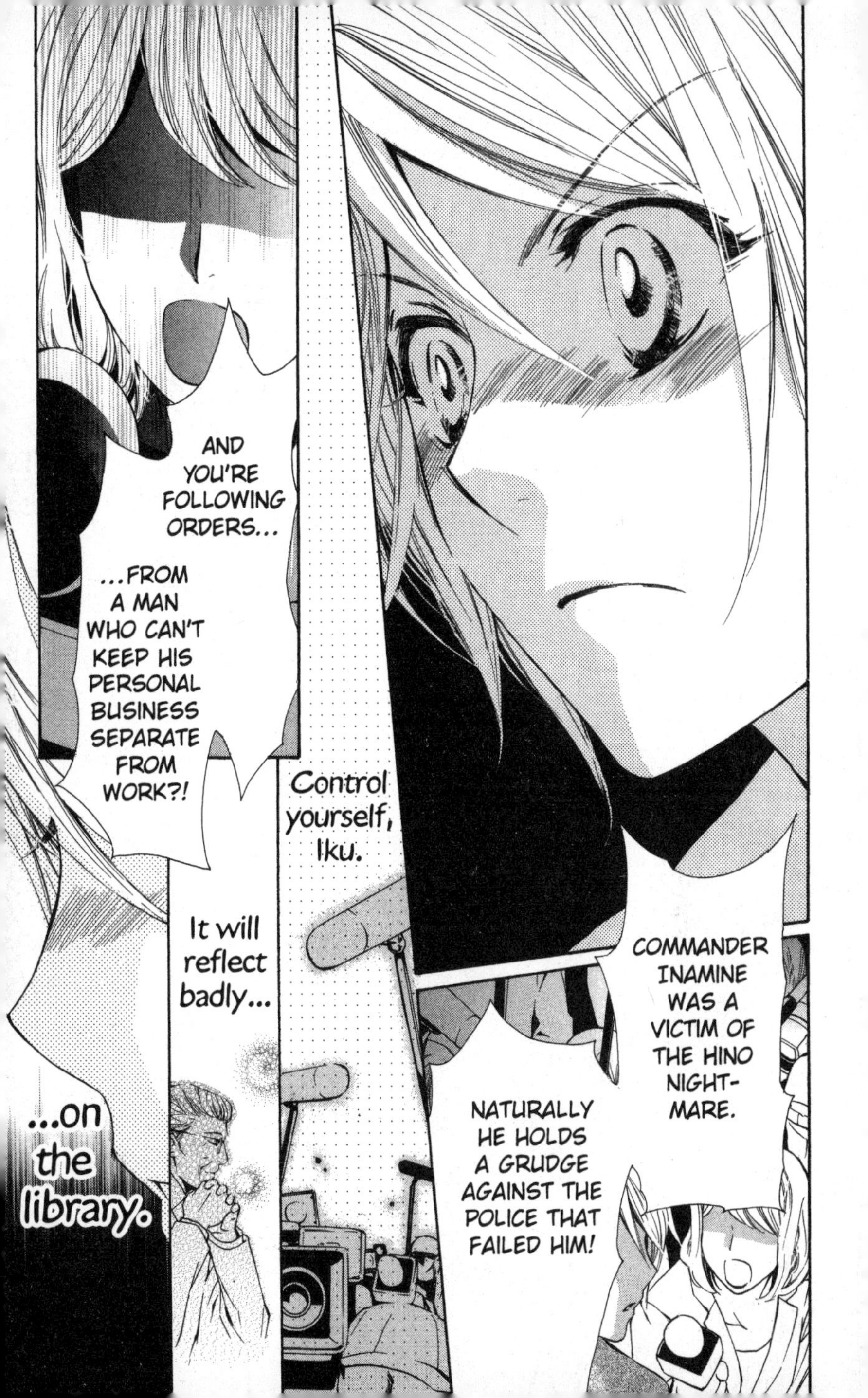
COMMANDER INAMINE WAS A VICTIM OF THE HINO NIGHT-MARE.
NATURALLY HE HOLDS A GRUDGE AGAINST THE POLICE THAT FAILED HIM!
AND YOU'RE FOLLOWING ORDERS...
...FROM A MAN WHO CAN'T KEEP HIS PERSONAL BUSINESS SEPARATE FROM WORK?!
Control yourself, Iku.
It will reflect badly...
...on the library.

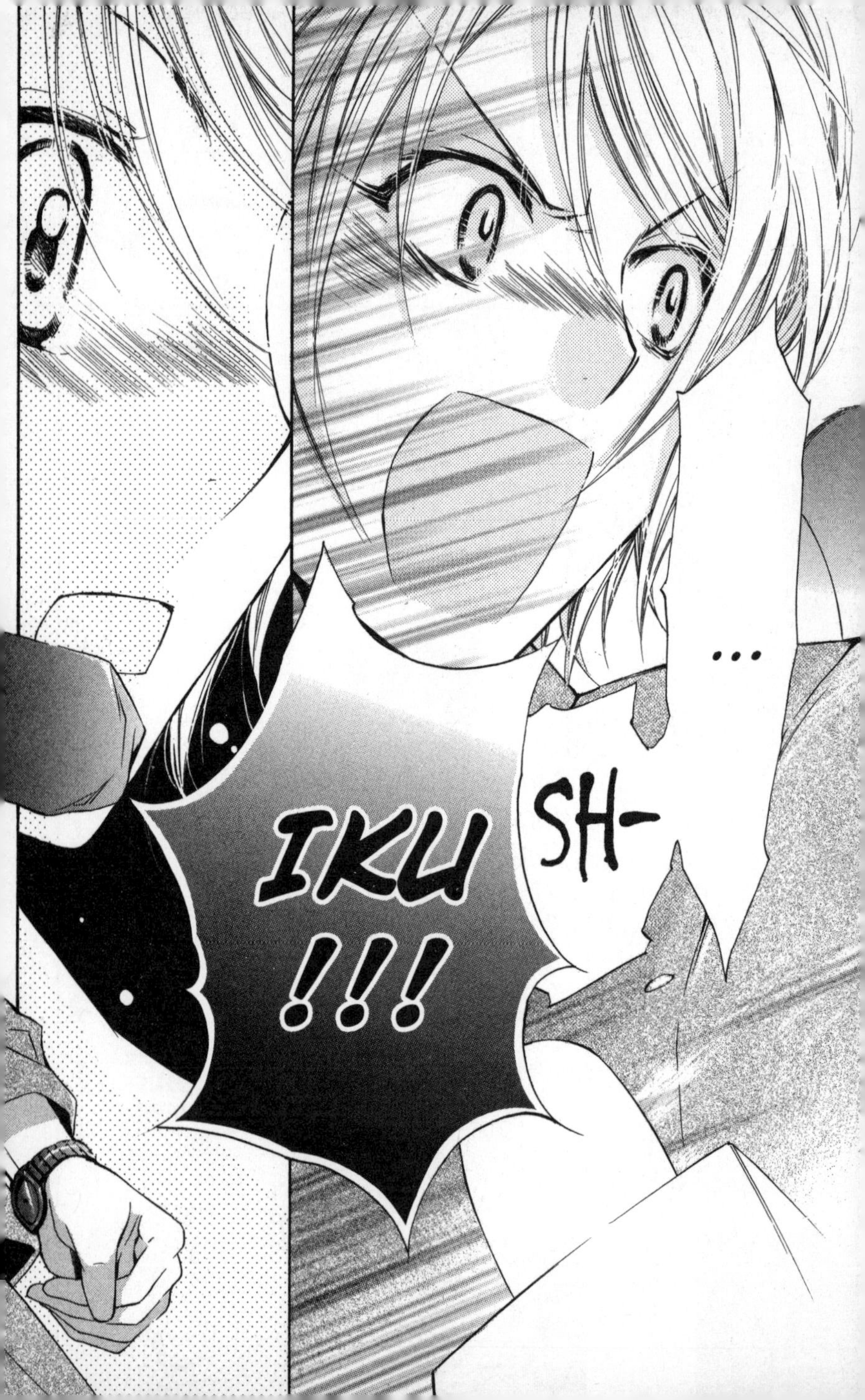
...
SH-
IKU !!!

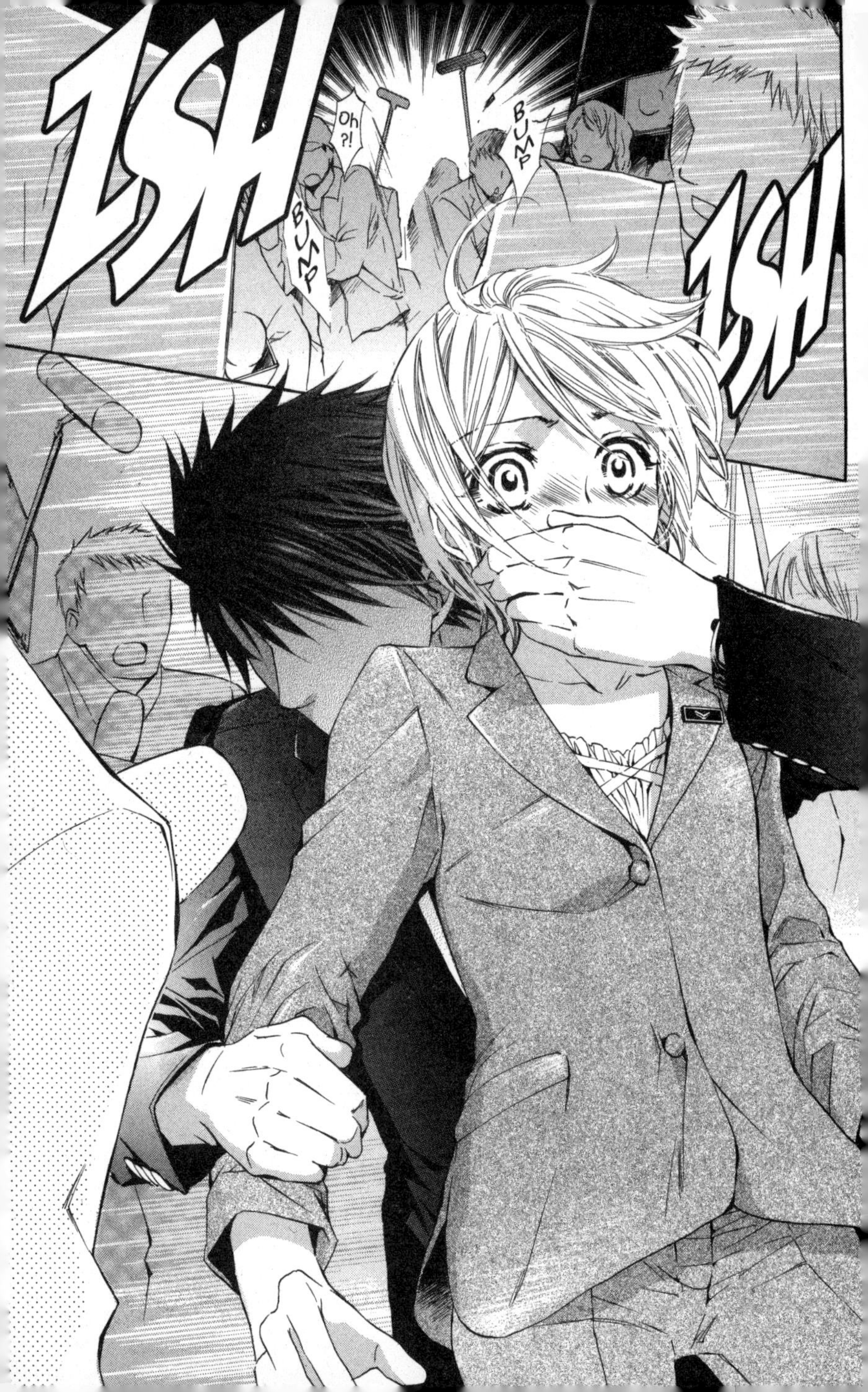
ZSH
BUMP
Oh?!
BUMP
ZSH

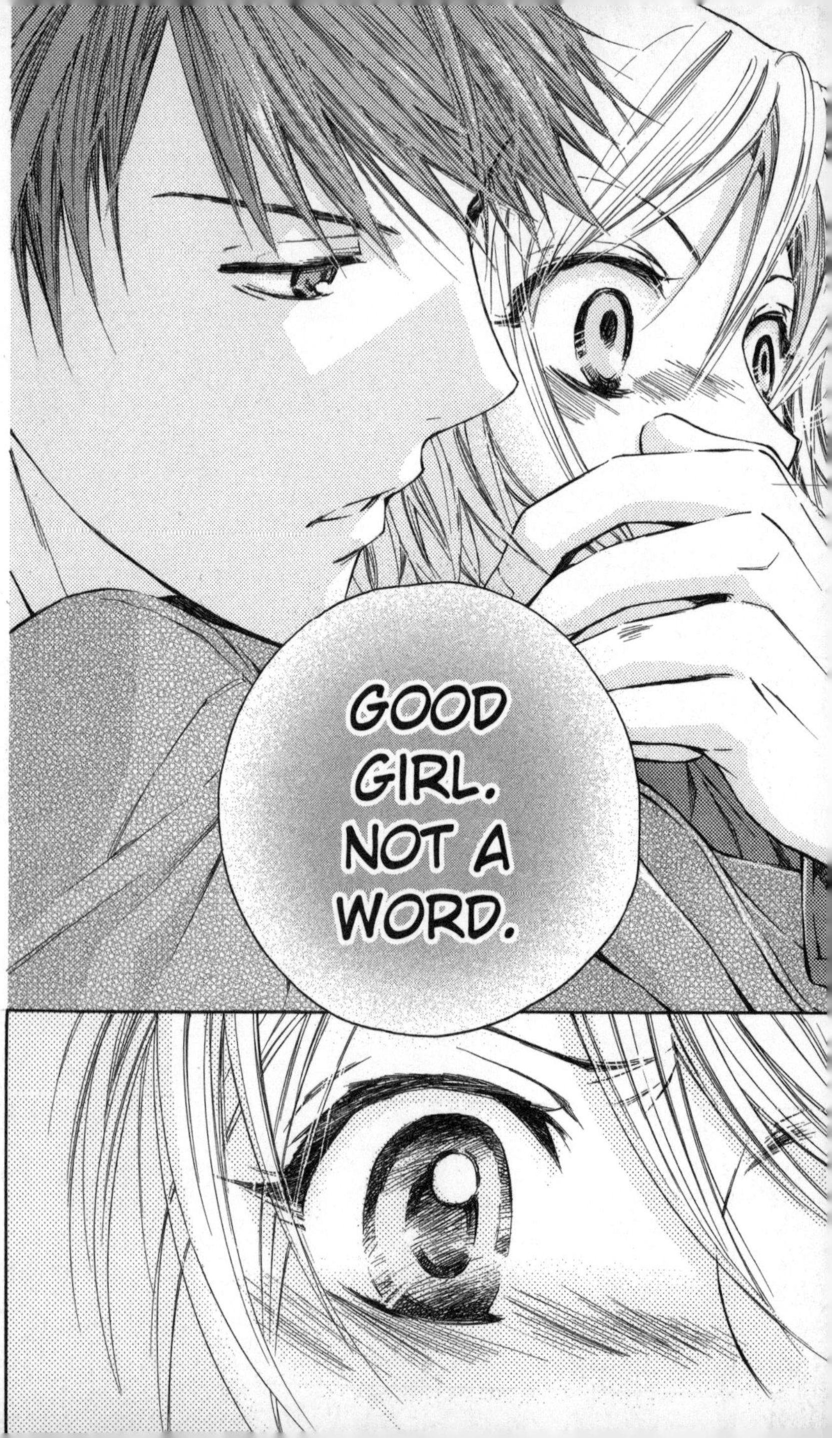
GOOD GIRL. NOT A WORD.

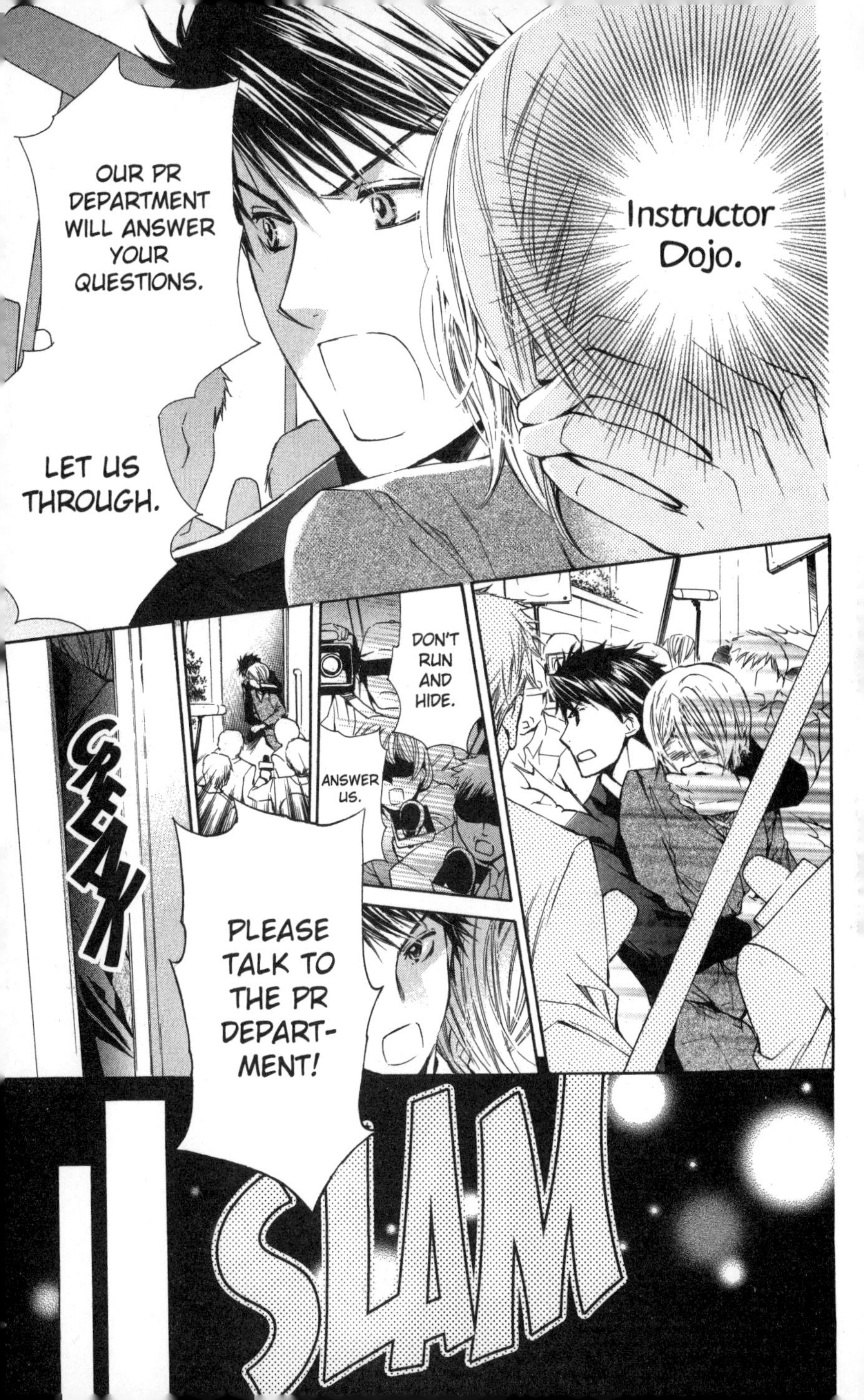
Instructor Dojo.
OUR PR DEPARTMENT WILL ANSWER YOUR QUESTIONS.
LET US THROUGH.
DON'T RUN AND HIDE.
ANSWER US.
PLEASE TALK TO THE PR DEPART-MENT!
CREAK
SLAM

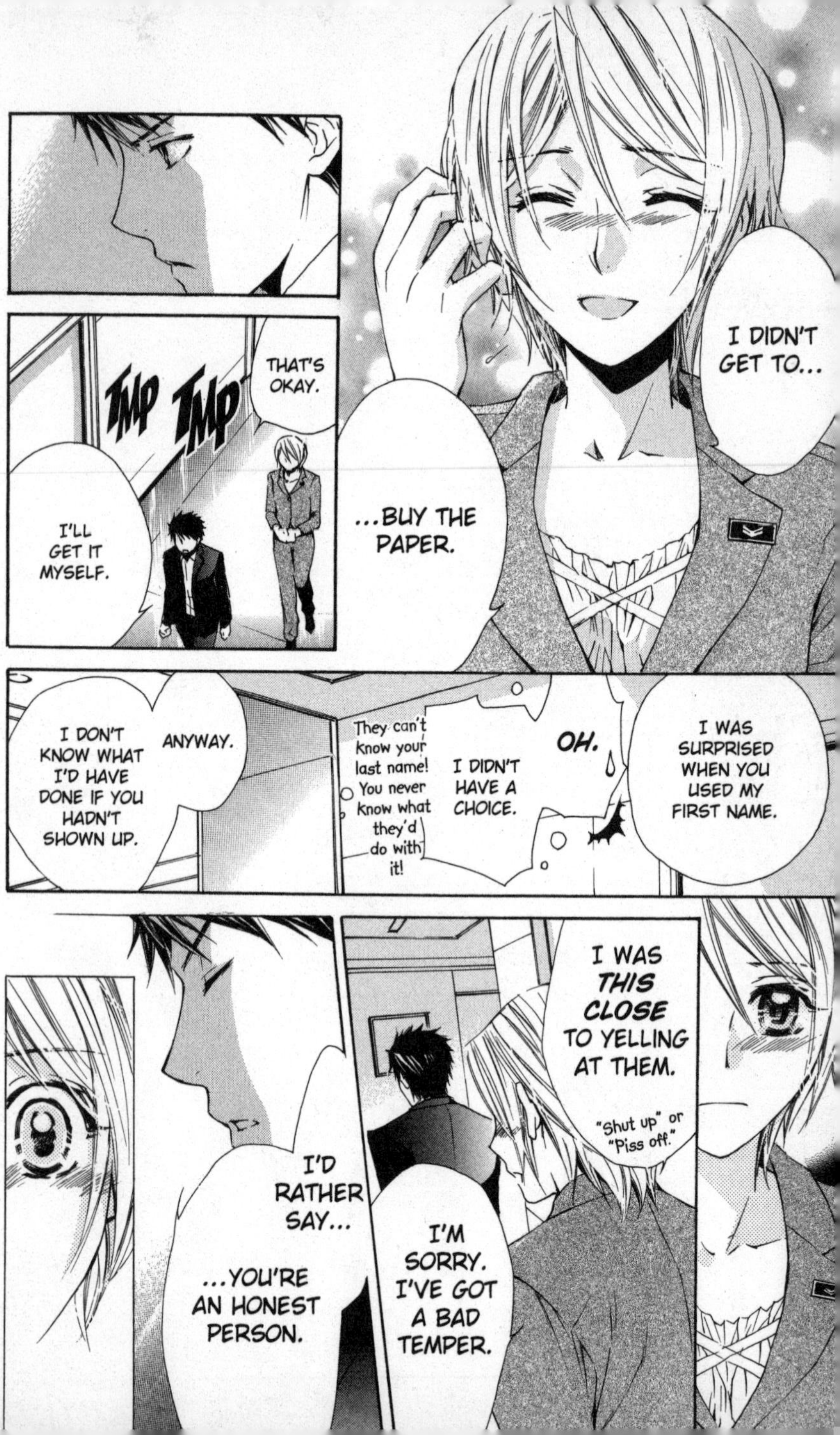
I DIDN'T GET TO...
...BUY THE PAPER.
TMP TMP
THAT'S OKAY.
I'LL GET IT MYSELF.
I WAS SURPRISED WHEN YOU USED MY FIRST NAME.
OH.
I DIDN'T HAVE A CHOICE.
They can't know your last name! You never know what they'd do with it!
ANYWAY.
I DON'T KNOW WHAT I'D HAVE DONE IF YOU HADN'T SHOWN UP.
I WAS THIS CLOSE TO YELLING AT THEM.
"Shut up" or "Piss off."
I'M SORRY. I'VE GOT A BAD TEMPER.
I'D RATHER SAY...
...YOU'RE AN HONEST PERSON.

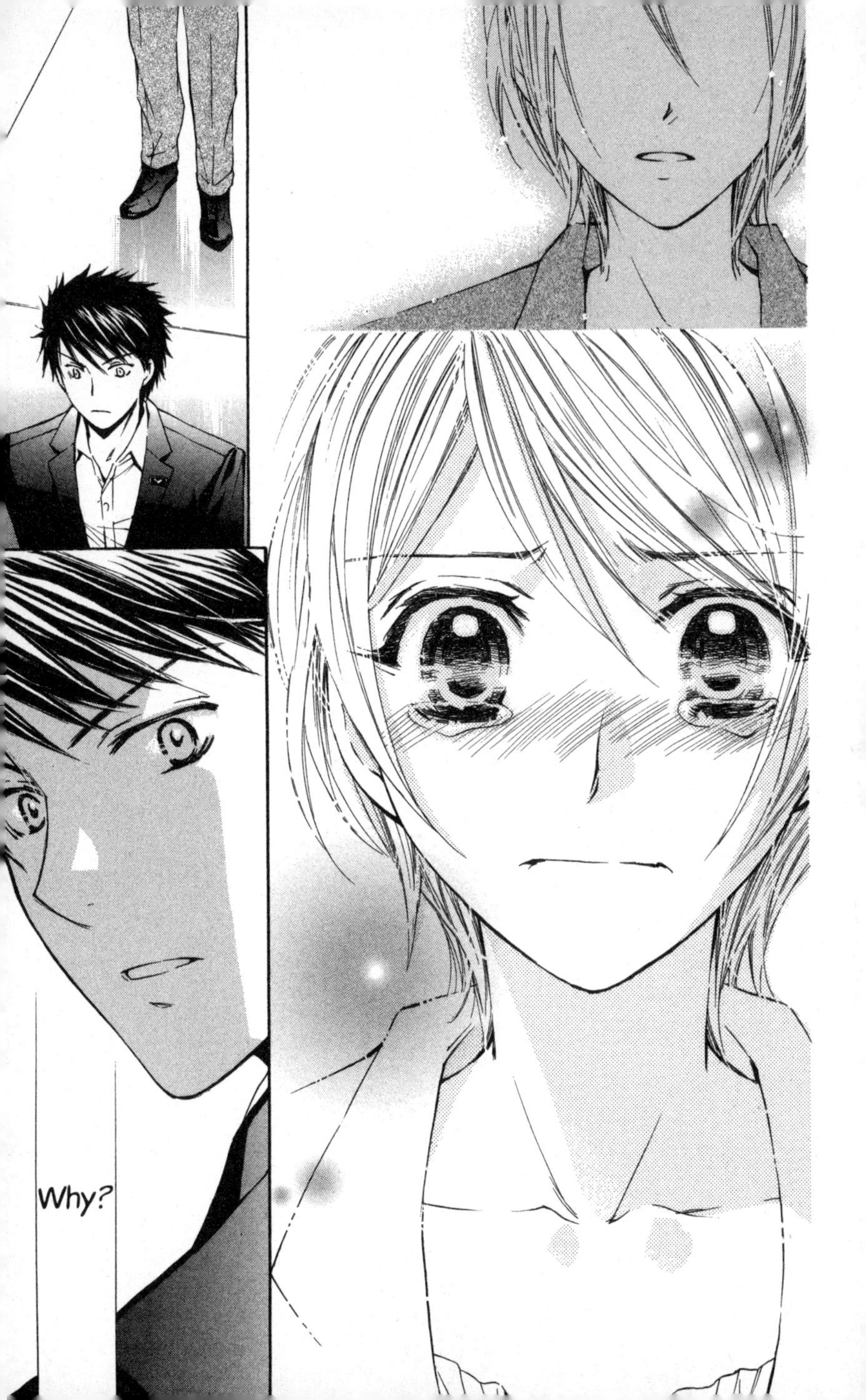
Why?

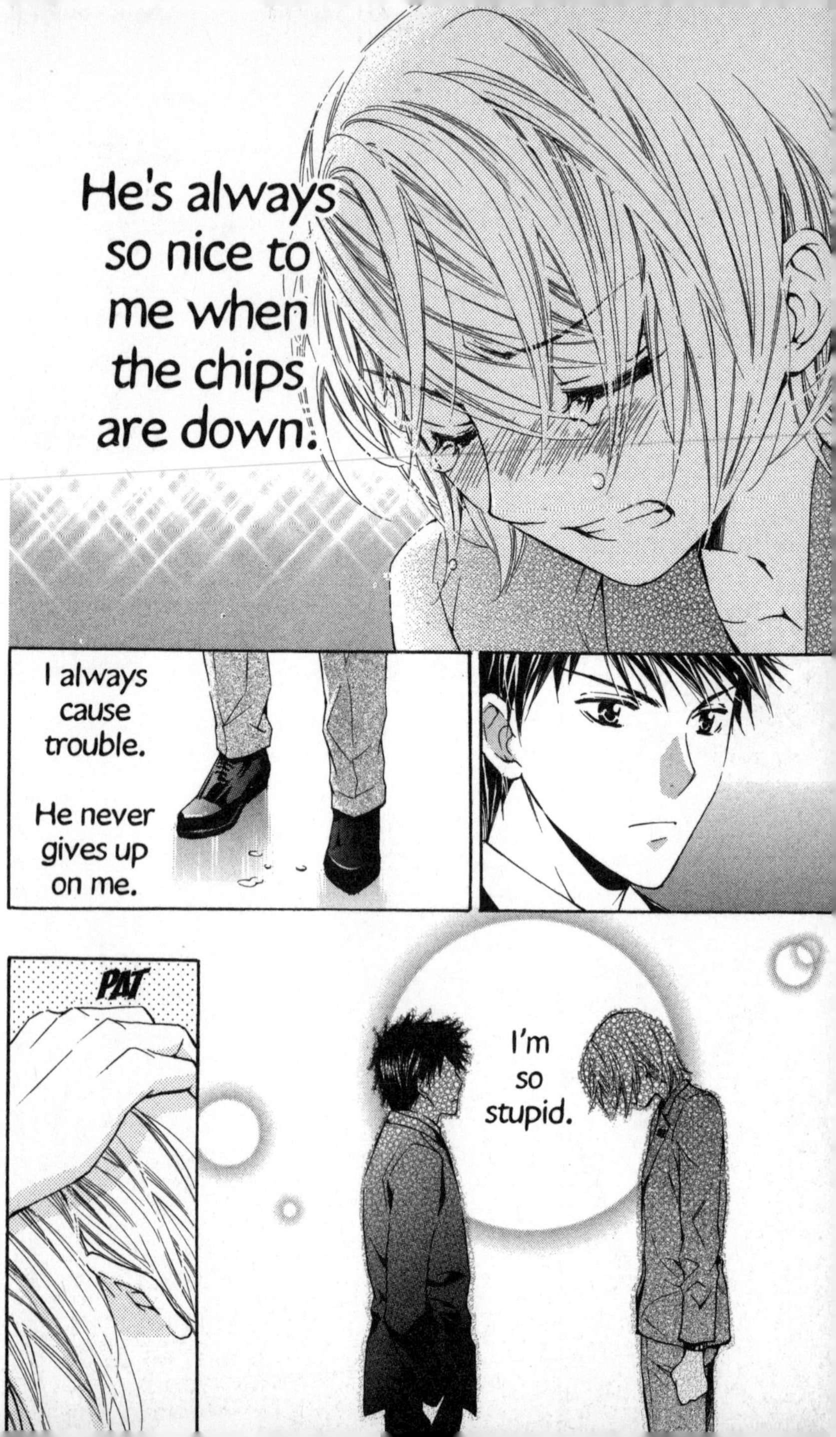
He's always so nice to me when the chips are down.
I always cause trouble.
He never gives up on me.
I'm so stupid.
PAT

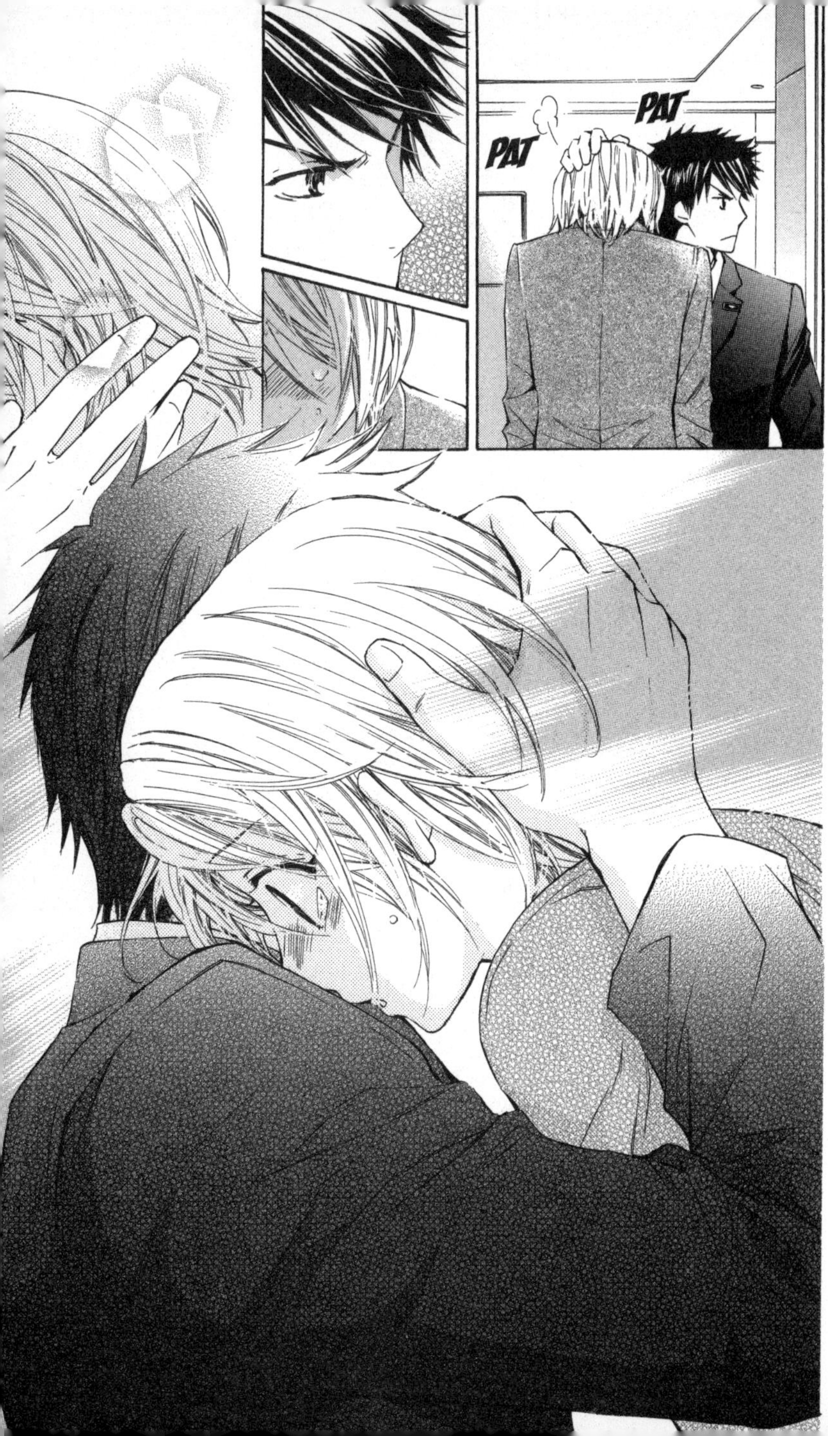
PAT
PAT

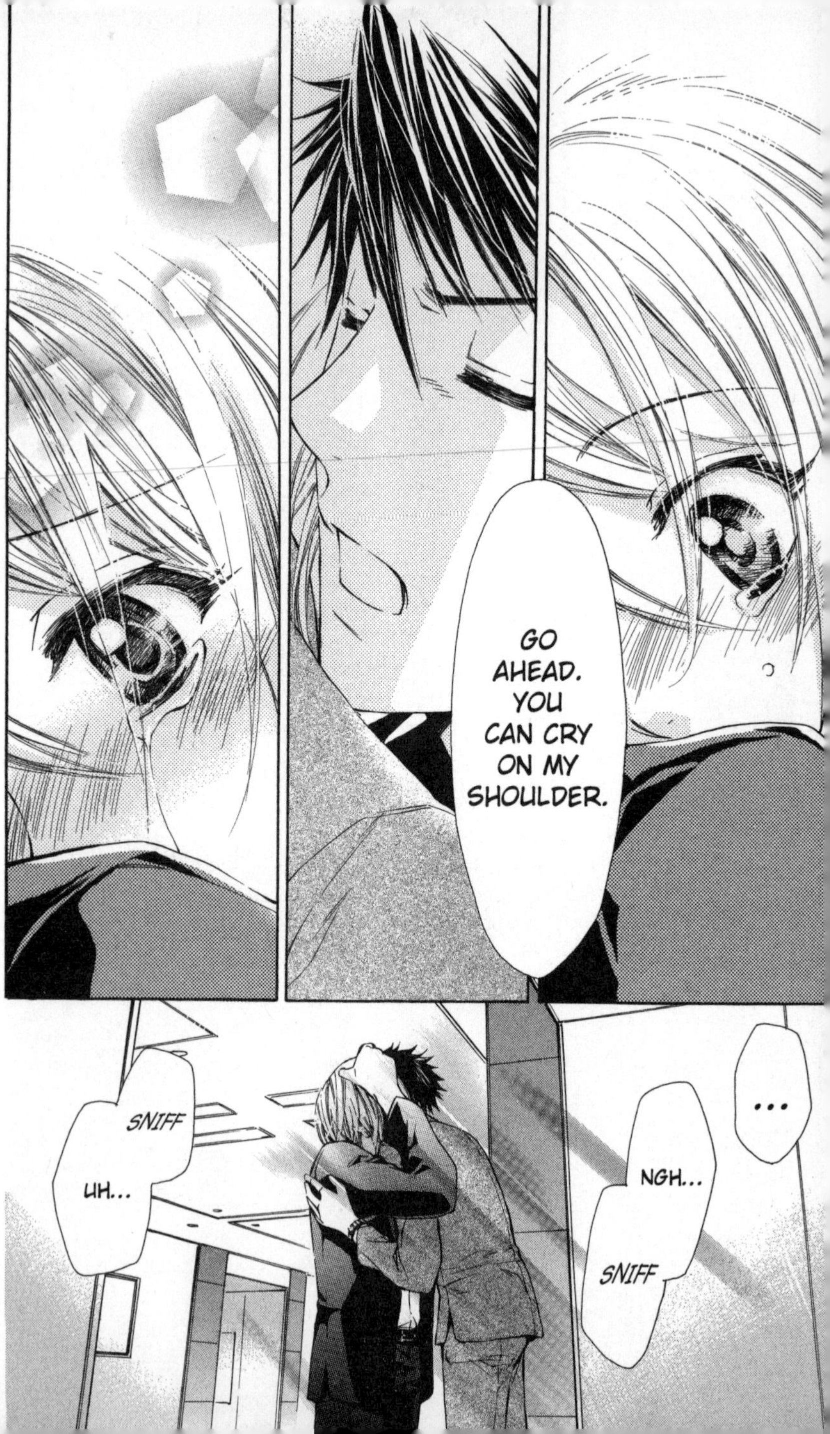
GO AHEAD. YOU CAN CRY ON MY SHOULDER.
...
NGH...
SNIFF
SNIFF
UH...

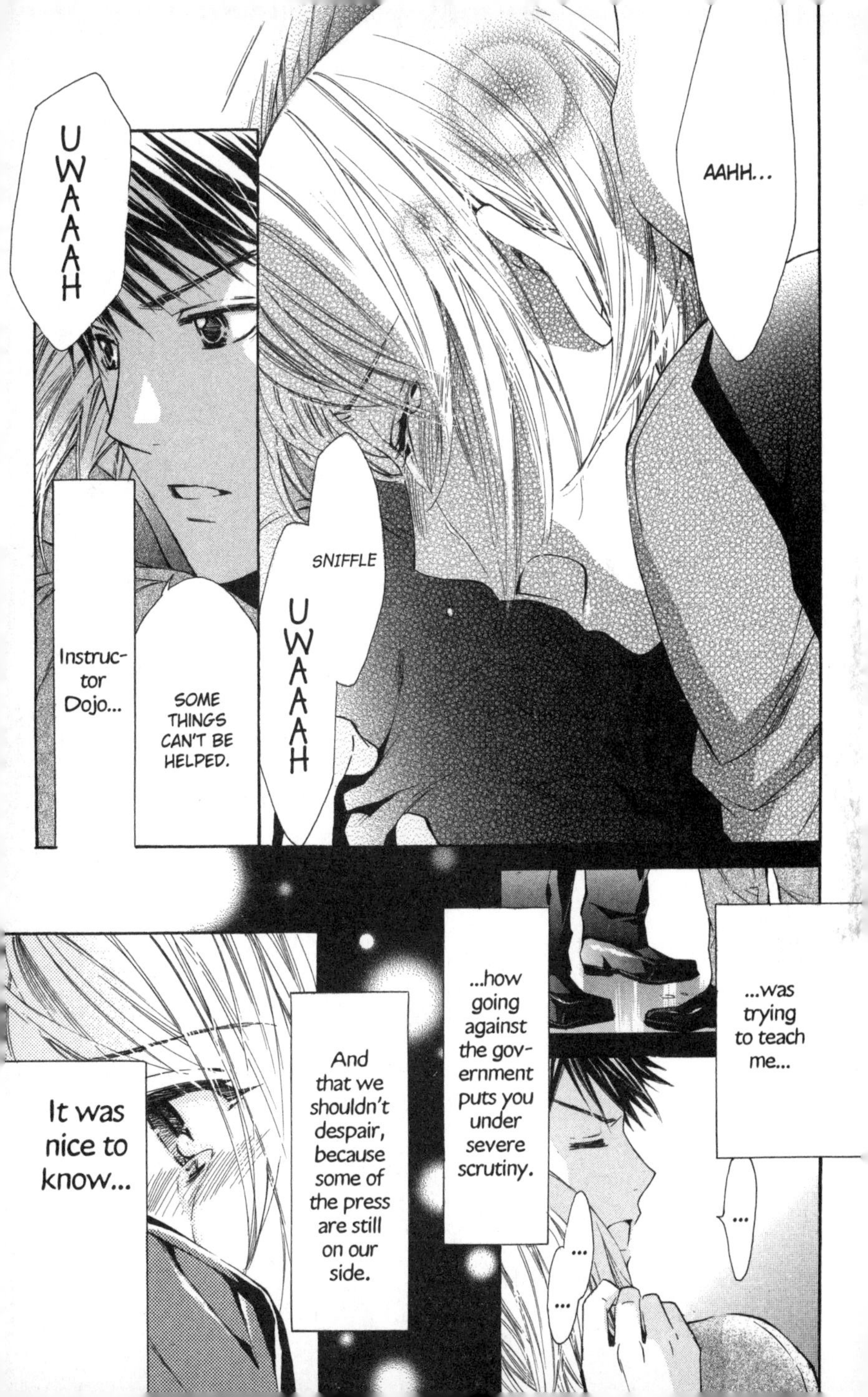

AAHH...
SNIFFLE
UWAAAAH
UWAAAAH
SOME THINGS CAN'T BE HELPED.
Instruc-tor Dojo...
...was trying to teach me...
...
...
...
...how going against the gov-ernment puts you under severe scrutiny.
And that we shouldn't despair, because some of the press are still on our side.
It was nice to know...

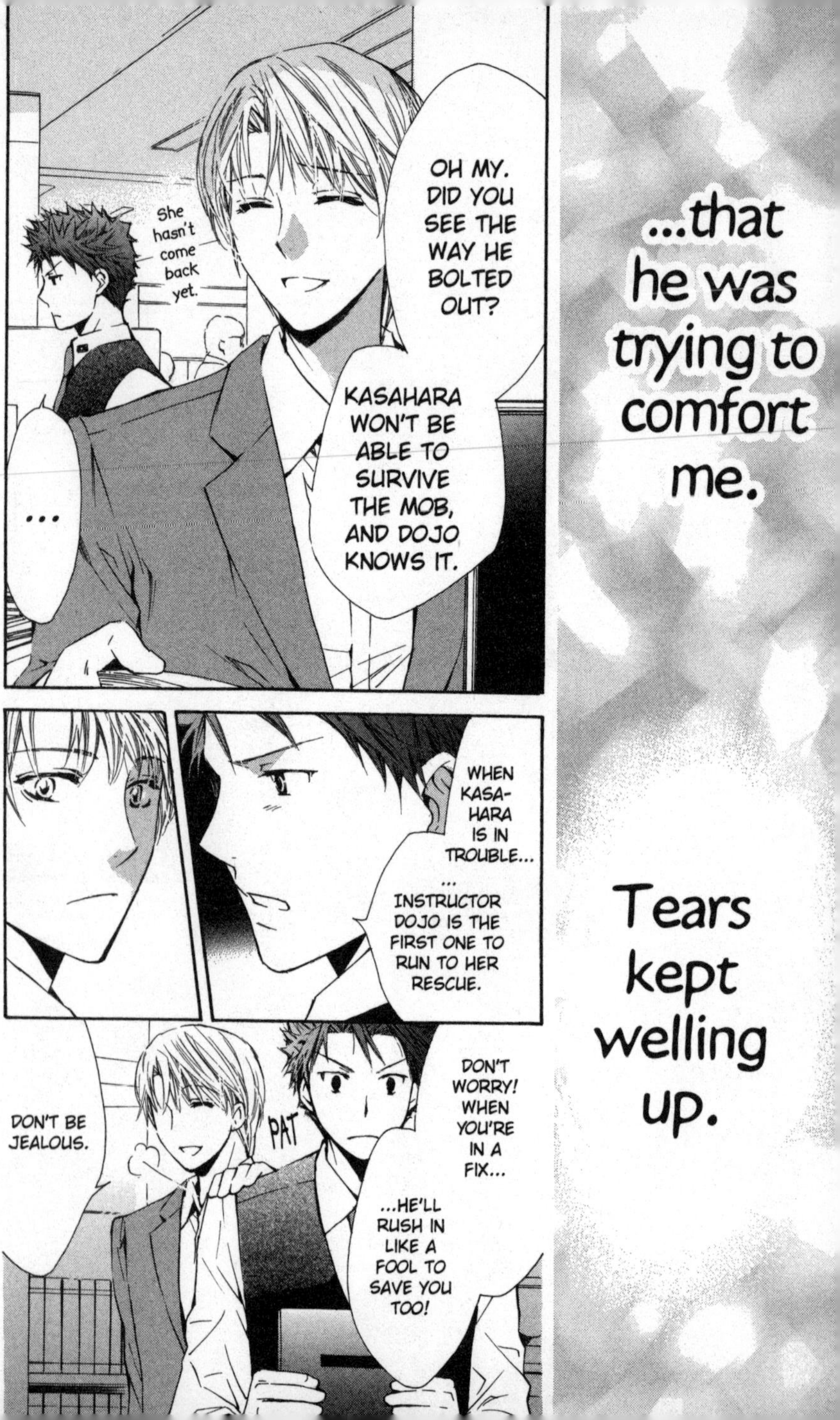
...that he was trying to comfort me.
Tears kept welling up.
OH MY. DID YOU SEE THE WAY HE BOLTED OUT?
KASAHARA WON'T BE ABLE TO SURVIVE THE MOB, AND DOJO KNOWS IT.
She hasn't come back yet.
...
WHEN KASAHARA IS IN TROUBLE...
...INSTRUCTOR DOJO IS THE FIRST ONE TO RUN TO HER RESCUE.
DON'T WORRY! WHEN YOU'RE IN A FIX...
...HE'LL RUSH IN LIKE A FOOL TO SAVE YOU TOO!
PAT
DON'T BE JEALOUS.

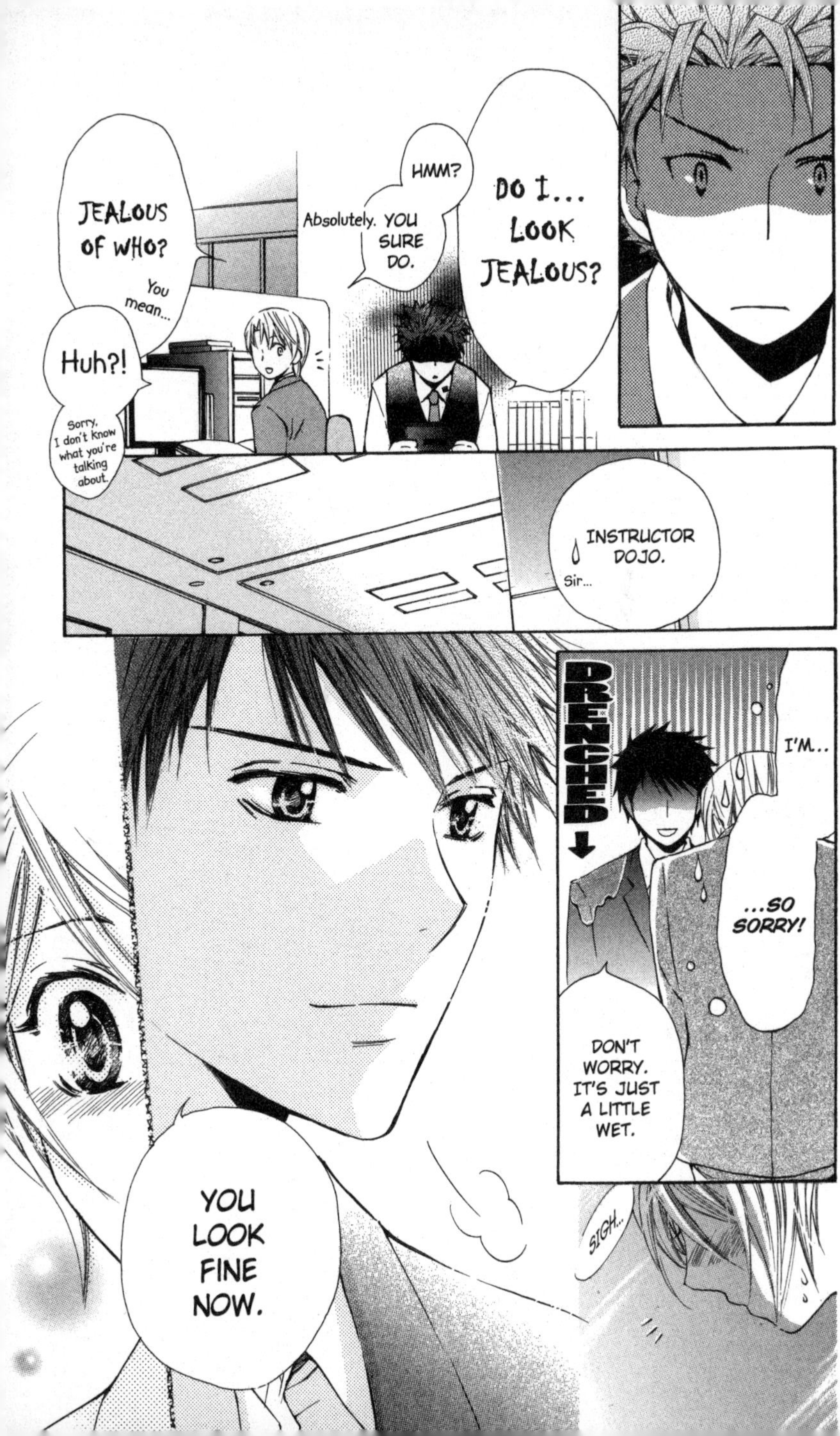
DO I... LOOK JEALOUS?
HMM?
Absolutely. YOU SURE DO.
JEALOUS OF WHO?
You mean...
Huh?!
Sorry, I don't know what you're talking about.
INSTRUCTOR DOJO.
Sir...
I'M...
...SO SORRY!
DRENCHED
DON'T WORRY. IT'S JUST A LITTLE WET.
SIGH...
YOU LOOK FINE NOW.

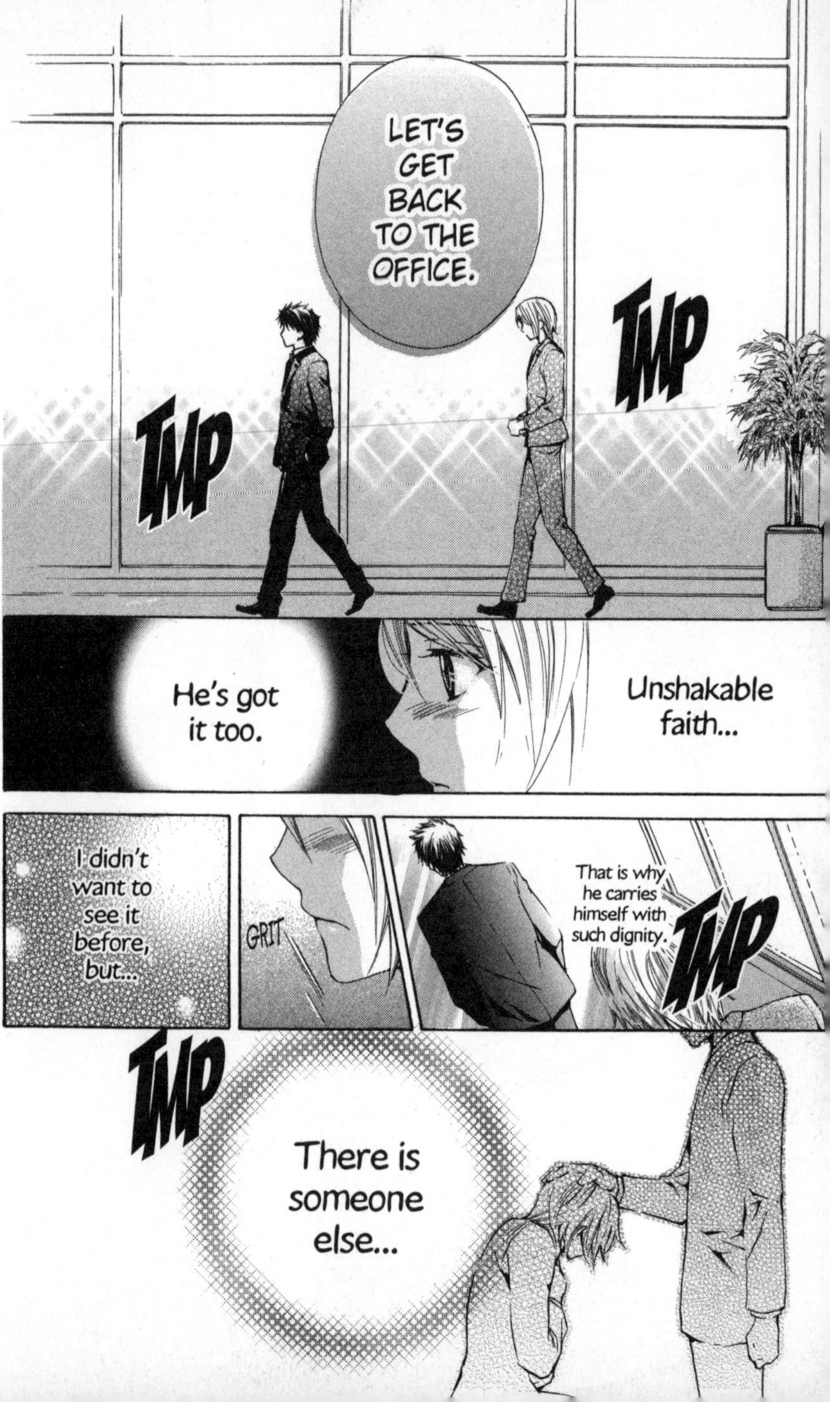
LET'S GET BACK TO THE OFFICE.
TMP
TMP
Unshakable faith...
He's got it too.
That is why he carries himself with such dignity.
TMP
GRIT
I didn't want to see it before, but...
TMP
There is someone else...

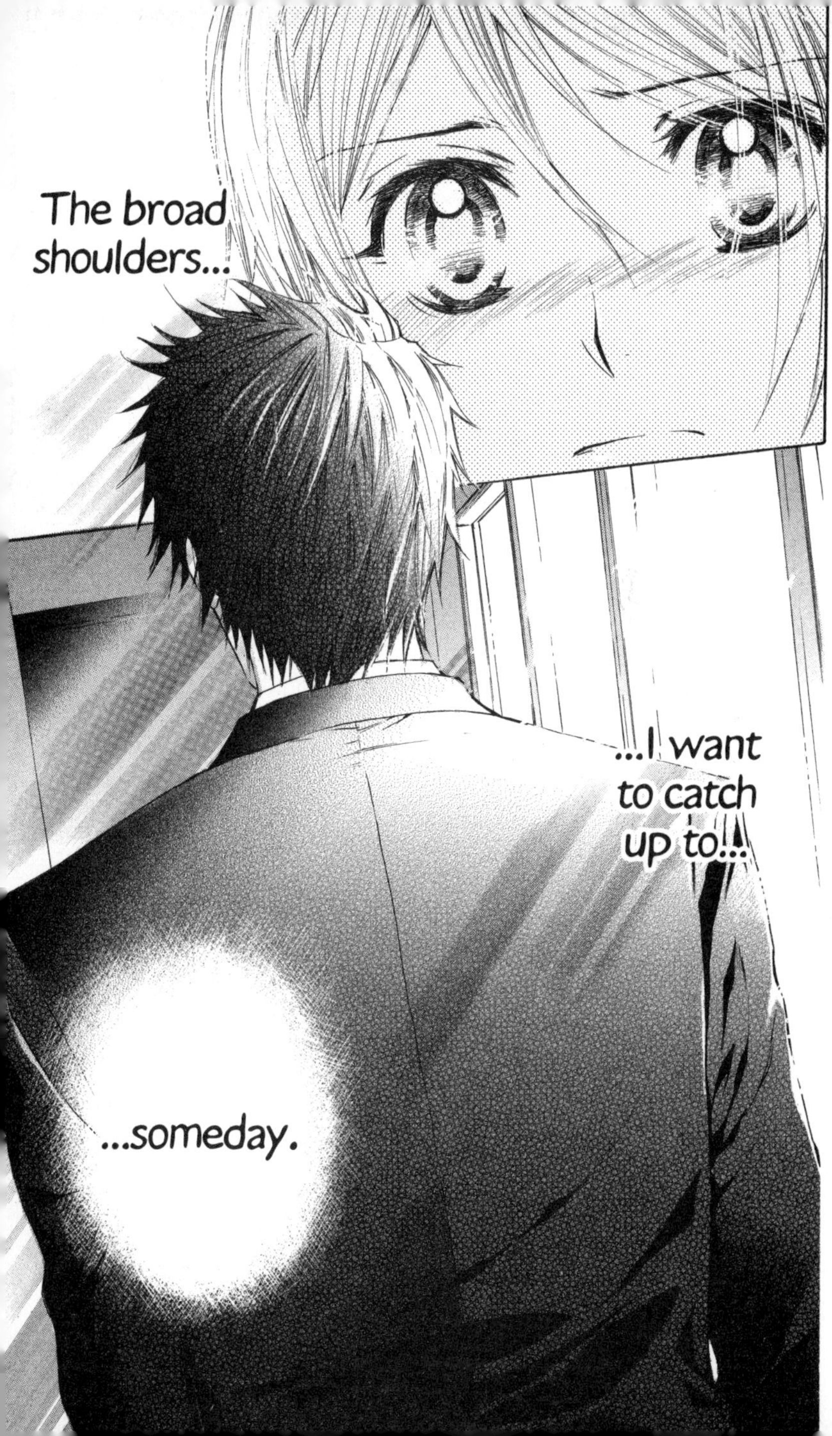
The broad shoulders...
...I want to catch up to...
...someday.

Secret Admirer

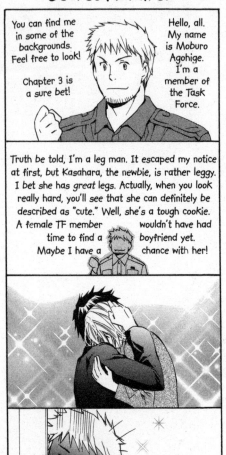

Hello, all. My name is Moburo Agohige. I'm a member of the Task Force.
You can find me in some of the backgrounds. Feel free to look!
Chapter 3 is a sure bet!
Truth be told, I'm a leg man. It escaped my notice at first, but Kasahara, the newbie, is rather leggy. I bet she has *great* legs. Actually, when you look really hard, you'll see that she can definitely be described as "cute." Well, she's a tough cookie.
A female TF member wouldn't have had time to find a boyfriend yet.
Maybe I have a chance with her!
Or not.

CHAPTER 9

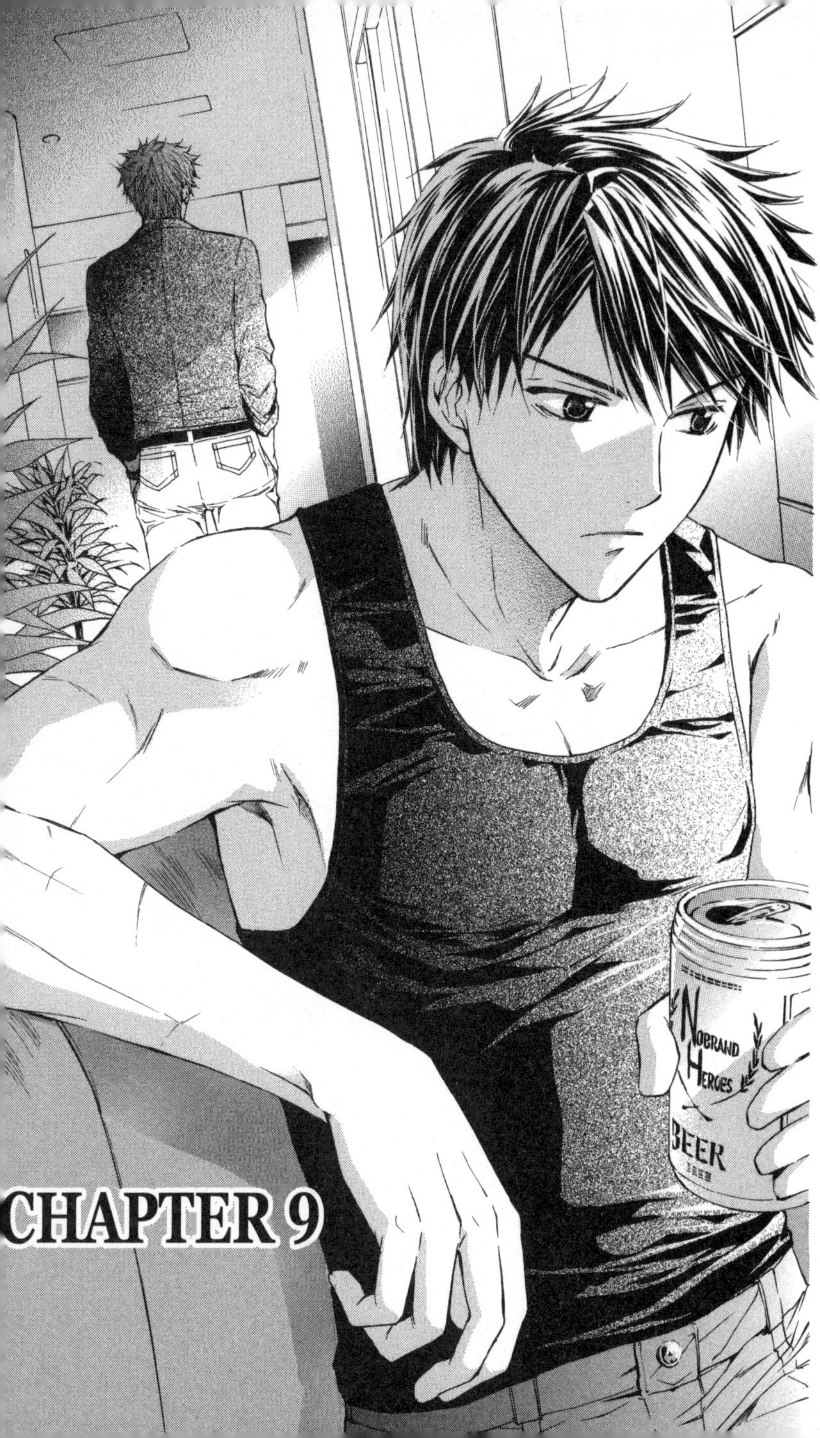
NOBRAND HEROES
BEER

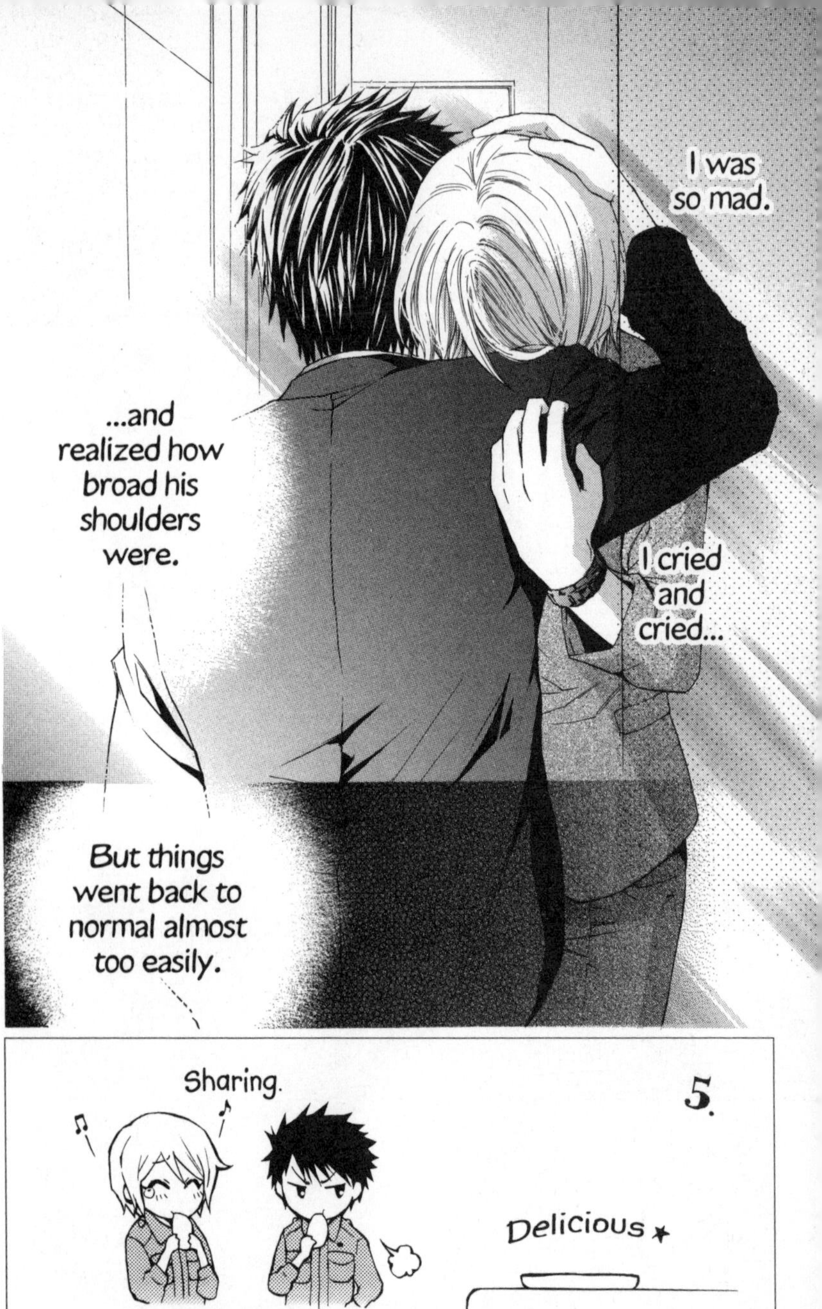
I was so mad.
I cried and cried...
...and realized how broad his shoulders were.
But things went back to normal almost too easily.
5.
Delicious★
Sharing.

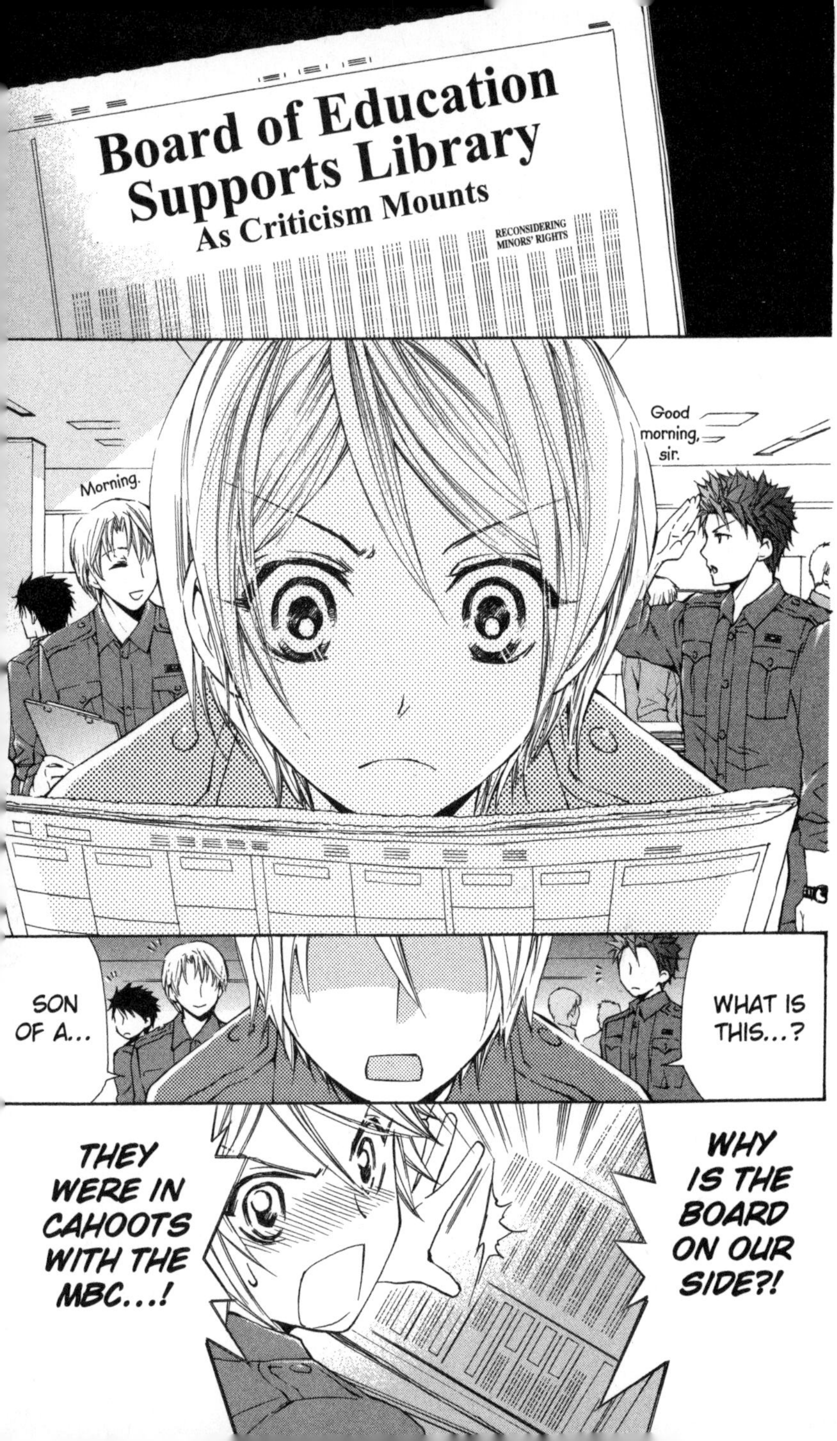
Board of Education Supports Library
As Criticism Mounts
RECONSIDERING MINORS' RIGHTS
Good morning, sir.
Morning.
WHAT IS THIS...?
SON OF A...
WHY IS THE BOARD ON OUR SIDE?!
THEY WERE IN CAHOOTS WITH THE MBC...!

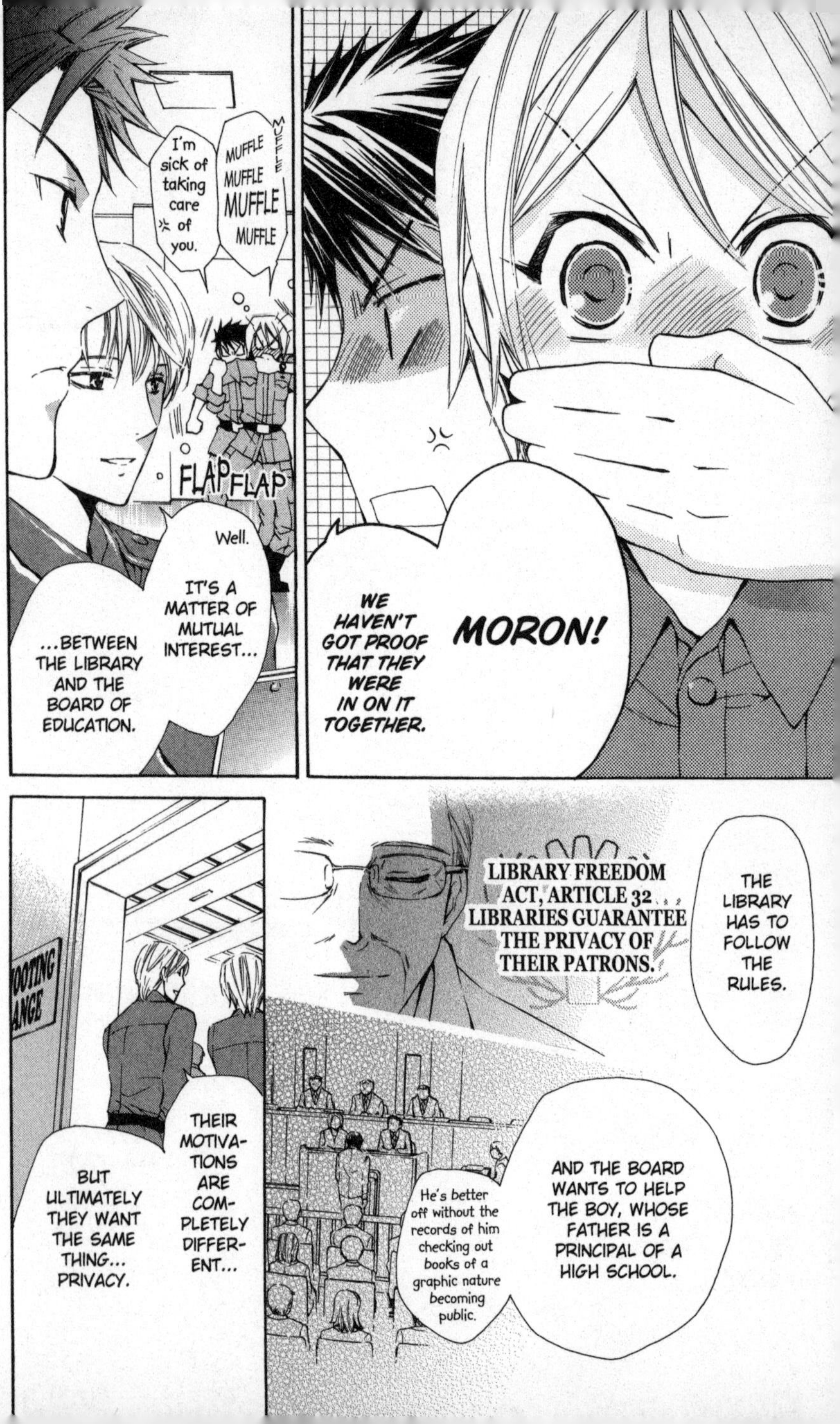
MORON!
WE HAVEN'T GOT PROOF THAT THEY WERE IN ON IT TOGETHER.
MUFFLE
MUFFLE MUFFLE MUFFLE MUFFLE
I'm sick of taking care of you.
FLAP FLAP
Well.
IT'S A MATTER OF MUTUAL INTEREST...
...BETWEEN THE LIBRARY AND THE BOARD OF EDUCATION.
THE LIBRARY HAS TO FOLLOW THE RULES.
LIBRARY FREEDOM ACT, ARTICLE 32 . . . LIBRARIES GUARANTEE THE PRIVACY OF THEIR PATRONS.
AND THE BOARD WANTS TO HELP THE BOY, WHOSE FATHER IS A PRINCIPAL OF A HIGH SCHOOL.
He's better off without the records of him checking out books of a graphic nature becoming public.
THEIR MOTIVATIONS ARE COMPLETELY DIFFERENT...
BUT ULTIMATELY THEY WANT THE SAME THING... PRIVACY.

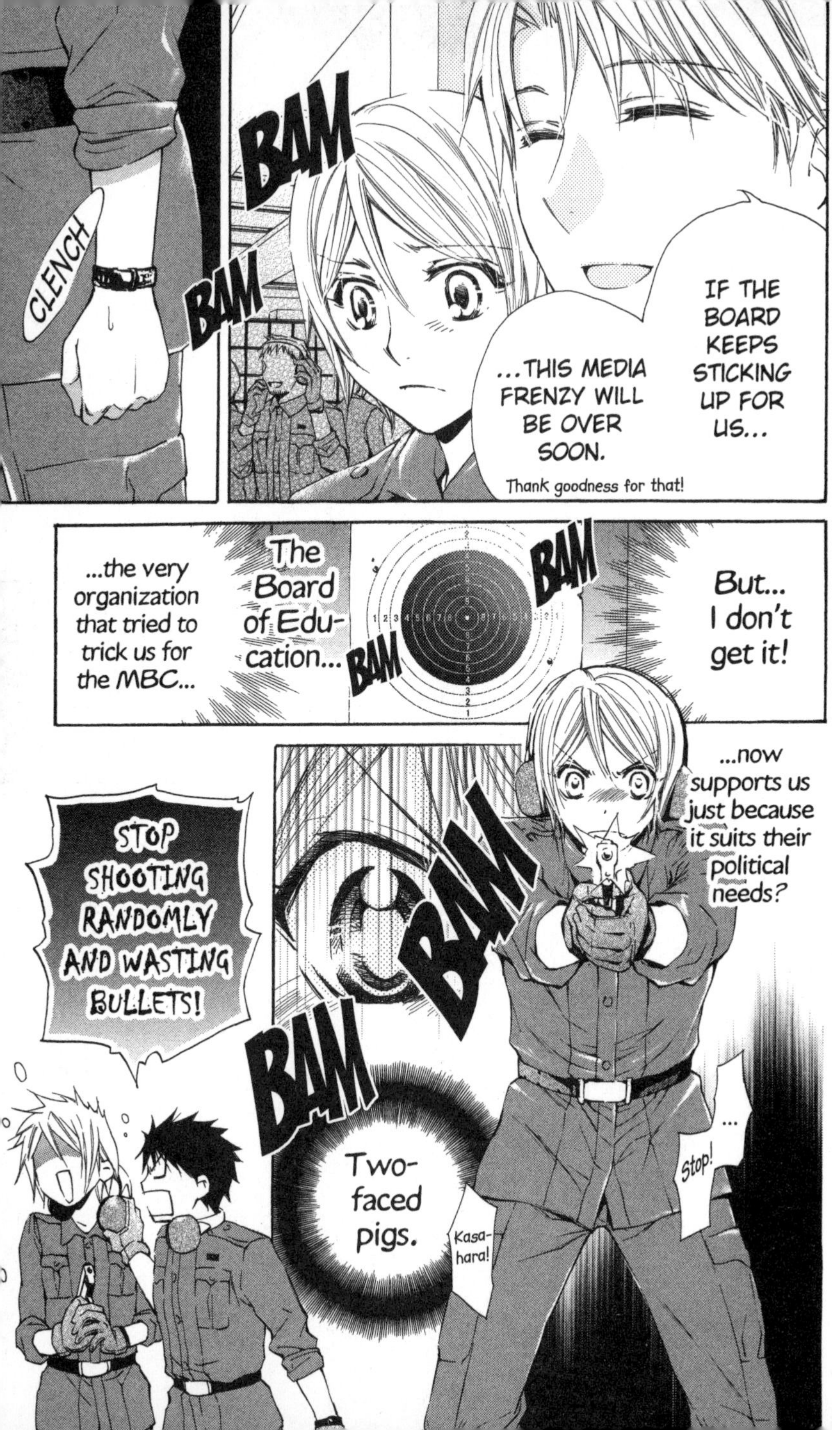
IF THE BOARD KEEPS STICKING UP FOR US...
...THIS MEDIA FRENZY WILL BE OVER SOON.
Thank goodness for that!
BAM
BAM
CLENCH
But... I don't get it!
BAM
BAM
The Board of Education...
...the very organization that tried to trick us for the MBC...
...now supports us just because it suits their political needs?
BAM
BAM
Two-faced pigs.
...
Stop!
Kasa-hara!
STOP SHOOTING RANDOMLY AND WASTING BULLETS!

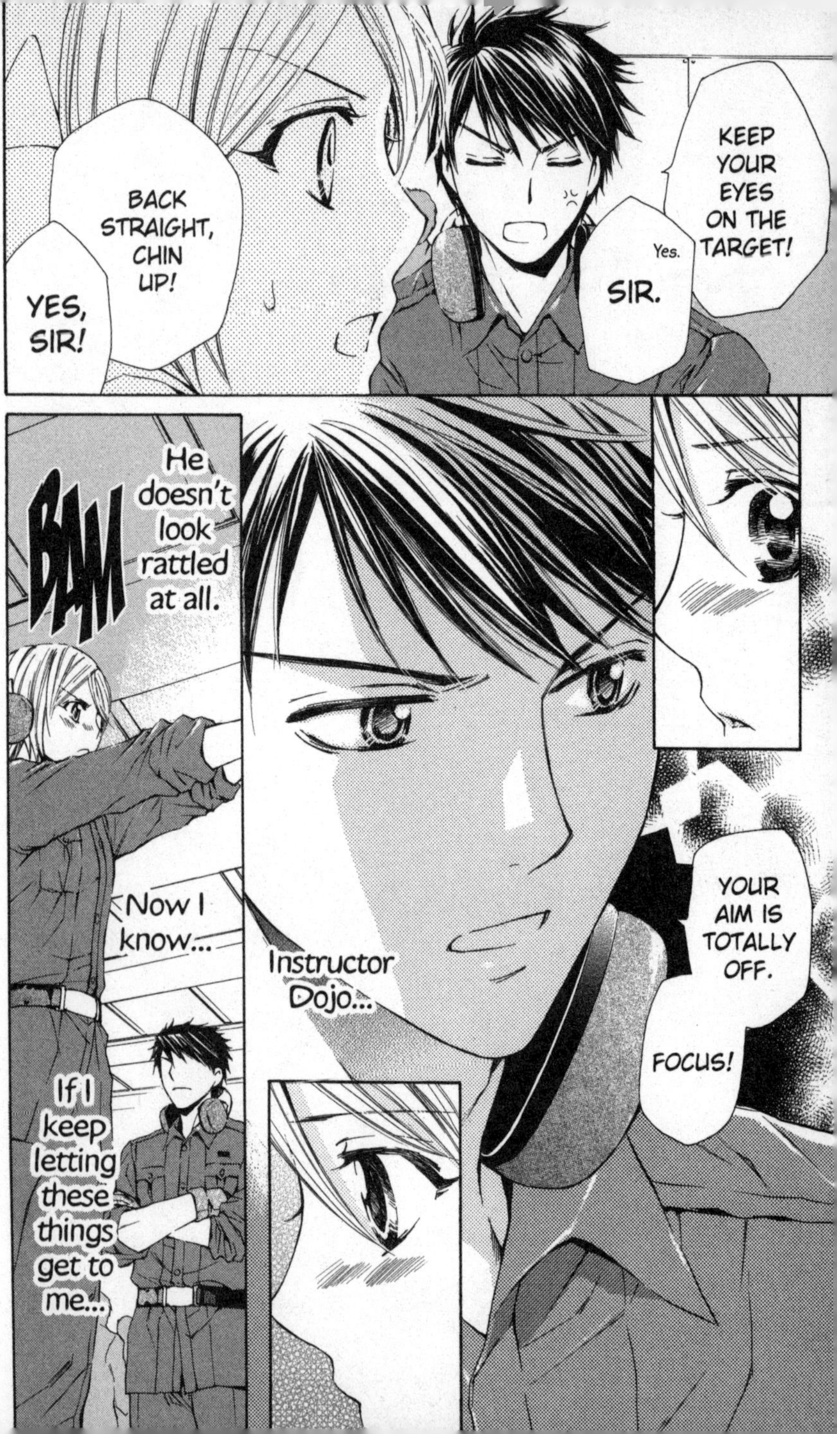
KEEP YOUR EYES ON THE TARGET!
Yes.
SIR.
BACK STRAIGHT, CHIN UP!
YES, SIR!
YOUR AIM IS TOTALLY OFF.
FOCUS!
Instructor Dojo...
BAM
He doesn't look rattled at all.
Now I know...
If I keep letting these things get to me...

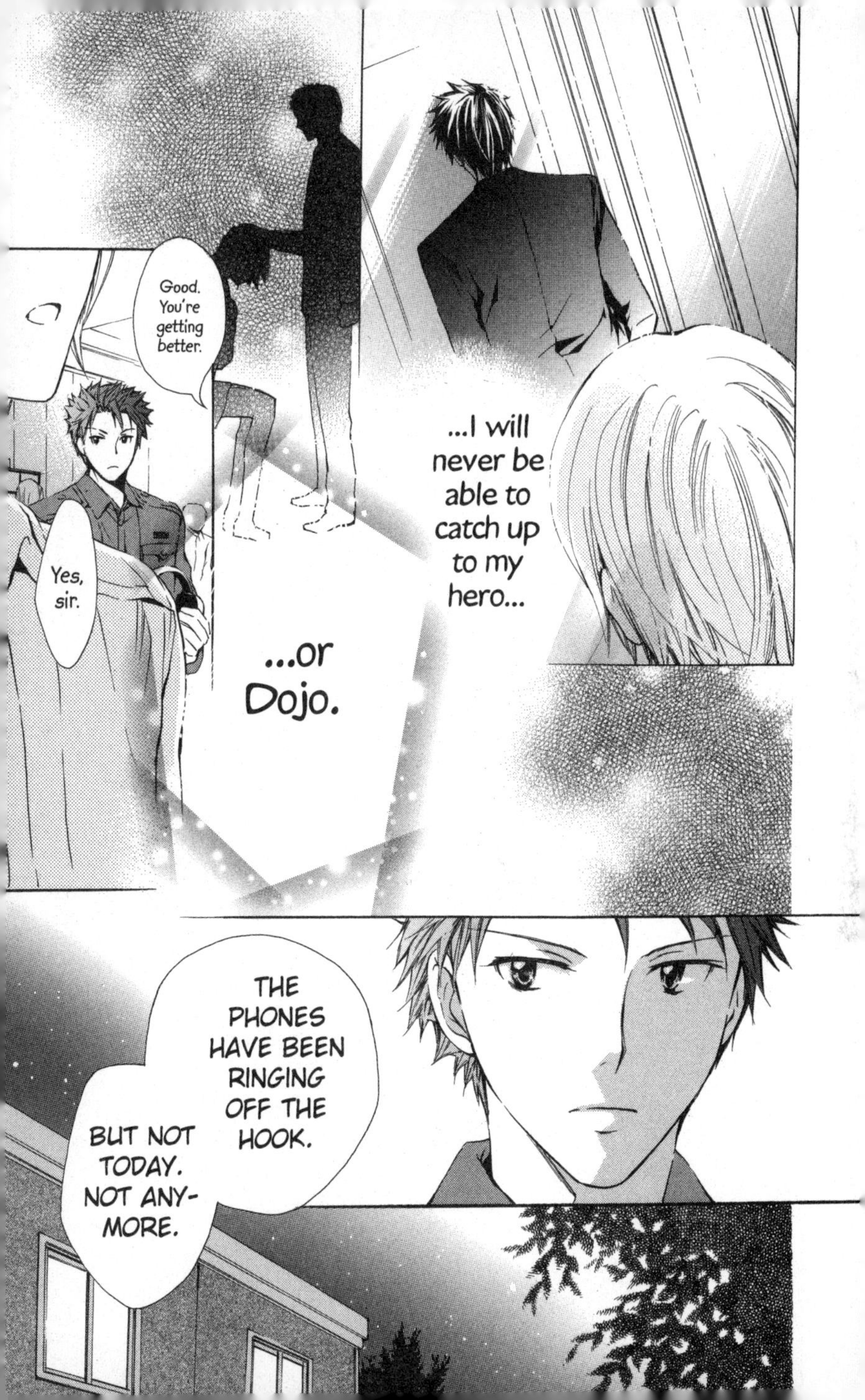
...I will never be able to catch up to my hero...
...or Dojo.
Good. You're getting better.
Yes, sir.
THE PHONES HAVE BEEN RINGING OFF THE HOOK.
BUT NOT TODAY. NOT ANY-MORE.

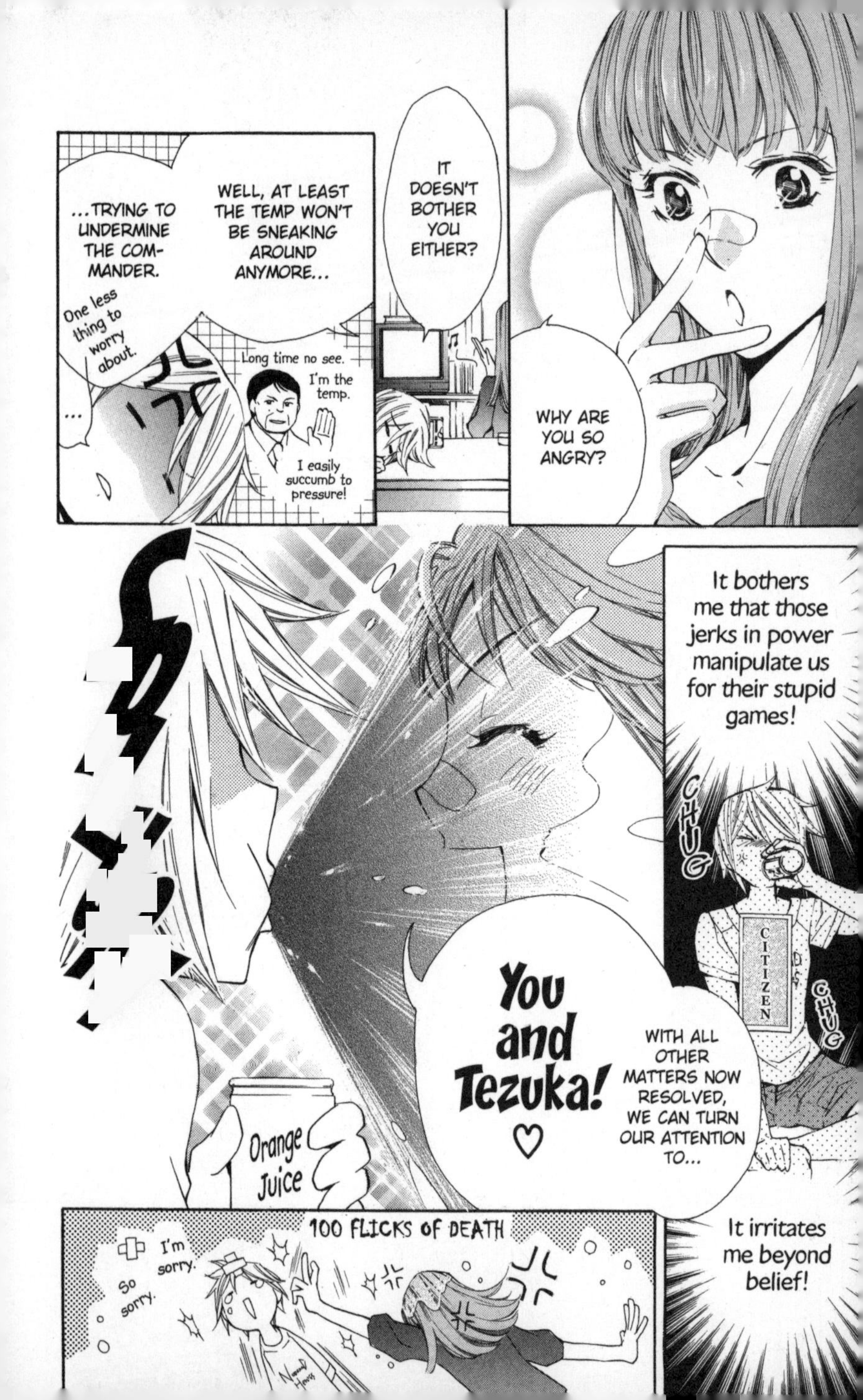
WHY ARE YOU SO ANGRY?
IT DOESN'T BOTHER YOU EITHER?
WELL, AT LEAST THE TEMP WON'T BE SNEAKING AROUND ANYMORE...
...TRYING TO UNDERMINE THE COM-MANDER.
One less thing to worry about.
...
Long time no see. I'm the temp.
I easily succumb to pressure!
It bothers me that those jerks in power manipulate us for their stupid games!
CHUG
CITIZEN
CHUG
WITH ALL OTHER MATTERS NOW RESOLVED, WE CAN TURN OUR ATTENTION TO...
You and Tezuka! ♡
Orange Juice
It irritates me beyond belief!
100 FLICKS OF DEATH
I'm sorry.
So sorry.

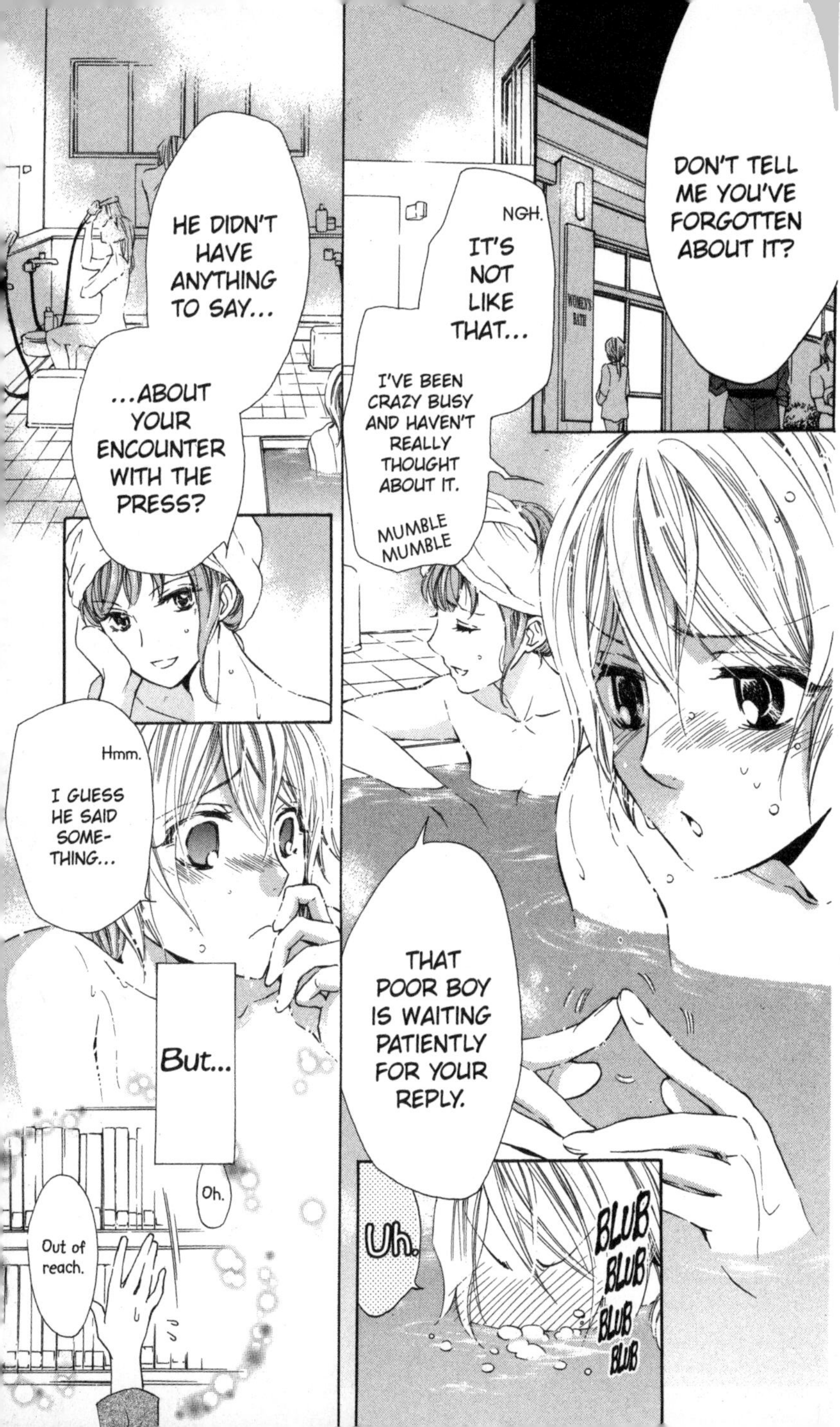
DON'T TELL ME YOU'VE FORGOTTEN ABOUT IT?
NGH.
IT'S NOT LIKE THAT...
I'VE BEEN CRAZY BUSY AND HAVEN'T REALLY THOUGHT ABOUT IT.
MUMBLE MUMBLE
THAT POOR BOY IS WAITING PATIENTLY FOR YOUR REPLY.
Uh.
BLUB BLUB BLUB BLUB
HE DIDN'T HAVE ANYTHING TO SAY...
...ABOUT YOUR ENCOUNTER WITH THE PRESS?
Hmm.
I GUESS HE SAID SOME-THING...
But...
Oh.
Out of reach.

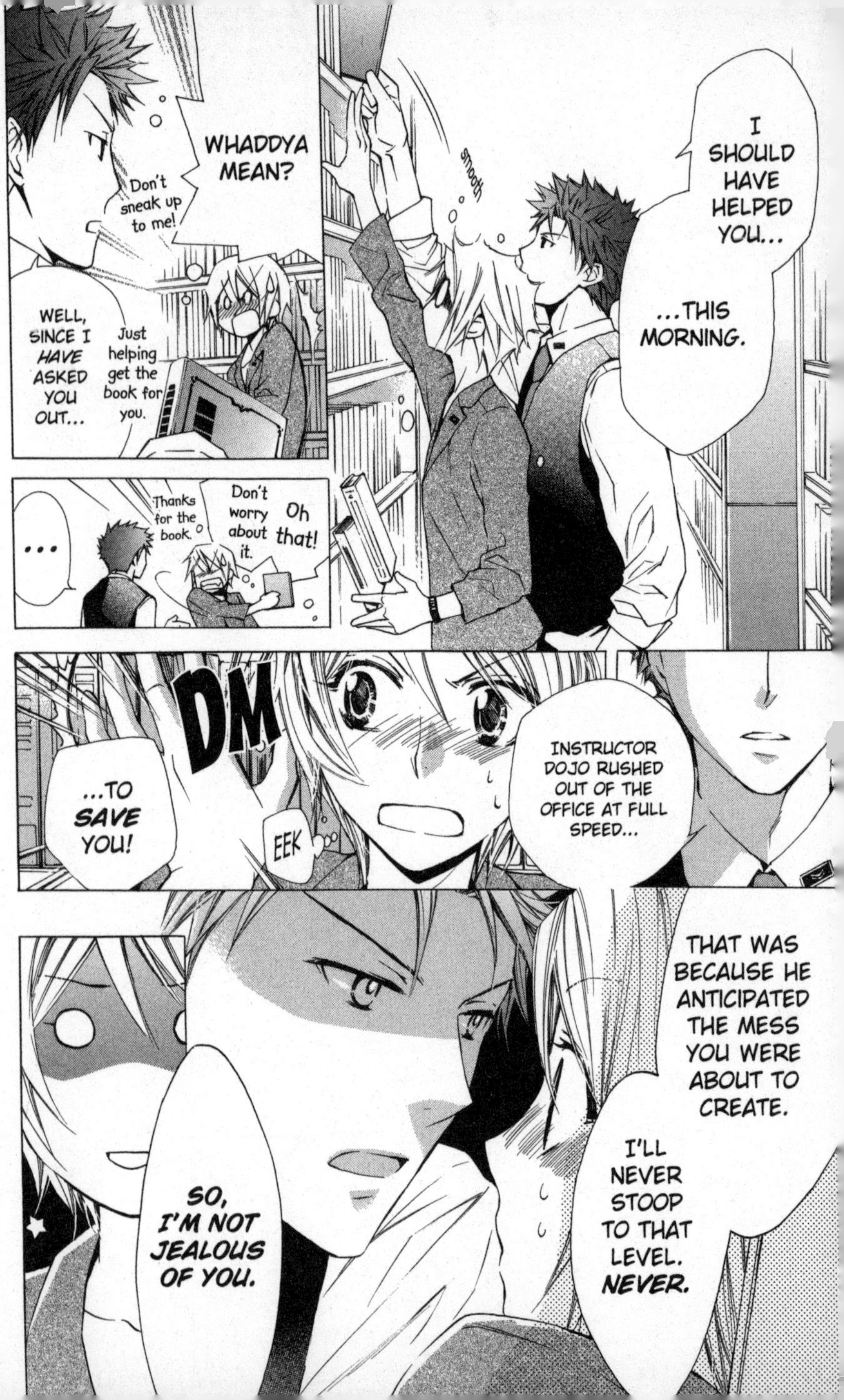

I SHOULD HAVE HELPED YOU...
...THIS MORNING.
smooth
WHADDYA MEAN?
Don't sneak up to me!
Just helping get the book for you.
WELL, SINCE I *HAVE* ASKED YOU OUT...
Oh that!
Don't worry about it.
Thanks for the book.
...
INSTRUCTOR DOJO RUSHED OUT OF THE OFFICE AT FULL SPEED...
DM
...TO *SAVE* YOU!
EEK
THAT WAS BECAUSE HE ANTICIPATED THE MESS YOU WERE ABOUT TO CREATE.
I'LL NEVER STOOP TO THAT LEVEL. ***NEVER.***
SO, I'M NOT JEALOUS OF YOU.

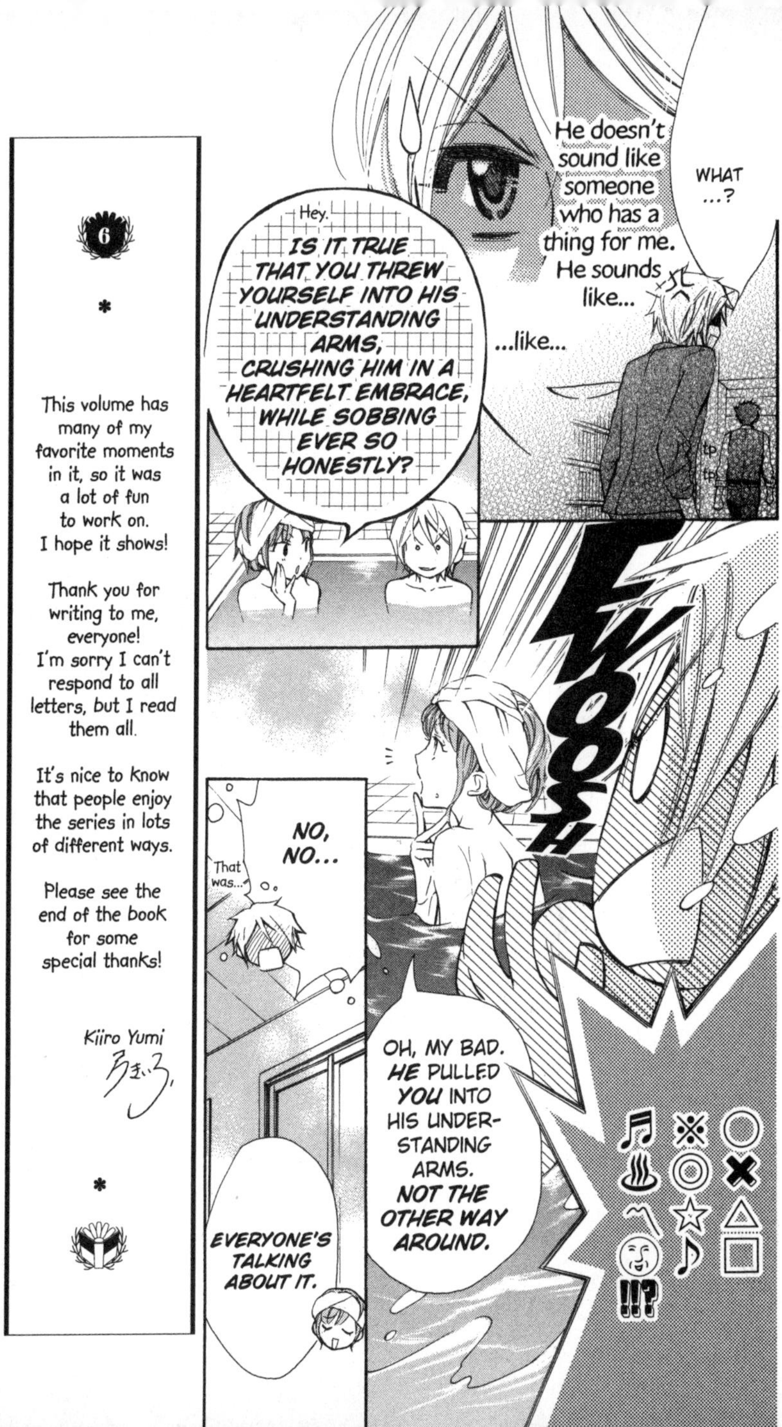
WHAT ...?
He doesn't sound like someone who has a thing for me. He sounds like...
...like...
tp tp
Hey.
IS IT TRUE THAT YOU THREW YOURSELF INTO HIS UNDERSTANDING ARMS, CRUSHING HIM IN A HEARTFELT EMBRACE, WHILE SOBBING EVER SO HONESTLY?
WHOOSH!
NO, NO...
That was...
OH, MY BAD. HE PULLED YOU INTO HIS UNDER-STANDING ARMS. NOT THE OTHER WAY AROUND.
EVERYONE'S TALKING ABOUT IT.

6

*

This volume has many of my favorite moments in it, so it was a lot of fun to work on. I hope it shows!

Thank you for writing to me, everyone! I'm sorry I can't respond to all letters, but I read them all.

It's nice to know that people enjoy the series in lots of different ways.

Please see the end of the book for some special thanks!

Kiiro Yumi

*

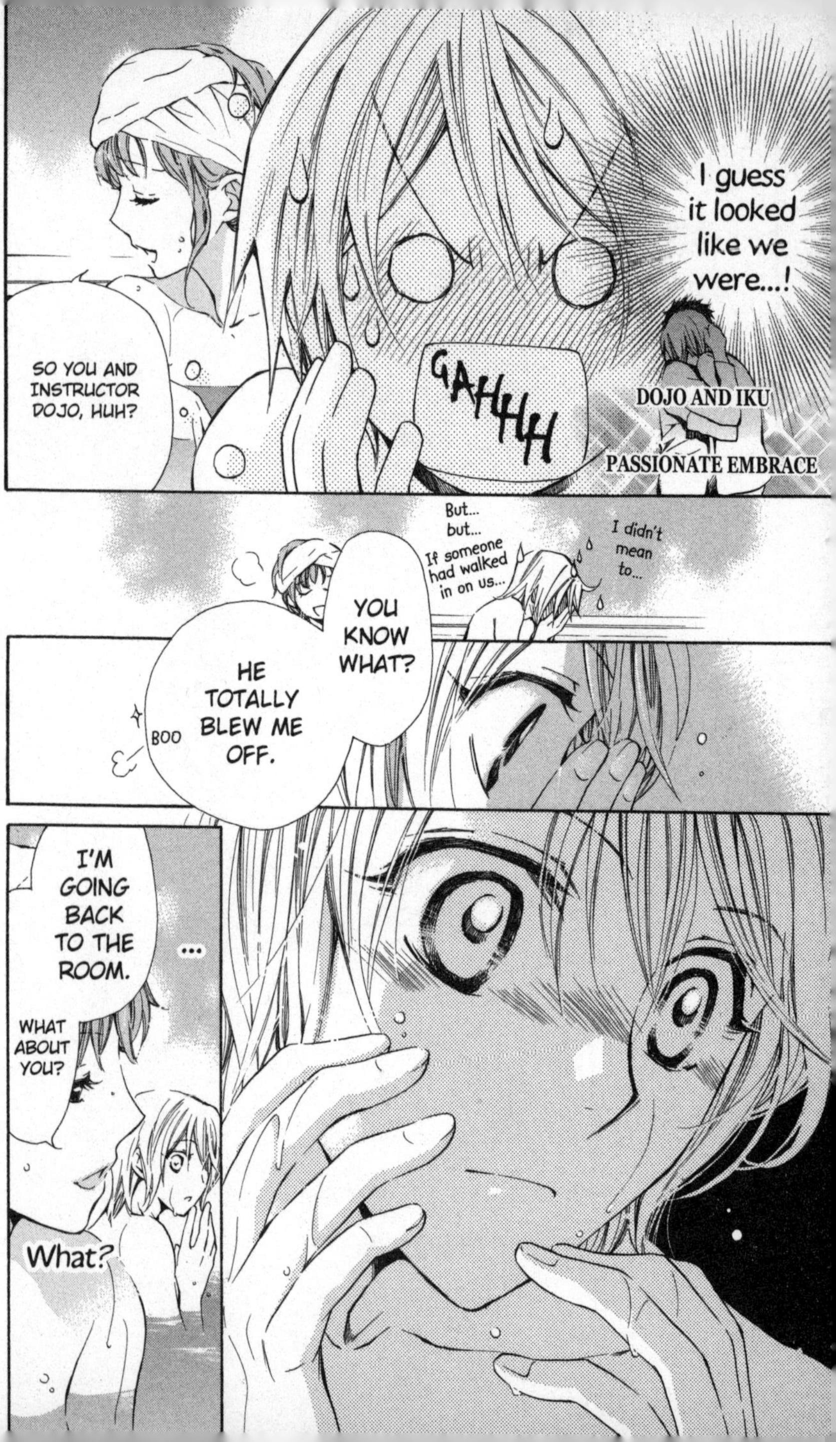
I guess it looked like we were...!
DOJO AND IKU
PASSIONATE EMBRACE
GAHHHH
SO YOU AND INSTRUCTOR DOJO, HUH?
I didn't mean to...
But... but... If someone had walked in on us...
YOU KNOW WHAT?
HE TOTALLY BLEW ME OFF.
BOO
...
I'M GOING BACK TO THE ROOM.
WHAT ABOUT YOU?
What?

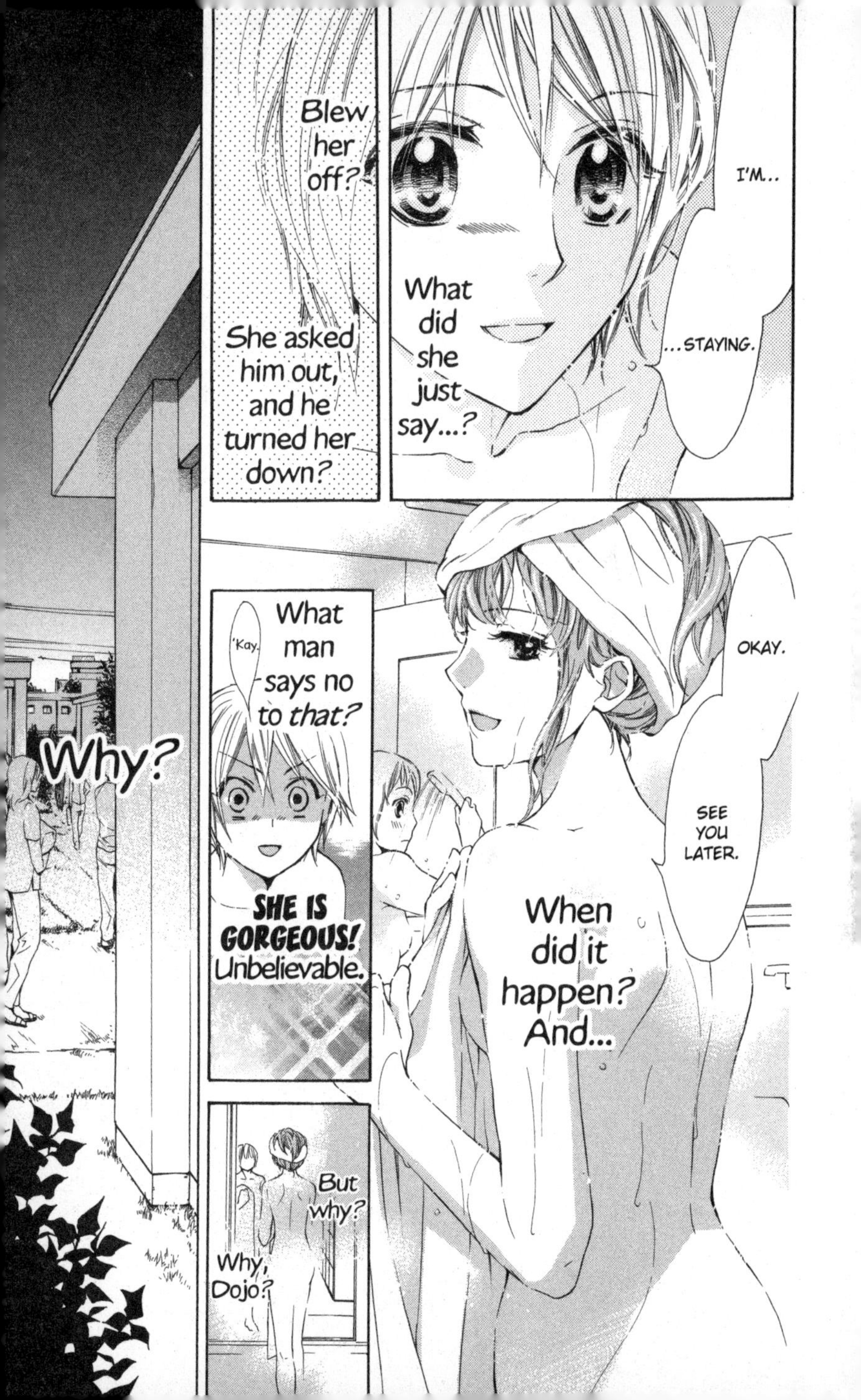
I'M...
...STAYING.
What did she just say...?
Blew her off?
She asked him out, and he turned her down?
OKAY.
SEE YOU LATER.
When did it happen? And...
What man says no to that?
'Kay.
SHE IS GORGEOUS! Unbelievable.
But why?
Why, Dojo?
Why?

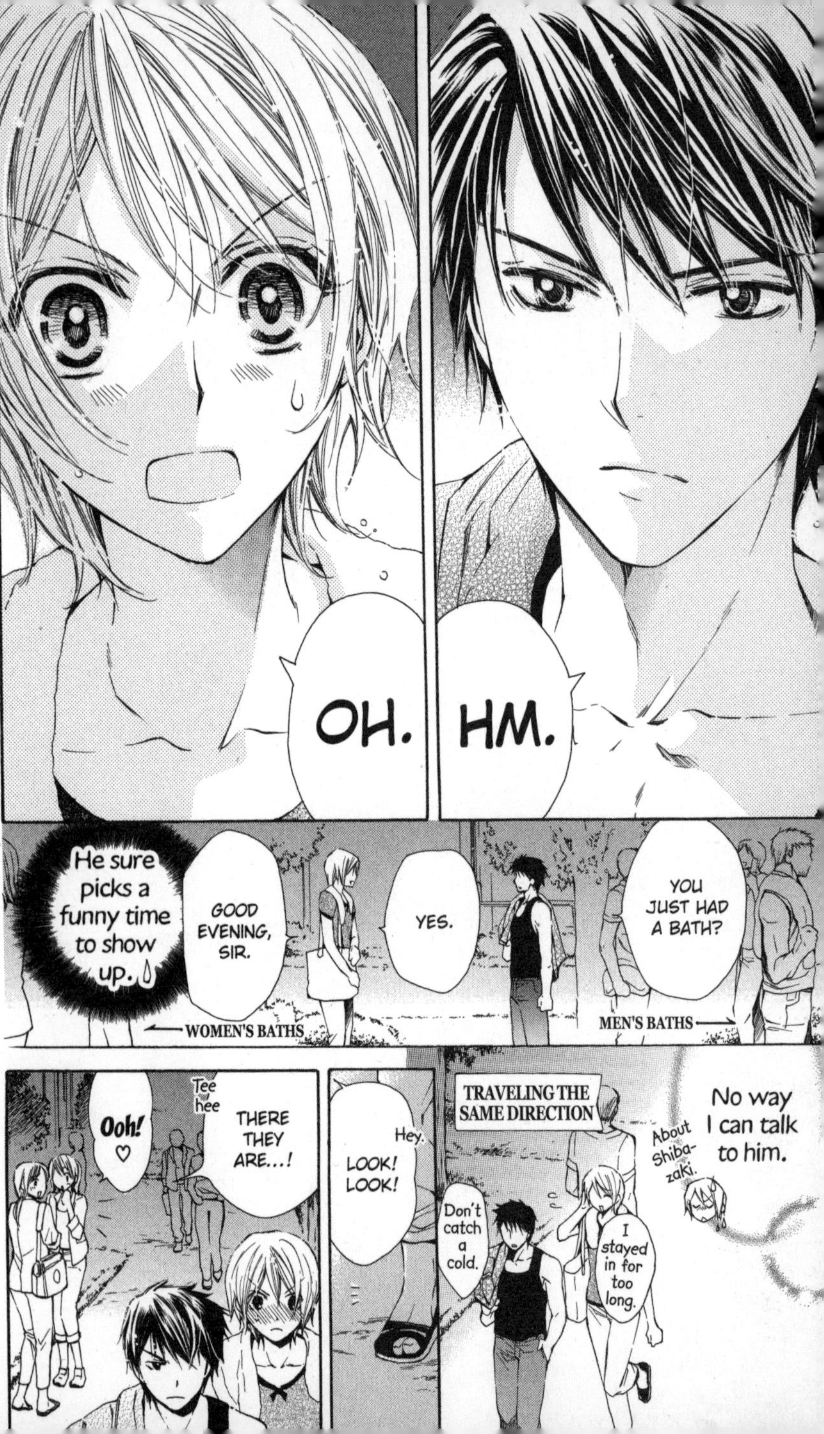
HM.
OH.
YOU JUST HAD A BATH?
MEN'S BATHS →
YES.
GOOD EVENING, SIR.
He sure picks a funny time to show up.
← WOMEN'S BATHS
No way I can talk to him.
About Shiba-zaki.
TRAVELING THE SAME DIRECTION
I stayed in for too long.
Don't catch a cold.
Hey.
LOOK! LOOK!
Tee hee
THERE THEY ARE...!
Ooh! ♡

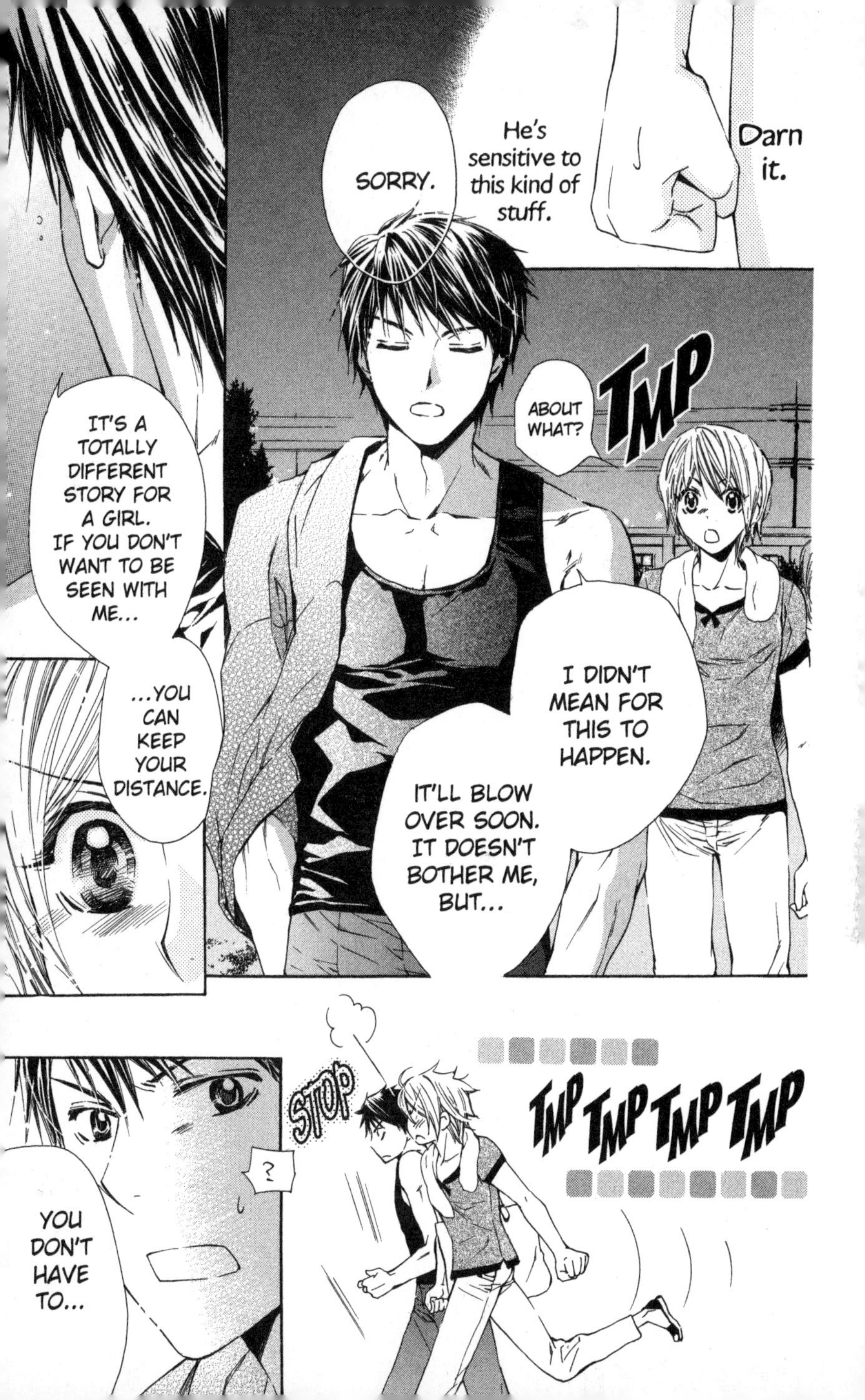
Darn it.
He's sensitive to this kind of stuff.
SORRY.
ABOUT WHAT?
TMP
I DIDN'T MEAN FOR THIS TO HAPPEN.
IT'LL BLOW OVER SOON. IT DOESN'T BOTHER ME, BUT...
IT'S A TOTALLY DIFFERENT STORY FOR A GIRL. IF YOU DON'T WANT TO BE SEEN WITH ME...
...YOU CAN KEEP YOUR DISTANCE.
TMP TMP TMP TMP
STOP
?
YOU DON'T HAVE TO...

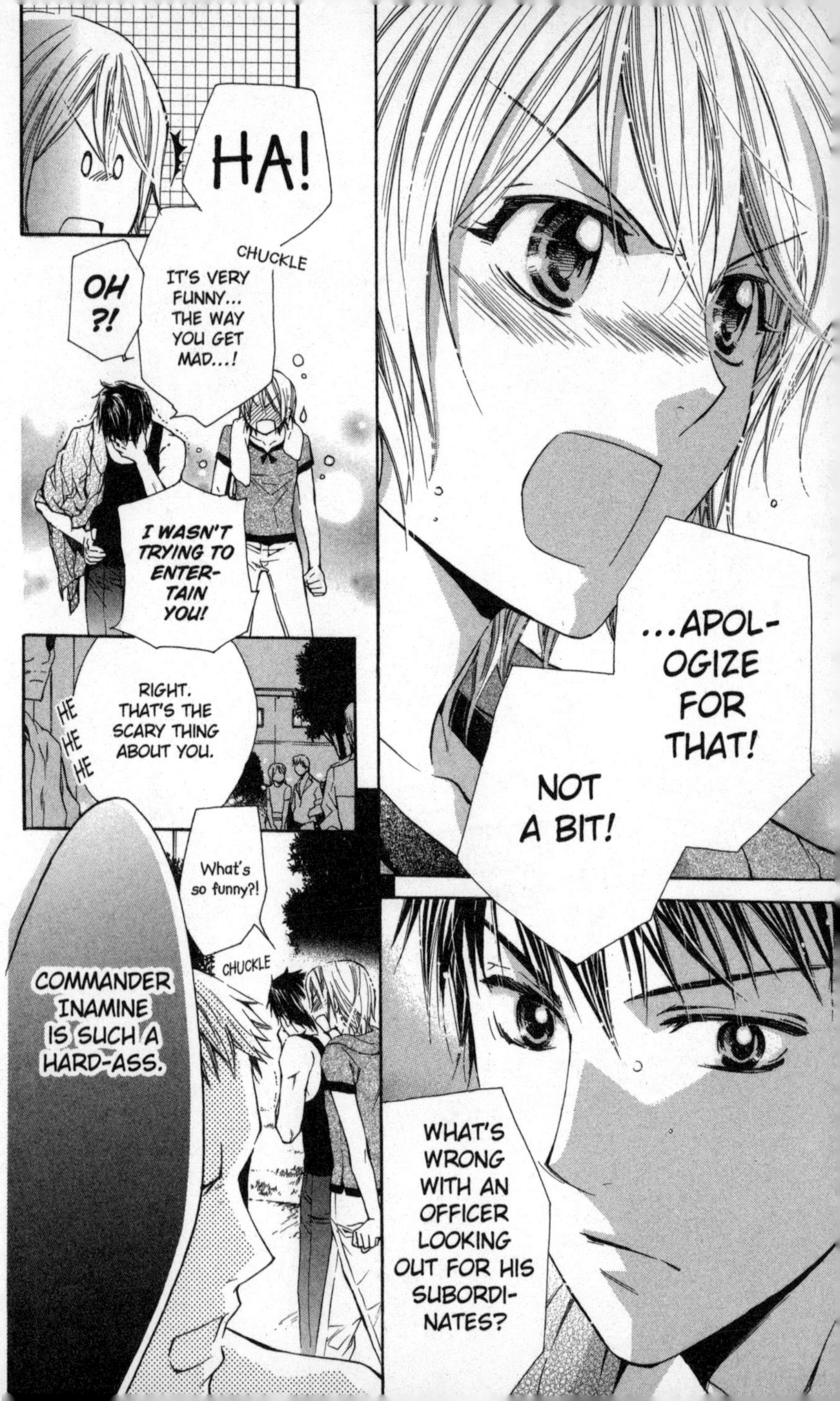
...APOLOGIZE FOR THAT!
NOT A BIT!
WHAT'S WRONG WITH AN OFFICER LOOKING OUT FOR HIS SUBORDINATES?
HA!
CHUCKLE
IT'S VERY FUNNY... THE WAY YOU GET MAD...!
OH ?!
I WASN'T TRYING TO ENTERTAIN YOU!
RIGHT. THAT'S THE SCARY THING ABOUT YOU.
HE HE HE
What's so funny?!
CHUCKLE
COMMANDER INAMINE IS SUCH A HARD-ASS.

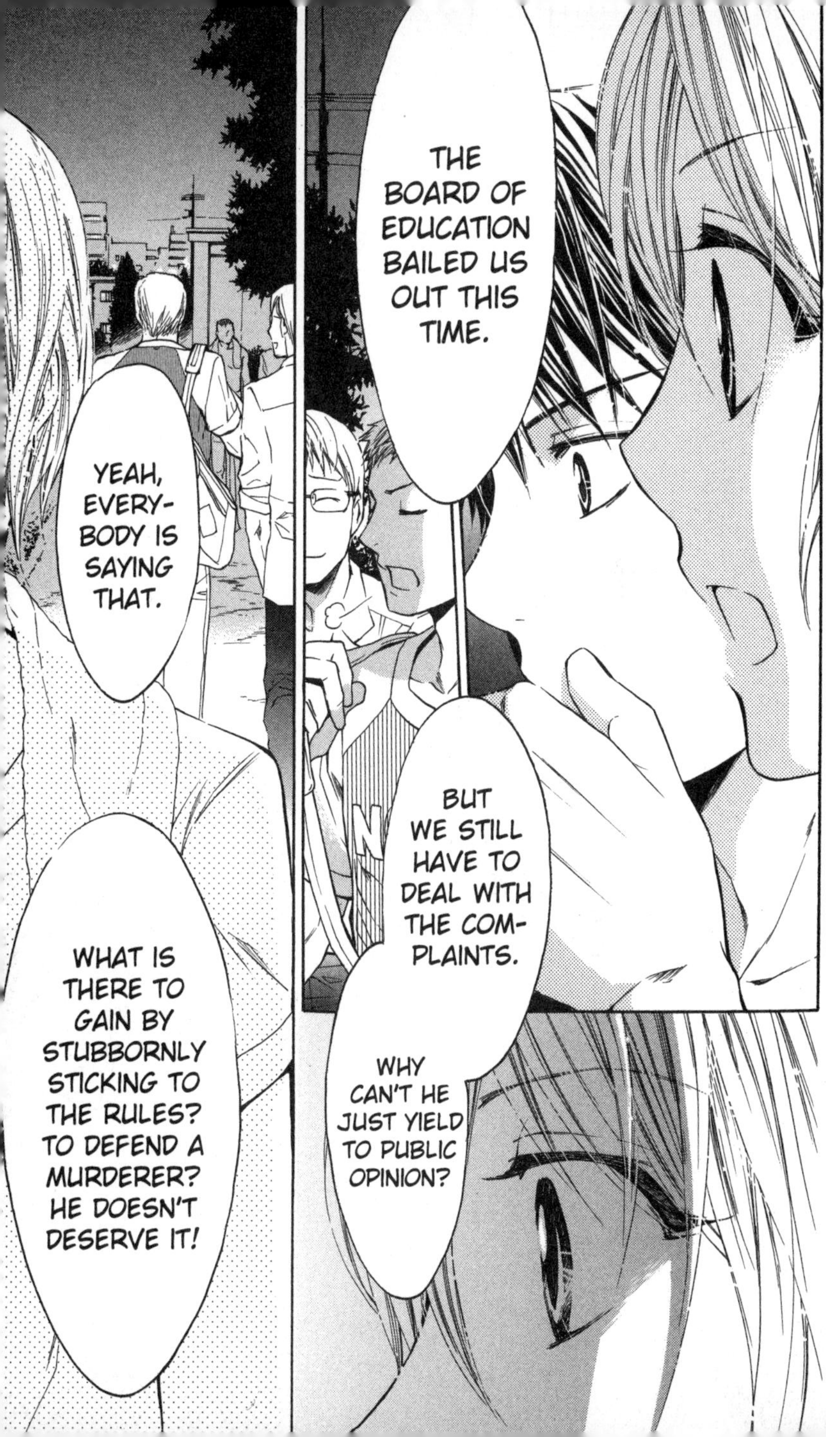
THE BOARD OF EDUCATION BAILED US OUT THIS TIME.
BUT WE STILL HAVE TO DEAL WITH THE COM-PLAINTS.
WHY CAN'T HE JUST YIELD TO PUBLIC OPINION?
YEAH, EVERY-BODY IS SAYING THAT.
WHAT IS THERE TO GAIN BY STUBBORNLY STICKING TO THE RULES? TO DEFEND A MURDERER? HE DOESN'T DESERVE IT!

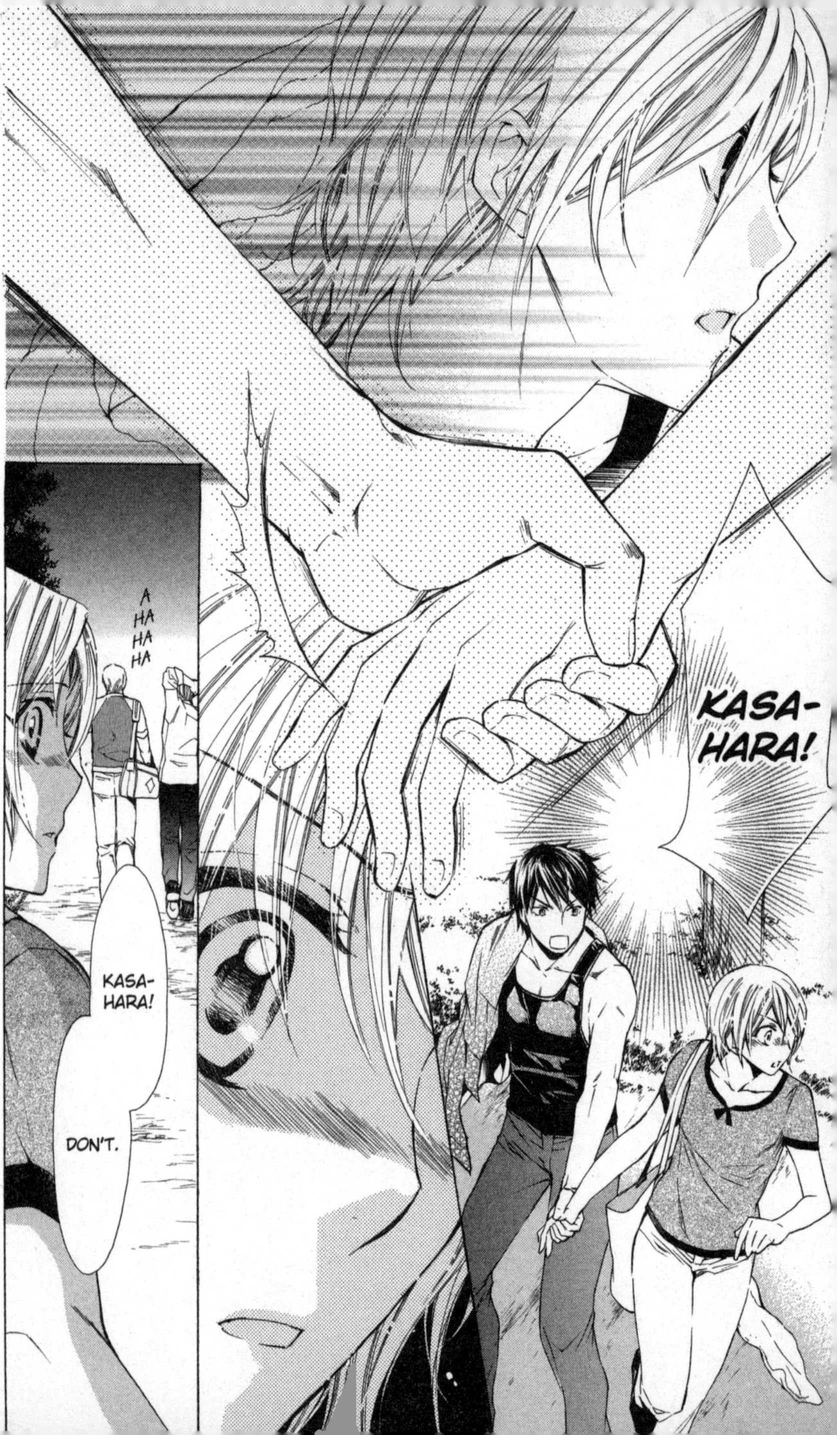
KASA-HARA!
A HA HA HA
KASA-HARA!
DON'T.

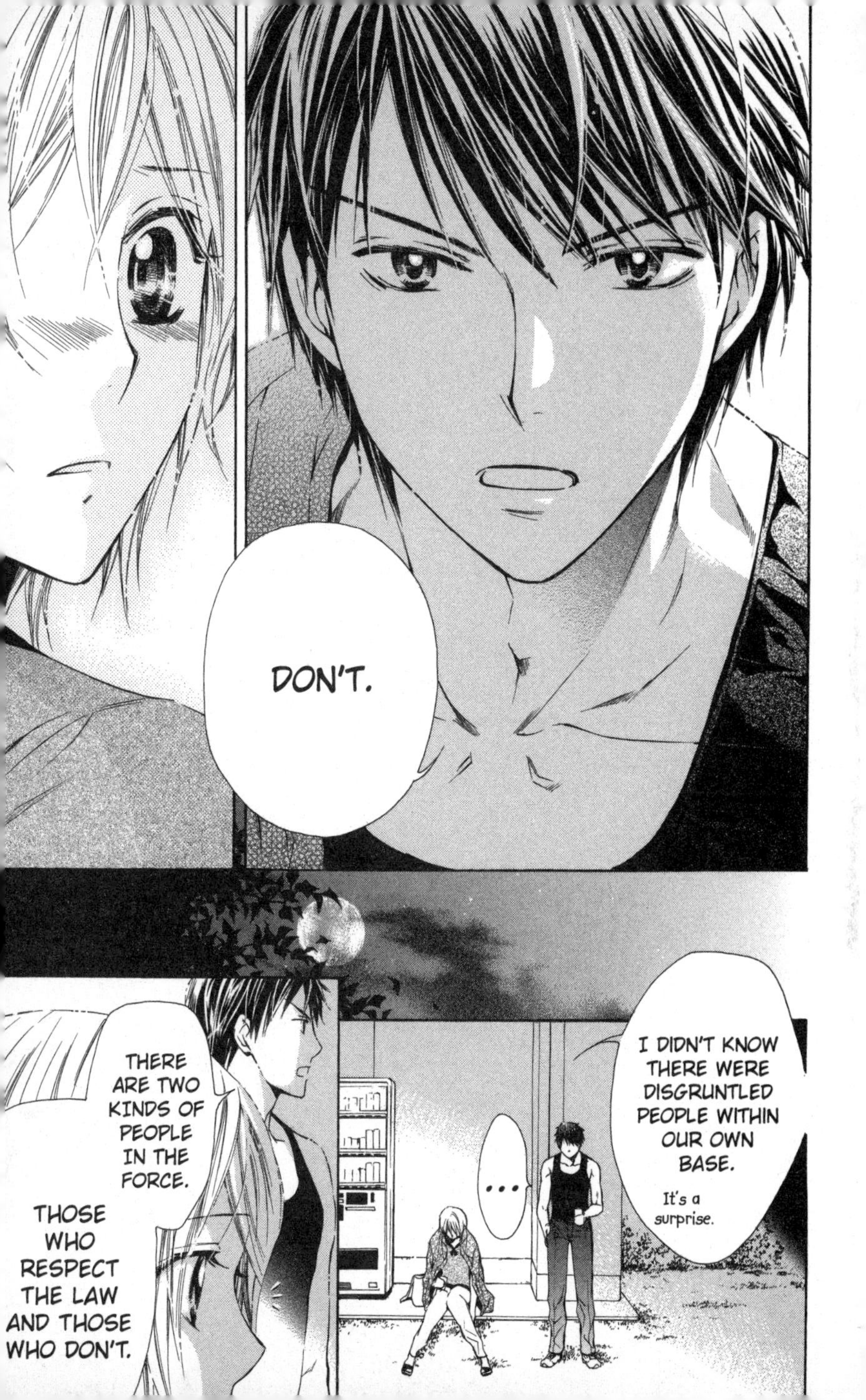
DON'T.
I DIDN'T KNOW THERE WERE DISGRUNTLED PEOPLE WITHIN OUR OWN BASE.
It's a surprise.
...
THERE ARE TWO KINDS OF PEOPLE IN THE FORCE.
THOSE WHO RESPECT THE LAW AND THOSE WHO DON'T.

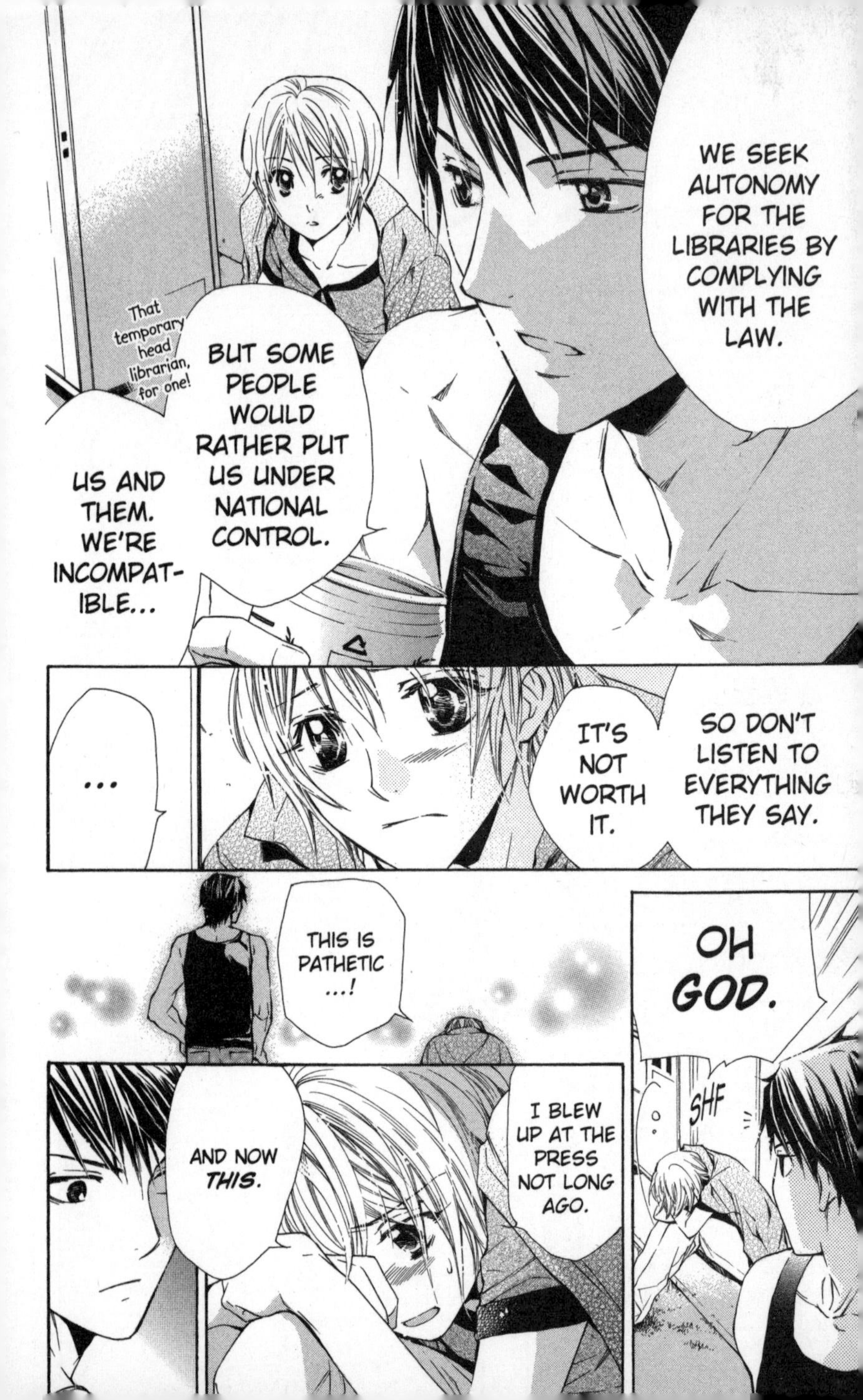
WE SEEK AUTONOMY FOR THE LIBRARIES BY COMPLYING WITH THE LAW.
BUT SOME PEOPLE WOULD RATHER PUT US UNDER NATIONAL CONTROL.
That temporary head librarian, for one!
US AND THEM. WE'RE INCOMPAT-IBLE...
SO DON'T LISTEN TO EVERYTHING THEY SAY.
IT'S NOT WORTH IT.
...
OH GOD.
SHF
THIS IS PATHETIC ...!
I BLEW UP AT THE PRESS NOT LONG AGO.
AND NOW *THIS*.

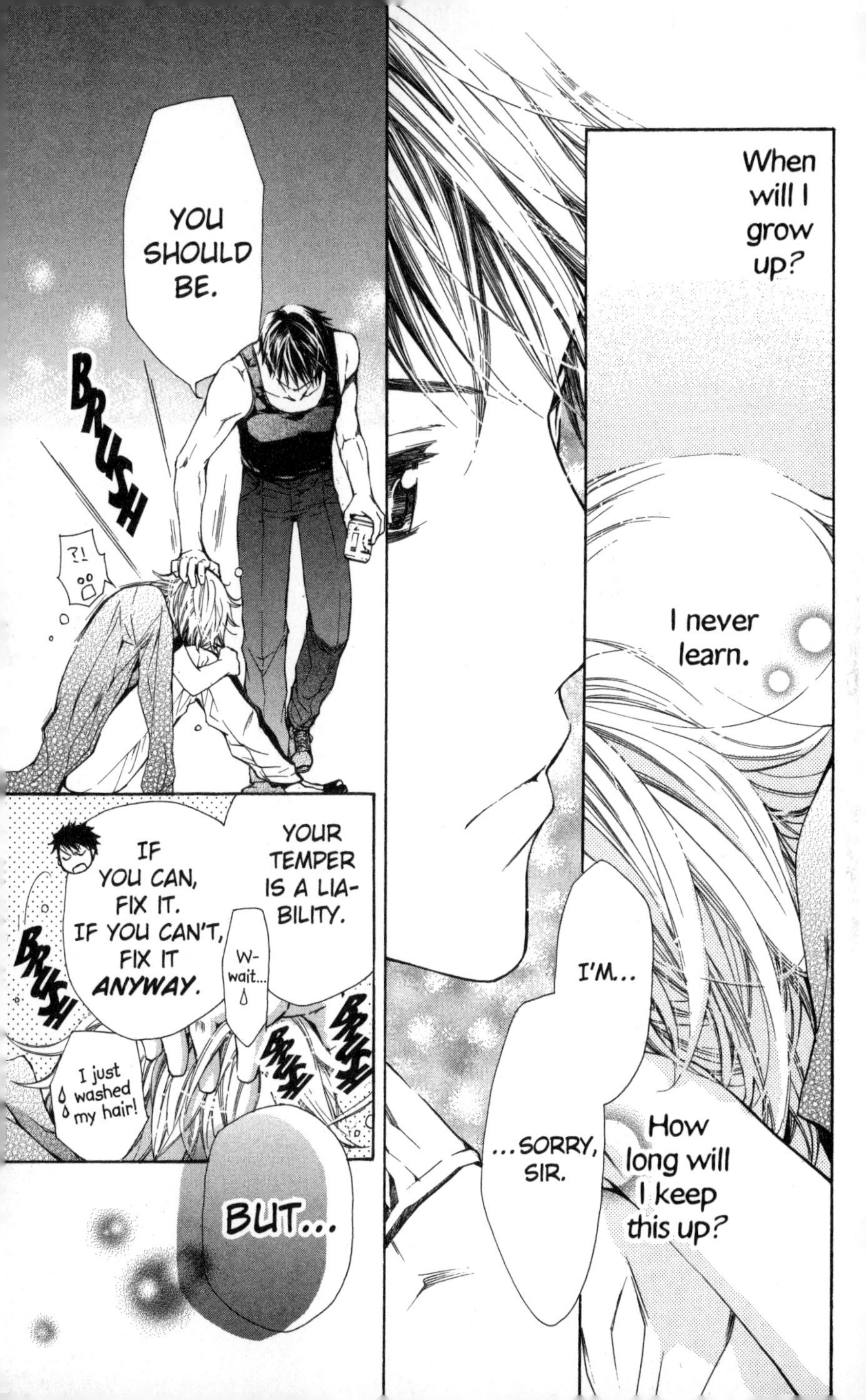
When will I grow up?
I never learn.
I'M...
...SORRY, SIR.
How long will I keep this up?
YOU SHOULD BE.
BRUSH
?!
YOUR TEMPER IS A LIA-BILITY.
IF YOU CAN, FIX IT. IF YOU CAN'T, FIX IT ANYWAY.
W-wait...
BRUSH
BRUSH
BRUSH
BRUSH
I just washed my hair!
BUT...

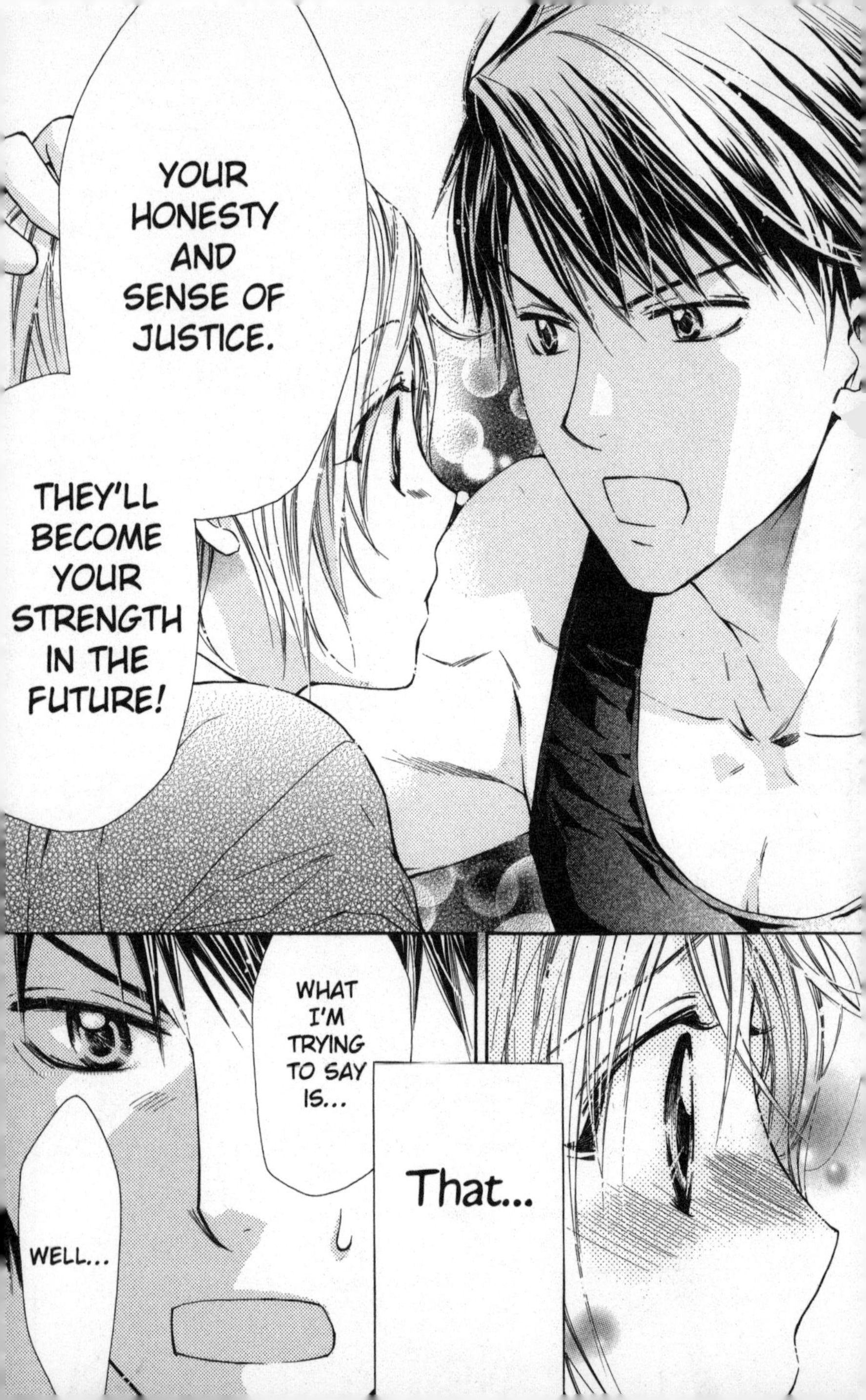
YOUR HONESTY AND SENSE OF JUSTICE.
THEY'LL BECOME YOUR STRENGTH IN THE FUTURE!
That...
WHAT I'M TRYING TO SAY IS...
WELL...

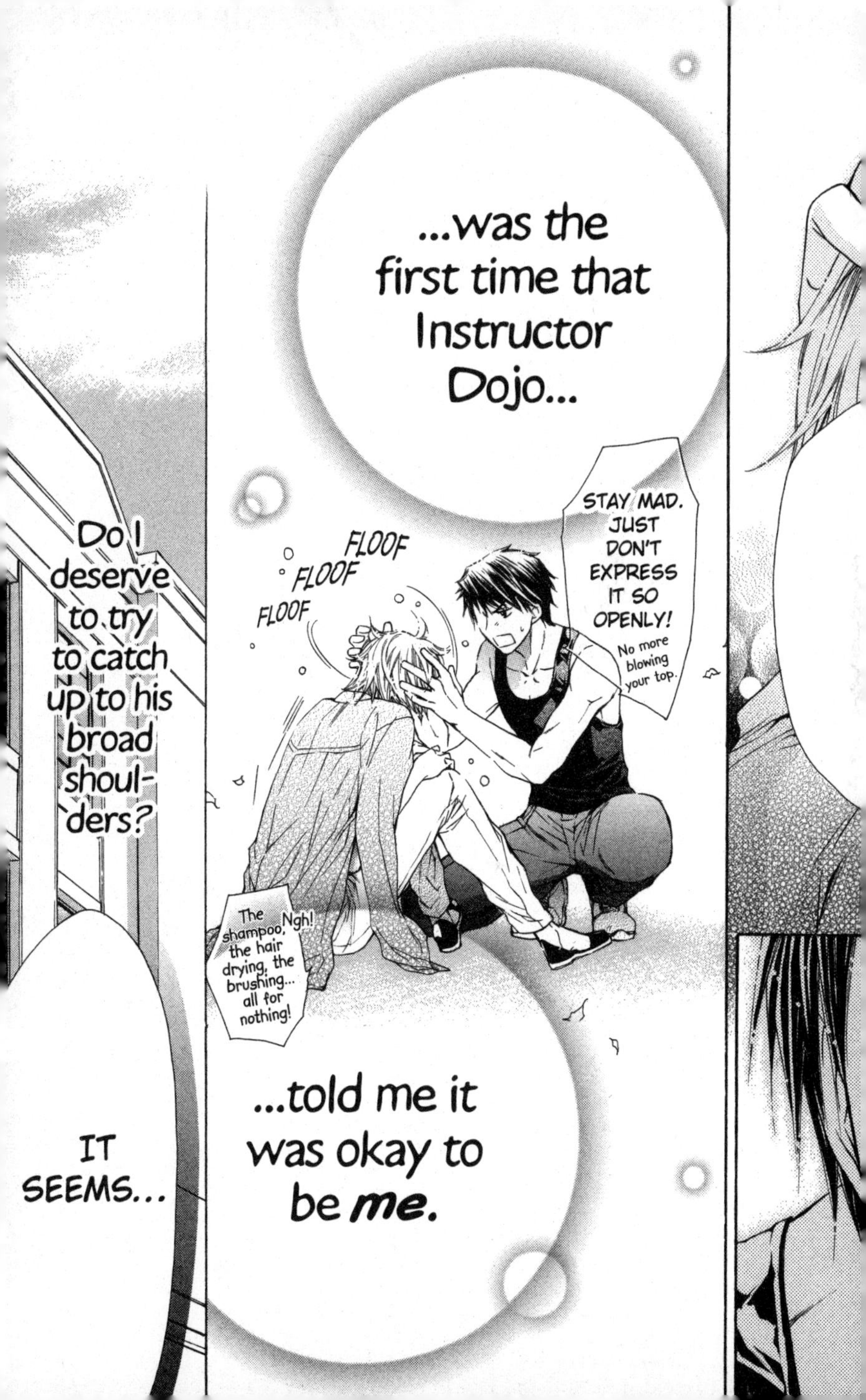
Do I deserve to try to catch up to his broad shoulders?
IT SEEMS...
...was the first time that Instructor Dojo...
STAY MAD. JUST DON'T EXPRESS IT SO OPENLY!
No more blowing your top.
FLOOF
FLOOF
FLOOF
Ngh!
The shampoo, the hair drying, the brushing... all for nothing!
...told me it was okay to be me.

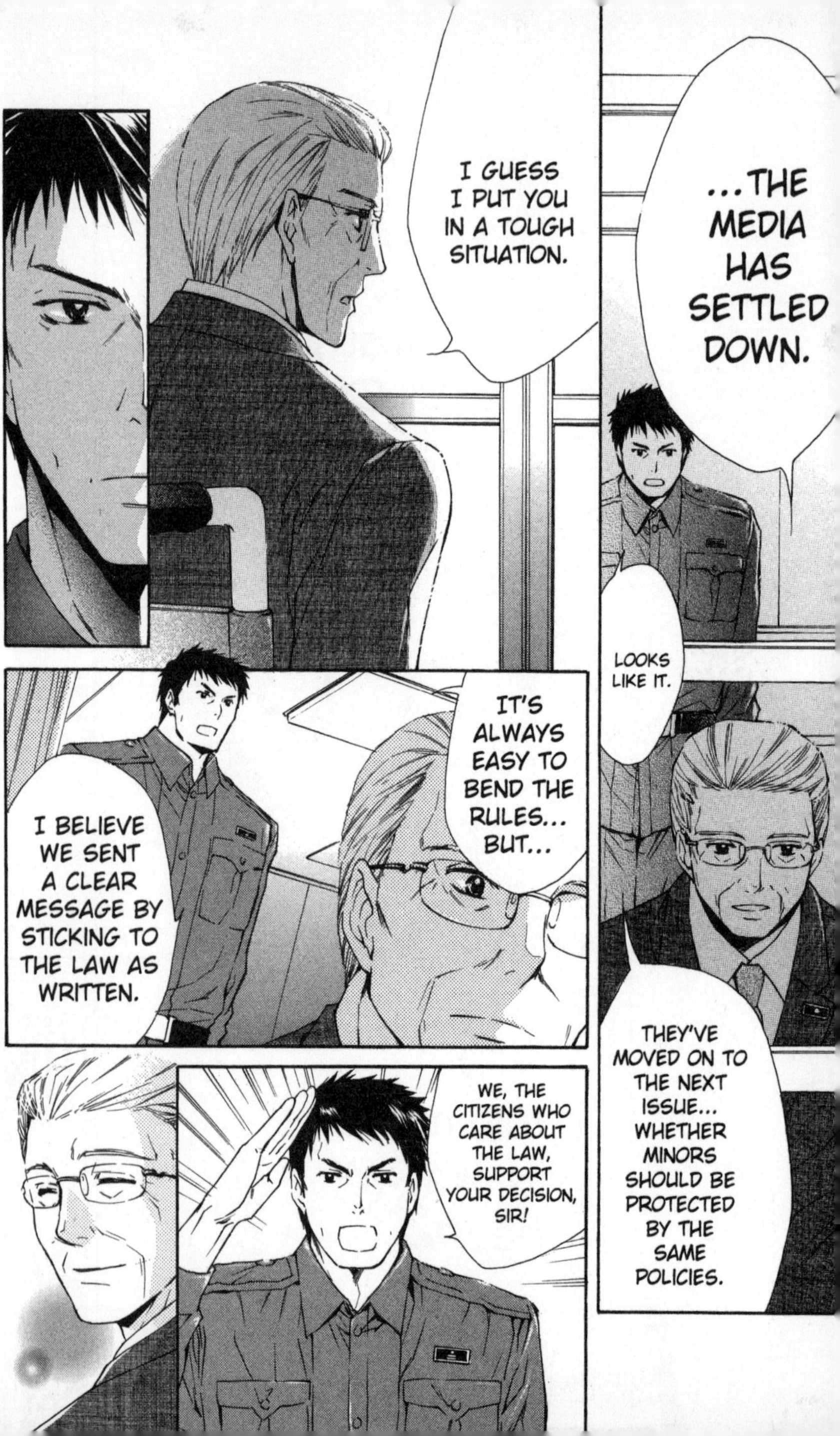
...THE MEDIA HAS SETTLED DOWN.
LOOKS LIKE IT.
I GUESS I PUT YOU IN A TOUGH SITUATION.
THEY'VE MOVED ON TO THE NEXT ISSUE... WHETHER MINORS SHOULD BE PROTECTED BY THE SAME POLICIES.
IT'S ALWAYS EASY TO BEND THE RULES... BUT...
I BELIEVE WE SENT A CLEAR MESSAGE BY STICKING TO THE LAW AS WRITTEN.
WE, THE CITIZENS WHO CARE ABOUT THE LAW, SUPPORT YOUR DECISION, SIR!

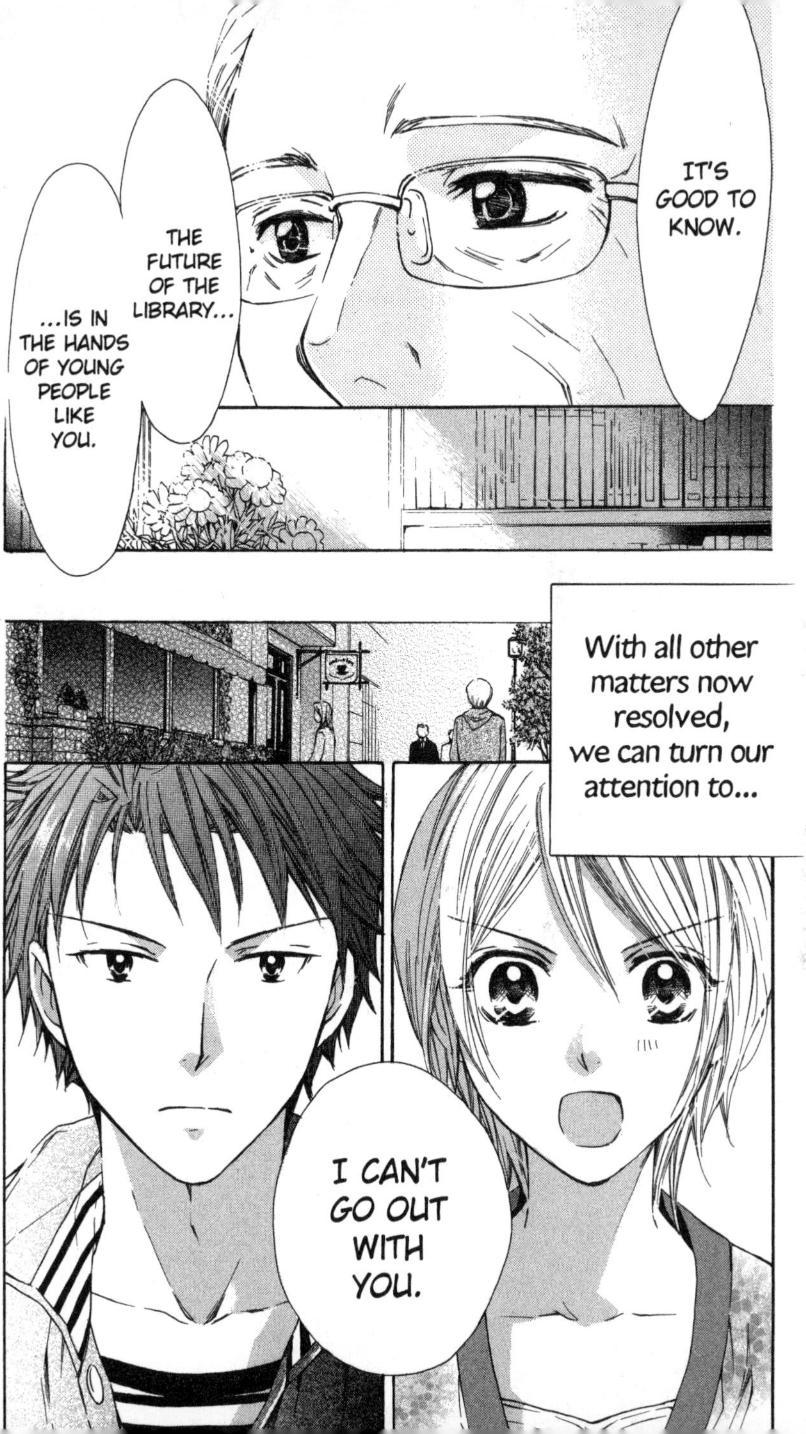
IT'S GOOD TO KNOW.
THE FUTURE OF THE LIBRARY...
...IS IN THE HANDS OF YOUNG PEOPLE LIKE YOU.
With all other matters now resolved, we can turn our attention to...
I CAN'T GO OUT WITH YOU.

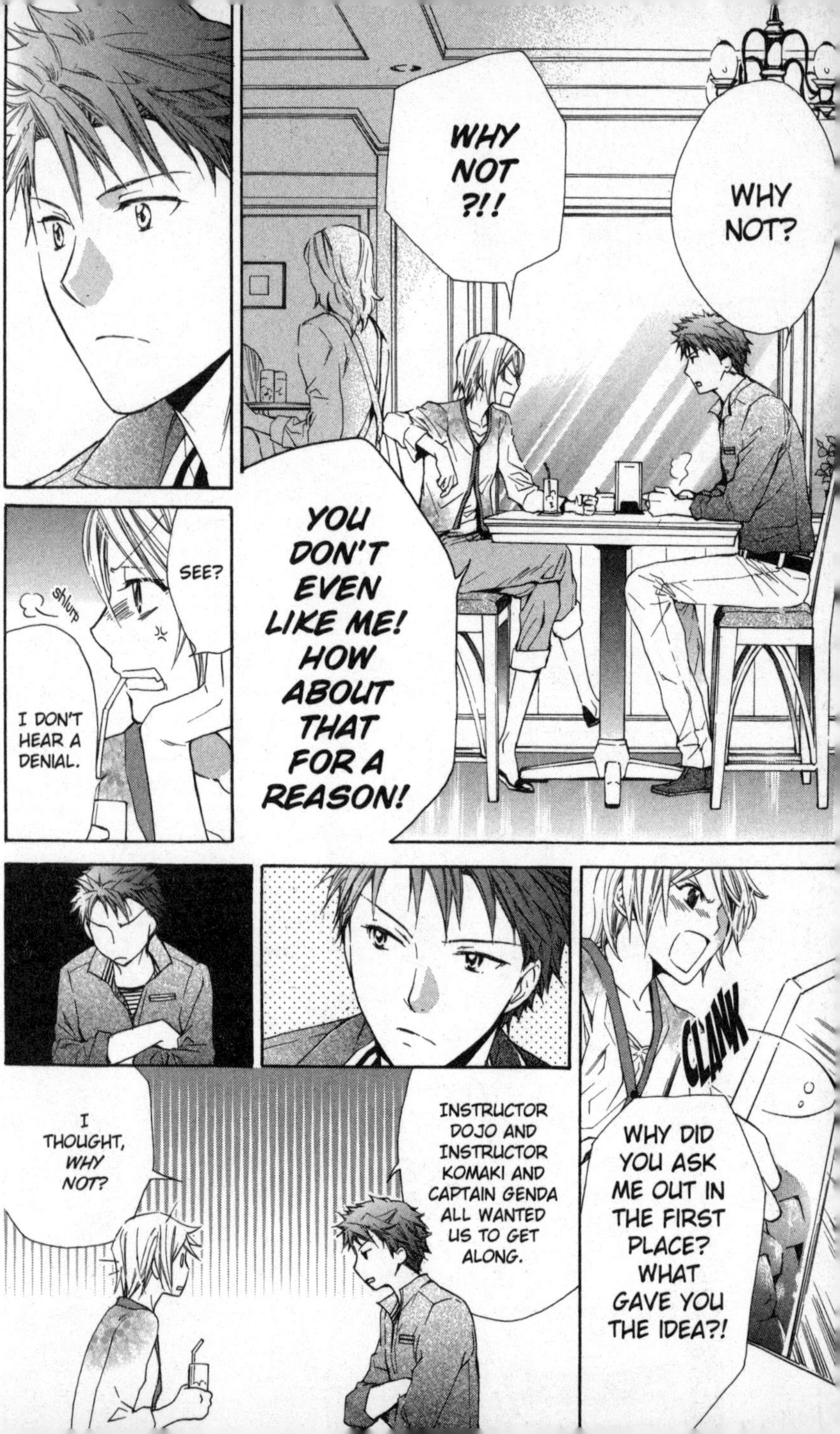
WHY NOT?
WHY NOT ?!!
YOU DON'T EVEN LIKE ME! HOW ABOUT THAT FOR A REASON!
SEE?
shlurp
I DON'T HEAR A DENIAL.
CLANK
WHY DID YOU ASK ME OUT IN THE FIRST PLACE? WHAT GAVE YOU THE IDEA?!
INSTRUCTOR DOJO AND INSTRUCTOR KOMAKI AND CAPTAIN GENDA ALL WANTED US TO GET ALONG.
I THOUGHT, *WHY NOT?*

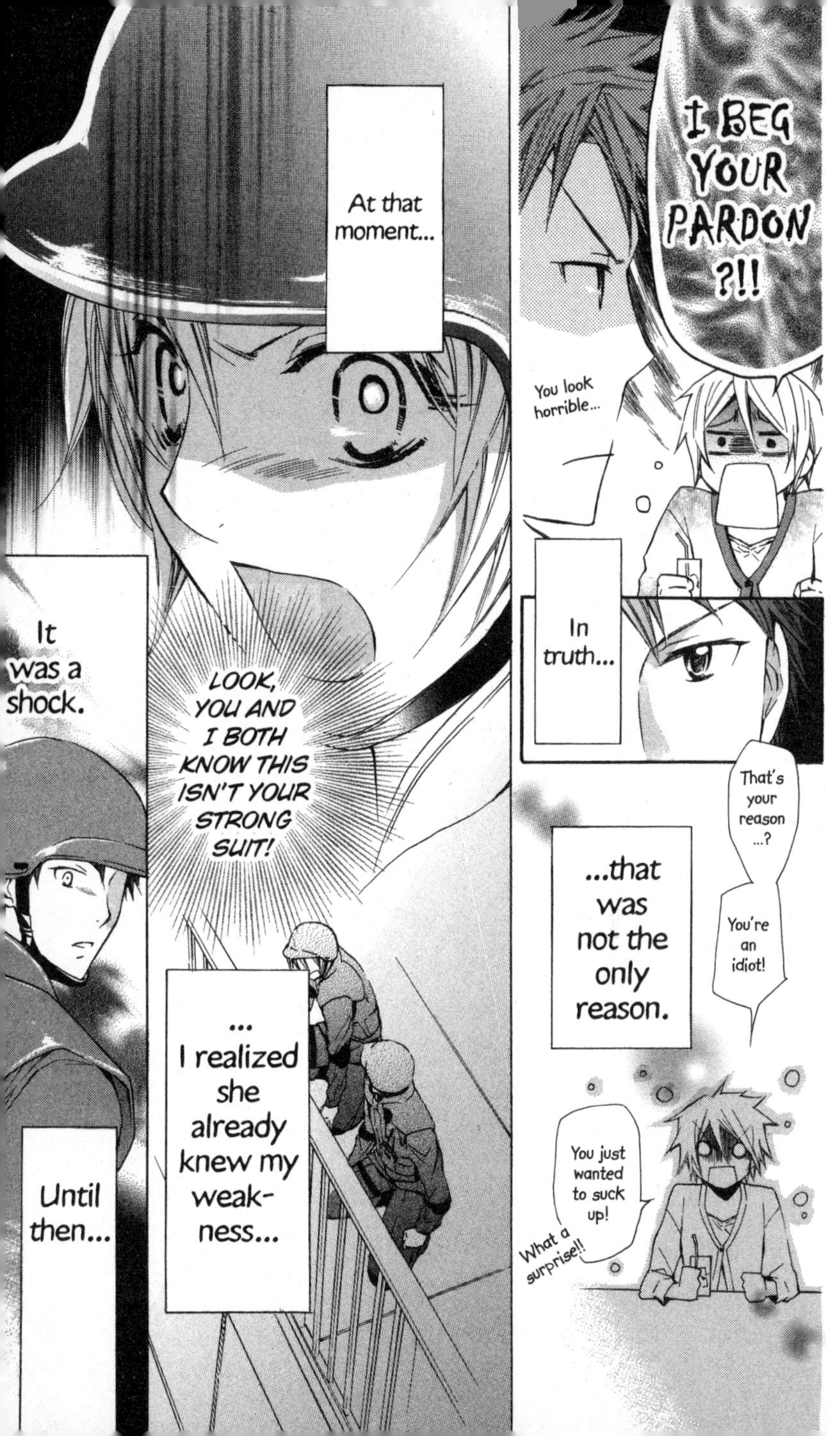
I BEG YOUR PARDON?!!
You look horrible...
In truth...
That's your reason...?
You're an idiot!
...that was not the only reason.
You just wanted to suck up!
What a surprise!!
At that moment...
LOOK, YOU AND I BOTH KNOW THIS ISN'T YOUR STRONG SUIT!
It was a shock.
...I realized she already knew my weak-ness...
Until then...

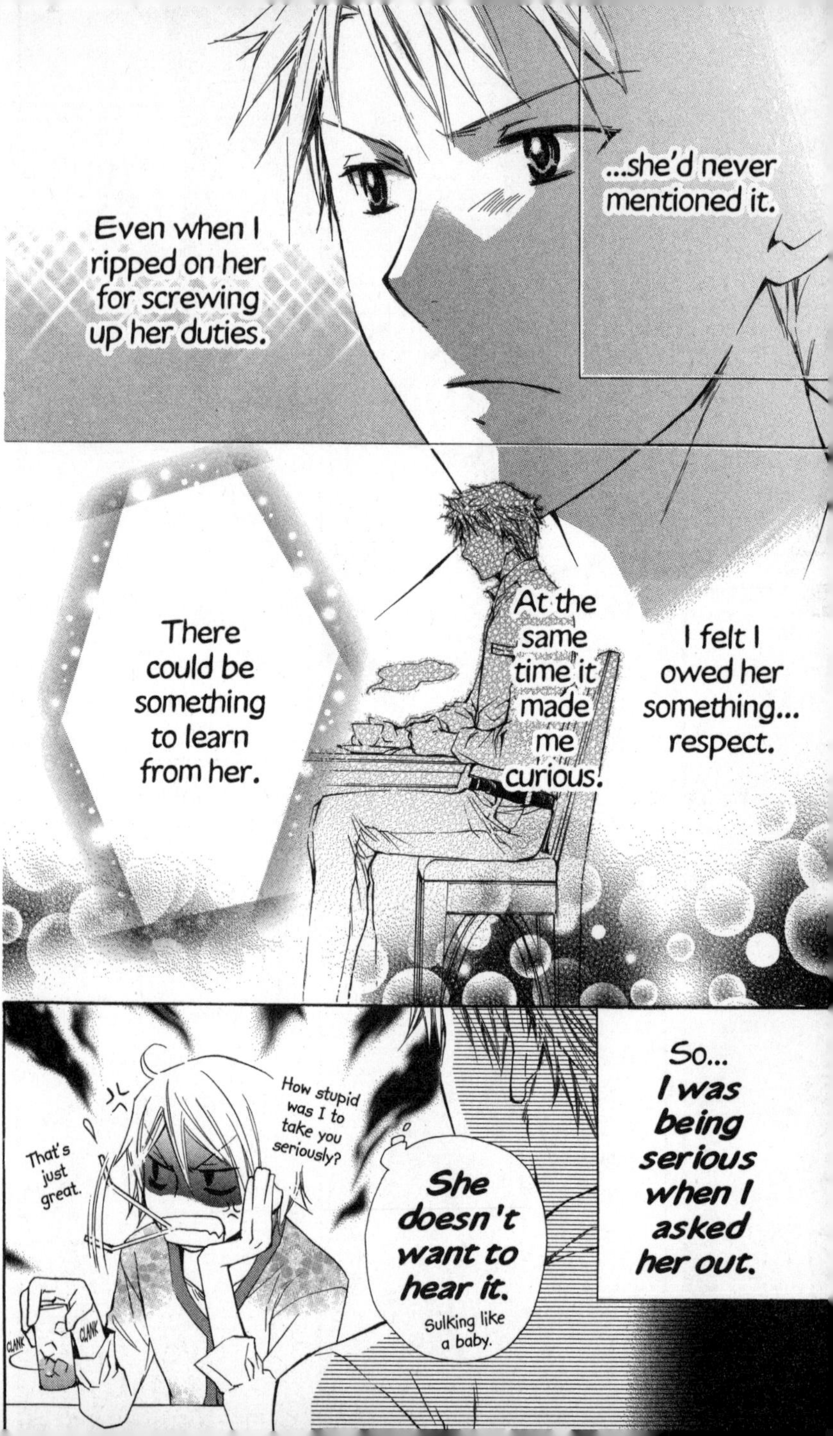
Even when I ripped on her for screwing up her duties.
...she'd never mentioned it.
I felt I owed her something... respect.
At the same time it made me curious.
There could be something to learn from her.
So... *I was being serious when I asked her out.*
She doesn't want to hear it.
Sulking like a baby.
How stupid was I to take you seriously?
That's just great.
CLANK
CLANK

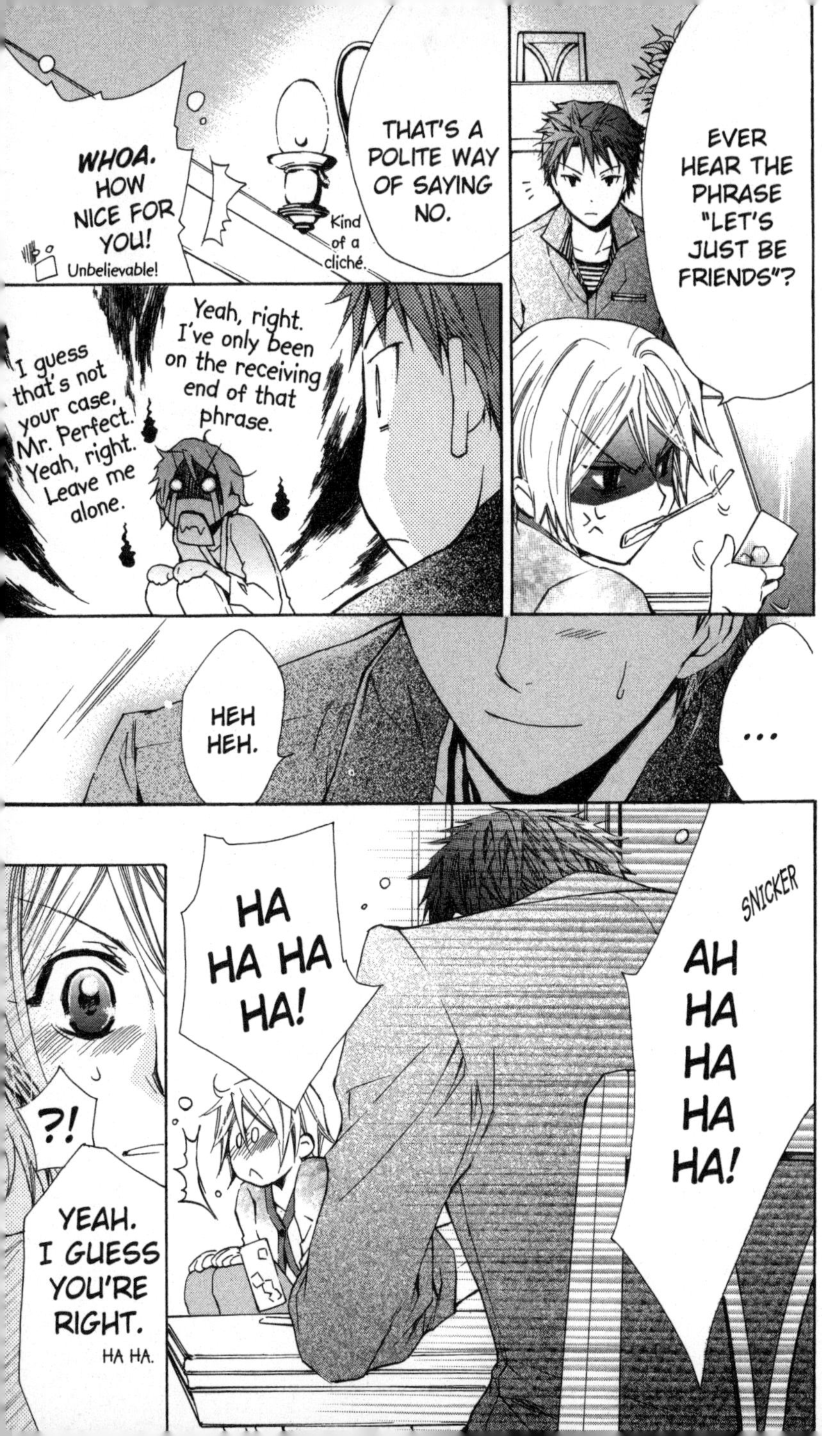
EVER HEAR THE PHRASE "LET'S JUST BE FRIENDS"?
THAT'S A POLITE WAY OF SAYING NO.
Kind of a cliché.
WHOA. HOW NICE FOR YOU!
Unbelievable!
Yeah, right. I've only been on the receiving end of that phrase.
I guess that's not your case, Mr. Perfect. Yeah, right. Leave me alone.
...
HEH HEH.
SNICKER
AH HA HA HA HA HA!
HA HA HA HA!
?!
YEAH. I GUESS YOU'RE RIGHT.
HA HA.

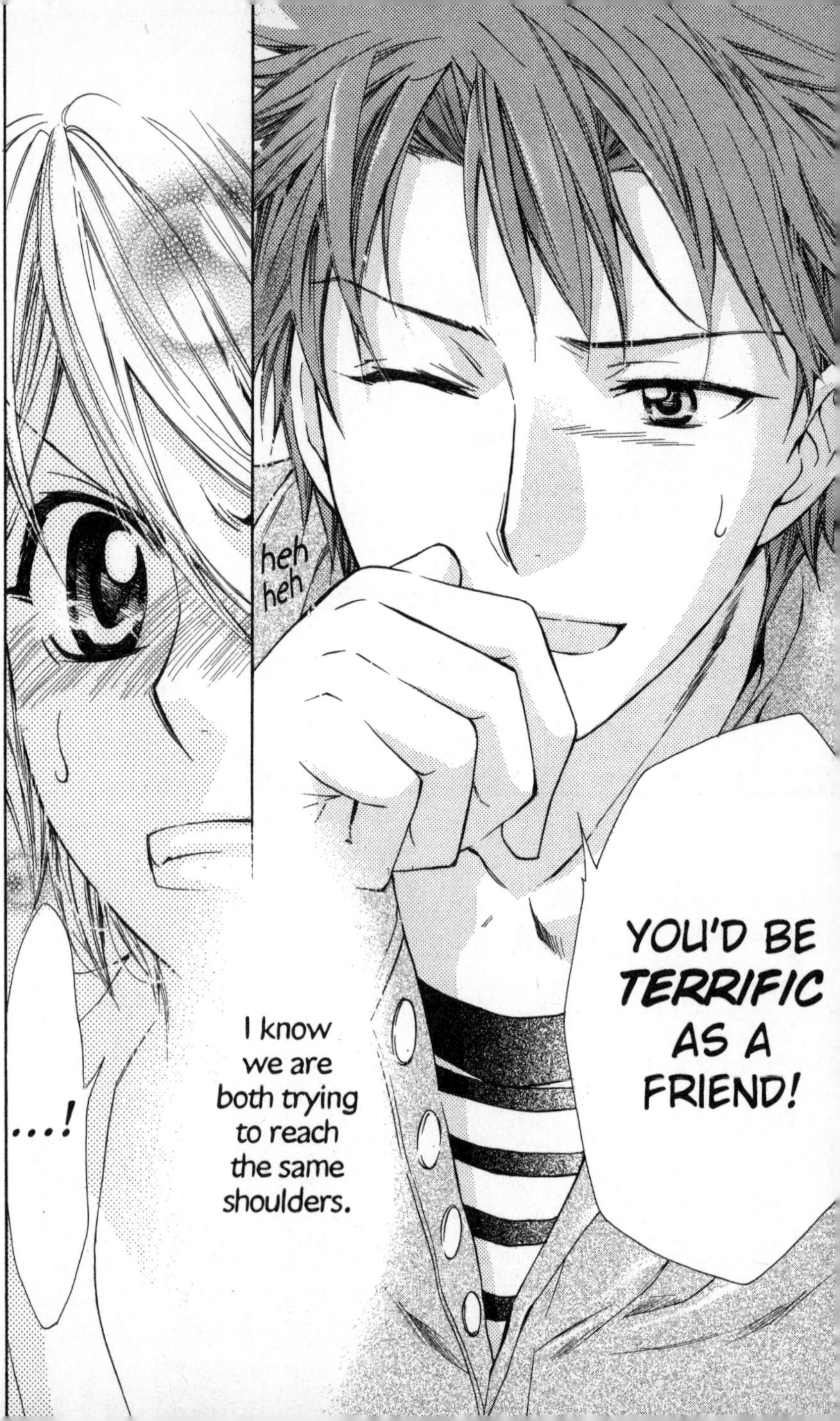
heh heh
YOU'D BE TERRIFIC AS A FRIEND!
I know we are both trying to reach the same shoulders.
...!

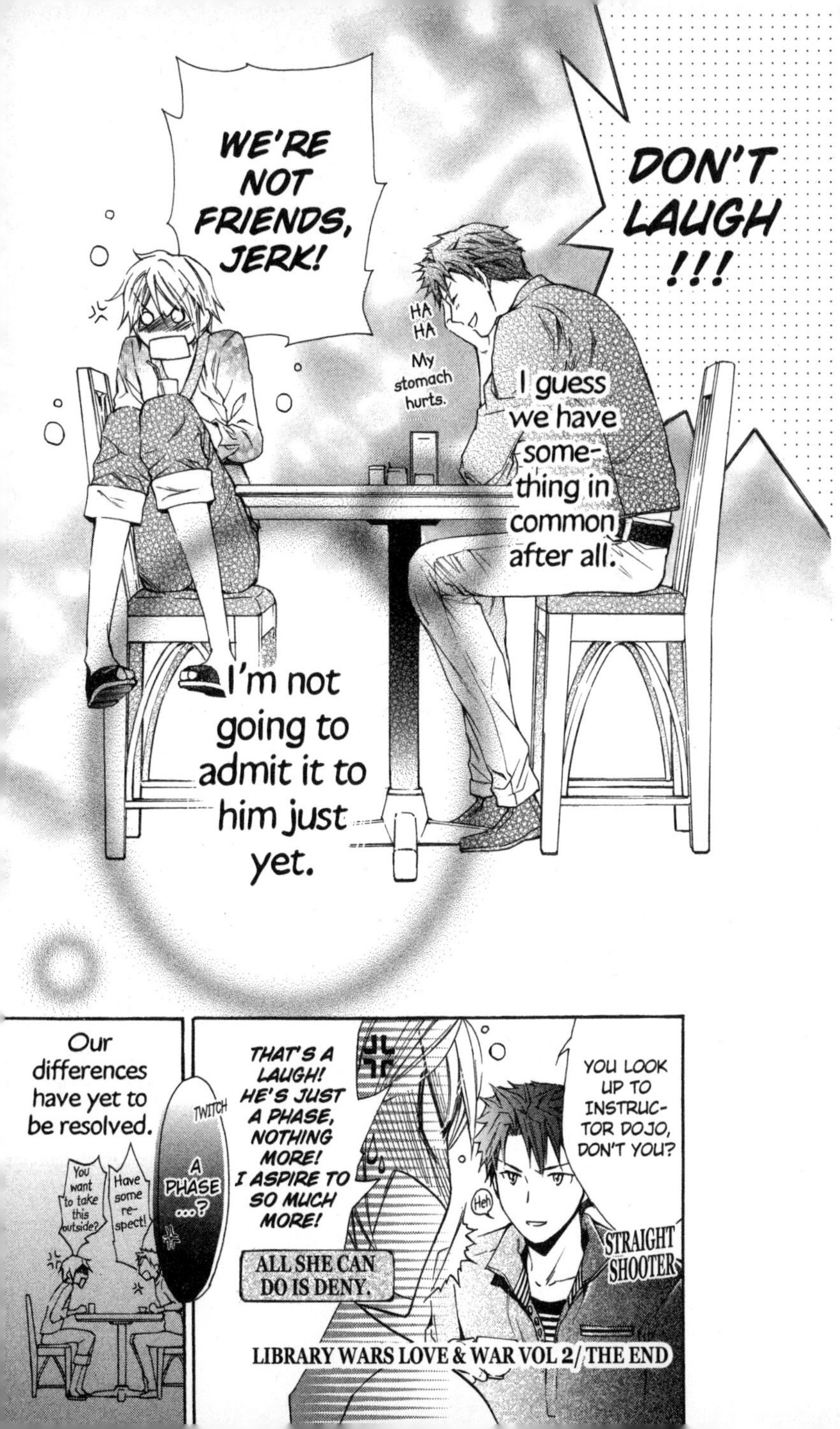

DON'T LAUGH!!!
WE'RE NOT FRIENDS, JERK!
HA HA
My stomach hurts.
I guess we have some-thing in common after all.
I'm not going to admit it to him just yet.
YOU LOOK UP TO INSTRUCTOR DOJO, DON'T YOU?
Heh
STRAIGHT SHOOTER
THAT'S A LAUGH! HE'S JUST A PHASE, NOTHING MORE! I ASPIRE TO SO MUCH MORE!
ALL SHE CAN DO IS DENY.
LIBRARY WARS LOVE & WAR VOL 2/THE END
TWITCH
A PHASE ...?
Our differences have yet to be resolved.
Have some re-spect!
You want to take this outside?

☆ BONUS MANGA 1 ☆

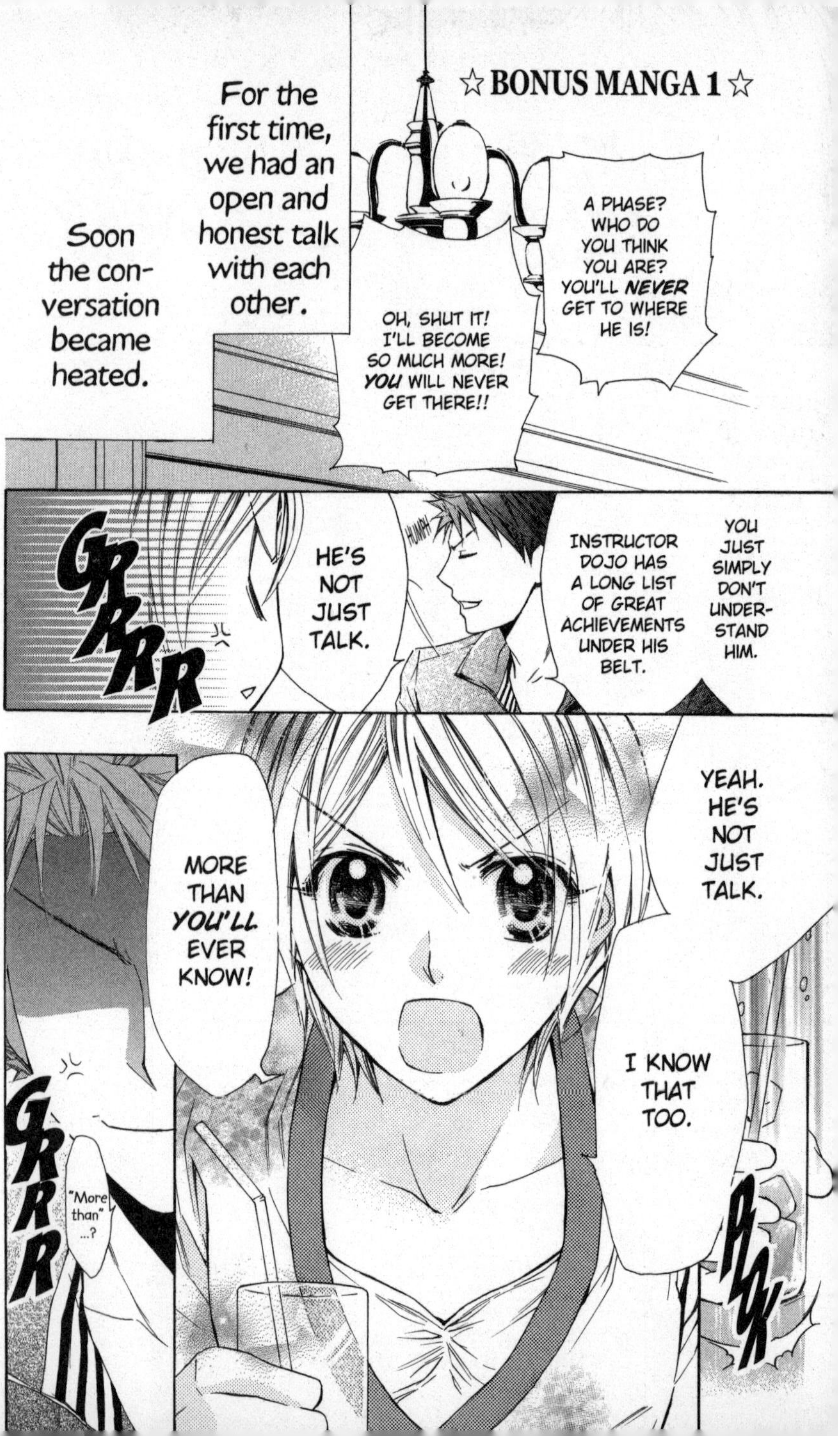
A PHASE? WHO DO YOU THINK YOU ARE? YOU'LL NEVER GET TO WHERE HE IS!
OH, SHUT IT! I'LL BECOME SO MUCH MORE! YOU WILL NEVER GET THERE!!
For the first time, we had an open and honest talk with each other.
Soon the con-versation became heated.
YOU JUST SIMPLY DON'T UNDER-STAND HIM.
INSTRUCTOR DOJO HAS A LONG LIST OF GREAT ACHIEVEMENTS UNDER HIS BELT.
HUMPH
HE'S NOT JUST TALK.
GRRRR
YEAH. HE'S NOT JUST TALK.
I KNOW THAT TOO.
PLOK
MORE THAN YOU'LL EVER KNOW!
GRRR
"More than" ...?

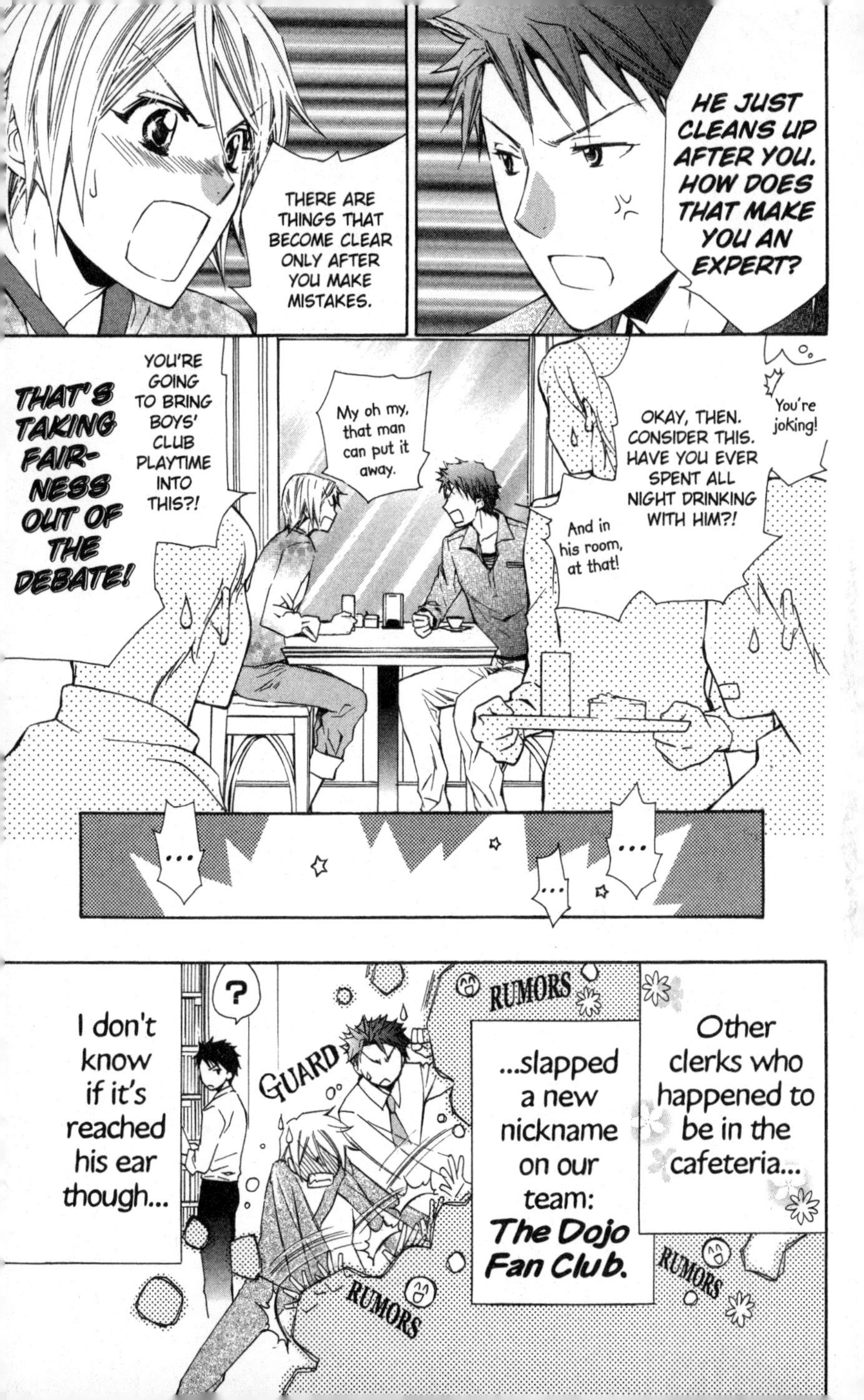
HE JUST CLEANS UP AFTER YOU. HOW DOES THAT MAKE YOU AN EXPERT?
THERE ARE THINGS THAT BECOME CLEAR ONLY AFTER YOU MAKE MISTAKES.
You're joking!
OKAY, THEN. CONSIDER THIS. HAVE YOU EVER SPENT ALL NIGHT DRINKING WITH HIM?!
And in his room, at that!
My oh my, that man can put it away.
YOU'RE GOING TO BRING BOYS' CLUB PLAYTIME INTO THIS?!
THAT'S TAKING FAIR-NESS OUT OF THE DEBATE!
...
...
...
Other clerks who happened to be in the cafeteria...
RUMORS
...slapped a new nickname on our team: The Dojo Fan Club.
RUMORS
GUARD
?
I don't know if it's reached his ear though...
RUMORS

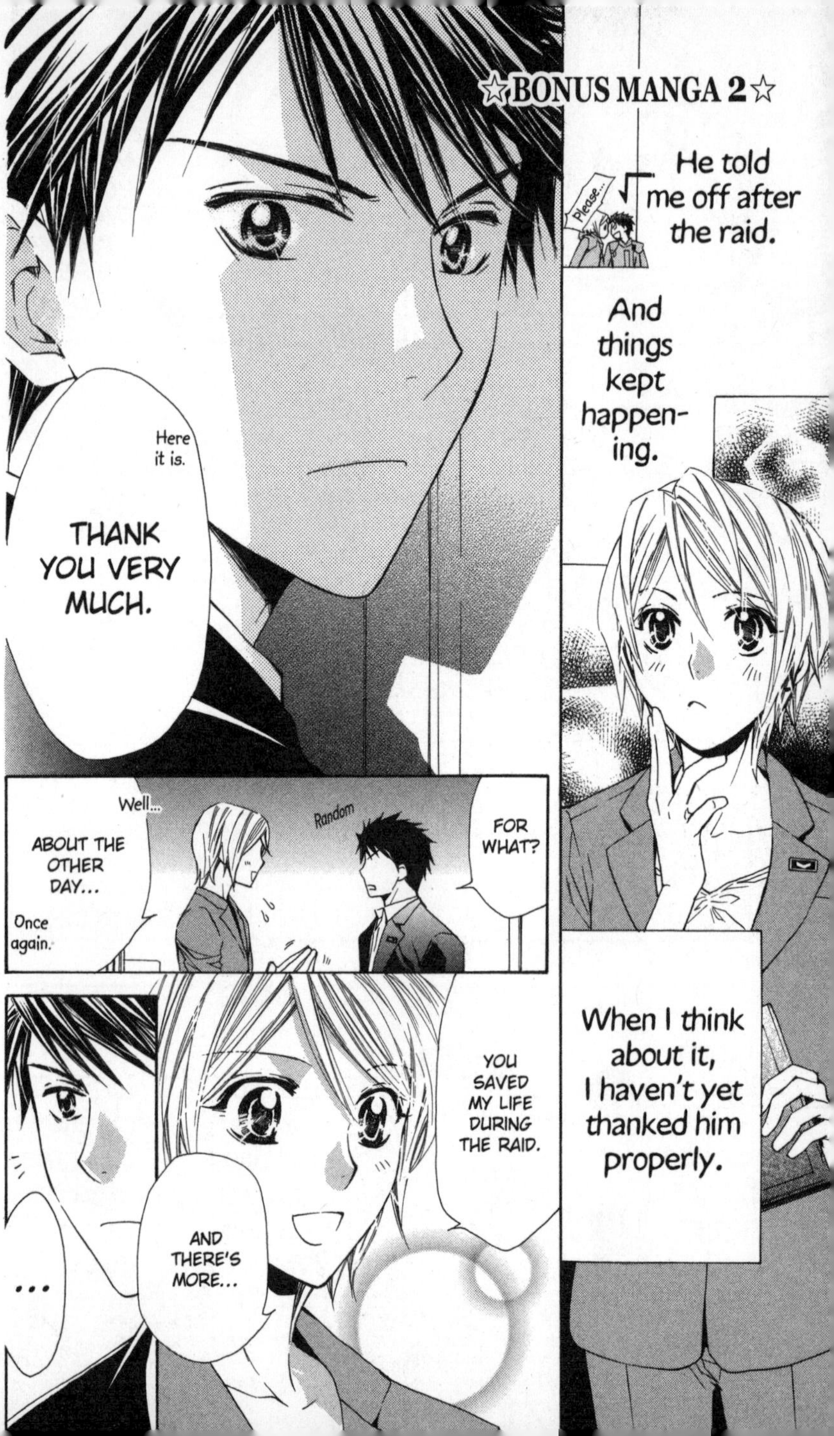
☆BONUS MANGA 2☆
He told me off after the raid.
Please...
And things kept happening.
When I think about it, I haven't yet thanked him properly.
Here it is.
THANK YOU VERY MUCH.
FOR WHAT?
Random
Well...
ABOUT THE OTHER DAY...
Once again.
YOU SAVED MY LIFE DURING THE RAID.
AND THERE'S MORE...
...

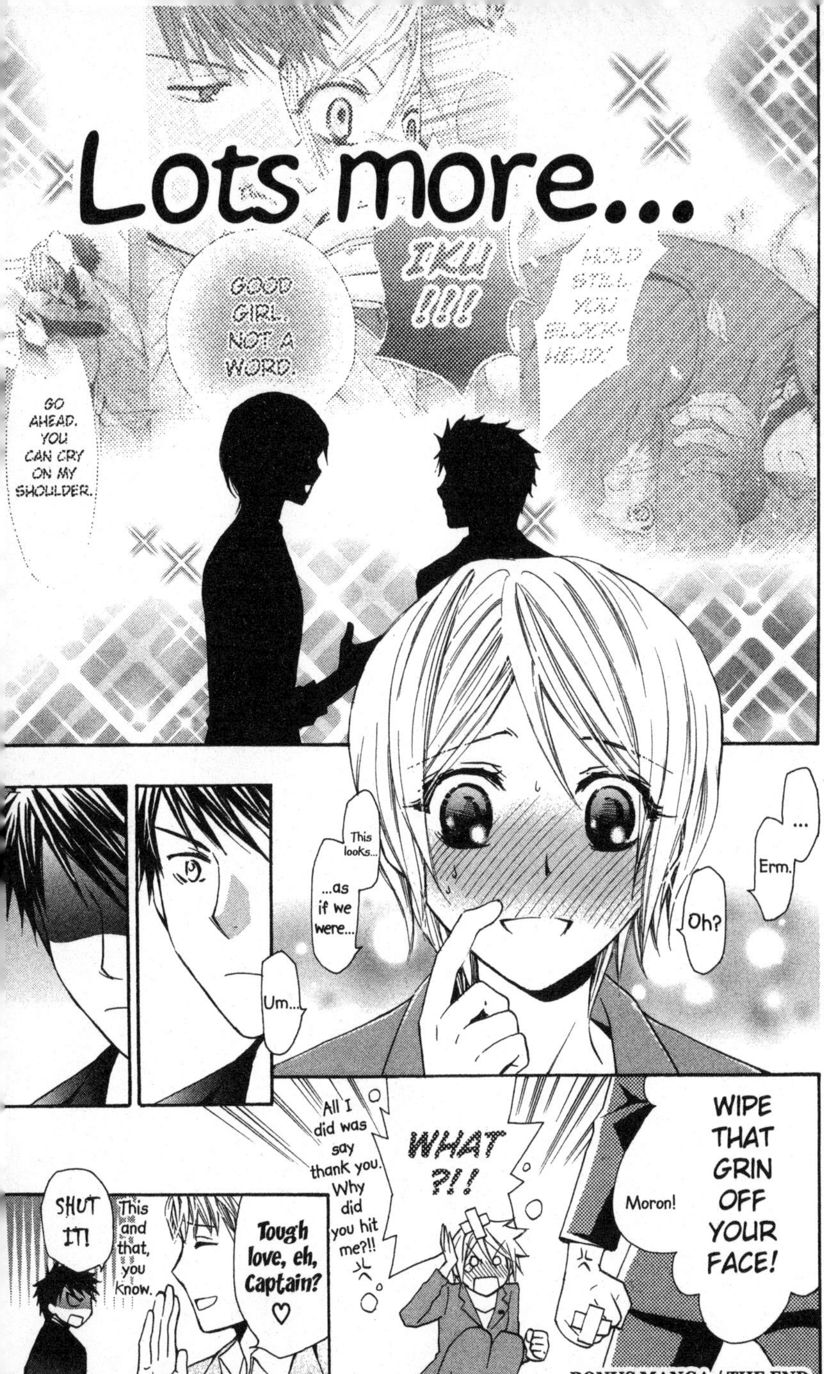
Lots more...
HOLD STILL YOU BLOCKHEAD!
IKU !!!
GOOD GIRL. NOT A WORD.
GO AHEAD. YOU CAN CRY ON MY SHOULDER.
... Erm.
Oh?
This looks... ...as if we were...
Um...
WIPE THAT GRIN OFF YOUR FACE!
Moron!
WHAT ?!!
All I did was say thank you. Why did you hit me?!!
Tough love, eh, Captain? ♡
This and that, you know.
SHUT IT!

BONUS MANGA / THE END

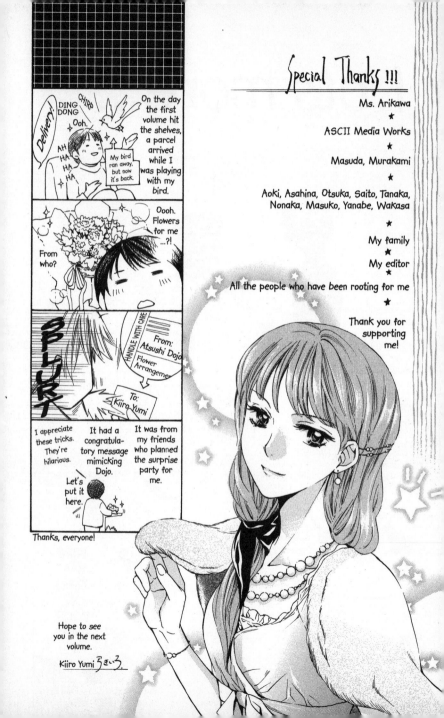

Special Thanks!!!

Ms. Arikawa

★

ASCII Media Works

★

Masuda, Murakami

★

Aoki, Asahina, Otsuka, Saito, Tanaka, Nonaka, Masuko, Yanabe, Wakasa

★

My family

★

My editor

★

All the people who have been rooting for me

★

Thank you for supporting me!

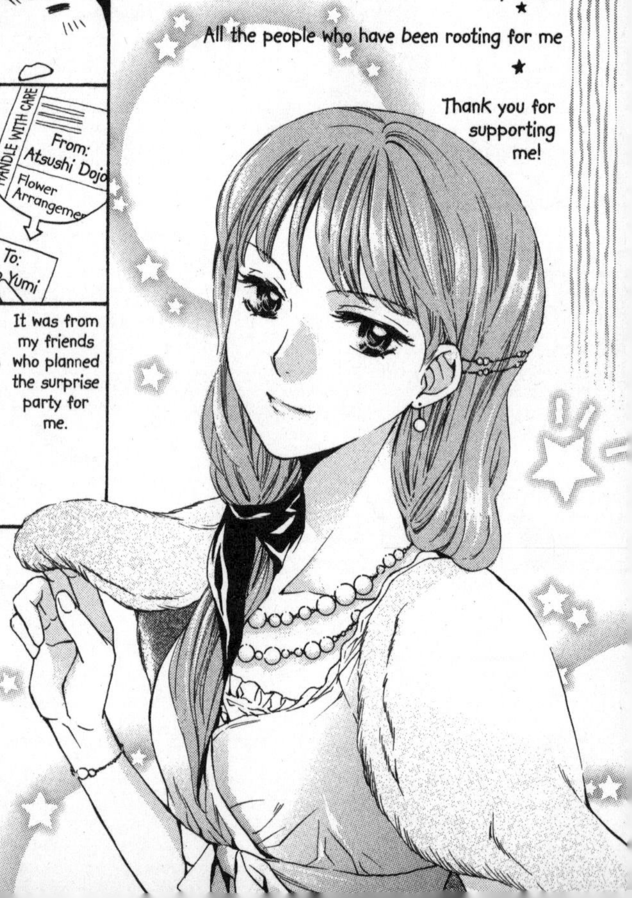

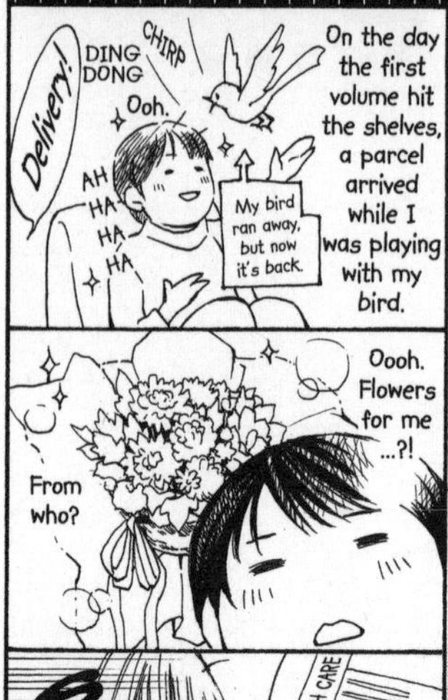
On the day the first volume hit the shelves, a parcel arrived while I was playing with my bird.
CHIRP
My bird ran away, but now it's back.
DING DONG
Ooh.
Delivery!
AH HA HA HA
Oooh. Flowers for me ...?!
From who?
HANDLE WITH CARE
From: Atsushi Dojo
Flower Arrangemen
To: Kiiro Yumi
SPLURT
It was from my friends who planned the surprise party for me.
It had a congratulatory message mimicking Dojo.
I appreciate these tricks. They're hilarious.
Let's put it here.

Thanks, everyone!

Hope to see you in the next volume.

Kiiro Yumi

End notes

Page 7, note: Babanuki
A card game like Go Fish.

Page 9, panel 3: Seika 31
In Japan, years are often identified by eras rather than the Western calendar. For example, 2010 is Heisei 22, or the 22nd year of the reign of the emperor Akihito. Seika is a fictional era name placed in the near future.

Page 57, side note: Tankobon
Japanese graphic novel.

Page 112, panel 1: Kanto
A region of Japan that includes Tokyo.

Page 117, panel 4: Hino
A district in central Tokyo.

Page 154, panel 1: Agohige
Agohige means "chin beard" and is a very unusual name.

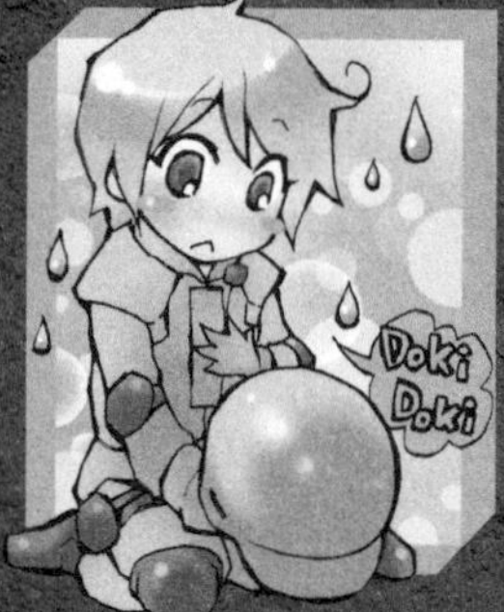
Doki
Doki

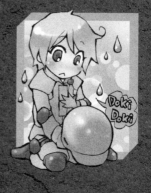

Kiiro Yumi won the 42nd *LaLa* Manga Grand Prix Fresh Debut award for her manga *Billy Bocchan no Yuutsu* (Little Billy's Depression). Her latest series is *Toshokan Senso Love&War (Library Wars: Love & War)*, which runs in *LaLa* magazine in Japan and is published in English by VIZ Media.

Hiro Arikawa won the 10th Dengeki Novel Prize for her work *Shio no Machi: Wish on My Precious* in 2003 and debuted with the same novel in 2004. Of her many works, Arikawa is best known for the *Library Wars* series and her *Jieitai Sanbusaku* trilogy, which consists of *Sora no Naka* (In the Sky), *Umi no Soko* (The Bottom of the Sea) and *Shio no Machi* (City of Salt).

library wars

Volume 2
Shojo Beat Edition

Story & Art by **Kiiro Yumi**
Original Concept by **Hiro Arikawa**

ENGLISH TRANSLATION Kinami Watabe
ADAPTATION & LETTERING Sean McCoy
DESIGN Courtney Utt
EDITOR Pancha Diaz

Toshokan Sensou LOVE&WAR by Kiiro Yumi and Hiro Arikawa
© Kiiro Yumi 2008
© 2008 Hiro Arikawa
Licensed BY KADOKAWA CORPORATION ASCII MEDIA WORKS
All rights reserved.
First published in Japan in 2008 by HAKUSENSHA, Inc., Tokyo.
English language translation rights arranged with HAKUSENSHA,
Inc., Tokyo.

Printed in the U.S.A.

Published by VIZ Media, LLC
P.O. Box 77010
San Francisco, CA 94107

10 9 8 7 6 5
First printing, September 2010
Fifth printing, March 2016

www.shojobeat.com   www.viz.com

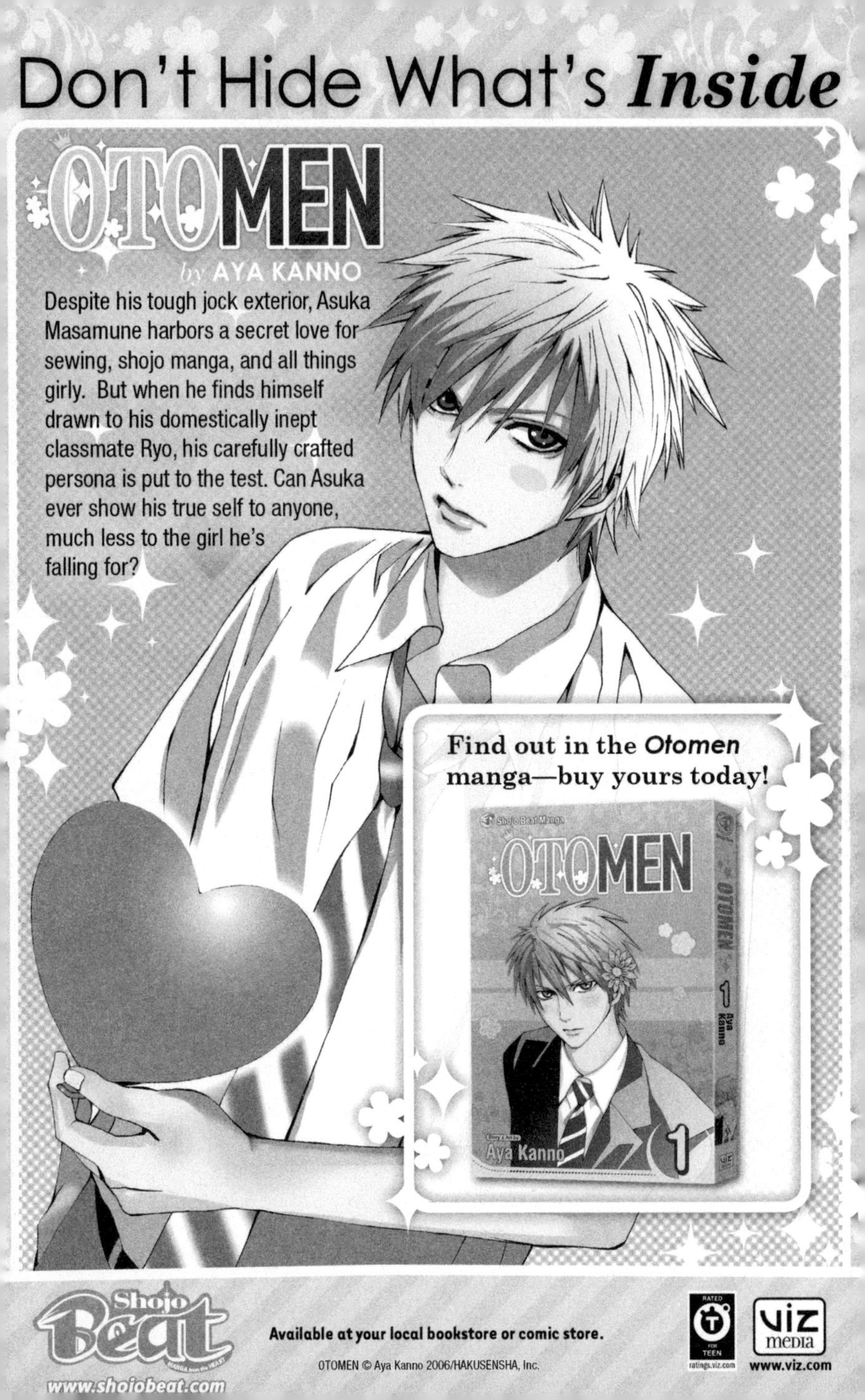
Don't Hide What's Inside
OTOMEN
by AYA KANNO
Despite his tough jock exterior, Asuka Masamune harbors a secret love for sewing, shojo manga, and all things girly. But when he finds himself drawn to his domestically inept classmate Ryo, his carefully crafted persona is put to the test. Can Asuka ever show his true self to anyone, much less to the girl he's falling for?
Find out in the Otomen manga—buy yours today!
Shojo Beat Manga
OTOMEN
1
Story & Art by
Aya Kanno
Shojo Beat
www.shojobeat.com
Available at your local bookstore or comic store.
OTOMEN © Aya Kanno 2006/HAKUSENSHA, Inc.
RATED T FOR TEEN
ratings.viz.com
VIZ media
www.viz.com

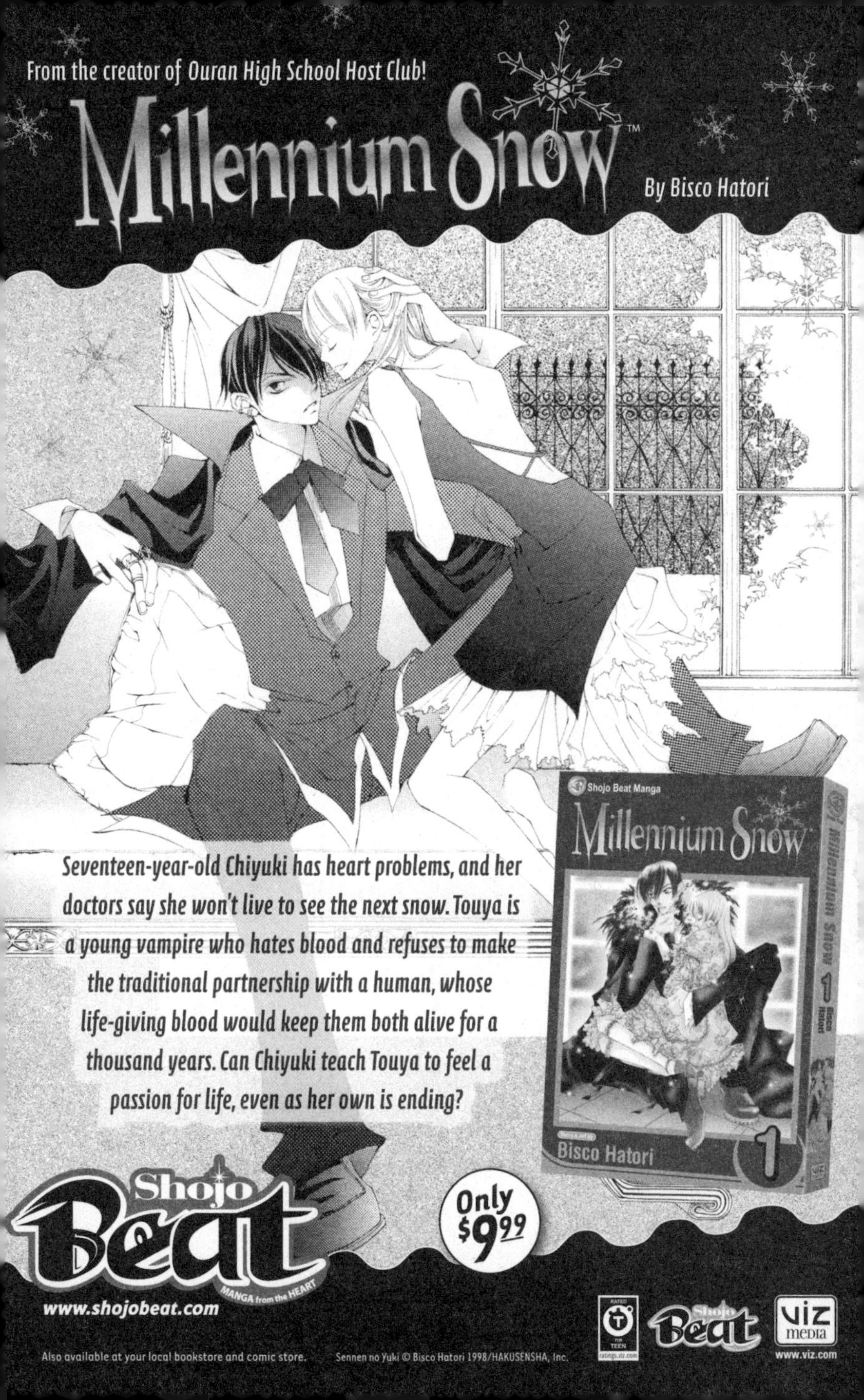
From the creator of Ouran High School Host Club!
Millennium Snow™
By Bisco Hatori
Seventeen-year-old Chiyuki has heart problems, and her doctors say she won't live to see the next snow. Touya is a young vampire who hates blood and refuses to make the traditional partnership with a human, whose life-giving blood would keep them both alive for a thousand years. Can Chiyuki teach Touya to feel a passion for life, even as her own is ending?
Shojo Beat Manga
Millennium Snow
Bisco Hatori
1
Shojo Beat
MANGA from the HEART
Only $9.99
www.shojobeat.com
Shojo Beat
VIZ media
www.viz.com
Also available at your local bookstore and comic store.
Sennen no Yuki © Bisco Hatori 1998/HAKUSENSHA, Inc.

This is the last page.

In keeping with the original Japanese comic format, this book reads from right to left—so action, sound effects, and word balloons are completely reversed. This preserves the orientation of the original artwork—plus, it's fun! Check out the diagram shown here to get the hang of things, and then turn to the other side of the book to get started!

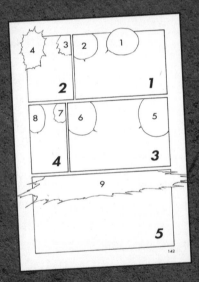